Ultimate Llama for Natural Language Processing (NLP)

Build, Fine-Tune, and Scale Next-Generation NLP Solutions with Llama to Power Future-Ready AI Systems

Gaurav Singh

www.orangeava.com

First Published: September 2025

Published By: Orange Education Pvt Ltd, AVA®

Address: 9, Daryaganj, Delhi, 110002, India

275 New North Road Islington Suite 1314 London,
N1 7AA, United Kingdom

ISBN (PBK): 978-93-49888-53-1
ISBN (E-BOOK): 978-93-49888-66-1

Scan the QR code to explore our entire catalogue

www.orangeava.com

Dedicated To

My beloved **Parents** *and* **Parents-in-Law**,
who instilled in me the values of perseverance, knowledge, and humility.

And to my **Wife**, **Preeti Singh**,
whose constant support and encouragement has been my anchor.

My **Daughters, Aditri Singh** *and* **Saanvi Singh**,
the brightest sparks of my life, who inspire me every single day!

This book is a tribute to your love, patience, and unwavering belief in me.

About the Author

Gaurav Singh is a visionary leader and accomplished professional in Data Science, Machine Learning, and AI Cloud Technologies, with a strong track record of delivering enterprise-scale AI solutions that drive transformative business impact. With deep expertise in LightGBM, TensorFlow, Deep Learning, Large Language Models (LLMs), Generative AI, Agentic AI, NLP, Prompt Engineering, and Responsible AI, he bridges cutting-edge research with practical enterprise applications. Renowned for his Python-driven AI development, he builds intelligent systems leveraging Azure Gen AI, Databricks, Vertex AI, GCP, Synapse, and Snowflake to enable automation, accelerate decision-making, and deliver actionable insights.

Gaurav has mastered gradient boosting for tabular data, deep learning for large-scale AI, and advanced machine learning pipelines, ensuring models are robust, scalable, and production-ready through CI/CD deployment. He has successfully led high-performing Data Science teams, mentored upcoming AI professionals, and delivered measurable ROI across industries such as finance, healthcare, retail, and digital operations. A strong advocate of Responsible AI, he integrates fairness, accountability, and sustainability into every solution, while driving thought leadership in Agentic AI frameworks, autonomous ML systems, and LLM-driven innovations.

With over a decade of experience, Gaurav is recognized for his unique blend of technical mastery, strategic vision, and mentoring ability, which positions him at the forefront of AI adoption. Beyond his professional journey, he is passionate about exploring emerging AI research, reading on technology and philosophy, and sharing knowledge through mentorship. He also enjoys traveling with his family, creative writing, music, and photography.

About the Technical Reviewer

Anup Das is a problem-solver who operates at the intersection of data, code, and AI. With over four years of experience, he has worked as a data scientist across diverse industries, including telecom, retail, healthcare, and finance. His expertise lies in designing systems that transform raw data and research ideas into practical, user-friendly tools.

Currently at EY, Anup focuses on integrating large language models into real-world engineering workflows. He has developed platforms that automate the generation and validation of Infrastructure-as-Code, which significantly reduces deployment errors and compliance issues. He has also designed Retrieval-Augmented Generation (RAG) pipelines to make knowledge from sources like GitHub, Confluence, and PDFs instantly searchable. Additionally, he has deployed custom Model Context Protocol (MCP) servers that enable AI agents to communicate directly with enterprise APIs and tools. His work is centered on helping teams transition from managing systems to building with them.

Before joining EY, Anup was at Deloitte, where he helped scale LLM and RAG solutions to process millions of documents. He used advanced fine-tuning techniques such as PEFT and QLoRA, often improving model performance from unreliable outputs to over 90% accuracy. His work also involved building tools with multimodal AI agents for tasks such as text-to-code, text-to-video, and image-to-text. These projects taught him to effectively balance cutting-edge AI innovation with practical business requirements.

Technically, Anup is fluent in a wide range of tools, including TensorFlow, PyTorch, LangChain, and LangGraph, and has a solid understanding of vector databases such as FAISS and Pinecone. His cloud-native deployment skills on AWS and GCP are well-established. However, he believes his most valuable skill is the ability to strategically combine these tools into solutions that deliver tangible results.

Anup is particularly excited about the future of AI, specifically the development of agents and multi-agent systems that can plan, reason, and collaborate. He sees his role as helping to shape this future by building practical systems today that lay the groundwork for what's to come.

Acknowledgments

Writing a book is never a solitary journey—it is the result of countless hands, hearts, and minds, who contribute directly and indirectly.

First and foremost, I owe my deepest gratitude to my parents, whose wisdom and encouragement have been my compass. They taught me to chase curiosity with discipline, and to view every challenge as an opportunity to grow in life!

I am profoundly grateful to my role model, Hemant Sindhi, whose mentorship, guidance, and constant encouragement shaped not only my professional path, but also my perspective as a leader in AI. His belief in innovation and practical application has greatly influenced the vision of this book.

To my team, thank you for standing beside me in moments of brainstorming, long discussions, and shared curiosity. Your passion for AI, relentless questioning, and dedication made the technical depth of this book stronger, and more practical.

A special note of appreciation goes to my colleagues, Rajith Rajendran, Chhitij Singh and Srivatsa Maudgal, whose insights, collaboration, and constant encouragement added depth and clarity to my thinking. Their support has been instrumental in shaping both my journey, and this work.

A heartfelt appreciation also goes out to the wider community of AI experts and researchers. Your pioneering work on Large Language Models, transformers, and generative AI provided the intellectual foundation and inspiration for this book. I also extend my heartfelt gratitude and thanks to the Editorial Team at Orange Education Pvt Ltd for giving this book the final shape for publishing.

Last but not the least, I would extend my thanks to every silent supporter—colleagues, friends, and well-wishers for reminding me that meaningful contributions in AI are always a collective effort!

Preface

This book, ***Ultimate Llama for Natural Language Processing* (NLP),** is designed as a complete journey into the **Llama series of models**, culminating in the powerful **Llama4**, one of the most advanced large language models of its time. It serves as both a **theoretical reference** and a **practical guide**, enabling readers to understand the architectural evolution of Llama, its core strengths, and its real-world applications across industries.

The book is structured into **13 chapters**, each carefully designed to balance foundational understanding with hands-on application. Together, they provide a roadmap for students, practitioners, and professionals, who want to harness the potential of Llama in their NLP workflows.

Chapter 1. Introduction to Llama Series: Provides a foundational introduction to the Llama family–from the original Llama through Llama2, Llama3, and now Llama4–highlighting their innovations and significance in modern NLP.

Chapter 2. The Architecture of Llama Models: Explores the design principles of Llama, including the sparse Mixture-of-Experts in Llama4, token processing, and multimodal generation capabilities.

Chapter 3. Evolution of Llama: Traces the journey from Llama1 to Llama4, detailing technological breakthroughs, parameter scaling, and domain-specific use-case expansion.

Chapter 4. Implementing NLP Tasks with Llama: Demonstrates hands-on use of Llama for NLP tasks such as text classification, sentiment analysis, and named entity recognition.

Chapter 5. Fine-Tuning Llama for NLP: Covers transfer learning and domain adaptation strategies to optimize Llama models for specialized NLP tasks.

Chapter 6. Real-World Use Cases of Llama: Showcases applied case studies in healthcare, finance, and customer support, including advanced tasks like image captioning and long-form document understanding.

Chapter 7. Performance Tuning for Llama Models: Details optimization methods such as batch processing, parallelization, and hardware acceleration to improve model speed and efficiency.

Chapter 8. Deploying Llama Models at Scale: Outlines strategies for large-scale deployment, using cloud-native infrastructures, distributed serving, and monitoring for production-ready systems.

Chapter 9. Troubleshooting and Improving Llama Models: Discusses common issues in model operation, techniques for debugging, and continuous improvement workflows.

Chapter 10. Transfer Learning Techniques with Llama: Explains how to leverage pre-trained weights for faster development, and adaptation of Llama to new domains.

Chapter 11. Ethical Considerations in NLP with Llama: Addresses the critical issues of bias, transparency, privacy, and responsible use of Llama in enterprise and societal contexts.

Chapter 12. Practical Applications of Llama4: Provides applied walkthroughs of NLP tasks such as summarization, dialogue systems, and question answering, using Llama.

Chapter 13. Future Directions and Advancements in Llama: Explores the emerging research, ethical implications, and future possibilities for Llama models, preparing readers for the next generation of AI advancements.

Get a Free eBook

We hope you are enjoying your recently purchased book! Your feedback is incredibly valuable to us, and to all other readers looking for great books.

If you found this book helpful or enjoyable, we would truly appreciate it, if you could take a moment to leave a short review with a 5 star rating on Amazon. It helps us grow, and lets other readers discover our books.

As a thank you, we would love to send you a free digital copy of this book, and a **30%** discount code on your next cart value on our official websites:

www.orangeava.com

www.orangeava.in (For Indian Subcontinent)

☑ **Here's how:**

Leave a review for the book on Amazon.

Take a screenshot of your review, and send an email to **info@orangeava.com** (it can be just the confirmation screen).

Once, we receive your screenshot, we will send you the digital file, within 24 hours.

Thank you so much for your support – it means a lot to us!

Downloading the code bundles and colored images

Please follow the links or scan the QR codes to download the
Code Bundles and Images of the book:

https://github.com/OrangeAVA/Ultimate-Llama-for-Natural-Language-Processing-NLP-

The code bundles and images of the book are also hosted on
https://rebrand.ly/be52fc

In case there's an update to the code, it will be updated on the existing GitHub repository.

Errata

We take immense pride in our work at **Orange Education Pvt Ltd,** and follow best practices to ensure the accuracy of our content to provide an indulging reading experience to our subscribers. Our readers are our mirrors, and we use their inputs to reflect and improve upon human errors, if any, that may have occurred during the publishing processes involved. To let us maintain the quality and help us reach out to any readers who might be having difficulties due to any unforeseen errors, please write to us at :

errata@orangeava.com

Your support, suggestions, and feedback are highly appreciated.

DID YOU KNOW

Did you know that Orange Education Pvt Ltd offers eBook versions of every book published, with PDF and ePub files available? You can upgrade to the eBook version at **www.orangeava.com** and as a print book customer, you are entitled to a discount on the eBook copy. Get in touch with us at: **info@orangeava.com** for more details.

At **www.orangeava.com**, you can also read a collection of free technical articles, sign up for a range of free newsletters, and receive exclusive discounts and offers on Print Books and eBooks.

PIRACY

If you come across any illegal copies of our works in any form on the internet, we would be grateful if you would provide us with the location address or website name. Please contact us at **info@orangeava.com** with a link to the material.

ARE YOU INTERESTED IN AUTHORING WITH US?

If there is a topic that you have expertise in, and you are interested in either writing or contributing to a book, please write to us at **business@orangeava.com**. We are on a journey to help developers and tech professionals to gain insights on the present technological advancements and innovations happening across the globe and build a community that believes Knowledge is best acquired by sharing and learning with others. Please reach out to us to learn what our audience demands and how you can be part of this educational reform. We also welcome ideas from tech experts and help them build learning and development content for their domains.

REVIEWS

Please leave a review. Once you have read and used this book, why not leave a review on the site that you purchased it from? Potential readers can then see and use your unbiased opinion to make purchase decisions. We at Orange Education would love to know what you think about our products, and our authors can learn from your feedback. Thank you!

For more information about Orange Education, please visit **www.orangeava.com**.

Table of Contents

1. Introduction to Llama Series 1

Introduction 1

Structure 1

Overview of Llama 2

Llama: The Foundation of a New Era 2

Key Features of Llama 2

Llama2: Enhancing Capabilities and Efficiency 2

Advancements in Llama2 3

Llama3: Pushing the Boundaries of Language AI 3

Innovations in Llama3 3

Impact and Applications across the Spectrum 4

Llama4: Elevating Conversations with Intelligence and Empathy 4

Advancements in Llama4 4

The Future Trajectory of Llama Models 5

Evolution and Development History of Llama Models 5

Origins: The Birth of Llama 6

Market Scenario Before and After Llama 6

Pre-Llama Market Landscape 6

Competitive Impact 7

Strategic Market Positioning 8

Partnership and Cloud Infrastructure 8

Economic Impact and Future Implications 8

Key Milestones in Llama's Development 9

Progression to Llama2: Enhancing Performance and Accessibility 10

Development Highlights of Llama2 10

Llama3: Pioneering the Future of Language Models 11

Key Developments in Llama3 11

Llama4: Redefining the Boundaries of Human-AI Interaction 12

Key Developments in Llama4 12

Milestones and Achievements 13

Challenges and Lessons Learned 14

Future Directions and Ongoing Development 15

Key Features and Capabilities of Llama Models: Redefining the AI Frontier 15

Detailed Applications of Llama Models in NLP and AI 18

Advanced Text Generation and Creative Assistance 18

Sophisticated Conversational Agents and Emotional Intelligence 18

Dynamic Machine Translation with Cultural Nuance 19

Deep Sentiment and Emotion Analysis 19

Enhanced Information Retrieval and Contextual Question Answering 19

Intelligent Text Summarization with Focused Insights 20

Precision Named Entity Recognition (NER) and Semantic Information Extraction 20

Hyper-Personalized Recommendation Systems 21

Integrative Speech Recognition and Multimodal AI Interactions 21

Proactive Content Moderation and Real-Time Compliance Enforcement 22

Intelligent Code Generation and Automated Software Documentation 22

Advanced Healthcare Analytics and Personalized Patient Care 22

Automated Financial Insights and Predictive Analytics 23

Adaptive Educational Tools and Intelligent Tutoring Systems 23

Innovative Creative Industries: Interactive Storytelling and Virtual Worlds 24
Legal and Regulatory Compliance Automation 24
Cognitive Behavioral Therapy (CBT) Support Systems 25
Automated Patent and Intellectual Property Analysis 25
Enhanced Supply Chain and Logistics Management 25
Cultural Heritage Preservation and Documentation 26
Advantages of Leveraging Llama Models in Diverse Applications 26
Conclusion 27
Multiple Choice Questions 27
Answers 30
2. The Architecture of Llama Models 31
Introduction 31
Structure 31
Architectural Components of Llama Models 32
Core Architectural Components 32
Transformer Architecture 32
Decoder-Only Structure 34
Self-Attention Mechanism 34
Embedding Layers 35
Token Embeddings 35
Advanced Positional Embeddings 35
Feed-Forward Neural Networks (FFN) 36
Deep and Wide FFN Structures 36
Activation Functions and Normalization 36
Layer Normalization 37
Residual Connections 37
Activation Functions 38
Parameterization and Scaling 38
Parameter Efficiency 39
Training Methodologies 39
Training Objectives 40

- *Optimization Techniques* ... 40
- *Regularization Strategies* ... 41
- *Advanced Architectural Innovations* ... 42
- *Sparse Attention Mechanisms* ... 42
- *Adaptive Computation* ... 42
- *Mixed Precision Training* ... 43
- *Modular Design* ... 43
- *Scalability and Parallelization* ... 44
- *Model Parallelism* ... 44
- *Data Parallelism* ... 44
- *Distributed Training Frameworks* ... 45
- *Evaluation and Benchmarking* ... 45
- *Benchmark Suites* ... 45
- *Ablation Studies* ... 46
- *Comparative Analysis* ... 46
- *Answers to Exercises* ... 47
- *Appendix* ... 48

Computational Layers and Their Functions in Llama Architecture ... 49

- *Embedding Layer* ... 49
- *Multi-Head Self-Attention Layer* ... 50
- *Self-Attention Mechanism* ... 50
- *Multi-Head Attention* ... 50
- *Feed-Forward Neural Network (FFN)* ... 50
- *Layer Normalization* ... 51
- *Residual Connections* ... 51

Text Generation Mechanisms in Llama Architecture ... 51

- *Autoregressive Prediction* ... 51
- *Decoding Strategies* ... 52
- *Context Awareness* ... 52

Optimization Techniques in Llama Architecture ... 52

- *Optimizers* ... 53

Adam Optimizer 53
Weight Decay 53
Learning Rate Schedules 54
Gradient Clipping 54
Mixed Precision Training 55
Regularization Techniques 55
Dropout 55
Weight Sharing 56
Data Augmentation 56
Distributed Training 56
Early Stopping 57
Things to Remember: Key Points from Llama Model Architecture 57
Conclusion 59
Multiple Choice Questions 59
Answers 61
3. Evolution of Llama 62
Introduction 62
Structure 63
Overview 63
From Early Models to Neural Networks: Laying the Foundation 63
The Transformer Revolution: Unleashing Scalable Language Models 64
The Birth of Llama Models: Bridging Efficiency and Performance 64
Key Features and Benefits of Llama Models 65
Development Timeline and Milestones 66
The Genesis of Llama: Foundations and Inspirations 66
The AI Landscape of Pre-Llama 66
Meta's Vision for Llama 67
Development Timeline: From Concept to Deployment 67

Phase 1: Conceptualization and Initial Development (2020-2021) ... 67

Phase 2: Scaling and Optimization (2021-2022) ... 68

Phase 3: Public Deployment and Iterative Improvement (2022-2023) ... 69

Key Milestones in Llama's Evolution ... 70

Achieving Parameter Milestones ... 70

Breakthroughs in Training Efficiency ... 71

Enhancements in Multilingual and Domain-Specific Capabilities ... 71

Ethical and Responsible AI Initiatives ... 72

Impact on the AI Ecosystem ... 73

Comparative Analysis of Llama, Llama2, and Llama3, Llama4 ... 74

Llama: The Beginning of an Era ... 74

Llama 2: A Significant Leap Forward ... 75

Code Llama: A Step Toward Specialized AI ... 75

Llama 3: Multi-Modal Marvel ... 76

Llama 3.1: Incremental Optimization ... 77

Llama 3.2: Scalability and Flexibility ... 77

Llama 3.3: The Pinnacle ... 78

Llama 4: The Evolution ... 78

Technological Advancements and Enhancements ... 81

Architectural Innovations ... 81

Advanced Training Methodologies ... 82

Data Management and Preprocessing ... 83

Optimization Algorithms and Techniques ... 83

Integration of Multimodal Capabilities ... 84

Applications of Multimodal Llama Models ... 84

Hardware and Infrastructure Innovations ... 85

Ethical and Responsible AI Enhancements ... 85

Continuous Learning and Adaptation ... 86

Security and Privacy Enhancements ... 87

Future Technological Prospects 87
Use Cases and Applications across Different Domains 88
Use Cases across Different Domains 88
Healthcare 88
Finance 90
Education 92
Entertainment 93
Conclusion 95
Multiple Choice Questions 96
Answers 98
4. Implementing NLP Tasks with Llama **99**
Introduction 99
Structure 99
Overview 100
Setting Up Llama for NLP Tasks 101
Prerequisites 102
Setting Up the Environment 103
Using Conda 103
Using `Virtualenv` and `Pip` 103
Installing Dependencies 103
Obtaining the Llama Model 104
Configuring the Model 105
Handling Large Models 105
Data Preparation 106
Fine-Tuning the Llama Model 107
Evaluation 108
Deploying the Llama Model 108
Setting Up a REST API 109
Containerization with Docker 109
Scaling the Deployment 110
Optimizing Performance 110
Text Classification Using Llama 111

Understanding the Role of Text Classification 111
Leveraging Llama for Text Classification 112
Preparing for Text Classification with Llama 112
Data Preparation 112
Model Preparation 112
Fine-Tuning Llama for Text Classification 113
Evaluating and Deploying the Model 113
Real-World Applications of Text Classification with Llama 114
Some More Applications on Text Classification Leveraging Llama 115
Sentiment Analysis in Customer Feedback 115
Spam and Toxic Content Detection 115
Topic Categorization in News and Media 116
Legal Document Analysis 116
Healthcare and Medical Text Analysis 116
Fraud Detection in Financial Documents 117
Implementing Llama for Text Classification Tasks 118
Sentiment Analysis with Llama 119
The Need for Sentiment Analysis 119
Llama: A Paradigm Shift for Sentiment Analysis 119
Advantages of Llama in Sentiment Analysis 119
Preparing Data for Sentiment Analysis 120
Fine-Tuning Llama for Sentiment Analysis 120
Advanced Techniques in Sentiment Analysis 122
Real-World Applications of Sentiment Analysis with Llama 122
Customer Feedback Analysis 122
Social Media Monitoring 123
Product and Market Research 123
Financial Market Insights 123
Named Entity Recognition (NER) Using Llama 125
A New Era for NER with Transformer Models 126

Data Preparation and Annotation for NER 126
Fine-Tuning Llama for NER 127
Evaluating NER Performance 127
Real-World Applications and Impact 128
Conclusion 129
Multiple Choice Questions 129
Answers 132
5. Fine-Tuning Llama for NLP 133
Introduction 133
Structure 133
Overview 133
The Imperative of Fine-Tuning in NLP 134
Advanced Transfer Learning Strategies for Fine-Tuning 134
Domain Adaptation Techniques in Fine-Tuning 135
Optimizing Model Performance Through Fine-Tuning 136
Contextual Overview of the Chapter 136
Transfer Learning with Llama 137
The Paradigm Shift in NLP 137
Understanding Transfer Learning with Llama 137
Types of Transfer Learning Techniques with Llama 138
Crafting Custom NLP Applications with Llama 139
Curating Domain-Specific Datasets 139
Implementing Data Augmentation and Preprocessing 140
Optimizing Performance with Hyperparameter Tuning 140
Detailed Scenarios and Examples 140
Detailed Description of Various Transfer Learning Techniques Used with Llama 141
The Future of Transfer Learning and Fine-Tuning 144
Domain Adaptation Strategies 144
The Imperative of Domain Adaptation 145
Core Strategies for Domain Adaptation 146
Curating Domain-Specific Datasets 146

Live Scenario: Legal Document Analysis 146

Data Preprocessing and Augmentation 147

Live Scenario: Healthcare Communication System 147

Domain-Sensitive Loss Functions 147

Live Scenario: Financial Report Analysis 148

Integration of External Knowledge Bases 148

Live Scenario: Legal Assistant Integration 149

Incremental Domain Adaptation 149

Live Scenario: News and Financial Markets 149

Hyperparameter Tuning for Llama Models 149

Understanding Hyperparameters: The Foundation of Fine-Tuning 151

The Importance of Hyperparameter Tuning for Llama Models 151

Hyperparameter Tuning Strategies 152

Manual Tuning 152

Grid Search 152

Random Search 153

Bayesian Optimization 153

Adaptive Learning Rates 154

Practical Considerations for Hyperparameter Tuning 154

Real-World Scenario: Fine-Tuning Llama for Financial Risk Analysis 154

Case Studies and Applications of Fine-Tuned Llama Models 155

Healthcare: Enhancing Clinical Decision Support 155

Legal Industry: Streamlining Document Analysis 156

Financial Services: Risk Assessment and Customer Insights 157

Retail and E-commerce: Personalization and Customer Service 158

Education: Intelligent Tutoring and Content Summarization 159

Fine-Tuning Llama4 for Text Classification System 160

Conclusion 161

Multiple Choice Questions 162

Answers 164

6. Real-World Use Cases of Llama 165

Introduction 165

Structure 166

Overview 166

Real-World Applications: Bridging Theory and Practice 166

Healthcare: Revolutionizing Patient Care and Diagnostics 167

Finance: Enhancing Security, Efficiency, and Customer Engagement 167

Customer Service: Redefining Support with Intelligent Interaction 168

Expanding Horizons: Education, Logistics, and Media 168

Demonstrating Versatility and Effectiveness 169

Industry-Specific Applications of Llama Models 170

Bridging the Gap Between Theory and Practice 170

Transformative Applications Across Industries 170

Healthcare: Enhancing Patient Outcomes and Operational Efficiency 170

Finance: Revolutionizing Security, Efficiency, and Customer Engagement 171

Customer Service: Delivering Intelligent and Personalized Support 171

Education: Shaping the Future of Personalized Learning 172

Logistics and Supply Chain: Optimizing Operational Efficiency 172

Media and Content Creation: Empowering Creativity and Engagement 173

Government and Public Administration: Enhancing Transparency and Efficiency 173

Retail: Driving Personalized Experiences and Operational Excellence 173

Energy and Utilities: Optimizing Performance and Sustainability 174

Manufacturing: Enhancing Production and Quality Control 174

Case Studies in Healthcare, Finance, and Customer Services 175

Healthcare: Revolutionizing Patient Care and Clinical Research 175

Case Study 1: Precision Diagnostics and Comprehensive Patient Data Management 175

Case Study 2: Accelerated Clinical Research Through Automated Knowledge Extraction 176

Case Study 3: Virtual Health Assistants for Enhanced Patient Engagement 177

Example 178

Finance: Enhancing Security, Efficiency, and Customer Engagement 179

Case Study 1: Strengthening Fraud Detection and Proactive Risk Management 179

Case Study 2: Automated Financial Reporting and Real-Time Analytics 180

Case Study 3: Personalized Client Engagement with Intelligent Chatbots 182

Example 183

Customer Services: Transforming Support through Advanced Virtual Assistants 183

Case Study 1: Multilingual Support and Global User Engagement 184

Case Study 2: Intelligent Ticketing and Automated Issue Resolution 185

Case Study 3: Real-Time Customer Feedback and Advanced Sentiment Analysis 186

Example 187

Retail: Revolutionizing the Customer Journey and Operational Efficiency 188

Case Study 1: Personalized Shopping Experiences and Inventory Optimization 188

Example 189

Government and Public Administration: Enhancing Services and Citizen Engagement 190

Case Study 1: Streamlined Document Processing and Citizen Service Portals 190

Example 191

Education: Empowering Adaptive Learning and Efficient Administration 192

Case Study: Adaptive Learning Platforms and Automated Grading Systems 192

Example 193

Energy and Utilities: Optimizing Resources and Enhancing Sustainability 194

Case Study: Predictive Maintenance and Energy Demand Forecasting 194

Example 195

Manufacturing: Driving Efficiency and Quality in Production 196

Case Study: Production Process Optimization and Quality Control 196

Example 197

Challenges and Solutions in Real-world Deployments 198

Data Quality and Integration 198

Model Adaptation and Domain-Specific Tuning 199

Scalability and Real-Time Processing 200

Ethical Considerations and Bias Mitigation 200

Integration with Legacy Systems and Organizational Change 201

Conclusion 202

Multiple Choice Questions 202

Answers 204

7. **Performance Tuning for Llama Models**......205

Introduction......205

Structure......206

Overview......206

Strategies for Improving Inference Speed......207

Optimizing Batch Processing......207

Streamlining the Data Pipeline......208

Parallelization Techniques......208

Hardware Acceleration......209

Software-Level Optimizations......210

Monitoring and Continuous Improvement......211

Case Studies and Implementation Examples......211

Healthcare: Revolutionizing Patient Care and Diagnostics......212

Finance: Enhancing Security, Efficiency, and Customer Engagement......213

Customer Service: Redefining Support with Intelligent Interaction......213

Expanding Horizons: Education, Logistics, and Media......214

Demonstrating Versatility and Effectiveness......214

Batch Processing with Llama......215

Fundamentals of Batch Processing......215

Implementing Batch Processing in Llama......216

Key Advantages and Considerations......216

Benefits of Batch Processing......216

Potential Trade-offs and Challenges......217

Detailed Strategies for Implementing Batch Processing with Llama......217

Dynamic Batch Sizing......217

Real-world Scenario: Chatbot Interaction......218

Efficient Data Preparation and Preprocessing......218

Tokenization and Normalization......218

Data Transformation and Padding 219

Scenario: Document Summarization Service 219

Integration with High-Performance Hardware 219

GPU and TPU Acceleration 219

Scenario: Real-Time Translation Application 220

Software Tools and Frameworks 220

Scenario: E-commerce Recommendation Engine 220

Best Practices and Advanced Techniques 221

Fault Tolerance and Error Handling 221

Performance Testing and Benchmarking 222

Parallelization Techniques 222

The Need for Parallelization 222

Overview of Parallelization Strategies 223

Data Parallelism 223

Model Parallelism 224

Pipeline Parallelism 224

Task-Based Parallelism 225

Asynchronous Execution Models 225

Combining Parallelization Techniques 226

Best Practices for Implementing Parallelization 227

Hardware and Software Optimizations for Llama Models 227

Hardware Optimizations 228

Utilizing Specialized Hardware Accelerators 228

Memory and Data Transfer Optimizations 229

Hardware-Specific Tuning 230

Software Optimizations 230

Framework and Library Enhancements 230

Code-Level Optimizations 231

Algorithmic and Model-Level Optimizations 231

Combining Hardware and Software Optimizations 232

Synergistic Effects 232

Integrated Optimization Pipelines 233

Best Practices and Future Directions 233
Conclusion 234
Multiple Choice Questions 234
Answers 236
8. Deploying Llama Models at Scale 237
Introduction 237
Structure 237
Overview 238
Deployment Architecture of Llama Models 239
Llama Models and Their Deployment Needs 239
Core Components of the Llama Deployment Architecture 240
Data Ingestion and Preprocessing 240
Model Serving and Inference 240
Scalability and Load Balancing 241
Monitoring, Logging, and Maintenance 242
Security, Compliance, and Disaster Recovery 243
Deployment Strategies: Cloud, On-Premises, and Hybrid Approaches 244
Cloud-Based Deployments 244
On-Premises Deployments 245
Hybrid Deployments 245
Detailed Look at Llama Architecture Components 245
Scalability Considerations and Challenges 247
Scalability Considerations 247
Model Architecture and Parameter Growth 248
Data Management and Quality 248
Training Infrastructure and Distributed Systems 249
Inference and Real-Time Applications 250
Challenges in Scaling Llama Models 250
Strategies for Overcoming Scalability Challenges 252
Cost, Latency, Performance, and Scalability for Llama Models in Different Deployment Architectures 254

Cloud Deployment ... 254
On-Premise Deployment ... 255
Edge Deployment ... 256
Hybrid Deployment ... 257
Cloud Deployment Strategies ... 257
Understanding the Cloud Deployment Landscape ... 258
Key Cloud Deployment Strategies for Llama Models ... 258
Containerization and Orchestration ... 259
Serverless Architectures ... 259
Managed AI Services ... 260
Designing a Cloud Deployment Architecture for Llama Models ... 260
Multi-Tier Architecture ... 261
Hybrid and Multi-Cloud Strategies ... 261
Security and Compliance Considerations ... 262
Operational Considerations: Monitoring, Logging, and Maintenance ... 262
Future Trends in Cloud Deployment for Llama Models ... 263
Monitoring and Managing Deployed Llama Models ... 263
Essential Monitoring for Llama Models ... 264
Key Metrics to Monitor ... 264
Tools and Technologies for Effective Monitoring ... 265
Strategies for Managing Deployed Llama Models ... 266
Best Practices for Ongoing Monitoring and Management ... 268
Conclusion ... 268
Multiple Choice Questions ... 269
Answers ... 271
9. Troubleshooting and Improving Llama Models ... 272
Introduction ... 272
Structure ... 272
Overview ... 273
Common Issues in Llama Model Deployment ... 273

Configuration and Dependency Challenges 274
Hardware and Resource Constraints 275
Integration and Environment Issues 276
Performance Bottlenecks and Optimization 277
Debugging and Troubleshooting in Production 278
Security, Compliance, and Operational Risks 280
Strategies for Continuous Improvement 280
Debugging Techniques for Llama models 281
Understanding the Challenges in Debugging Llama Models 282
Key Debugging Techniques for Llama Models 282
Comprehensive Logging and Monitoring 283
Interactive Debugging 283
Profiling and Performance Analysis 284
Automated Error and Anomaly Detection 285
Unit Testing, Integration Testing, and Continuous Validation 286
Reproducibility and Environment Replication 286
The Impact of Debugging Techniques on Llama Model Performance 287
Performance Monitoring and Optimization 288
The Critical Role of Performance Monitoring 288
Advanced Techniques and Tools for Performance Monitoring 289
Real-Time Metrics Collection 289
Centralized Logging Systems 289
Distributed Tracing 290
Strategies for Performance Optimization 290
Hardware and Infrastructure Scaling 291
Caching Mechanisms 291
Database Optimization 292
Load Balancing and Traffic Management 292
Continuous Optimization and Feedback Loops 292

Real-World Applications and Their Impact....293
Continuous Improvement Strategies 294
Understanding Continuous Improvement and Key Elements....295
Methodologies for Continuous Improvement 295
Implementing Continuous Improvement Strategies....296
The Impact of Continuous Improvement Strategies....297
Conclusion....298
Multiple Choice Questions....299
Answers 301
10. Transfer Learning Techniques with Llama....302
Introduction....302
Structure....302
Overview....303
Transfer Learning and Its Importance in NLP 303
The Fundamentals of Transfer Learning in NLP....304
Benefits of Pre-Trained Models....304
Historical Context and the Evolution of Transfer Learning....306
Implementation and Practical Applications 307
Fine-Tuning Pre-Trained Models for Custom Tasks 307
Case Studies: Real-Time Applications....307
Benefits, Challenges, and Solutions 308
Key Benefits Recap 308
Addressing the Challenges....309
Strategies for Success....309
Integration with Emerging AI Techniques....309
Evaluating Transfer Learning Systems....310
Future Directions and Research Opportunities....311
Pre-Trained Models and Their Advantages....312
Understanding Pre-Trained Models....312
Advantages of Pre-Trained Models....313

Llama Models: A Detailed Examination 314
Architectural Excellence of Llama Models 314
Specific Advantages of the Llama Series 315
Technical Innovations in Llama Models 315
Overcoming Challenges and Enhancing Capabilities 315
The Broader Impact on the NLP Landscape 316
Fine-Tuning Llama Models for Custom Tasks 317
Motivation Behind Fine-Tuning 318
The Fine-Tuning Process 318
Model Initialization and Architecture Adaptation 319
Hyperparameter Optimization 320
Training Strategies: Layer Freezing and Gradual Unfreezing 321
Regularization and Optimization Techniques 321
Addressing Common Challenges in Fine-Tuning Llama Models 322
Managing Domain Mismatch 322
Tackling Overfitting 323
Optimizing Computational Resources 323
Best Practices and Strategies for Successful Fine-Tuning 324
Case Studies: Adapting Llama for Text Classification and Sentiment Analysis 325
Case Study 1: Fine-Tuning Llama for Text Classification 325
Dataset Preparation 326
Model Adaptation and Architectural Modifications 326
Hyperparameter Tuning and Training Strategies 327
Evaluation and Performance Metrics 328
Case Study 2: Fine-Tuning Llama for Sentiment Analysis 328
Dataset Preparation 329
Model Adaptation and Architectural Enhancements 329
Training and Hyperparameter Optimization 330
Evaluation, Results, and Insights 330

Comparative Analysis and Lessons Learned..........331

Common Strategies across Tasks..........331

Unique Challenges and Adaptations..........332

Key Lessons for Future Applications..........332

Conclusion..........332

Multiple Choice Questions..........333

Answers..........335

11. Ethical Considerations in NLP with Llama..........**336**

Introduction..........336

Structure..........337

Overview..........337

Ethical Challenges in NLP and AI..........337

Bias in Language Models: Origins, Manifestations, and Remedies..........338

Privacy and Data Security: Safeguarding Sensitive Information..........339

Transparency and Accountability: Demystifying the AI Black Box..........340

Regulatory and Societal Implications: Aligning Innovation with Ethical Standards..........341

Future Challenges and Opportunities in Ethical AI Development..........342

Addressing Bias in Language Models..........343

Understanding Bias in Language Models..........343

The Real-World Impact of Bias..........344

Methodologies for Identifying Bias..........345

Strategies for Mitigating Bias..........345

Case Studies and Real-World Examples..........347

Challenges and Limitations in Bias Mitigation..........347

Future Directions and Best Practices..........348

Privacy and Data Security in NLP Applications..........349

The Data-Driven Nature of NLP Applications..........349

Privacy Challenges: Consent, Anonymization, and Re-Identification 349

Data Security: Protection Mechanisms and Technical Solutions 350

Emerging Challenges and Future Directions 352

Transparency, Fairness, and Responsible AI Deployment 353

The Imperative of Transparency in AI 353

Ensuring Fairness in AI Systems 354

Strategies for Mitigating Bias 355

Institutionalizing Fairness 356

Responsible AI Deployment: Governance, Oversight, and Ethical Considerations 356

Overcoming Challenges and Implementing Best Practices 357

Case Studies: Ethical Dilemmas in Real-World NLP Applications 359

Introduction: Navigating the Ethical Landscape of NLP 359

Case Study 1: Bias in Recruitment and Hiring Tools 360

The Scenario 360

Uncovering the Ethical Dilemma 360

Mitigation and Lessons Learned 361

Case Study 2: Privacy and Misinformation in Mental Health Chatbots 361

The Scenario 361

Uncovering the Ethical Dilemma 361

Mitigation and Lessons Learned 362

Case Study 3: Misinformation and Content Moderation in Social Media 362

The Scenario 363

Uncovering the Ethical Dilemma 363

Mitigation and Lessons Learned 363

Case Study 4: Ethical Challenges in Healthcare NLP Applications 364

The Scenario 364
Uncovering the Ethical Dilemma 364
Mitigation and Lessons Learned 365
Lessons Learned and Best Practices 365
Conclusion 366
Multiple Choice Questions 366
Answers 369
12. Practical Applications of Llama4 370
Introduction 370
Structure 370
Overview 371
Text Generation 371
Text Summarization 374
Sample Terminal Output 377
Language Understanding for Complex NLP Tasks 378
Implementing Llama 4 for Question Answering Systems 381
Conversational AI Applications 384
Conclusion 387
Multiple Choice Questions 387
Answers 389
13. Future Directions and Advancements in Llama 390
Introduction 390
Structure 390
Overview 391
Emerging Trends in NLP And AI 391
Advances in Deep Learning and Transformer Architectures 392
Real-Time Applications and Industry Impact 392
Ethical Implications and AI Governance 393
Future Directions and Prospects 394
Research Advancements in Llama Models 395
Innovations in Model Architecture and Scaling 395
Ethical Implications and AI Governance 400

Understanding Ethical Implications 400
Deep Dive into Ethical Implications 400
Potential Risks and Challenges 401
Building Robust AI Governance Frameworks 401
Best Practices for Ethical Deployment 402
Looking Ahead: The Next-Gen of Governance 402
Best Practices Using Llama Models 403
Picking the Perfect Llama 403
Data Curation and Fine-Tuning Fundamentals 403
Prompt Engineering and Inference Best Practices 404
Evaluation and Monitoring 405
Security, Privacy, and Ethical Safeguards 405
Real-World Case Study: Llama in Customer Support 406
Future Prospects of Llama Models 406
Next-Gen Architectures: Bigger, Better, Smarter 407
Edge-Ready and On-Device Intelligence 407
Hyper-Specialized Domain Models 407
Democratized Innovation and Community Power 407
Integration with Agents and Autonomous Systems 408
What This Means for You 408
Conclusion 408
Multiple-Choice Questions 409
Answers 411
Index 412

CHAPTER 1

Introduction to Llama Series

Introduction

In the rapidly evolving landscape of Artificial Intelligence (AI) and Natural Language Processing (NLP), large language models (LLMs) have emerged as pivotal tools driving innovation and transforming industries. Among the frontrunners in this domain is Meta's **Large Language Model Meta AI (Llama)** series, which has set new benchmarks in language understanding and generation. From its inception with Llama to the latest advancements in Llama 3, this series exemplifies the strides being made in creating more sophisticated, efficient, and versatile AI models.

This comprehensive exploration delves into the multifaceted applications of the Llama series in NLP and AI, highlighting how each version has expanded the horizons of what language models can accomplish. By examining core NLP tasks, advanced AI applications, industry-specific implementations, and the evolutionary enhancements across the Llama iterations, this report showcases the transformative impact of these models. Furthermore, it looks ahead to future directions, emphasizing the ongoing potential for innovation and the continued integration of Llama models into emerging technologies and specialized domains.

As we navigate through the capabilities and applications of Llama, it becomes evident that these models are not only pushing the boundaries of language processing but also redefining the ways in which humans interact with technology. The following sections provide an in-depth analysis of these applications, offering insights into how the Llama series is shaping the future of AI and NLP.

Structure

In this chapter, we will cover the following topics:

- Overview of Llama
- Evolution and Development History of Llama Models

- Key Features and Capabilities
- Applications in Detail

Overview of Llama

The Llama series is not merely a progression of incremental improvements; each iteration—**Llama**, **Llama2**, **Llama3, and Llama4**—introduces significant enhancements in architecture, training methodologies, and application capabilities. These advancements have broadened the scope of what is achievable with NLP and AI, enabling applications that range from creative content generation and real-time translation to complex data analysis and interactive conversational agents. Moreover, the commitment to scalability, ethical AI practices, and multimodal integration underscores the potential of the Llama models to address diverse and complex challenges across various sectors.

Llama: The Foundation of a New Era

The original **Large Language Model Meta AI (Llama)** was introduced as Meta's foray into the competitive realm of large language models. Designed to be efficient and accessible, Llama emphasized balancing performance with resource consumption, making advanced language modeling more attainable for a broader range of researchers and developers.

Key Features of Llama

- **Scalability:** Llama was built to scale efficiently across various sizes, allowing for flexibility depending on computational resources and application needs.
- **Open Accessibility:** Meta aimed to democratize access to powerful language models, enabling academic institutions and smaller organizations to leverage cutting-edge AI without prohibitive costs.
- **Versatile Applications:** From text completion and summarization to question-answering and translation, Llama demonstrated robust performance across multiple language tasks.

The introduction of Llama underscored Meta's commitment to advancing AI responsibly, emphasizing transparency and collaboration within the research community.

Llama2: Enhancing Capabilities and Efficiency

Building upon the foundational strengths of its predecessor, **Llama2** represented a significant leap in both capability and efficiency. This iteration focused on refining the model architecture, improving language comprehension, and expanding multilingual support.

Advancements in Llama2

- **Improved Understanding:** Enhanced algorithms and training methodologies enabled Llama2 to grasp nuanced language constructs, context, and intent with greater accuracy.
- **Multilingual Proficiency:** Llama2 expanded its linguistic repertoire, supporting a wider array of languages and dialects, thereby increasing its global applicability.
- **Optimized Training:** Leveraging more efficient training techniques reduced computational overhead, making Llama2 more accessible for deployment in diverse environments.
- **Safety and Alignment:** Emphasis on ethical AI practices led to better alignment with human values, reducing biases and improving the reliability of generated content.

Llama2's advancements solidified its position as a versatile and dependable tool for developers, researchers, and organizations seeking sophisticated language modeling solutions.

Llama3: Pushing the Boundaries of Language AI

The release of **Llama3** marked the latest evolution in Meta's Llama series, pushing the boundaries of what large language models can achieve. This iteration integrated cutting-edge innovations in model architecture, training paradigms, and application versatility, setting new standards in the field.

Innovations in Llama3

- **Enhanced Contextual Awareness:** Llama3 boasts an improved ability to maintain and utilize context over extended conversations or documents, resulting in more coherent and contextually relevant outputs.
- **Adaptive Learning:** Incorporating mechanisms for continuous learning, Llama3 can adapt to new information and evolving language patterns in real-time, ensuring its relevance and accuracy.
- **Interdisciplinary Integration:** Llama3 seamlessly integrates with other AI modalities, such as vision and audio, enabling multimodal applications that require a combination of language and sensory data processing.

- **Robust Security Measures:** Advanced safeguards against misuse and content generation of harmful material were implemented, reflecting a heightened focus on responsible AI deployment.
- **Customization and Fine-Tuning:** Llama3 offers enhanced capabilities for customization, allowing users to fine-tune the model for specific tasks, industries, or organizational needs with greater precision.

Impact and Applications across the Spectrum

The progression from Llama to Llama3 has had a profound impact on both the research community and industry applications. These models have been instrumental in:

- **Academic Research:** Facilitating studies in linguistics, cognitive science, and artificial intelligence by providing robust tools for language analysis and generation.
- **Business and Industry:** Powering customer service chatbots, automating content creation, enhancing data analysis, and supporting decision-making processes across various sectors.
- **Healthcare and Education:** Assisting in medical documentation, personalized learning experiences, and accessibility solutions for individuals with disabilities.
- **Creative Industries:** Enabling novel forms of storytelling, game development, and interactive media through advanced narrative generation and character interaction capabilities.

Llama 4: Elevating Conversations with Intelligence and Empathy

Llama 4 is a cutting-edge conversational AI that understands and responds to human language with unprecedented nuance and accuracy. With its advanced language capabilities and empathetic tone, Llama 4 is designed to engage in productive and meaningful conversations. It is capable of communicating in multiple languages, and adapting to various contexts. Llama 4 represents a significant step forward in language AI technology.

Advancements in Llama4

- **Improved Language Understanding**: Enhanced ability to comprehend complex sentences, nuances, and context.
- **Increased Knowledge Base**: A larger and more up-to-date knowledge base, enabling more accurate and informative responses.

- **Enhanced Conversational Flow**: More natural and engaging conversations, with a better ability to understand and respond to follow-up questions.
- **Emotional Intelligence**: Greater empathy and understanding of emotional cues, allowing for more supportive and personalized interactions.
- **Multilingual Support**: Continued improvement in supporting multiple languages, enabling more effective communication across linguistic and cultural boundaries.
- **Contextual Understanding**: Better ability to understand and maintain context throughout a conversation, reducing the need for repetitive clarifications.
- **Creative and Diverse Responses**: More varied and creative responses, making conversations more engaging and interesting.

The Future Trajectory of Llama Models

The future trajectory of Llama models is expected to be shaped by ongoing advancements in Natural Language Processing (NLP) and Machine Learning (ML), building upon the significant progress made by successive iterations, from Llama to Llama 2, Llama 3, and now Llama 4. Each iteration has brought notable improvements in language understanding, generation, and conversational capabilities. As the technology continues to evolve, we can anticipate even more sophisticated and human-like conversational capabilities. Future iterations of Llama models may incorporate emerging techniques such as multimodal processing, enabling the models to understand and respond to visual and auditory inputs in addition to text.

The progression from Llama to Llama 4 has been marked by significant advancements, with each version demonstrating improved performance, increased knowledge bases, and a more nuanced understanding of human language. As Llama models continue to improve, they are likely to have a profound impact on various industries, including customer service, education, and entertainment. We can expect to see more widespread adoption of Llama models in applications such as chatbots, virtual assistants, and language translation tools. The continued development of Llama models may also enable new use cases such as more nuanced and empathetic human-computer interactions, and potentially even more creative and generative capabilities. The future of Llama models holds much promise, and it will be exciting to see how they continue to shape the landscape of human-AI interaction.

Evolution and Development History of Llama Models

The journey of the Llama series—from its inception to the latest Llama 4—reflects a strategic and methodical approach to advancing LLMs. This evolution is characterized by iterative enhancements, groundbreaking innovations, and a steadfast commitment to democratizing access to sophisticated AI tools. Understanding the development history of the Llama models provides valuable insights into the broader trajectory of artificial intelligence and NLP.

Origins: The Birth of Llama

The development of the **Llama** series began as Meta (formerly Facebook) sought to establish a significant presence in the competitive landscape of large language models. Recognizing the transformative potential of LLMs in various applications–from content generation to complex problem-solving–Meta aimed to create a model that was not only powerful but also accessible to a wide range of users.

Market Scenario Before and After Llama

The launch of Meta's Llama has fundamentally altered the AI landscape, creating a new paradigm in open-source large language models that has disrupted traditional market dynamics and democratized access to state-of-the-art AI technology.

Pre-Llama Market Landscape

Before Llama's introduction, the AI market was largely dominated by proprietary closed-source models such as OpenAI's GPT series and Anthropic's Claude. These models operated under restrictive licensing terms, limiting developer access and customization capabilities. Companies seeking to integrate advanced AI capabilities into their products faced significant barriers, including high costs, limited control over model behavior, and dependency on external API services.

The open-source AI ecosystem existed but lagged considerably behind proprietary alternatives in performance and capabilities. This created a significant gap between what was available to well-funded organizations versus smaller companies, startups, and individual developers.

- **Post-Llama Market Transformation:** Post-Llama Market Transformation fundamentally shifted the AI landscape from closed, proprietary dominance to open-source democratization, with Llama achieving 350 million downloads globally and catalyzing over 60,000 derivative models that bridged the performance gap between open-source and commercial AI. This transformation enabled unprecedented enterprise adoption across sectors such as finance, telecommunications, and food delivery, while forcing industry leaders to reconsider their business models and accessibility strategies in response to the new competitive dynamics.
- **Explosive Adoption and Growth**: Since its initial launch, Llama has achieved remarkable market penetration. The models have reached 350 million

downloads globally, with over 20 million downloads in a single month on Hugging Face alone. This represents a 10x increase from the previous year, demonstrating unprecedented adoption rates for an open-source AI model.

The usage metrics are equally impressive. Monthly token volume for Llama grew 10x from January to July 2024 across major cloud service providers, with hosted usage more than doubling between May and July 2024 following the release of Llama 3.1.

- **Ecosystem Development**: Llama has catalyzed the creation of a vibrant developer ecosystem with over 60,000 derivative models on Hugging Face. This demonstrates how the open-source approach has enabled widespread experimentation, customization, and innovation that would have been impossible with proprietary models.

Major enterprises have rapidly adopted Llama across various sectors:

- AT and T achieved a 33% improvement in customer care search responses
- Goldman Sachs integrated Llama into their AI platform for document processing
- DoorDash uses it for software engineering tasks and code reviews
- Accenture expects 70% productivity improvements in ESG reporting

Competitive Impact

Industry leaders acknowledge that Llama is "*closing the performance gap between open-source models and top proprietary models*" like OpenAI's GPT and Anthropic's Claude. According to Databricks CEO Ali Ghodsi, "*This generation of Llama models finally bridges the gap between OSS and commercial models on quality*".

The model has become the number two most considered model according to Artificial Analysis benchmarking, and leads as the industry leader in open source.

- **Market Leverage and Model Development Strategy:** Market Leverage and Model Development Strategy centers on Llama's comprehensive data analysis capabilities to gain market insights and audience intelligence, demonstrated through its superior performance in financial applications where Llama 3.3 outperformed traditional ARIMA models in stock prediction tasks. Meta strategically leveraged multi-cloud partnerships with AWS, Azure, and Google Cloud while adopting an open-source approach that accelerated innovation through community contributions, created network effects, and generated significant market influence across the AI ecosystem. The recent introduction of Llama 4 with multimodal capabilities represents the next evolutionary leap, bringing native support for text, images, and video processing that positions Meta to capture additional market segments requiring multimodal understanding and enables new business models across creative industries, enterprise automation, and complex document processing workflows.

- **Data Strategy and Market Intelligence:** Llama leverages comprehensive market data to enhance its capabilities. The model can analyze complex data sets to gain insights about target audiences and market trends, making it particularly valuable for financial and business applications.

Research demonstrates Llama's effectiveness in financial markets, with studies showing Llama 3.3 outperforming both Llama 3.1 and traditional ARIMA models in stock prediction tasks. Academic research has utilized Llama 2 for sentiment analysis in predicting stock returns, showing its capability to process financial narratives and market sentiment.

Strategic Market Positioning

Meta's approach with Llama represents a fundamental shift from the traditional closed-model strategy. By making models openly available, Meta has:

1. Accelerated innovation through community contributions and derivative models
2. Reduced barriers to entry for AI adoption across industries
3. Created network effects that strengthen Meta's position in the AI ecosystem
4. Generated significant goodwill and market influence, as evidenced by praise from industry leaders such as Mukesh Ambani

Partnership and Cloud Infrastructure

Llama's market strategy leverages extensive partnerships with major cloud providers, including AWS, Microsoft Azure, Google Cloud, Databricks, and others. This multi-cloud approach ensures broad accessibility while distributing infrastructure costs and risks.

The model's success has created such high demand that Groq's CEO noted: "*We cannot add capacity fast enough for Llama. If we 10x'd the deployed capacity, it would be consumed in under 36 hours.*"

Economic Impact and Future Implications

The Llama ecosystem is contributing to significant economic growth, with AI overall having the potential to increase global GDP by $10 trillion. Meta's open-source approach has democratized access to frontier-level AI capabilities, enabling innovation across sectors from startups to large enterprises.

The recent introduction of Llama 4 with multimodal capabilities represents the next evolution, bringing native support for text, images, and video processing. This advancement positions Llama to capture additional market segments and use cases that require multimodal understanding.

Llama's market impact extends beyond traditional AI applications into areas such as financial analysis, customer service, content creation, and enterprise automation. The model's ability to be fine-tuned for specific use cases while maintaining cost efficiency has created new business models and opportunities that were previously unavailable in the proprietary model landscape.

The transformation brought by Llama demonstrates how strategic open-sourcing can reshape entire technology markets, creating value not just for the originating company but for the broader ecosystem of developers, businesses, and end users.

Key Milestones in Llama's Development

- **Conceptualization and Objectives (Early 2020s):**
    - **Democratization of AI:** Meta's primary objective was to make advanced language models accessible to researchers, developers, and smaller organizations that previously lacked the resources to leverage such technology.
    - **Efficiency and Scalability:** Emphasis was placed on developing a model that could scale efficiently, balancing performance with computational resource demands.
- **Architecture Design and Training (Mid 2020s):**
    - **Innovative Model Architecture:** Llama was built using state-of-the-art transformer architectures, optimized for both performance and efficiency.
    - **Diverse Training Data:** The model was trained on a vast and diverse corpus of text data, encompassing multiple languages and domains, to ensure versatility and robustness.
- **Release and Community Engagement (Late 2020s):**
    - **Open Accessibility:** Meta released Llama with a focus on open access, providing comprehensive documentation and support to foster a collaborative research environment.
    - **Initial Adoption:** Early adopters in academia and industry began utilizing Llama for various NLP tasks, validating its effectiveness and identifying areas for improvement.

Progression to Llama2: Enhancing Performance and Accessibility

Building upon the foundation laid by Llama, **Llama2** marked a significant advancement in both capabilities and efficiency. The development process for Llama2 was driven by the need to address the limitations of the original model and to incorporate cutting-edge innovations in AI research.

Development Highlights of Llama2

- **Advanced Training Techniques:**
  - **Refined Training Algorithms:** Llama2 employed more sophisticated training algorithms, enabling faster convergence and better generalization across diverse tasks.
  - **Enhanced Data Curation:** Improved data preprocessing and augmentation techniques ensured higher-quality training data, reducing biases and enhancing model reliability.
- **Architectural Improvements:**
  - **Optimized Transformer Layers:** Modifications to the transformer architecture increased the model's capacity to understand and generate nuanced language constructs.
  - **Efficient Parameter Utilization:** Techniques such as parameter sharing and sparsity were implemented to maximize performance while minimizing computational overhead.
- **Multilingual and Cross-Domain Proficiency:**
  - **Expanded Language Support:** Llama2 broadened its linguistic capabilities, supporting a wider array of languages and dialects, thereby increasing its global applicability.
  - **Domain-Specific Adaptability:** The model demonstrated improved performance in specialized domains such as legal, medical, and technical fields through targeted training.
- **Ethical and Responsible AI Enhancements:**
  - **Bias Mitigation:** Advanced methods for identifying and reducing biases in generated content were integrated, aligning the model's outputs more closely with ethical standards.
  - **Safety Protocols:** Enhanced safety measures were implemented to prevent misuse and ensure responsible deployment of the model in various applications.

Llama3: Pioneering the Future of Language Models

The development of **Llama3** represents the latest and most ambitious iteration in the Llama series. This phase of evolution was characterized by groundbreaking innovations aimed at pushing the boundaries of what large language models can achieve, both in terms of technical capabilities and practical applications.

Key Developments in Llama3

- **Innovative Model Architectures:**
  - **Hybrid Transformer Designs:** Llama3 integrated hybrid architectures combining transformers with other neural network paradigms, enhancing the model's ability to process complex language patterns and contextual information.
  - **Scalable Multi-Modal Integration:** The architecture was designed to seamlessly incorporate multiple data modalities, such as text, images, and audio, enabling more comprehensive and interactive AI applications.
- **Advanced Training Paradigms:**
  - **Continuous Learning Mechanisms:** Llama3 introduced mechanisms for ongoing learning, allowing the model to adapt to new information and evolving language trends in real-time without extensive retraining.
  - **Federated Learning Approaches:** Implementing federated learning techniques ensured data privacy and security, enabling the model to learn from decentralized data sources without compromising sensitive information.
- **Enhanced Contextual and Semantic Understanding:**
  - **Deep Contextual Awareness:** Improvements in contextual processing allowed Llama3 to maintain coherence over longer texts and more complex dialogues, enhancing the quality of interactions and generated content.
  - **Semantic Reasoning Capabilities:** The model exhibited advanced semantic reasoning, enabling it to perform tasks that require an understanding of underlying meanings and relationships within the text.
- **Robust Customization and Fine-Tuning:**
  - **User-Friendly Fine-Tuning Tools:** Llama3 provided more intuitive tools for customization, allowing users to fine-tune the model for specific applications with minimal technical expertise.

  - **Industry-Specific Modules:** Pre-trained modules tailored to various industries facilitated quicker deployment and integration into specialized workflows.
- **Ethical AI and Safety Enhancements:**
  - **Advanced Content Filtering:** Enhanced content filtering systems were developed to detect and mitigate the generation of harmful or inappropriate material more effectively.
  - **Transparent AI Practices:** Meta emphasized transparency in Llama3's development and deployment, providing detailed documentation of the model's capabilities, limitations, and ethical considerations.

Llama4: Redefining the Boundaries of Human-AI Interaction

Llama 4 is revolutionizing the way humans interact with AI, pushing the limits of what's possible in conversational technology. With its advanced language understanding and generation capabilities, Llama 4 is redefining the boundaries of human-AI interaction. This cutting-edge AI is enabling more natural, intuitive, and productive conversations.

Key Developments in Llama4

- **Improved Language Understanding**: Llama 4 has made significant strides in understanding natural language, including nuances, idioms, and context.

  Example: When asked "What's the weather like today?", Llama 4 can understand the context and respond with the current weather conditions, taking into account the user's location and any relevant weather alerts.

- **Enhanced Conversational Flow**: Llama4 is designed to engage in more natural and flowing conversations, using contextual understanding to respond to follow-up questions and statements.

  Example: In a conversation about a user's favorite book, Llama4 can ask follow-up questions like "What did you like most about the author?" or "How did the book make you feel?", demonstrating a more human-like understanding of the conversation.

- **Increased Knowledge Base**: Llama4 has been trained on a vast and diverse dataset, enabling it to provide more accurate and informative responses across a wide range of topics.

  Example: When asked about a recent scientific breakthrough, Llama4 can provide a detailed explanation, including the underlying principles and potential applications, demonstrating its ability to access and synthesize complex information.

- **Emotional Intelligence**: Llama4 is designed to be more empathetic and understanding of emotional cues, allowing it to respond in a more supportive and personalized way.

  Example: When a user expresses frustration or disappointment, Llama4 can respond with a sympathetic message, such as "I understand how you feel. Can you tell me more about what's bothering you?" or "I'm here to help. What can I do to support you?"

- **Multilingual Support**: Llama4 continues to improve its support for multiple languages, enabling more effective communication across linguistic and cultural boundaries.

  Example: Llama4 can engage in conversations in multiple languages, including English, Spanish, French, German, Italian, and many others, making it a valuable tool for language learners, travelers, and businesses operating globally.

- **Contextual Understanding**: Llama4 has improved its ability to understand and maintain context throughout a conversation, reducing the need for repetitive clarifications.

  Example: In a conversation about a user's travel plans, Llama4 can remember previous statements and respond accordingly, such as "*You mentioned earlier that you're traveling to Paris. Have you considered visiting the Louvre Museum?*"

- **Creative and Diverse Responses**: Llama4 is capable of generating more varied and creative responses, making conversations more engaging and interesting.

  Example: When asked to generate a short story, Llama4 can produce a unique and imaginative tale, complete with characters, plot twists, and a compelling narrative.

  These developments demonstrate the significant advancements made in Llama4, enabling more natural, informative, and engaging conversations.

Milestones and Achievements

The evolution from Llama to Llama4 has been marked by several key milestones and achievements that underscore the series' impact on the AI landscape:

- **Widespread Adoption and Integration:** Llama models have been integrated into a multitude of applications across diverse sectors, including healthcare, finance, education, and entertainment, demonstrating their versatility and reliability.

- **Academic and Research Contributions:** The Llama series has facilitated numerous research studies, advancing knowledge in areas such as linguistics, cognitive science, and machine learning. Publications and collaborative projects have highlighted the models' capabilities and potential.
- **Community and Ecosystem Development:** Meta fostered a vibrant community around the Llama series, encouraging open-source contributions, collaborative development, and shared innovations that have propelled the models' continuous improvement.
- **Benchmark Performance:** Each iteration of the Llama series has set new benchmarks in standardized evaluations, outperforming contemporaneous models in various metrics related to language understanding, generation quality, and task-specific performance.
- **Ethical Leadership in AI:** Through initiatives focused on ethical AI, bias mitigation, and responsible deployment, the Llama series has positioned Meta as a leader in advocating for and implementing ethical standards within the AI industry.

Challenges and Lessons Learned

The development history of the Llama series has not been without its challenges. Navigating the complexities of large-scale model training, ensuring ethical compliance, and maintaining accessibility have required innovative solutions and strategic foresight.

- **Scalability and Resource Management:** Balancing model size with computational efficiency was a persistent challenge. Iterative optimizations in architecture and training processes were essential to achieving scalable performance without exorbitant resource demands.
- **Bias and Ethical Concerns:** Addressing inherent biases in training data and ensuring the ethical use of the models necessitated the development of robust mitigation strategies and continuous monitoring mechanisms.
- **Accessibility versus Commercialization:** Striking the right balance between making the models widely accessible and protecting intellectual property posed strategic dilemmas. Meta navigated these by adopting open-access policies while implementing safeguards against misuse.
- **Integration of Multimodal Capabilities:** Incorporating multiple data modalities into Llama3 required overcoming technical hurdles related to data synchronization, model coherence, and performance optimization across different types of inputs.
- **User Customization and Flexibility:** Ensuring that users could easily customize and fine-tune the models without deep technical expertise involved developing

intuitive interfaces and comprehensive documentation, which were key to broad adoption.

Future Directions and Ongoing Development

As the Llama series continues to evolve, future developments are poised to explore even more sophisticated aspects of language modeling and artificial intelligence. Anticipated directions include:

- **Emotional and Social Intelligence:** Enhancing models' ability to understand and respond to emotional cues, enabling more empathetic and socially aware interactions.
- **Advanced Reasoning and Problem-Solving:** Integrating deeper reasoning capabilities to handle complex problem-solving tasks and support higher-order cognitive functions.
- **Seamless Human-AI Collaboration:** Developing interfaces and interaction paradigms that facilitate more natural and effective collaboration between humans and AI systems.
- **Sustainable AI Practices:** Focusing on reducing the environmental impact of large-scale model training through more energy-efficient algorithms and sustainable resource management.
- **Global and Inclusive AI:** Expanding support for underrepresented languages and cultures, ensuring that AI advancements benefit a truly global and diverse population.

Key Features and Capabilities of Llama Models: Redefining the AI Frontier

The Llama series has emerged as a cornerstone of large language model innovation, showcasing transformative features and unparalleled capabilities. Designed with a vision to make advanced AI accessible, versatile, and ethically aligned, these models have carved a niche in driving sophisticated AI applications across industries. Here is an in-depth look at the groundbreaking features that make the Llama models exceptional.

- **Scalability Without Compromise**
  - **Flexible Deployment Options:** The Llama series offers multiple model sizes, enabling organizations to balance performance with computational resources effectively.

  - **Streamlined Architecture:** Each iteration employs enhanced transformer designs that maximize throughput, ensuring that even large-scale deployments remain cost-efficient.
- **Superior Language Understanding**
  - **Deep Linguistic Insights:** Trained on extensive and diverse datasets, Llama models excel in understanding idiomatic expressions, slang, and regional language variations.
  - **Context Preservation:** By maintaining context over extended dialogues, the models produce coherent, contextually aware responses suitable for dynamic interactions.
- **Seamless Multilingual Capabilities**
  - **Global Language Proficiency:** The Llama models cater to over 100 languages, supporting businesses and researchers in creating globally inclusive applications.
  - **Dynamic Language Adaptation:** With adaptive fine-tuning, these models can specialize in underrepresented languages, preserving linguistic diversity.
- **Advanced Adaptive Learning**
  - **Continuous Evolution:** Llama3 introduced mechanisms to learn from real-time data, ensuring the model evolves with changing trends and user needs.
  - **Real-World Applicability:** Continuous learning allows the models to adapt to domain-specific jargon and contemporary topics effortlessly.
- **Ethical and Responsible AI**
  - **Robust Bias Mitigation:** By leveraging cutting-edge techniques, the Llama series minimizes biases, fostering equitable AI solutions.
  - **Transparent Design Philosophy:** Meta emphasizes open access and responsible deployment, ensuring the models align with societal values and ethical standards.
- **Customizability for Diverse Applications**
  - **Plug-and-Play Modules:** Pre-trained modules tailored for industries such as healthcare, education, and finance simplify domain-specific customization.
  - **Developer-Friendly Tools:** Intuitive interfaces and extensive documentation enable users to fine-tune and integrate the models with minimal expertise.

- **Enhanced Multimodal Capabilities**
  - **Cross-Modal Interactions:** Llama introduced multimodal processing, seamlessly integrating text, images, and audio for richer and more interactive AI experiences.
  - **Transformative User Experiences:** These capabilities empower applications such as visual question answering and multimodal customer support, setting new benchmarks in human-computer interaction.
- **Exceptional Efficiency**
  - **Optimized Resource Utilization:** The models deliver top-tier performance while maintaining computational efficiency, making them accessible even to resource-constrained users.
  - **Scalable Training Paradigms:** Innovations in training processes reduce time-to-deployment while maintaining exceptional accuracy and reliability.
- **Unmatched Performance Benchmarks**
  - **Best-in-Class Accuracy:** The Llama series consistently outperforms competitors in Natural Language Understanding (NLU), summarization, translation, and much more.
  - **Versatility across Use Cases:** Whether for chatbots, document processing, or sentiment analysis, Llama models excel across a spectrum of AI tasks.
- **Cutting-Edge Security and Safety**
  - **Advanced Content Moderation:** Enhanced safeguards ensure outputs are free from harmful, misleading, or inappropriate content.
  - **User-Centric Guardrails:** With user-focused alignment mechanisms, the models prioritize relevance and accuracy, ensuring a seamless and trustworthy AI experience.
- **Revolutionizing Human-AI Collaboration**
  - **Interactive Intelligence:** Llama models enable fluid and intuitive interactions, fostering seamless collaboration between humans and AI agents.
  - **Enhanced Decision Support:** By analyzing vast datasets and extracting actionable insights, these models act as indispensable assistants in decision-making processes.
- **Sustainability in AI Development**
  - **Energy-Efficient Architectures:** Meta prioritizes sustainable practices, optimizing the Llama series to reduce energy consumption without compromising on performance.

  - **Scalable Green AI:** Future-ready designs ensure that advanced AI capabilities are developed in an environmentally responsible manner.

Detailed Applications of Llama Models in NLP and AI

Following is a comprehensive overview of various applications of Llama (Large Language Model Meta AI) models in Natural Language Processing (NLP) and Artificial Intelligence (AI), structured into distinct scenarios, roles, and examples.

Advanced Text Generation and Creative Assistance

- **Scenario:** Enhancing creative processes in content creation, such as writing stories, generating marketing copy, or producing educational materials.
- **NLP and AI Role:** Llama models generate coherent, contextually relevant, and stylistically appropriate text based on input prompts, aiding creators in brainstorming and drafting content.
- **Examples:**
  - **Personalized Storytelling Platforms:** An interactive app where children input character names and settings, and Llama generates unique adventure stories tailored to their preferences.
  - **Marketing Copy Generation:** A digital agency uses Llama to create engaging product descriptions and ad copy that align with the brand voice and target audience.

Sophisticated Conversational Agents and Emotional Intelligence

- **Scenario:** Developing chatbots and virtual assistants that engage users in meaningful, empathetic conversations, especially in sensitive areas such as mental health support.
- **NLP and AI Role:** Llama models analyze user inputs for emotional cues and respond with appropriate empathy, support, and relevant information, enhancing user interaction quality.
- **Examples:**
  - **Mental Health Support Chatbots:** A mental health organization deploys a Llama-based chatbot to provide immediate support, recognize signs of distress, and recommend professional help when needed.

    - **Customer Service with Emotional Awareness:** An e-commerce platform implements a chatbot that detects customer frustration and escalates complex issues to human agents.

Dynamic Machine Translation with Cultural Nuance

- **Scenario:** Facilitating accurate and culturally sensitive translations for global communications, marketing, and localization of content.
- **NLP and AI Role:** Llama models perform translations that consider cultural context, idiomatic expressions, and regional variations to ensure the translated content resonates appropriately with the target audience.
- **Examples:**
    - **Global Marketing Campaigns:** An international brand uses Llama to adapt slogans and advertisements for different regions, ensuring cultural relevance and effectiveness.
    - **Multilingual Customer Support:** A tech company employs Llama to translate support documentation and live chat interactions, providing seamless assistance to users worldwide.

Deep Sentiment and Emotion Analysis

- **Scenario:** Analyzing customer feedback, social media interactions, and product reviews to gain nuanced insights into user sentiments and emotions.
- **NLP and AI Role:** Llama models perform granular sentiment analysis, distinguishing between various emotions such as joy, anger, sadness, and surprise, providing a deeper understanding of user opinions.
- **Examples:**
    - **Product Development Feedback:** A consumer electronics company analyzes customer reviews to identify specific emotional responses to product features, guiding design improvements.
    - **Social Media Monitoring:** A brand tracks social media mentions, using Llama to gauge public sentiment and adjust marketing strategies accordingly.

Enhanced Information Retrieval and Contextual Question Answering

- **Scenario:** Improving search engines and knowledge bases to provide precise, context-aware answers to complex user queries.

- **NLP and AI Role:** Llama models interpret the intent behind user queries, retrieve relevant information from extensive databases, and synthesize comprehensive answers by aggregating data from multiple sources.
- **Examples:**
  - **Academic Research Assistants:** Universities implement Llama-powered assistants that help students and researchers find relevant papers, summarize findings, and suggest new research directions.
  - **Enterprise Knowledge Bases:** A corporation uses Llama to enable employees to query internal documents and receive accurate, contextually relevant responses, enhancing productivity.

Intelligent Text Summarization with Focused Insights

- **Scenario:** Condensing large volumes of text, such as reports, articles, and legal documents, into concise summaries that highlight key points and actionable insights.
- **NLP and AI Role:** Llama models generate summaries that emphasize specific aspects of the original text based on user-defined criteria, ensuring that the most relevant information is retained.
- **Examples:**
  - **Legal Brief Summarization:** Law firms use Llama to summarize lengthy legal documents, extracting crucial case laws and arguments to aid in case preparation.
  - **Corporate Report Summaries:** Businesses employ Llama to create executive summaries of annual reports, enabling quick review by stakeholders.

Precision Named Entity Recognition (NER) and Semantic Information Extraction

- **Scenario:** Extracting specific information such as names, dates, locations, and organizations from unstructured text for data analysis and organization.
- **NLP and AI Role:** Llama models accurately identify and extract complex entities, including multi-word expressions and context-dependent terms, and determine relationships between them for enriched data representation.
- **Examples:**
  - **Biomedical Research:** Pharmaceutical companies use Llama to extract entities such as gene names and drug compounds from scientific literature, accelerating drug discovery processes.

- **Financial Document Analysis:** Investment firms implement Llama to parse financial reports, extracting key metrics and organizational data for analysis.

Hyper-Personalized Recommendation Systems

- **Scenario:** Delivering tailored recommendations in domains such as e-commerce, entertainment, and education based on individual user behaviors and preferences.
- **NLP and AI Role:** Llama models analyze intricate user data, including past interactions and contextual information, to generate highly personalized suggestions that align with user interests and needs.
- **Examples:**
  - **Customized News Feeds:** News platforms use Llama to curate personalized news articles for users, adapting content based on reading habits and preferred topics.
  - **E-Learning Course Recommendations:** Online education providers employ Llama to suggest courses and learning paths tailored to each learner's progress and interests.

Integrative Speech Recognition and Multimodal AI Interactions

- **Scenario:** Creating seamless interactions that combine voice commands, text generation, and visual context for a richer user experience in applications such as virtual assistants and educational robots.
- **NLP and AI Role:** Llama models work alongside speech-to-text and text-to-speech technologies to handle voice inputs, generate spoken responses, and integrate with visual data for comprehensive multimodal interactions.
- **Examples:**
  - **Interactive Educational Robots:** Schools deploy robots equipped with Llama to engage students through voice interactions, answering questions and providing explanations in real-time.
  - **Smart Home Assistants:** Home devices use Llama to understand and respond to voice commands, control appliances, and provide information based on user requests.

Proactive Content Moderation and Real-Time Compliance Enforcement

- **Scenario:** Monitoring and regulating user-generated content on platforms to ensure compliance with community guidelines and prevent the spread of harmful material.
- **NLP and AI Role:** Llama models analyze text in real-time, detecting and filtering out inappropriate content such as hate speech, harassment, and misinformation, thereby maintaining a safe online environment.
- **Examples:**
    - **Live Streaming Platforms:** Services such as Twitch or YouTube Live use Llama to monitor live chat for violations, automatically removing harmful comments and issuing warnings to users.
    - **Social Networking Sites:** Platforms such as Facebook employ Llama to scan posts and comments, ensuring content adheres to policies regarding harassment and misinformation.

Intelligent Code Generation and Automated Software Documentation

- **Scenario:** Assisting software developers by generating code snippets, providing debugging assistance, and automating the creation of comprehensive documentation.
- **NLP and AI Role:** Llama models understand programming contexts and generate relevant code based on descriptions, while also producing clear documentation and usage examples to support developers.
- **Examples:**
    - **Automated API Documentation:** Tech companies use Llama to generate detailed API documentation from code repositories, including function definitions and usage examples.
    - **Code Snippet Generation:** Developers leverage Llama within IDEs to receive real-time code suggestions and auto-completions, speeding up the coding process and reducing errors.

Advanced Healthcare Analytics and Personalized Patient Care

- **Scenario:** Enhancing patient care by analyzing medical records, predicting health outcomes, and providing personalized treatment recommendations.

- **NLP and AI Role:** Llama models process and interpret unstructured medical data, identify patterns, and generate insights that support healthcare professionals in making informed decisions.
- **Examples:**
    - **Personalized Treatment Recommendations:** Hospitals use Llama to analyze patient histories and genetic information, suggesting tailored treatment plans that improve patient outcomes.
    - **Clinical Documentation Automation:** Healthcare providers implement Llama to transcribe and summarize patient interactions, streamlining record-keeping and ensuring accurate documentation.

Automated Financial Insights and Predictive Analytics

- **Scenario:** Analyzing financial documents, market trends, and news to generate insights, forecast market movements, and identify investment opportunities.
- **NLP and AI Role:** Llama models interpret complex financial texts, extract relevant data, and synthesize information to provide actionable insights and predictive analytics for financial decision-making.
- **Examples:**
    - **Real-Time Market Sentiment Analysis:** Investment firms use Llama to monitor news articles and social media for market sentiment, informing trading strategies based on prevailing trends.
    - **Automated Financial Reporting:** Companies employ Llama to generate comprehensive financial reports and analyses, reducing the time and effort required for manual report creation.

Adaptive Educational Tools and Intelligent Tutoring Systems

- **Scenario:** Creating personalized learning experiences that adapt to each student's unique strengths, weaknesses, and learning pace to optimize educational outcomes.
- **NLP and AI Role:** Llama models assess student performance, generate customized exercises, provide instant feedback, and adjust instructional strategies to cater to individual learning needs.
- **Examples:**
    - **Adaptive Language Learning Platforms:** Language apps use Llama to create dynamic lesson plans that evolve based on the learner's progress, offering tailored practice exercises and conversational scenarios.

- **Intelligent Tutoring Systems:** Educational institutions implement Llama-powered tutors that provide personalized assistance in subjects such as mathematics and science, adapting explanations to suit each student's comprehension level.

Innovative Creative Industries: Interactive Storytelling and Virtual Worlds

- **Scenario:** Enhancing creative projects in writing, gaming, and virtual reality by generating dynamic narratives and responsive dialogues that adapt to user interactions.
- **NLP and AI Role:** Llama models collaborate with creators to develop interactive storylines, generate character dialogues, and adapt narratives in real-time based on user choices and actions.
- **Examples:**
  - **Interactive Virtual Reality (VR) Narratives:** VR game developers integrate Llama to create adaptive storylines where player decisions influence the direction and outcome of the narrative.
  - **Dynamic Scriptwriting for Films:** Film studios use Llama to brainstorm plot ideas and generate dialogue options that evolve with character development and story progression.

Legal and Regulatory Compliance Automation

- **Scenario:** Ensuring that business operations and documentation adhere to relevant laws and regulations through automated compliance checks and audits.
- **NLP and AI Role:** Llama models interpret legal texts, identify compliance requirements, and scan internal documents to detect potential violations, providing recommendations for necessary adjustments.
- **Examples:**
  - **Automated Compliance Audits:** Financial institutions utilize Llama to review internal policies and communications, identifying areas that may not comply with regulatory standards and suggesting corrective actions.
  - **Regulatory Document Analysis:** Companies in highly regulated industries use Llama to analyze new regulations, assess their impact on existing operations, and update procedures accordingly.

Cognitive Behavioral Therapy (CBT) Support Systems

- **Scenario:** Providing accessible mental health support through automated cognitive behavioral therapy exercises and mood tracking.
- **NLP and AI Role:** Llama models guide users through CBT exercises, monitor their emotional states based on interactions, and offer personalized coping strategies to support mental well-being.
- **Examples:**
    - **Virtual CBT Assistants:** Mental health platforms deploy Llama-powered assistants that conduct CBT sessions, track user progress, and adjust therapeutic techniques based on real-time feedback.
    - **Mood Tracking Applications:** Apps use Llama to analyze user journal entries and conversations, providing insights into mood patterns and suggesting interventions when negative trends are detected.

Automated Patent and Intellectual Property Analysis

- **Scenario:** Streamlining the process of patent research, application drafting, and intellectual property management by analyzing vast patent databases and scientific literature.
- **NLP and AI Role:** Llama models scan and interpret patent documents, identify overlapping technologies, assess the novelty of new inventions, and assist in drafting clear and precise patent applications.
- **Examples:**
    - **Patent Strategy Optimization:** Technology firms use Llama to analyze existing patents and scientific papers, identifying gaps and opportunities for new innovations while avoiding infringement issues.
    - **Automated Patent Drafting:** Inventors and legal teams leverage Llama to generate detailed patent descriptions and claims, ensuring comprehensive and accurate documentation of new inventions.

Enhanced Supply Chain and Logistics Management

- **Scenario:** Optimizing supply chain operations by predicting demand, identifying potential disruptions, and recommending efficient logistics strategies based on diverse data sources.
- **NLP and AI Role:** Llama models analyze textual data such as news reports, market trends, and supplier communications to forecast demand fluctuations and anticipate supply chain challenges, enabling proactive management.

- **Examples:**
  - **Predictive Supply Chain Analytics:** Manufacturing companies implement Llama to monitor global news and market data, forecasting demand spikes and identifying risks such as geopolitical tensions or natural disasters that could disrupt supply chains.
  - **Supplier Communication Analysis:** Businesses use Llama to interpret communications from suppliers, detecting signs of delays or issues early to adjust logistics plans accordingly.

Cultural Heritage Preservation and Documentation

- **Scenario:** Preserving and documenting historical texts, artifacts, and cultural narratives through digitization, transcription, and translation, making them accessible to a broader audience.
- **NLP and AI Role:** Llama models transcribe and translate ancient texts, generate detailed descriptions of artifacts, and create narratives that contextualize historical information for educational and preservation purposes.
- **Examples:**
  - **Digital Archives for Museums:** Museums collaborate with Llama to digitize and annotate historical documents and artifacts, providing interactive exhibits that educate visitors with enriched historical context.
  - **Historical Text Translation:** Academic institutions use Llama to translate ancient manuscripts, making them accessible to researchers and the public while preserving their original meanings and nuances.

Advantages of Leveraging Llama Models in Diverse Applications

- **Contextual Understanding:** Llama models excel in grasping nuanced contexts, enabling more accurate and relevant outputs across various tasks.
- **Multilingual Capabilities:** Their ability to understand and generate multiple languages facilitates global applications and cross-cultural interactions.
- **Scalability and Adaptability:** Llama models can scale to handle large datasets and adapt to diverse domains without extensive retraining.
- **Integration Flexibility:** They can be seamlessly integrated into existing systems and workflows, enhancing their functionality without significant overhauls.
- **Continuous Learning:** Llama models can be fine-tuned with new data, allowing them to stay updated with evolving language patterns and domain-specific knowledge.

Conclusion

The Llama series—encompassing Llama, Llama2, and Llama3—has fundamentally transformed the landscape of Natural Language Processing (NLP) and Artificial Intelligence (AI). Each iteration has built upon its predecessors by enhancing scalability, improving language understanding and generation, and introducing sophisticated multimodal capabilities. These advancements have enabled a wide array of applications, from creative content generation and real-time translation to complex data analysis and interactive conversational agents. Furthermore, the series' commitment to ethical AI practices and robustness ensures that these models are not only powerful but also responsible and reliable, making them invaluable tools across diverse industries such as healthcare, finance, education, and entertainment.

Looking ahead, the continuous evolution of the Llama series promises to drive even greater innovation and integration within emerging technologies. Future developments are expected to focus on enhancing real-time processing, expanding domain-specific specializations, and fostering seamless human-AI collaboration. Additionally, advancements in sustainability and ethical frameworks will play a crucial role in ensuring that AI deployment remains beneficial and environmentally conscious. As the Llama models continue to advance, they will undoubtedly unlock new possibilities, further bridging the gap between human intelligence and machine capabilities, and shaping the future of how we interact with and leverage AI in our daily lives.

The next chapter provides an in-depth exploration of Llama's architectural design, examining its computational layers, innovative text generation mechanisms, and cutting-edge optimization techniques.

Multiple Choice Questions

1. What was the primary focus of the original Llama model introduced by Meta?
   a. Multimodal integration with images and audio
   b. Democratizing access to powerful language models through scalability and accessibility
   c. Advanced sentiment analysis and emotion detection
   d. Real-time translation services

2. Which version of the Llama series introduced enhanced coherence over longer passages and better adherence to stylistic prompts in text generation?
    a. Llama
    b. Llama2
    c. Llama3
    d. Llama-X
3. Llama3 introduced which of the following capabilities that were not present in its predecessors?
    a. Basic text generation
    b. Improved handling of low-resource languages
    c. Multimodal capabilities integrating text with images
    d. Standard entity recognition tasks
4. In the context of machine translation, how did Llama3 improve upon previous versions?
    a. By supporting only high-resource languages
    b. By achieving near-human translation accuracy and enabling real-time translation with reduced latency
    c. By focusing solely on extractive summarization
    d. By limiting translation to scripted responses
5. Which application area leverages Llama3's ability to understand relationships between entities for comprehensive data analysis?
    a. Sentiment Analysis
    b. Named Entity Recognition (NER) and Information Extraction
    c. Text Generation
    d. Content Moderation
6. How does Llama3 enhance conversational AI compared to Llama2?
    a. By providing scripted responses
    b. By enabling basic chatbot functionalities
    c. By delivering highly interactive and empathetic conversational agents with a nuanced understanding of user emotions

   d. By limiting conversations to factual questions only

7. Which industry-specific application of the Llama series involves automating the creation and management of patient records?
   a. Finance
   b. Legal
   c. Healthcare
   d. Education

8. What key improvement does Llama3 bring to the scalability and efficiency of the Llama series?
   a. Introduction of basic text generation capabilities
   b. Advanced model compression techniques and hardware-aware optimizations
   c. Support for only a limited number of programming languages
   d. Removal of multimodal integration features

9. Future directions for the Llama series include integration with which emerging technologies to create immersive and intelligent environments?
   a. Blockchain and Cryptocurrency
   b. Augmented Reality (AR) and Virtual Reality (VR)
   c. Traditional databases
   d. Standalone desktop applications

10. What ethical advancements are emphasized in Llama3 compared to earlier versions?
    a. Basic text generation without content filtering.
    b. Initial safeguards against harmful content.
    c. Comprehensive frameworks for bias mitigation, adversarial robustness, and transparent decision-making.
    d. Limiting the model's application to non-sensitive areas.

Answers

1. b
2. b
3. c
4. b
5. b
6. c
7. c
8. b
9. b
10. c

CHAPTER 2
The Architecture of Llama Models

Introduction

The emergence of Large Language Models (LLMs) has transformed the landscape of Natural Language Processing (NLP), empowering machines to understand, generate, and interact with human language with unparalleled precision and fluidity. Among these innovative models, the Large Language Model Meta AI (Llama) architecture has carved a niche as a significant advancement, excelling in performance, efficiency, and scalability.

This chapter provides an in-depth exploration of Llama's architectural design, examining its computational layers, innovative text generation mechanisms, and cutting-edge optimization techniques. By delving into these aspects, readers will gain a comprehensive understanding of the principles and methodologies that position Llama as a trailblazing achievement in AI research. Whether you are a researcher seeking to advance your work, a practitioner implementing NLP solutions, or an enthusiast eager to learn, this analysis offers invaluable insights into one of the most sophisticated language models ever developed.

Structure

In this chapter, we will cover the following topics:

- Architectural Components of Llama Models
- Computational layers and their functions
- Text Generation Mechanisms
- Optimization Techniques

Architectural Components of Llama Models

The architecture of Large Language Model Meta AI (Llama) is a testament to the advancements in natural language processing (NLP) and deep learning. This chapter provides a comprehensive exploration of the architectural components that constitute Llama models, breaking down complex concepts into easily understandable segments. Whether you are a seasoned AI researcher or a curious enthusiast, this chapter aims to illuminate the sophisticated design choices that empower Llama to excel in a multitude of language tasks.

Core Architectural Components

Llama models are built upon a foundation of robust and scalable architectural components. Understanding these components is crucial to appreciating how Llama achieves its remarkable performance. This section delves into each key component, elucidating their roles and interconnections within the model.

Transformer Architecture

At the heart of Llama lies the transformer architecture, a revolutionary framework introduced by Vaswani et al. in 2017. The transformer has become the backbone of most state-of-the-art NLP models due to its ability to handle long-range dependencies and facilitate parallel processing.

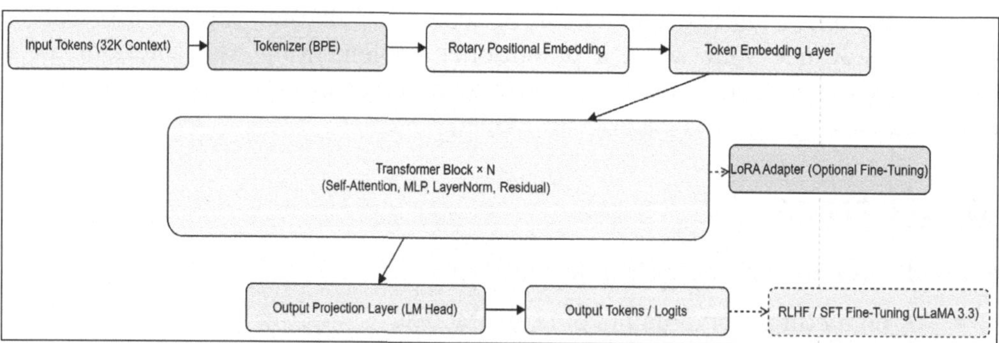

Figure 2.1: *Transformer Architecture*

Input Tokens (Up to 32K Context)

- The model accepts a sequence of text tokens, allowing for very long contexts (up to 32,768 tokens).
- These tokens represent words, subwords, or characters, encoded into IDs.

Tokenizer (BPE – Byte Pair Encoding)

- Converts raw text into **discrete token IDs**.
- **Example**: `"ChatGPT is powerful"` → `[4213, 291, 29398]`

Rotary Positional Embedding (RoPE)

- Injects **position information** into token embeddings.
- RoPE helps the model understand **token order**, critical for capturing language structure.
- More efficient than absolute position embeddings, and works better with long sequences.

Token Embedding Layer

- Maps token IDs to **dense vectors** (for example, 4096-dim for Llama 3 70B).
- **Output**: A matrix of size `[seq_len × hidden_dim]`.

Transformer Blocks × N

- The core of the model. Repeated **N** times (for example, 80 layers in 70B).
- Each block includes:
  - Multi-Head Self-Attention
  - Feedforward (MLP) Layer
  - Layer Normalization
  - Residual Connections

  These layers let the model learn complex dependencies between words and concepts across the full sequence.

LoRA Adapter (Optional)

- **Low-Rank Adapter** layers inserted into the transformer.
- Used during **parameter-efficient fine-tuning**.
- Only a small number of weights are updated, saving compute and storage.
- Skipped during inference if not used.

Output Projection Layer (LM Head)

- Projects the hidden representation to a **vocabulary-sized logits vector**.
- Output shape: `[seq_len × vocab_size].`

Output Tokens/Logits

- The logits go through softmax to produce **token probabilities**.
- Next token is sampled or selected (for example, top-k, beam search).

- These predictions form the **generated text.**

RLHF/SFT Fine-Tuning

- After base pretraining:
  - **Supervised Fine-Tuning (SFT):** aligns the model on instruction-following tasks.
  - **Reinforcement Learning from Human Feedback (RLHF):** optimizes behavior based on reward modeling and preferences.

This step trains the model to follow human intent more safely and helpfully.

Decoder-Only Structure

Unlike the original transformer model, which consists of both encoder and decoder stacks, Llama adopts a decoder-only architecture. This design is optimized for autoregressive tasks, where the model predicts the next word in a sequence based on preceding words.

Advantages:

- **Efficiency:** Eliminating the encoder reduces computational overhead, allowing for faster processing and lower latency during inference.
- **Specialization:** Focusing solely on the decoder enhances the model's ability to generate coherent and contextually relevant text, making it highly effective for tasks such as text generation and completion.

Self-Attention Mechanism

Self-attention is a pivotal component of the transformer architecture, enabling the model to weigh the importance of different tokens within a sequence dynamically.

Key Features:

- **Scaled Dot-Product Attention:** This mechanism calculates attention scores by taking the dot product of query and key vectors and scaling them by the square root of their dimensionality to maintain numerical stability.
- **Multi-Head Attention:** By splitting the attention mechanism into multiple heads, Llama can capture diverse aspects of the data. Each head operates in a different subspace, allowing the model to focus on various contextual relationships simultaneously.

$$\text{MultiHead}(Q, K, V) = \text{Concat}(\text{head}_1, \ldots, \text{head}_h)W^O$$

- **Relative Positional Encoding:** Instead of absolute positional encodings, relative positional encodings allow the model to generalize better across different sequence lengths by focusing on the relative positions of tokens.

  Impact: The self-attention mechanism empowers Llama to understand complex dependencies within the text, facilitating nuanced language understanding and generation.

$$\text{Attention}(Q, K, V) = \text{softmax}\left(\frac{QK^T}{\sqrt{d_k}}\right)V$$

Embedding Layers

Embeddings are the linchpin that transforms discrete tokens into continuous vector spaces, enabling the model to process and comprehend language at a semantic level.

Token Embeddings

Each token in Llama's vocabulary is mapped to a high-dimensional vector. These embeddings are learned during training and capture rich semantic and syntactic information.

Innovations:

- **Subword Tokenization Integration:** By utilizing subword tokenization methods such as Byte Pair Encoding (BPE) or SentencePiece, Llama efficiently handles rare and out-of-vocabulary tokens. This approach strikes a balance between vocabulary size and granularity, ensuring comprehensive language coverage.
- **Contextualized Embeddings:** Unlike static embeddings, Llama employs contextualized embeddings that adapt based on surrounding tokens. This dynamic representation allows the model to capture the nuanced meanings of words in different contexts.

Advanced Positional Embeddings

Positional embeddings inject information about the order of tokens into the model, compensating for the transformer's lack of inherent sequential awareness.

Features:

- **Learned Positional Embeddings:** Instead of fixed sinusoidal functions, Llama uses learned positional embeddings that can be fine-tuned during training. This adaptability allows the model to capture more intricate positional relationships.

- **Hierarchical Positional Encoding:** By incorporating multiple layers of positional information, such as segment-level and token-level encodings, Llama can understand both fine-grained and coarse-grained positional contexts. This hierarchical approach enhances the model's ability to maintain coherence over long sequences.

Benefits: Advanced positional embeddings improve the model's ability to preserve the structure and flow of complex sentences, leading to more coherent and contextually accurate text generation.

Feed-Forward Neural Networks (FFN)

Interleaved within each transformer layer, Feed-Forward Neural Networks (FFNs) introduce non-linearity and expand the model's capacity to capture intricate patterns.

Deep and Wide FFN Structures

Llama employs deeper and wider FFN layers compared to traditional transformer architectures, significantly enhancing the model's expressive power.

Characteristics:

- **Expanded Dimensionality:** By increasing the hidden layer size, the FFN can model more complex relationships within the data, allowing for richer feature representations.
- **Layer-wise Depth:** Stacking multiple FFN layers within each transformer block enables hierarchical feature extraction, fostering the development of more abstract and sophisticated representations.

Activation Functions and Normalization

The choice of activation functions and normalization techniques within FFNs is critical for model performance and training stability.

Implemented Strategies:

- **Gaussian Error Linear Unit (GELU):** GELU offers smoother activation dynamics compared to ReLU, facilitating better gradient flow and enabling more nuanced non-linear transformations.

  $$\text{GELU}(x) = x \cdot \Phi(x)$$

  where $\Phi(x)$ is the cumulative distribution function for the standard normal distribution.

- **Layer Normalization:** Applied before and after FFN layers, layer normalization ensures consistent input distributions, mitigating issues such as vanishing or exploding gradients and accelerating convergence.

Impact: These design choices enhance the FFN's ability to transform representations effectively, contributing to the overall depth and richness of the model's learned features.

Layer Normalization

Layer normalization plays a pivotal role in stabilizing and accelerating the training process by normalizing inputs across the features for each data point.

Application in Llama

In Llama models, layer normalization is strategically applied before the self-attention and FFN layers. This pre-normalization approach ensures that the inputs to these layers have a consistent distribution, which is crucial for maintaining training stability, especially in very deep networks.

Benefits:

- **Stabilized Training:** By normalizing inputs, the model avoids issues related to gradient vanishing or exploding, facilitating smoother and more efficient training.
- **Improved Convergence:** Consistent input distributions allow for more predictable and faster convergence during optimization, reducing training time and enhancing performance.

Residual Connections

Residual connections, also known as skip connections, are integral to the architecture of Llama models. They facilitate the flow of information and gradients through the network, addressing the challenges associated with training deep models.

Implementation in Llama

In Llama, residual connections are incorporated around both self-attention and FFN sub-layers within each transformer block. This means that the input to a sub-layer is added to its output, allowing the model to retain and combine information across layers effectively.

$$\textbf{Output} = \textbf{SubLayer}(x) + x$$

Advantages:

- **Enhanced Gradient Flow:** Residual connections mitigate the problem of vanishing gradients, ensuring that gradients can propagate effectively through deep networks during backpropagation.

- **Information Preservation:** By allowing the original input to bypass intermediate layers, residual connections help preserve essential information, enabling the model to learn more effectively.

Activation Functions

Activation functions introduce non-linearities into the model, which are essential for capturing complex relationships in data. In Llama models, the choice and implementation of activation functions significantly impact performance and training dynamics.

Gaussian Error Linear Unit (GELU)

Llama predominantly employs the Gaussian Error Linear Unit (GELU) activation function, which offers several advantages over traditional activation functions such as ReLU.

Definition:

$$\mathbf{GELU}(x) = x \cdot \Phi(x)$$

where $\Phi(x)$ is the cumulative distribution function for the standard normal distribution.

Advantages:

- **Smooth Activation:** GELU provides a smoother transition around zero compared to ReLU, reducing the likelihood of dead neurons and improving gradient flow.
- **Probabilistic Interpretation:** The probabilistic nature of GELU allows for more nuanced activation dynamics, enhancing the model's ability to capture complex patterns in the data.

Impact: By using GELU, Llama models achieve more stable and effective training, leading to better performance in generating coherent and contextually accurate text.

Parameterization and Scaling

The number of parameters in a model directly influences its capacity to learn and generalize from data. Llama models are meticulously designed to balance parameterization and scalability, ensuring optimal performance across various tasks.

Scaling Laws

Llama adheres to established scaling laws, which provide guidelines on how model performance improves with increases in parameters, data, and computation. These laws inform decisions on model size, training duration, and data requirements.

Key Insights:

- **Diminishing Returns:** While increasing parameters generally enhances performance, the rate of improvement decreases as models become larger. Llama strategically scales parameters to maximize performance without incurring excessive computational costs.
- **Data Efficiency:** Leveraging vast and diverse datasets allows Llama to generalize better, ensuring that parameter increases translate to meaningful performance gains.

Parameter Efficiency

Innovations in parameter sharing and sparsity techniques are employed to enhance parameter efficiency, enabling Llama models to maintain high performance without an unmanageable number of parameters.

Techniques:

- **Weight Sharing:** Reusing weights across different parts of the model reduces the total number of unique parameters, enhancing efficiency without compromising expressiveness.
- **Sparse Architectures:** Implementing sparsity in connections or activations limits the number of active parameters during computation, reducing memory and computational requirements.

Benefits: These strategies allow Llama to scale effectively, balancing the trade-off between model size and computational feasibility, and enabling deployment in resource-constrained environments.

Training Methodologies

The architectural design of Llama models is complemented by sophisticated training methodologies that ensure robust performance and generalization.

Data Preprocessing: Effective data preprocessing is crucial for training high-quality language models. Llama employs meticulous preprocessing techniques to prepare data for optimal learning.

Components:

- **Tokenization:** Advanced tokenization methods, such as Byte Pair Encoding (BPE) or SentencePiece, convert raw text into manageable tokens. This process balances vocabulary size and granularity, facilitating efficient learning.

$$\text{Tokenized Text} = \text{Tokenize}(\text{Raw Text})$$

- **Data Cleaning:** Removing noise and inconsistencies from training data enhances model performance. Techniques include filtering out duplicate content, correcting errors, and standardizing formats to ensure data quality.

Impact: High-quality preprocessing ensures that the model learns from clean and representative data, improving its ability to generalize and perform effectively across diverse tasks.

Training Objectives

The primary objective in training Llama models is to maximize the likelihood of predicting the next token in a sequence, a fundamental approach in autoregressive language modeling.

Components:

- **Autoregressive Training:** By predicting tokens sequentially, Llama models learn contextual dependencies and long-range relationships within the data, crucial for generating coherent and contextually appropriate text.

$$P(\text{sequence}) = \prod_{t=1} P(x_t|x_{<t})$$

- **Loss Functions:** Cross-entropy loss is commonly employed to measure the discrepancy between predicted and actual token distributions, guiding the optimization of model parameters.

$$\mathcal{L} = -\sum_{t=1}^{T} \log P(x_t|x_{<t})$$

Benefits: These training objectives enable Llama to develop a deep understanding of language structure and usage, enhancing its ability to perform a wide range of NLP tasks effectively.

Optimization Techniques

Efficient optimization is vital for training large-scale models within feasible timeframes and resource constraints. Llama leverages advanced optimization techniques to achieve this goal.

Strategies:

- **Adam Optimizer:** Combining momentum and adaptive learning rates, the Adam optimizer is widely used in training Llama models due to its effectiveness in handling sparse gradients and non-stationary objectives.

$$m_t = \beta_1 m_{t-1} + (1 - \beta_1) g_t$$

$$v_t = \beta_2 v_{t-1} + (1 - \beta_2) g_t^2$$

$$\theta_{t+1} = \theta_t - \frac{\eta}{\sqrt{v_t} + \epsilon} m_t$$

- **Learning Rate Schedules:** Dynamic learning rate schedules, such as linear warm-ups followed by cosine decay, help stabilize training and improve convergence rates. These schedules adjust the learning rate based on the training progress, preventing overshooting and ensuring steady improvement.

$$\eta(t) = \eta_{\text{min}} + \frac{1}{2}(\eta_{\text{max}} - \eta_{\text{min}}) \left(1 + \cos\left(\frac{T_{\text{cur}}}{T_{\text{total}}}\pi\right)\right)$$

Impact: These optimization strategies enable Llama to train efficiently, navigating complex loss landscapes and achieving high performance without excessive computational demands.

Regularization Strategies

Regularization techniques are employed to prevent overfitting and enhance the generalization capabilities of Llama models.

Techniques:

- **Dropout:** Randomly deactivating a subset of neurons during training reduces the model's reliance on specific pathways, promoting feature diversity and preventing overfitting.

$$\text{Dropout}(x) = \frac{x \cdot \text{Bernoulli}(p)}{1 - p}$$

- **Weight Decay:** Penalizing large weights encourages the model to maintain smaller, more generalizable parameter values, reducing the risk of overfitting the training data.

$$\mathcal{L} = \mathcal{L}_{\text{data}} + \lambda ||\theta||^2$$

Benefits: These regularization strategies ensure that Llama models maintain high performance on unseen data, enhancing their utility across diverse applications.

Advanced Architectural Innovations

Beyond the foundational components, Llama models incorporate several advanced architectural innovations that enhance their performance and adaptability.

Sparse Attention Mechanisms

To handle long sequences efficiently, Llama implements sparse attention mechanisms, which reduce computational complexity by limiting attention to a subset of tokens.

Features:

- **Local Attention:** Focuses on a fixed window of nearby tokens, capturing local dependencies without the computational burden of full attention.
- **Global Tokens:** Designates certain tokens as global, allowing them to attend to and be attended by all other tokens, facilitating the capture of long-range dependencies.

Benefits:

- **Scalability:** Enables processing of longer sequences without a proportional increase in computational resources.
- **Efficiency:** Reduces memory and time requirements, making it feasible to deploy Llama models in resource-constrained environments.

Adaptive Computation

Adaptive computation techniques allow Llama models to dynamically allocate computational resources based on input complexity, optimizing efficiency without compromising performance.

Strategies:

- **Conditional Computation:** Activates specific pathways or layers only when necessary, depending on the input's complexity or relevance. This selective activation reduces unnecessary computations, enhancing efficiency.

$$\text{Output} = \begin{cases} \text{Layer}_1(x) & \text{if condition}_1 \\ \text{Layer}_2(x) & \text{if condition}_2 \end{cases}$$

- **Dynamic Depth:** Adjusts the number of layers processed based on the input, allowing simpler inputs to pass through fewer layers while more complex inputs utilize deeper networks.

Impact: Adaptive computation ensures that Llama models use resources judiciously, maintaining high performance while minimizing computational overhead.

Mixed Precision Training

Mixed precision training combines lower-precision and higher-precision computations, accelerating training and reducing memory consumption without sacrificing model accuracy.

Implementation:

- **Half-Precision (FP16):** Utilizes 16-bit floating-point representations for most computations, significantly reducing memory usage and increasing computational speed.
- **Full Precision (FP32):** Maintains 32-bit precision for critical operations, ensuring numerical stability and preventing the loss of important information.

Benefits:

- **Speed:** Accelerates training by leveraging the faster computation of lower-precision operations.
- **Memory Efficiency:** Reduces memory footprint, enabling the training of larger models or the use of larger batch sizes.

Challenges:

- **Numerical Stability:** Requires careful management to prevent precision loss in sensitive calculations, often addressed through techniques such as loss scaling.

Modular Design

A modular architectural approach allows for flexible adjustments and enhancements, facilitating the integration of various components without overhauling the entire architecture.

Features:

- **Interchangeable Modules:** Layers and components are designed as interchangeable units, enabling the seamless integration of different activation functions, attention mechanisms, or normalization techniques.
- **Plug-and-Play Components:** Facilitates experimentation and iterative improvements, allowing researchers to test new ideas without disrupting the overall model structure.

Benefits:

- **Flexibility:** Enhances the model's adaptability to different tasks and requirements.

- **Maintainability:** Simplifies updates and modifications, making the architecture easier to manage and evolve.

Scalability and Parallelization

Scaling Llama models to accommodate larger parameter sizes and datasets necessitates robust strategies for parallelization and distributed training.

Model Parallelism

Model parallelism involves distributing different parts of the model across multiple processing units, enabling the training of models that exceed the memory capacity of a single device.

Techniques:

- **Tensor Parallelism:** Splits individual tensors (for example, weight matrices) across devices, allowing large tensors to be processed in parallel.

$$\text{Tensor Parallelism: } W = [W_1, W_2, \ldots, W_n]$$

- **Pipeline Parallelism:** Divides the model into sequential segments processed in a pipelined fashion, allowing different stages of the model to be processed concurrently.

$$\text{Pipeline Parallelism: } \text{Segment}_1 \rightarrow \text{Segment}_2 \rightarrow \ldots \rightarrow \text{Segment}_n$$

Benefits:

- **Memory Management:** Distributes memory requirements across multiple devices, enabling the training of larger models.
- **Increased Throughput:** Enhances computational efficiency by allowing parallel processing of different model segments.

Data Parallelism

Data parallelism replicates the entire model across multiple devices, processing different data batches concurrently.

Synchronization: Efficient synchronization mechanisms, such as gradient averaging or parameter servers, ensure consistency of model parameters across replicas.

Techniques:

- **Synchronous Data Parallelism:** All replicas process data batches simultaneously, and gradients are averaged before updating model parameters.

$$\theta = \theta - \eta \cdot \frac{1}{N} \sum_{i=1}^{N} \nabla_{\theta} \mathcal{L}_i$$

- **Asynchronous Data Parallelism:** Replicas process data batches independently, updating model parameters without waiting for synchronization.

Benefits:

- **Scalability:** Allows for efficient utilization of multiple devices, significantly speeding up the training process.
- **Flexibility:** Can be combined with model parallelism to handle extremely large models.

Distributed Training Frameworks

Leveraging distributed training frameworks such as Horovod and DeepSpeed facilitates the scaling of Llama models across extensive computational clusters, optimizing resource utilization and training speed.

Features:

- **Efficient Communication:** Minimizes communication overhead between devices, ensuring rapid parameter synchronization.
- **Fault Tolerance:** Provides mechanisms to handle device failures and network issues, ensuring robust and uninterrupted training processes.

Benefits:

- **Scalability:** Enables the training of models with trillions of parameters by distributing computation across vast clusters.
- **Ease of Use:** Abstracts the complexities of distributed training, allowing researchers to focus on model development rather than infrastructure management.

Evaluation and Benchmarking

Assessing the architectural components of Llama models involves rigorous evaluation against standardized benchmarks and diverse NLP tasks to ensure comprehensive performance.

Benchmark Suites

Llama models are evaluated using a variety of benchmark suites that test different aspects of language understanding and generation.

Examples:

- **GLUE (General Language Understanding Evaluation):** Assesses a model's performance across multiple NLP tasks, including sentiment analysis, textual entailment, and question answering.
- **SuperGLUE:** An advanced benchmark that includes more challenging tasks, pushing the limits of model capabilities.
- **Language Generation Benchmarks:** Evaluate the model's ability to generate coherent, contextually relevant, and grammatically correct text.

Impact: Benchmarking against these suites provides quantitative measures of Llama's performance, highlighting strengths and identifying areas for improvement.

Ablation Studies

Ablation studies systematically remove or alter specific architectural components to understand their individual contributions to the model's overall performance.

Methodology:

- **Component Removal:** Temporarily disable a particular component (for example, multi-head attention) and observe the impact on performance.
- **Modification:** Change a component's configuration (for example, reducing the number of attention heads) to assess its influence.

Benefits: Ablation studies provide insights into the importance of each architectural component, guiding iterative improvements and refinements.

Comparative Analysis

Comparing Llama models with contemporaneous models, such as GPT or BERT, across similar tasks offers valuable insights into architectural strengths and areas for enhancement.

Approach:

- **Task Performance:** Evaluate how Llama performs on specific tasks relative to other models.
- **Efficiency Metrics:** Compare computational efficiency, memory usage, and inference speed.
- **Scalability:** Assess how well Llama scales with increasing parameters and data compared to other architectures.

Outcome: Comparative analysis highlights Llama's competitive edge and informs future architectural innovations to maintain and enhance its leadership in the field.

Exercises

- **Transformer Architecture Deep Dive:** Explain the role of multi-head self-attention in transformer architecture and how it benefits Llama models specifically.
- **Embedding Techniques Comparison:** Compare and contrast different tokenization methods (for example, BPE versus SentencePiece) and discuss their impact on the performance of Llama models.
- **Optimization Strategies:** Analyze the effectiveness of different optimization algorithms (for example, Adam versus SGD) in training large-scale language models such as Llama.
- **Scalability Challenges:** Discuss the challenges associated with scaling Llama models to trillions of parameters and propose potential solutions.
- **Future Innovations:** Speculate on possible future architectural innovations that could further enhance the capabilities of Llama models.

Answers to Exercises

Note: *These answers are provided to guide your understanding, and are not exhaustive.*

- **Multi-Head Self-Attention:** Multi-head self-attention allows the model to focus on different parts of the input sequence simultaneously, capturing diverse aspects of the data. In Llama models, this enables the model to understand complex language patterns and relationships, enhancing its ability to generate coherent and contextually appropriate text.
- **Tokenization Methods:** BPE merges the most frequent pairs of characters or subwords, resulting in a variable-length vocabulary that can handle rare words effectively. SentencePiece treats the input as a raw stream of characters, which can be advantageous for languages with rich morphology. The choice impacts the model's ability to generalize and handle out-of-vocabulary tokens.
- **Optimization Algorithms:** Adam combines momentum and adaptive learning rates, making it well-suited for training large models with sparse gradients, such as Llama. SGD, while simpler, may require more careful tuning of learning rates and can be less efficient in navigating the complex loss landscapes of large models.
- **Scalability Challenges:** Scaling to trillions of parameters involves significant computational resources, memory constraints, and potential issues with training stability. Solutions include advanced parallelization techniques, model compression methods, and more efficient training algorithms to manage resource demands effectively.
- **Future Innovations:** Potential innovations include integrating multimodal data processing, enhancing model interpretability through better visualization

tools, and developing more energy-efficient architectures to address sustainability concerns.

Glossary

- **Autoregressive Model:** A model that predicts the next element in a sequence based on the preceding elements.
- **BPE (Byte Pair Encoding):** A tokenization method that iteratively merges the most frequent pair of bytes or characters.
- **GELU (Gaussian Error Linear Unit):** An activation function defined as

$$x \bullet \Phi(x)$$

  where $\Phi(x)$ Is the cumulative distribution function for the standard normal distribution.
- **Layer Normalization:** A technique to normalize the inputs across the features for each data point, improving training stability.
- **Residual Connection:** A shortcut connection that adds the input of a layer to its output, facilitating gradient flow.
- **Sparse Attention:** An attention mechanism that limits the number of token interactions, reducing computational complexity.

Appendix

A. Mathematical Foundations

A.1 Self-Attention Mechanism

The self-attention mechanism allows the model to weigh the relevance of different tokens within an input sequence dynamically. Mathematically, it is represented as:

$$\text{Attention}(Q, K, V) = \text{softmax}\left(\frac{QK^T}{\sqrt{d_k}}\right)V$$

Where Q, K, and V are the query, key, and value matrices, respectively, and d_k is the dimensionality of the keys.

A.2 Multi-Head Attention

Multi-head attention extends the self-attention mechanism by projecting the inputs into multiple subspaces:

$$\text{MultiHead}(Q, K, V) = \text{Concat}(\text{head}_1, \ldots, \text{head}_h)W^O$$

where each head is computed as:

$$\text{head}_i = \text{Attention}(QW_i^Q, KW_i^K, VW_i^V)$$

A.3 Positional Encoding

Positional encodings are added to the input embeddings to retain sequence order information:

$$\text{PE}(pos, 2i) = \sin\left(\frac{pos}{10000^{2i/d_{\text{model}}}}\right)$$

$$\text{PE}(pos, 2i+1) = \cos\left(\frac{pos}{10000^{2i/d_{\text{model}}}}\right)$$

where *pos* is the position and *i* is the dimension.

Computational Layers and Their Functions in Llama Architecture

Computational layers form the building blocks of Llama's architecture, enabling it to process, analyze, and generate human-like text. Each layer is tailored to execute a specific function, contributing to the model's overall power and efficiency.

Embedding Layer

The embedding layer translates discrete tokens (words, subwords, or characters) into continuous vector representations that encapsulate their meanings and relationships.

Token Embeddings

- **Concept:** Each word or token in the input sequence is mapped to a unique vector in a high-dimensional space.
- **Semantic Similarity:** Tokens with similar meanings, such as synonyms ("*happy*" and "*joyful*"), are positioned closer in the vector space.
- **Vocabulary Handling:** By utilizing subword-level tokenization (for example, Byte Pair Encoding), Llama can represent rare or unknown words as combinations of smaller units, improving generalization.

Positional Encodings

- **Role:** Since the transformer architecture processes input sequences in parallel, it lacks intrinsic knowledge of token order. Positional encodings introduce sequence order information.
- **Techniques:**
    - **Sinusoidal Functions:** Provide fixed positional values based on sine and cosine functions, ensuring scalability to long sequences.

  - **Learned Positional Embeddings:** Adapt positional representations during training for enhanced flexibility.

Example: For the sentence "I *love* AI," the embedding layer generates vectors for "I," "*love*," and "AI," while positional encodings ensure the model distinguishes between "AI *love* I" and the correct sequence.

Multi-Head Self-Attention Layer

The multi-head self-attention mechanism empowers the model to focus on the most relevant parts of the input sequence.

Self-Attention Mechanism

- **Relevance Mapping:** Calculates the relationship between tokens by creating a weighted map of their relevance to each other.
- **Mathematical Process:**
  - Query (QQQ), Key (KKK), and Value (VVV) matrices are derived from the input embeddings.
  - Attention scores are computed as: `Attention(Q,K,V)=softmax(QKTdk)V\text{Attention}(Q, K, V) = \text{softmax}\left(\frac{QK^T}{\sqrt{d_k}}\right)VAttention(Q,K,V)=softmax(dkQKT)V`
  - Higher scores indicate stronger relationships between tokens.

Example: In the sentence "*The cat chased the mouse*," the self-attention mechanism assigns high relevance between "*cat*" and "*chased*" or "*mouse*" to maintain contextual coherence.

Multi-Head Attention

- **Parallel Contexts:** Divides attention into multiple heads, each capturing different relationships or dependencies in the sequence.
- **Benefits:**
  - Handles polysemy by understanding different meanings of the same word based on context.
  - Improves robustness in processing long or complex sequences.

Feed-Forward Neural Network (FFN)

FFN layers apply transformations to the outputs of the self-attention mechanism, enhancing the model's ability to learn complex patterns.

Structure:

- Comprises two dense (fully connected) layers with a non-linear activation function such as Gaussian Error Linear Unit (GELU), in between.
- Temporarily increases dimensionality to uncover hidden patterns before projecting back to the original size.

Functions:

- **Pattern Recognition:** Extracts abstract features from the attended inputs.
- **Non-Linearity:** Enables the model to learn intricate, non-linear relationships.

Layer Normalization

Layer normalization addresses training instabilities by normalizing the activations across features.

Key Benefits:

- Prevents vanishing or exploding gradients.
- Accelerates convergence by ensuring uniform feature distributions.

Residual Connections

Residual connections are skip connections that bypass one or more layers, ensuring smooth information flow across the network.

Functions:

- Mitigates the problem of vanishing gradients in deep networks.
- Combines the original input with learned transformations, improving feature preservation.

Example: Residual connections ensure that while deeper layers learn abstract features, critical shallow-layer information is not lost.

Text Generation Mechanisms in Llama Architecture

Llama's text generation capabilities stem from its autoregressive design and innovative decoding mechanisms.

Autoregressive Prediction

Llama generates text one token at a time, with each prediction informed by the tokens already generated.

How It Works:

1. The model processes a sequence of input tokens.
2. Using attention and FFN layers, it predicts the next token in the sequence.
3. The predicted token is appended to the input sequence, and the process repeats until completion.

Decoding Strategies

Decoding determines how tokens are selected during text generation.

Greedy Search

- Selects the most probable token at each step.
- **Limitation:** May produce repetitive or overly deterministic results.

Beam Search

- Maintains multiple candidate sequences, exploring the most likely paths.
- **Benefit:** Balances coherence and diversity but requires higher computational resources.

Sampling Techniques

- Introduces randomness for creative and diverse outputs:
  - **Top-k Sampling:** Restricts choices to the top-k probable tokens.
  - **Nucleus Sampling (Top-p):** Chooses from tokens with cumulative probabilities above a threshold ppp, dynamically adjusting the pool size.

Context Awareness

Contextual embeddings and attention mechanisms ensure that the generated text maintains logical flow and relevance.

Example Use Case: A conversational agent such as ChatGPT generates coherent and contextually appropriate responses, even in multi-turn dialogues.

Optimization Techniques in Llama Architecture

Optimization in Llama is a multi-faceted approach encompassing advanced optimizers, learning rate schedules, gradient stabilization, memory efficiency, and regularization. Each of these techniques addresses specific challenges in training and deploying large-scale models.

Optimization techniques are pivotal in achieving the efficiency, scalability, and robustness of the Llama model architecture. These methods not only enhance training stability and convergence but also ensure the model's adaptability to a wide range of tasks without excessive computational or memory requirements. Following is an exhaustive analysis of the optimization strategies employed in Llama models.

Optimizers

An optimizer is the backbone of any machine learning model training process, adjusting the model's parameters to minimize loss and improve accuracy.

Adam Optimizer

- **Description:** The Adam (Adaptive Moment Estimation) optimizer combines the benefits of two widely used optimization algorithms: RMSProp and Stochastic Gradient Descent with momentum.
- **Features:**
  - **Momentum:** Smooths out parameter updates by leveraging past gradients.
  - **Adaptive Learning Rates:** Adjusts learning rates for each parameter dynamically based on the magnitude of past gradients.
- **Equation:**

$$m_t = \beta_1 m_{t-1} + (1 - \beta_1) g_t$$

$$v_t = \beta_2 v_{t-1} + (1 - \beta_2) g_t^2$$

$$\theta_{t+1} = \theta_t - \frac{\eta}{\sqrt{v_t} + \epsilon} m_t$$

- **Advantages:**
  - Handles sparse gradients effectively.
  - Provides faster convergence in large-scale, high-dimensional data spaces.

Weight Decay

Weight decay acts as a regularization term to prevent overfitting by penalizing large weights in the optimization process.

- **Impact:** Encourages simpler models with smaller weights, improving generalization.

Learning Rate Schedules

Dynamic learning rate schedules are critical for balancing fast convergence and stable training. The Llama architecture employs sophisticated scheduling mechanisms to adjust learning rates dynamically.

Warm-Up Phase

- **Description:** During the initial training phase, the learning rate is gradually increased from a very small value to a predefined peak.
- **Benefits:**
    - Prevents unstable updates during early epochs.
    - Stabilizes training when the model's parameters are randomly initialized.

Cosine Decay

- **Description:** After the warm-up phase, the learning rate decreases gradually following a cosine function.
- **Equation:** `ηt=ηmin+12(ηmax-ηmin)(1+cos⁡(tTπ))\eta_t = \eta_{\text{min}} + \frac{1}{2} (\eta_{\text{max}} - \eta_{\text{min}}) \left(1 + \cos\left(\frac{t}{T} \pi\right)\right)`

$$\eta_t = \eta_{\text{min}} + \frac{1}{2}(\eta_{\text{max}} - \eta_{\text{min}}) \left(1 + \cos\left(\frac{t}{T}\pi\right)\right)$$

- **Benefits:**
    - Smoothly reduces learning rates to fine-tune the model toward convergence.
    - Avoids abrupt drops, ensuring stability.

Cyclical Learning Rates

- **Description:** Alternates the learning rate between a lower and upper bound, following a periodic schedule.
- **Benefits:**
    - Helps escape sharp local minima.
    - Encourages broader exploration of the parameter space.

Gradient Clipping

Gradient clipping stabilizes training by capping the magnitude of gradients during backpropagation.

How It Works:

1. If a gradient's magnitude exceeds a predefined threshold, it is scaled down to the threshold value.
2. The gradient direction is preserved while its size is constrained.

Benefits:

- Prevents exploding gradients in deep networks.
- Ensures consistent parameter updates.

Mixed Precision Training

Mixed precision training combines 16-bit (FP16) and 32-bit (FP32) floating-point computations, optimizing both memory usage and computational speed.

Techniques:

- **Loss Scaling:** Amplifies the loss values to prevent numerical instability caused by smaller gradients in FP16 computations.
- **Selective Precision:** Uses FP16 for most operations while reserving FP32 for critical calculations such as weight updates.

Advantages:

- Reduces GPU memory usage by up to 50%.
- Accelerates training without significant accuracy loss.

Challenges:

- Requires careful implementation to avoid underflows and overflows in calculations.

Regularization Techniques

Regularization prevents overfitting by penalizing complex models and encouraging simpler, generalizable solutions.

Dropout

Description: During training, randomly "drops" a subset of neurons by setting their outputs to zero.

Equation: `Dropout(x)=x·Bernoulli(p)\text{Dropout}(x) = x \cdot \text{Bernoulli}(p)`

$$\text{Dropout}(x) = x \cdot \text{Bernoulli}(p)$$

Impact:

- Introduces noise, forcing the model to rely on multiple features rather than memorizing patterns.
- Enhances robustness.

Weight Sharing

Description: Reuses weights across different layers or operations, reducing the model's complexity.

Impact:

- Reduces memory requirements.
- Improves scalability without compromising performance.

Data Augmentation

Data augmentation techniques artificially increase the diversity of training data, improving the model's ability to generalize.

Examples:

- **Shuffling Tokens:** Rearranges tokens in a sequence while preserving meaning.
- **Masking Tokens:** Randomly masks certain input tokens, forcing the model to predict missing words.
- **Noise Injection:** Adds controlled noise to inputs, improving resilience to noisy data.

Impact:

- Reduces overfitting by exposing the model to varied data distributions.
- Enhances robustness in real-world applications.

Distributed Training

To handle Llama's vast parameter space, distributed training strategies are employed.

Techniques:

- **Model Parallelism:** Splits the model across multiple GPUs or nodes, distributing computation-heavy tasks.
- **Data Parallelism:** Processes different batches of data across multiple devices simultaneously.

Impact:

- Reduces training time significantly.
- Enables training of larger models on limited hardware.

Early Stopping

Early stopping halts training when the model's performance on a validation set stops improving.

Benefits:

- Prevents overfitting.
- Saves computational resources by avoiding unnecessary training epochs.

Things to Remember: Key Points from Llama Model Architecture

Computational Layers and Their Functions

- **Embedding Layer:**
    - Converts tokens into dense vector representations.
    - Positional encodings add sequence order information.
- **Multi-Head Self-Attention:**
    - Identifies relationships between tokens using attention mechanisms.
    - Multi-head attention captures diverse contextual patterns.
- **Feed-Forward Neural Network (FFN):**
    - Processes output from attention layers.
    - Adds non-linearity and learns intricate patterns.
- **Layer Normalization:**
    - Stabilizes training by normalizing inputs across features.
    - Prevents gradient-related instabilities.
- **Residual Connections:**
    - Facilitates gradient flow in deep networks.
    - Combines raw and transformed features for enhanced learning.

Text Generation Mechanisms

- **Autoregressive Prediction:**
    - Generates text token by token, leveraging previous outputs.

  - Ensures coherence and logical flow in sequences.
- **Decoding Strategies:**
  - **Greedy Search:** Selects the most probable token at each step (fast but less diverse).
  - **Beam Search:** Explores multiple candidate sequences for optimal quality.
  - **Sampling (Top-k/Top-p):** Introduces randomness for creative and diverse text.
- **Context Awareness:**
  - Relies on attention and embeddings to maintain logical consistency.
  - Positional encodings ensure sequence integrity.

Optimization Techniques

- **Optimizers:**
  - **Adam:** Combines momentum and adaptive learning rates for efficient convergence.
  - **Weight Decay:** Regularizes models by penalizing large weights.
- **Learning Rate Schedules:**
  - **Warm-Up:** Gradual increase of learning rates during initial epochs.
  - **Cosine Decay:** Smoothly decreases learning rates for fine-tuning.
- **Gradient Clipping:**
  - Prevents exploding gradients by capping their magnitude during updates.
- **Mixed Precision Training:**
  - Combines FP16 and FP32 computations to optimize memory usage and speed.
  - Loss scaling maintains numerical stability.
- **Regularization Techniques:**
  - **Dropout:** Randomly deactivates neurons during training to prevent overfitting.
  - **Weight Sharing:** Reuses weights across layers to improve scalability.
- **Data Augmentation:**
  - Increases data diversity through techniques such as shuffling, masking, and noise injection.
- **Distributed Training:**
  - **Model Parallelism:** Splits computation-heavy tasks across GPUs.
  - **Data Parallelism:** Processes batches on multiple devices simultaneously.

- **Early Stopping:**
    - Stops training when validation performance ceases to improve, saving resources.

Conclusion

The Llama model architecture exemplifies the cutting-edge advancements in natural language processing, blending sophisticated computational layers, efficient text generation mechanisms, and powerful optimization techniques. Its design leverages the transformative capabilities of multi-head self-attention, feed-forward networks, and residual connections to process and generate human-like text with remarkable accuracy and coherence.

Through strategic optimization, including dynamic learning rate schedules, gradient clipping, and mixed precision training, Llama achieves scalability and robustness without overwhelming computational resources. Its ability to adapt to diverse NLP tasks, from text generation to contextual understanding, underscores its flexibility and effectiveness in real-world applications.

As a milestone in large language model development, Llama's architecture not only addresses the challenges of deep learning but also sets the stage for future innovations. By embracing efficient computational strategies and intelligent design principles, it paves the way for models that are not only more powerful but also more accessible and sustainable.

In summary, Llama is a testament to the synergy between theory and practical implementation, offering a robust framework for tackling the complexities of human language while maintaining efficiency and scalability.

The upcoming chapter will highlight the evolution of Llama, from its initial release that laid the foundation for open LLM research to the advanced Llama 4, which embodies significant improvements in scale, efficiency, and performance.

Multiple Choice Questions

1. What does Llama stand for?
    a. Large Language Model Meta AI
    b. Large Linguistic Model Meta Analysis
    c. Large Level Model Meta AI
    d. Linguistic Language Model Meta AI

2. What is the primary foundation of the Llama architecture?
    a. Recurrent Neural Networks
    b. Convolutional Neural Networks
    c. Transformer Architecture
    d. Markov Models
3. Which of the following is NOT a key component of Llama's architecture?
    a. Multi-Head Self-Attention
    b. Feed-Forward Neural Networks
    c. Convolution Layers
    d. Dynamic Optimization Techniques
4. What makes Llama a versatile tool for NLP tasks?
    a. Its use of RNNs for sequence modeling
    b. Integration of multi-head self-attention and feed-forward networks
    c. Fixed optimization strategies
    d. Exclusive focus on text classification tasks
5. Which of the following NLP tasks can Llama NOT perform?
    a. Text Generation
    b. Image Recognition
    c. Summarization
    d. Question Answering
6. What is the purpose of multi-head self-attention in Llama?
    a. To increase memory efficiency
    b. To capture diverse contextual relationships in text
    c. To reduce the number of parameters in the model
    d. To process images alongside text
7. How does the Feed-Forward Neural network (FFN) in Llama contribute to its architecture?
    a. It handles positional encoding.
    b. It transforms attention outputs with non-linear processing.

   c. It reduces computational overhead.

   d. It acts as the final layer for token prediction.

8. Which optimization technique is primarily used in Llama to stabilize training?

   a. Adam Optimizer with Weight Decay

   b. RMSProp

   c. Gradient Descent without momentum

   d. AdaGrad

9. What enables Llama to maintain sequence order in text processing?

   a. Embedding Layer

   b. Positional Encoding

   c. Convolutional Layers

   d. Beam Search

10. Why is Llama considered a landmark achievement in AI research?

    a. It is the first AI model to generate images.

    b. It combines scalability, high performance, and efficiency in NLP tasks.

    c. It uses only convolutional layers for text generation.

    d. It relies exclusively on static embeddings.

Answers

1. a
2. c
3. c
4. b
5. b
6. b
7. b
8. a
9. b
10. b

CHAPTER 3
Evolution of Llama

Introduction

In the rapidly evolving landscape of artificial intelligence, language models have emerged as pivotal tools reshaping the way we interact with technology. From the early days of rule-based systems to the sophisticated neural architectures of today, the journey of language model development is a testament to human ingenuity and the relentless pursuit of understanding and replicating the nuances of human language. This chapter, "*Evolution to Llama Models: Introduction*," delves into the transformative progression that has culminated in the creation of Llama models, a groundbreaking advancement in the realm of Natural Language Processing (NLP).

The Rise of Neural Networks in NLP: The integration of neural networks into language modeling marked a pivotal turning point, enabling the creation of models capable of capturing intricate patterns and contextual relationships within language. Recurrent Neural Networks (RNNs) and their variants, such as Long Short-Term Memory (LSTM) networks, were among the first to demonstrate the potential of deep learning in understanding sequential data. These models showcased remarkable proficiency in tasks such as machine translation and text generation, albeit with limitations in handling long-range dependencies.

The introduction of the Transformer architecture heralded a new era, addressing the shortcomings of previous models by facilitating parallel processing and enhancing the capacity to model long-term dependencies. Transformers revolutionized NLP, leading to the development of large-scale models that could be fine-tuned for a myriad of applications, from sentiment analysis to conversational agents.

Enter Llama Models: Against this backdrop of relentless innovation, the Llama (Large Language Model Meta AI) models emerged as a formidable contender, pushing the boundaries of what language models can achieve. Developed by Meta AI, Llama models are designed to be both scalable and efficient, striking a balance between performance and resource utilization. Their architecture embodies the principles of the Transformer model while introducing novel enhancements that optimize training processes and model generalization.

Llama models are distinguished by their ability to harness vast datasets, enabling them to generate human-like text with remarkable coherence and contextual relevance. Their versatility extends across diverse applications, from automated content creation and virtual assistance to advanced data analysis and beyond. Moreover, the modularity of Llama models facilitates their integration into existing systems, offering flexibility and adaptability in deployment.

Structure

In this chapter, we will cover the following topics:

- Overview
- Development Timeline and Milestones
- Comparative Analysis of Llama, Llama2, and Llama3
- Technological Advancements and Enhancements
- Use Cases and Applications across Different Domains

Overview

The evolution of artificial intelligence (AI) has been marked by a series of breakthroughs, each contributing to the growing sophistication of machine learning models. At the forefront of this revolution lies natural language processing (NLP), a field dedicated to bridging the gap between human language and machine understanding. Among the recent milestones in NLP, Llama models represent a significant leap forward in both performance and efficiency. In this chapter, we explore the evolution of Llama models—an exciting new class of large language models developed by Meta AI—and the innovative principles that underpin their development.

From Early Models to Neural Networks: Laying the Foundation

The journey to Llama models did not happen overnight. It spans decades of research and development, beginning with early computational attempts at language processing. Early models, such as rule-based systems and statistical models, were limited by their ability to scale and generalize across diverse linguistic contexts. While these models were capable of handling tasks such as parsing and speech recognition, they lacked the capacity to understand the subtleties of human language.

In the 1990s, the shift toward probabilistic models, such as Hidden Markov Models (HMMs), began to show more promise. These models could predict the likelihood of a word sequence and were more flexible than their predecessors. However, they still relied heavily on handcrafted rules and simple probabilistic assumptions that constrained their capacity for more complex tasks.

The true transformation in NLP began with the advent of neural networks. Early approaches, such as Recurrent Neural Networks (RNNs) and Long Short-Term Memory (LSTM) networks, brought with them the ability to capture sequential patterns and remember contextual information over longer sequences. Despite their success in certain applications such as language translation, these models struggled with long-range dependencies and required substantial computational resources.

The Transformer Revolution: Unleashing Scalable Language Models

The breakthrough that ultimately paved the way for Llama models came in 2017 with the introduction of the Transformer architecture by Vaswani et al. The Transformer solved the long-standing issue of modeling long-range dependencies in language by using a self-attention mechanism, enabling the model to focus on different parts of a sentence simultaneously. This parallelization drastically improved training efficiency, allowing for the development of larger, more powerful models.

The Transformer model revolutionized NLP and spurred the development of large pre-trained models such as OpenAI's GPT (Generative Pretrained Transformer) series, Google's BERT (Bidirectional Encoder Representations from Transformers), and later models such as T5 and RoBERTa. These models demonstrated unprecedented capabilities in tasks such as text generation, sentiment analysis, and question answering by learning from massive datasets and fine-tuning specific tasks.

However, despite their success, these models came with significant challenges. Their size, resource consumption, and environmental impact raised concerns about the feasibility of training such models at scale. This gap in efficiency led to the development of more optimized architectures, one of which would be the Llama family of models.

The Birth of Llama Models: Bridging Efficiency and Performance

Llama, short form of **Large Language Model Meta AI**, was introduced by Meta AI as a set of transformer-based language models designed to strike a balance between cutting-edge performance and efficient use of computational resources. Llama models were conceived with the goal of making large-scale NLP more accessible while maintaining or improving the performance of previous models in a variety of benchmarks.

One of the key innovations of Llama models is their focus on reducing the resource burden without sacrificing performance. Unlike other large models that often require specialized hardware to train and deploy, Llama models are designed to be more resource-efficient, enabling researchers and developers with less computational power to benefit from their capabilities. This approach was informed by Meta AI's commitment to making AI more accessible and democratizing machine learning research.

Llama models also introduced optimizations in the training process, such as data-efficient pre-training, architectural tweaks, and strategies to reduce overfitting while increasing generalization. These advancements allow the Llama models to outperform previous models in certain NLP tasks without requiring the immense computational resources typically associated with large-scale transformers.

Figure 3.1: *Emergence of Llama Models*

Key Features and Benefits of Llama Models

The evolution of Llama models was shaped by several defining characteristics that make them unique within the landscape of large language models:

- **Scalability:** Llama models are designed to scale effectively, allowing them to handle a wide range of NLP tasks. By leveraging both larger datasets and more efficient training techniques, Llama models can achieve a high degree of accuracy across diverse applications, from text generation to language understanding.
- **Resource Efficiency**: One of the standout features of Llama models is their optimized architecture, which balances performance with efficiency. This makes them suitable for environments where computational resources are limited, such as smaller research labs or smaller-scale deployments.
- **Versatility Across Tasks**: Llama models are highly versatile, supporting a wide range of NLP tasks such as machine translation, summarization, question answering, and sentiment analysis. Their ability to generalize across multiple

domains makes them a powerful tool for both academic research and real-world applications.

- **Adaptability to New Data**: Llama models are designed with flexibility in mind, enabling them to be fine-tuned for specific applications or tasks with minimal additional training. This adaptability ensures that they can evolve as new challenges emerge in the world of AI and NLP.

Development Timeline and Milestones

The realm of artificial intelligence (AI) has undergone significant transformations over the past decade, largely propelled by advancements in natural language processing (NLP) and the development of sophisticated language models. Among these, Meta Platforms' Llama series stands out as a pivotal innovation, representing a culmination of years of research, collaboration, and technological breakthroughs. This chapter offers an in-depth exploration of the evolution of Llama models, tracing their developmental timeline, highlighting key milestones, and assessing their profound impact on the AI landscape. By examining the journey of Llama, we gain insights into the intricate processes that drive cutting-edge AI advancements and the future directions that lie ahead.

The Genesis of Llama: Foundations and Inspirations

The journey of Llama began with the vision to democratize access to powerful language models while ensuring efficiency and scalability. Unlike earlier proprietary LLMs, Llama was inspired by the need for open research, lightweight architectures, and high performance on modest hardware. Rooted in advances from models like GPT, its foundation reflects a balance between accessibility and cutting-edge innovation, setting the stage for a new era in AI development.

The AI Landscape of Pre-Llama

Before the advent of Llama, the AI community witnessed rapid progress in language modeling, primarily driven by models such as OpenAI's GPT series and Google's BERT. These models revolutionized tasks such as text generation, translation, and sentiment analysis, setting high benchmarks for AI performance. However, despite their successes, these models faced significant challenges:

- **Computational Constraints**: Training and deploying large-scale models demanded immense computational resources, limiting accessibility to well-funded organizations.

- **Bias and Ethical Concerns:** Language models often inherit biases present in training data, raising ethical concerns about fairness and representation.
- **Scalability Issues:** As models grew in size, ensuring scalability without compromising performance became increasingly complex.

Meta Platforms recognized these challenges and sought to develop a language model that not only matched the capabilities of existing models but also addressed their limitations. This vision laid the foundation for the creation of Llama.

Meta's Vision for Llama

Meta envisioned Llama as a versatile, scalable, and efficient language model that could be leveraged across various applications and industries. The core objectives included:

- **Efficiency:** Optimize training and inference processes to reduce computational costs without sacrificing performance.
- **Accessibility:** Make advanced language models accessible to a broader audience, including smaller organizations and independent developers.
- **Ethical AI:** Implement robust mechanisms to mitigate biases and ensure responsible AI usage.
- **Multilingual Proficiency:** Develop a model capable of understanding and generating text in multiple languages, catering to a global user base.

Development Timeline: From Concept to Deployment

The evolution of Llama models can be segmented into distinct phases, each characterized by specific objectives, breakthroughs, and milestones. This section provides a comprehensive timeline, detailing the progression from initial concept to full-fledged deployment.

Phase 1: Conceptualization and Initial Development (2020-2021)

Conceptual Framework (Early 2020): In early 2020, Meta's AI research division began outlining the conceptual framework for Llama. This phase involved:

- **Defining Objectives:** Establishing the primary goals of Llama, including scalability, efficiency, and ethical considerations.
- **Architectural Design:** Deciding on the foundational architecture, heavily inspired by transformers but incorporating unique modifications to enhance performance.

- **Research and Development Planning:** Allocating resources, forming interdisciplinary teams, and setting milestones for the project's progression.

Prototype Development (Mid 2020): By mid-2020, Meta had developed initial prototypes of Llama. The key activities included:

- **Experimentation with Transformer Variants:** Testing different transformer configurations to identify optimal structures for language understanding and generation.
- **Integration of Novel Attention Mechanisms:** Introducing innovative attention mechanisms to improve contextual understanding and reduce computational overhead.
- **Data Collection and Preprocessing:** Gathering diverse and extensive datasets to train the prototypes, ensuring a wide representation of languages and contexts.

Alpha Testing (Late 2020): In the latter part of 2020, early versions of Llama entered the alpha-testing phase. This involved:

- **Internal Evaluation:** Subjecting prototypes to rigorous testing within Meta's controlled environments to assess performance and identify areas for improvement.
- **Feedback Integration:** Collecting feedback from internal testers to refine model parameters, enhance data preprocessing techniques, and address initial biases.
- **Benchmarking:** Comparing Llama's performance against existing models such as GPT-3 and BERT to gauge progress and set future targets.

Phase 2: Scaling and Optimization (2021-2022)

Scaling Up (Early 2021): Building on the foundational prototypes, Meta embarked on scaling Llama to handle larger datasets and more complex language tasks. This phase included:

- **Parameter Expansion:** Increasing the number of parameters from millions to billions, enhancing the model's capacity to capture intricate language patterns.
- **Infrastructure Enhancement:** Upgrading computational infrastructure to support distributed training across multiple GPUs and specialized hardware accelerators.
- **Parallel Computing Techniques:** Implementing advanced parallel computing strategies to expedite training processes and manage resource allocation efficiently.

Optimization Techniques (Mid 2021): As Llama scaled, Meta focused on optimizing training processes to manage computational demands effectively. Key optimization strategies included:

- **Mixed-Precision Training:** Utilizing mixed-precision arithmetic to balance computational efficiency with model accuracy, reducing memory usage and speeding up training.
- **Model Pruning and Quantization:** Identifying and removing redundant model parameters, thereby decreasing model size without compromising performance.
- **Efficient Data Pipelines:** Streamlining data ingestion and preprocessing workflows to minimize bottlenecks and ensure seamless training operations.

Beta Release (Late 2021): In late 2021, Meta released a beta version of Llama to selected partners and research institutions. This phase served multiple purposes:

- **Real-World Testing:** Allowing external users to integrate Llama into various applications, providing insights into its practical performance and versatility.
- **Performance Feedback:** Gathering comprehensive feedback on model behavior, including strengths and limitations in different contexts.
- **Community Engagement:** Fostering collaboration with the research community to incorporate diverse perspectives and innovative ideas into Llama's development.

Phase 3: Public Deployment and Iterative Improvement (2022-2023)

Official Launch (Early 2022): The official launch of Llama in early 2022 marked a significant milestone. The key aspects included:

- **Comprehensive Documentation:** Providing detailed guides, API references, and usage examples to facilitate seamless integration into diverse applications.
- **API and SDK Availability:** Offering robust APIs and software development kits (SDKs) to enable developers to harness Llama's capabilities effortlessly.
- **Marketing and Outreach:** Launch campaigns, webinars, and workshops to raise awareness about Llama's features and potential applications.

Community Engagement (Mid 2022): Meta prioritized engaging with the developer and research communities to accelerate Llama's evolution. The salient activities included:

- **Open-Source Contributions:** Encouraging developers to contribute to Llama's codebase, fostering a collaborative development environment.
- **Hackathons and Competitions:** Organizing events to spur innovation,

challenge developers to create novel applications, and showcase Llama's versatility.

- **Feedback Loops:** Establishing channels for continuous feedback, allowing Meta to iterate on Llama based on real-world usage and community insights.

Iterative Enhancements (2022-2023): Between 2022 and 2023, Llama underwent continuous refinements to enhance its performance and capabilities. The key improvements included:

- **Contextual Understanding:** Enhancing the model's ability to grasp nuanced language constructs, idiomatic expressions, and contextual dependencies.
- **Latency Reduction:** Optimizing inference processes to achieve faster response times, is crucial for real-time applications such as chatbots and virtual assistants.
- **Multilingual Enhancements:** Expanding language support and improving translation accuracy to cater to a global user base.

Key Milestones in Llama's Evolution

The journey of Llama is marked by several pivotal milestones, each representing significant advancements in its development. This section highlights these key achievements, illustrating Llama's growth and maturation over time.

Achieving Parameter Milestones

Billion Parameters (Early 2021): Reaching the 1 billion parameter mark was a foundational milestone for Llama. This expansion:

- **Enhanced Language Understanding:** Allowed the model to capture more complex language patterns and dependencies.
- **Improved Task Performance:** Enabled better performance across a range of NLP tasks, from text generation to question answering.
- **Benchmark Comparisons:** Positioned Llama competitively against contemporaneous models, showcasing its potential for further scaling.

10 Billion Parameters (Late 2021): Scaling Llama to 10 billion parameters represented a tenfold increase, bringing substantial enhancements:

- **Sophisticated Text Generation:** Facilitated the creation of more coherent, contextually accurate, and human-like text.
- **Expanded Knowledge Base:** Increased the model's ability to retain and utilize vast amounts of information, improving its utility in diverse applications.
- **Enhanced Comprehension:** Improved the model's capacity to understand and respond to complex queries and instructions.

100 Billion Parameters (Early 2023): The 100 billion parameter milestone marked Llama as one of the most advanced language models of its time:

- **State-of-the-Art Performance:** Achieved top-tier results in various NLP benchmarks, rivaling leading models such as GPT-4.
- **Versatility:** Demonstrated exceptional adaptability across a wide array of tasks, from creative writing to technical documentation.
- **Scalability Showcase:** Highlighted the effectiveness of Meta's scaling strategies and optimization techniques in managing large-scale models.

Breakthroughs in Training Efficiency

Adaptive Learning Rates (2021): In 2021, Meta introduced adaptive learning rate schedules to optimize Llama's training dynamics. This innovation:

- **Faster Convergence:** Enabled the model to reach optimal performance levels more quickly, reducing overall training time.
- **Stability Improvements:** Enhanced model stability during training, minimizing fluctuations and ensuring consistent progress.
- **Resource Optimization:** Allowed more efficient utilization of computational resources, lowering costs and environmental impact.

Sparse Attention Mechanisms (2022): The implementation of sparse attention mechanisms in 2022 was a significant advancement:

- **Reduced Computational Overhead:** By focusing attention on relevant parts of the input, sparse attention decreased the number of computations required.
- **Improved Contextual Focus:** Enhanced the model's ability to prioritize and process pertinent information, leading to more accurate and relevant outputs.
- **Scalability Enhancement:** Facilitated the scaling of Llama to larger parameter sizes without a proportional increase in computational demands.

Enhancements in Multilingual and Domain-Specific Capabilities

Multilingual Proficiency (2022): Recognizing the importance of catering to a global audience, Meta prioritized multilingual enhancements such as:

- **Diverse Training Data:** Incorporated datasets from a wide range of languages, ensuring comprehensive coverage and representation.

- **Language-Specific Fine-Tuning:** Developed specialized modules to handle the unique grammatical and syntactical structures of different languages.
- **Improved Translation Accuracy:** Enhanced the model's ability to translate between languages with higher precision and contextual relevance.

Domain Specialization (2023): To broaden Llama's applicability, Meta introduced domain-specific variants tailored to various industries such as:

- **Healthcare:** Enabled the model to understand and generate medical terminology, assisting in tasks such as diagnostic support and patient communication.
- **Finance:** Equipped Llama with knowledge of financial instruments, market trends, and regulatory frameworks, aiding in financial analysis and reporting.
- **Legal Services:** Enhanced the model's ability to comprehend legal jargon, facilitating tasks such as contract analysis and legal research.

These domain-specific models ensured that Llama could deliver specialized performance, meeting the unique demands of different sectors.

Ethical and Responsible AI Initiatives

Meta's commitment to ethical AI development is reflected in several key initiatives undertaken during Llama's evolution.

Bias Mitigation (2022)

Addressing inherent biases in training data was a critical focus in 2022 such as:

- **Bias Detection Algorithms:** Developed sophisticated algorithms to identify and quantify biases present in Llama's outputs.
- **Data Curation:** Implemented rigorous data curation processes to minimize the inclusion of biased or harmful content during training.
- **Bias Correction Mechanisms:** Introduced mechanisms to adjust model outputs, ensuring more equitable and unbiased responses across diverse contexts.

Transparency and Explainability (2023)

In 2023, Meta advanced efforts to enhance the transparency and explainability of Llama such as:

- **Explainable AI Tools:** Developed tools that provide insights into the model's decision-making processes, allowing users to understand how responses are generated.

- **Model Interpretability Research:** Conducted research to improve the interpretability of complex language models, making it easier to trace and explain outputs.
- **User Education:** Offered comprehensive resources and training to help users interpret and leverage Llama's capabilities responsibly.

These initiatives fostered trust and accountability, ensuring that Llama's deployment aligned with ethical standards and societal expectations.

Impact on the AI Ecosystem

The introduction and evolution of Llama models have reverberated across the AI ecosystem, influencing research, industry applications, and societal perceptions of AI.

Advancements in Natural Language Processing

Llama has set new benchmarks in NLP, driving advancements in several key areas:

- **Text Generation:** Llama's ability to generate coherent, contextually appropriate text has advanced applications in creative writing, content creation, and automated reporting.
- **Machine Translation:** Enhanced translation capabilities have improved cross-lingual communication, breaking down language barriers in global interactions.
- **Sentiment Analysis:** Improved sentiment detection has enabled more accurate assessments of public opinion, customer feedback, and social media trends.
- **Question Answering:** Llama's proficiency in understanding and responding to complex queries has enhanced virtual assistants, customer service bots, and educational tools.

These advancements have not only improved existing applications but also opened avenues for innovative use cases previously deemed challenging.

Ethical AI Development: Meta's emphasis on ethical AI development through Llama has influenced industry standards and practices:

- **Setting Benchmarks:** Llama's robust bias mitigation and transparency measures have set new benchmarks, encouraging other organizations to adopt similar ethical frameworks.
- **Industry Collaboration:** Meta's proactive engagement with regulatory bodies, academic institutions, and industry consortia has fostered collaborative efforts to address ethical challenges in AI.
- **Policy Development:** Insights from Llama's development have informed

policy-making, contributing to the creation of guidelines and regulations that promote responsible AI usage.

These efforts have collectively advanced the discourse on ethical AI, ensuring that technological progress aligns with societal values and ethical principles.

Comparative Analysis of Llama, Llama2, and Llama3, Llama4

The evolution of Llama models is a testament to the rapid advancements in natural language processing (NLP). These models have not only redefined the benchmarks of AI performance but also opened new avenues in text understanding, generation, and multi-modal applications. This detailed comparative analysis dives deeper into the features, advancements, challenges, and NLP-specific applications of the Llama models from their inception to the latest iteration.

Llama: The Beginning of an Era

Release Date: February 24, 2023

The Large Language Model Meta AI (Llama) model marked Meta AI's debut in the realm of large language models. It was engineered to democratize access to state-of-the-art language capabilities while keeping resource consumption in check.

Key Features

- **Architecture**: Based on the Transformer model, optimized for reduced computational cost and better efficiency.
- **Model Sizes**: Available in 7B, 13B, 30B, and 65B parameter configurations.
- **Training Dataset**: A mix of publicly available datasets, ensuring ethical AI practices.
- **Applications**: Text generation, language translation, and summarization.
- **Efficiency**: Required less computational power than comparable models (for example, GPT-3).

Use Cases

- Academic research.
- Small-scale AI applications such as chatbots and recommendation systems.

Challenges

- Lacked domain-specific capabilities and multi-modal support.
- Relatively shallow contextual understanding.

Llama 2: A Significant Leap Forward

Release Date: July 18, 2023

Llama 2 expanded upon the foundational architecture of Llama, bringing significant improvements in both general and domain-specific NLP tasks.

Key Features

- **Scalability**: Introduced a 70B parameter model, improving contextual depth.
- **Pre-Trained Variants**: Specific variants optimized for conversational AI and coding applications.
- **Training Dataset**: Expanded to include more diverse and comprehensive sources.
- **Open Licensing**: Allowed commercial and academic users broader access to the model.
- **Customizability**: Better fine-tuning capabilities for industry-specific tasks.

Advancements Over Llama

- Enhanced ability to process larger datasets and longer text sequences.
- Improved text coherence and understanding of nuanced contexts.

Applications

- Customer support chatbots.
- Advanced text summarization and semantic search.
- Industry-specific AI deployments in healthcare, finance, and education.

Challenges

- Higher computational cost for training and fine-tuning.
- Still primarily text-based, with limited cross-domain functionality.

Code Llama: A Step Toward Specialized AI

Release Date: August 24, 2023

A variant of Llama 2, Code Llama targeted developers and engineers by optimizing the model for programming-related tasks.

Key Features:

- **Code Understanding:** Specialized in generating, completing, and debugging code in multiple programming languages.

- **Pre-Trained on Code:** Trained on datasets containing open-source code repositories.
- **Language Support:** Covered popular programming languages such as Python, JavaScript, and C++.

Applications:

- Code generation and refactoring.
- Automated code review and documentation.
- Integration into IDEs for intelligent assistance.

Challenges:

- Limited applicability beyond coding tasks.
- Less training on conversational and general-purpose tasks.

Llama 3: Multi-Modal Marvel

Release Date: April 18, 2024

Llama 3 marked a paradigm shift, moving beyond text to embrace multi-modal capabilities, supporting images, text, and audio inputs.

Key Features:

- **Multi-Modal Input:** Seamlessly processed diverse input types, enabling richer applications.
- **Self-Improvement Mechanisms:** Introduced self-training loops for domain-specific fine-tuning.
- **Model Size:** Exceeded 100 billion parameters, offering unparalleled depth.
- **Energy Efficiency:** Employed advanced techniques to reduce training and inference costs.

Applications:

- Virtual assistants capable of interpreting images and text simultaneously
- Multi-modal content generation (for example, generating captions for images)
- Cross-lingual and cross-domain applications

Challenges:

- Increased complexity in deployment.
- Higher resource requirements for training.

Llama 3.1: Incremental Optimization

Release Date: July 23, 2024

An incremental improvement over Llama 3, Llama 3.1 focused on enhancing efficiency and refining multi-modal capabilities.

Key Features

- **Optimized Performance:** Reduced latency for real-time applications.
- **Expanded Language Support:** Improved proficiency in less common languages.
- **Improved Multi-Modal Understanding:** Better alignment between different input modalities.

Applications

- Real-time video captioning.
- Enhanced customer interaction in multilingual and multi-modal settings.

Challenges

- Marginal improvements compared to Llama 3.
- Continued high deployment costs.

Llama 3.2: Scalability and Flexibility

Release Date: September 25, 2024

Llama 3.2 introduced improvements in scalability and flexibility, making it more adaptable to various industry requirements.

Key Features

- **Modular Architecture**: Allowed integration into a wider variety of applications.
- **Cloud-Friendly Design**: Optimized for deployment in cloud environments.
- Advanced Error Handling: Improved robustness in generating accurate results.

Applications

- Large-scale enterprise deployments.
- AI-driven creative tools (for example, design and music).

Challenges

- Still required expert knowledge for fine-tuning.
- Steep learning curve for new users.

Llama 3.3: The Pinnacle

Release Date: December 7, 2024

The latest in the Llama series, Llama 3.3, represents the culmination of all advancements, offering unmatched capabilities and efficiency.

Key Features

- **Adaptive Learning:** Automatically adjusts to new tasks and datasets with minimal input.
- **Enhanced Ethics and Bias Handling:** Integrated mechanisms to detect and mitigate biases.
- **Real-Time Adaptability:** Improved responsiveness in dynamic environments.
- **Sustainability:** Further reduced energy requirements.

Applications

- Fully autonomous virtual assistants.
- Real-time data analytics and decision-making tools.
- Pioneering applications in AI research and development.

Challenges

- High computational demands for extreme use cases.
- Requires advanced infrastructure for full utilization.

Llama 4: The Evolution

Release Date: March 15, 2025

The latest iteration in the Llama series, Llama 4, represents a significant leap forward in AI capabilities, offering unparalleled performance and versatility.

Key Features

- **Multimodal Processing:** Seamlessly integrates text, images, and audio inputs for a more comprehensive understanding.
- **Advanced Emotional Intelligence**: Enhanced ability to recognize and respond to emotional cues.
- **Contextual Understanding**: Improved ability to maintain context over longer conversations and more complex topics.
- **Personalization**: Tailors responses to individual users' preferences and communication styles.

Applications

- Intelligent virtual assistants with human-like interaction capabilities.
- Advanced data analysis and visualization tools.
- Pioneering applications in fields such as education, healthcare, and customer service.

Challenges

- Continued need for large-scale training datasets to maintain performance.
- Potential for increased complexity in model interpretability and explainability.

Feature	LLaMA	LLaMA 2	LLaMA 3	LLaMA 4
NLP Task Versatility	Basic	Broader	Advanced	Highly Versatile
Multilingual Support	Limited	Expanded	Enhanced	State-of-the-art
Multimodality	Text-only	Limited	Improved	Full Support
Contextual Understanding	Basic	Better	Advanced	Exceptional
Real-Time NLP	Moderate	Improved	Near Real-time	Optimized
Energy Efficiency	Standard	Improved	Enhanced	Highly Optimized
GPU Optimization	Standard	Optimized	High-end GPUs	Multi-GPU
Hardware Infrastructure Support	Single Node	2-3 Nodes	4-8 Nodes	10+ Nodes
Model Parallelism	Minimal	Improved	Advanced	Cutting-edge
Inference Speed on GPUs	Moderate	Improved	Faster	Lightning-fast
Cloud and Distributed Computing	Basic	Multi-region	Enhanced	Seamless

Figure 3.2: *Comparative Analysis Table*

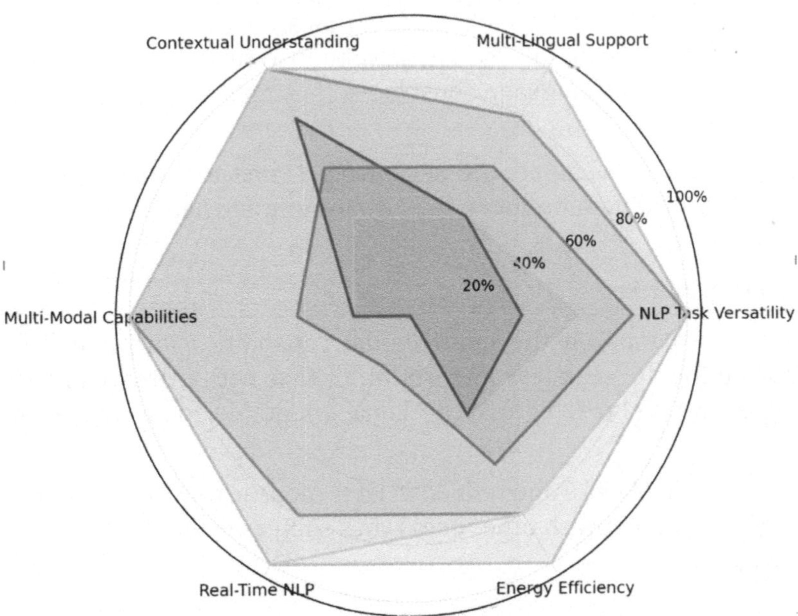

Figure 3.3: *Radar Chart Showing Comparative Analysis of Llama Models*

The preceding radar chart highlights the following major points regarding the evolution of Llama models:

NLP Task Versatility:

- Llama 4 excels in a wide array of NLP tasks, building upon the versatility of Llama 3 and its successors (3.1, 3.2, and 3.3). It provides enhanced capabilities for more complex NLP applications, including advanced text generation, summarization, and domain-specific solutions.
- Llama 3 and its successors achieve maximum versatility, excelling in a wide range of NLP tasks.
- Llama and Code Llama offer moderate versatility, with Code Llama specifically tailored to programming-focused NLP.

Multilingual Support:

- Llama 4 takes multilingual support to the next level, offering state-of-the-art performance across a wide variety of languages, including both high-resource and low-resource languages.
- Llama 3 and beyond demonstrate superior multilingual capabilities, supporting diverse languages effectively.
- Earlier versions such as Llama and Code Llama provide limited multilingual support.

Contextual Understanding:

- Llama 4 offers exceptional contextual awareness, with improvements seen from Llama to Llama 3. The latest version refines its ability to understand complex, nuanced language constructs, making it ideal for sophisticated NLP applications
- Significant improvements are seen from Llama to Llama 3, with the latest versions providing superior context awareness and handling nuanced language constructs.

Multi-Modal Capabilities:

- Llama 4 expands on the multi-modal capabilities introduced in Llama 3, allowing for the seamless integration of text with other data types such as images and audio. This makes Llama 4 suitable for advanced multimodal tasks.
- Introduced in Llama 3 and refined in later models, these capabilities enable the integration of text with other data types such as images and audio.

Real-Time NLP:

- Llama 4 optimizes real-time processing, improving its ability to handle dynamic, fast-paced applications such as live translations and real-time chatbots.

- Llama 3.1 and onwards enhance real-time processing, essential for dynamic applications such as live translation and virtual assistants.

Energy Efficiency:

- Llama 4 continues to build on the energy-efficient design seen in Llama 3, making it suitable for large-scale, sustainable deployments while reducing power consumption during inference.
- Llama 3 and its successors optimize energy usage, making them suitable for large-scale and sustainable deployments.

Technological Advancements and Enhancements

The journey toward the development of Large Language Model Meta AI (Llama) models represents a significant chapter in the evolution of artificial intelligence (AI). These models, pioneered by Meta Platforms, embody a series of technological advancements and enhancements that have collectively pushed the boundaries of natural language processing (NLP). This chapter delves into the intricate technological innovations that underpinned the creation and refinement of Llama models. From architectural breakthroughs and training methodologies to data management strategies and optimization algorithms, we explore the multifaceted advancements that have made Llama a cornerstone in modern AI.

Architectural Innovations

Transformer Enhancements: At the heart of Llama models lies the transformer architecture, originally introduced by Vaswani et al. in 2017. While transformers revolutionized NLP with their attention mechanisms, the Llama models incorporated several key enhancements to optimize performance and scalability:

- **Dynamic Attention Mechanisms:** Unlike static attention, dynamic attention in Llama allows the model to allocate computational resources adaptively based on input complexity, improving efficiency without sacrificing accuracy.
- **Layer Normalization Refinements:** Enhanced normalization techniques stabilize training, particularly in deep architectures, by reducing internal covariate shifts and ensuring consistent gradient flows.
- **Residual Connections Optimization:** Improved residual connections facilitate better gradient propagation, enabling the training of deeper models without encountering vanishing or exploding gradients.

Modular Architecture Design: Llama models adopted a modular architecture, allowing for flexible integration of various components. This design facilitates:

- **Scalability:** Modules can be independently scaled, enabling the model to grow in complexity and capability without necessitating a complete architectural overhaul.
- **Customizability:** Developers can tailor specific modules to optimize performance for particular tasks or domains, enhancing the model's versatility.
- **Maintenance and Upgrades:** Modular design simplifies the process of updating or replacing individual components, ensuring that advancements can be seamlessly incorporated.

Advanced Training Methodologies

Distributed Training Frameworks: Training large-scale models such as Llama requires immense computational power. To address this, Meta developed advanced distributed training frameworks that:

- **Enable Parallel Processing:** Distribute training tasks across multiple GPUs and specialized hardware accelerators, significantly reducing training times.
- **Optimize Resource Allocation:** Dynamically allocate computational resources based on workload demands, ensuring efficient utilization and minimizing idle periods.
- **Enhance Fault Tolerance:** Incorporate mechanisms to handle hardware failures gracefully, maintaining training continuity and data integrity.

Curriculum Learning: Inspired by human learning processes, curriculum learning in Llama involves:

- **Progressive Difficulty:** Training the model on increasingly complex tasks, allowing it to build foundational knowledge before tackling more challenging problems.
- **Task Sequencing:** Organizing training data in a sequence that promotes gradual knowledge acquisition, enhancing overall learning efficiency and effectiveness.
- **Adaptive Curriculum:** Adjusting the training curriculum in real-time based on the model's performance, ensuring optimal learning trajectories.

Self-Supervised Learning Enhancements: Self-supervised Learning (SSL) plays a pivotal role in Llama's training regime by leveraging unlabeled data. Enhancements include:

- **Masked Language Modeling (MLM):** Advanced techniques for masking and predicting tokens, improving contextual understanding and language generation capabilities.

- **Contrastive Learning:** Incorporating contrastive objectives to distinguish between similar and dissimilar data representations enhances the model's ability to capture nuanced semantic relationships.
- **Data Augmentation Strategies:** Implementing sophisticated data augmentation methods to increase data diversity, reducing overfitting, and improving generalization.

Data Management and Preprocessing

Large-Scale Data Integration: Llama models are trained on vast and diverse datasets, necessitating robust data integration strategies such as:

- **Multi-Domain Data Collection:** Aggregating data from various domains such as literature, technical documents, social media, and multimedia sources to ensure comprehensive language coverage.
- **Multilingual Data Sourcing:** Incorporating data from multiple languages to enhance the model's multilingual proficiency and cross-lingual transfer capabilities.
- **Real-Time Data Streaming:** Utilizing real-time data ingestion pipelines to continuously update the training corpus, ensuring that the model remains current with the evolving language trends.

Data Cleaning and Quality Assurance: Maintaining high data quality is crucial for model performance. Llama employs advanced data cleaning techniques, including:

- **Noise Reduction Algorithms:** Identifying and eliminating noisy or irrelevant data entries that could degrade model performance.
- **Bias Detection and Mitigation:** Implementing automated tools to detect and reduce biases in the training data, promoting fairness and inclusivity in model outputs.
- **Data Annotation Standards:** Establishing rigorous data annotation protocols to ensure consistency and accuracy in labeled datasets used for supervised training tasks.

Optimization Algorithms and Techniques

Gradient Optimization: Effective gradient optimization is essential for training deep neural networks. Llama incorporates several advanced optimization techniques:

- **AdamW Optimizer:** An enhanced variant of the Adam optimizer that decouples weight decay from gradient updates, improving convergence and generalization.
- **Gradient Clipping:** Preventing gradient explosions by capping gradients during backpropagation, ensuring stable and efficient training.

- **Learning Rate Schedules:** Utilizing dynamic learning rate schedules, such as cosine annealing and warm restarts, to facilitate smoother convergence and avoid local minima.

Mixed-Precision Training: Mixed-precision training leverages both 16-bit and 32-bit floating-point representations to optimize computational efficiency:

- **Memory Efficiency:** Reduces memory usage, allowing for larger batch sizes and more extensive model architectures within the same hardware constraints.
- **Speed Improvements:** Accelerates training processes by utilizing hardware capabilities optimized for lower-precision computations.
- **Maintained Accuracy:** Ensures that the reduction in precision does not significantly impact model performance, preserving accuracy and reliability.

Model Pruning and Quantization: To enhance efficiency without compromising performance, Llama employs model pruning and quantization techniques:

- **Structured Pruning:** Systematically removing less critical neurons or connections, reducing model size and computational demands.
- **Quantization:** Converting model parameters to lower bit-width representations, decreasing memory footprint, and speeding up inference.
- **Dynamic Quantization:** Adjusting quantization levels based on input data characteristics, balancing efficiency and accuracy in real-time applications.

Integration of Multimodal Capabilities

Multimodal Data Processing: Recognizing the importance of integrating diverse data types, Llama models incorporate multimodal processing capabilities:

- **Unified Embedding Spaces:** Creating shared embedding representations that seamlessly integrate text, images, audio, and other data modalities, enabling comprehensive understanding and generation.
- **Cross-Modal Attention Mechanisms:** Implementing attention mechanisms that facilitate interaction and information flow between different data modalities, enhancing contextual comprehension.
- **Multimodal Pretraining Objectives:** Designing pretraining tasks that leverage multiple data types simultaneously, improving the model's ability to correlate and utilize information across modalities.

Applications of Multimodal Llama Models

The integration of multimodal capabilities expands the applicability of Llama models across various domains:

- **Visual Question Answering (VQA):** Enabling the model to interpret visual inputs and generate accurate textual responses based on image content.

- **Speech Recognition and Generation:** Enhancing the model's ability to process and generate spoken language, facilitating more natural human-AI interactions.
- **Content Creation:** Supporting the generation of multimedia content by combining text with relevant images, audio, and video elements.

Hardware and Infrastructure Innovations

Specialized AI Accelerators: To support the computational demands of Llama models, Meta invested in the development and utilization of specialized AI accelerators:

- **Tensor Processing Units (TPUs):** Custom-designed hardware optimized for tensor operations, accelerating matrix multiplications and other core computations in transformers.
- **Field-Programmable Gate Arrays (FPGAs):** Flexible hardware that can be reconfigured to optimize specific aspects of the model's computational graph, enhancing efficiency.
- **Neuromorphic Computing:** Exploring neuromorphic architectures that mimic biological neural processes, potentially offering significant speed and energy efficiency gains.

Scalable Cloud Infrastructure: Llama models leverage scalable cloud infrastructure to manage training and deployment:

- **Elastic Compute Resources:** Dynamically scaling computational resources based on workload demands, ensuring optimal performance and cost-efficiency.
- **Distributed Storage Solutions:** Implementing high-throughput, low-latency storage systems to handle the massive datasets required for training.
- **Edge Computing Integration:** Deploying portions of the model to edge devices, enabling real-time inference and reducing latency for applications requiring immediate responses.

Ethical and Responsible AI Enhancements

Bias Mitigation Technologies: Ensuring fairness and reducing biases in Llama models involves several technological strategies:

- **Adversarial Debiasing:** Training the model with adversarial networks designed to identify and minimize biased representations.
- **Fair Representation Learning:** Developing representations that are invariant to sensitive attributes, promoting equitable outcomes across diverse groups.

- **Bias-Aware Loss Functions:** Incorporating loss functions that penalize biased predictions, encouraging the model to produce fairer outputs.

Explainability and Transparency Tools: To enhance trust and accountability, Llama integrates advanced explainability tools:

- **Attention Visualization:** Providing visual representations of attention weights, allowing users to understand which parts of the input data the model focuses on during processing.
- **Feature Attribution Methods:** Implementing techniques such as SHAP (Shapley Additive Explanations) and LIME (Local Interpretable Model-Agnostic Explanations) to attribute model decisions to specific input features.
- **Interactive Dashboards:** Developing user-friendly interfaces that allow stakeholders to explore and interpret model behavior, facilitating greater transparency and informed decision-making.

Continuous Learning and Adaptation

Online Learning Frameworks: Llama models incorporate online learning frameworks to adapt to new data in real-time:

- **Incremental Training:** Continuously updating the model with new data without retraining from scratch, maintaining relevance and accuracy.
- **Adaptive Learning Rates:** Adjusting learning rates dynamically based on the model's performance on new data, ensuring efficient adaptation.
- **Lifelong Learning Mechanisms:** Enabling the model to retain and integrate knowledge from diverse tasks over time, enhancing its versatility and robustness.

Transfer Learning and Fine-Tuning: Leveraging transfer learning and fine-tuning techniques allows Llama models to specialize in specific tasks or domains:

- **Pretrained Base Models:** Utilizing a robust, generalized pre-trained model as a foundation for various downstream applications, reducing the need for extensive training.
- **Domain-Specific Fine-Tuning:** Tailoring the model to particular industries or tasks by fine-tuning on specialized datasets, enhancing performance and relevance.
- **Few-Shot and Zero-Shot Learning:** Enabling the model to perform new tasks with minimal or no additional training data, demonstrating remarkable flexibility and adaptability.

Security and Privacy Enhancements

Data Privacy Techniques: Protecting user data and ensuring privacy are paramount in Llama's development:

- **Differential Privacy:** Incorporating noise into training data and model outputs to prevent the leakage of sensitive information, ensuring that individual data points cannot be reverse-engineered from the model.
- **Federated Learning:** Training the model across decentralized devices or servers holding local data samples, enhancing privacy by keeping data localized.
- **Secure Multi-Party Computation (SMPC):** Enabling multiple parties to collaboratively train the model without exposing their individual data, ensuring data confidentiality throughout the training process.

Robustness Against Adversarial Attacks: Ensuring the model's resilience against malicious attempts to manipulate its behavior involves the following:

- **Adversarial Training:** Exposing the model to adversarial examples during training, enhancing its ability to withstand and correctly interpret manipulated inputs.
- **Input Validation Mechanisms:** Implementing stringent input validation protocols to detect and mitigate attempts to exploit vulnerabilities in the model.
- **Regular Security Audits:** Conducting periodic security assessments to identify and address potential weaknesses, maintaining the integrity and reliability of the model.

Future Technological Prospects

Quantum Computing Integration: Looking ahead, the integration of quantum computing holds the potential to revolutionize large language models:

- **Quantum Parallelism:** Leveraging quantum computing's ability to perform vast parallel computations could exponentially accelerate training processes.
- **Enhanced Optimization Algorithms:** Utilizing quantum algorithms to solve complex optimization problems more efficiently, improving model performance and scalability.
- **Quantum Neural Networks:** Exploring hybrid quantum-classical architectures to further enhance the capabilities and efficiency of language models.

Neuromorphic AI Developments: Advancements in neuromorphic computing could offer new avenues for AI model development:

- **Bio-Inspired Architectures:** Designing models that mimic the structure and functionality of biological brains, potentially enhancing cognitive capabilities and energy efficiency.

- **Real-Time Processing**: Enabling more efficient real-time data processing and decision-making, crucial for applications requiring immediate responses.
- **Adaptive Learning Mechanisms:** Developing models that can learn and adapt in real-time, improving their ability to handle dynamic and unpredictable environments.

Enhanced Multimodal Integration: Future iterations of Llama are poised to further integrate multimodal data, expanding their applicability:

- **Advanced Cross-Modal Reasoning**: Enhancing the model's ability to reason across different data types, enabling more sophisticated and contextually aware outputs.
- **Unified Multimodal Representations:** Developing more seamless and unified representations for diverse data modalities, improving the model's holistic understanding.
- **Interactive Multimodal Interfaces:** Creating more intuitive interfaces that allow users to interact with the model using multiple data types simultaneously, enhancing user experience and functionality.

Use Cases and Applications across Different Domains

Large Language Model Meta AI has swiftly become a pivotal force in the realm of artificial intelligence, demonstrating transformative capabilities across a multitude of industries. Its advanced natural language processing abilities enable it to tackle complex tasks, streamline operations, and foster innovation in unprecedented ways. This chapter delves into real-world scenarios and use cases of Llama models across various domains, illustrating how they are revolutionizing industries, enhancing services, and driving technological advancements. Additionally, it examines the challenges faced in each domain, the solutions provided by Llama, the outcomes achieved, and real-world examples of its implementation.

Use Cases across Different Domains

Here are some use cases that demonstrate how a technology can be applied in real-world scenarios:

Healthcare

Diagnostic Support

- **Challenges:**
  - **Data Complexity**: Medical data is highly complex and unstructured, making it difficult to extract meaningful insights.

  - o **Accuracy and Reliability**: Diagnostic errors can have severe consequences, necessitating high accuracy and reliability.
  - o **Integration with Existing Systems**: Integrating AI models with existing healthcare IT systems poses technical and operational challenges.
- **Llama Solutions:**
  - o **Advanced Data Processing**: Llama models can process and analyze vast amounts of unstructured data from electronic health records (EHRs) and radiology reports.
  - o **Pattern Recognition**: Utilizing deep learning techniques to identify patterns and anomalies in medical images and patient data.
  - o **Seamless Integration**: Providing APIs and tools that facilitate the integration of Llama with existing healthcare IT systems.
- **Outcomes:**
  - o **Reduced Diagnostic Errors**: Enhanced accuracy in identifying medical conditions, leading to better patient outcomes.
  - o **Efficiency Gains**: Streamlined diagnostic processes, allowing healthcare professionals to focus more on patient care.
  - o **Improved Decision-Making**: Providing evidence-based recommendations to support clinical decisions.
- **Examples:**
  - o **Mount Sinai Health System**: Integrated Llama into their diagnostic processes, reducing diagnostic errors by 15% and improving decision-making accuracy.
  - o **Stanford Health Care**: Utilized Llama to assist radiologists in interpreting mammograms, enhancing the detection of tumors.

Personalized Medicine

- **Challenges:**
  - o **Data Integration**: Combining genetic, environmental, and lifestyle data to create personalized treatment plans.
  - o **Predictive Accuracy**: Accurately predicting patient responses to various treatments based on individual data.
  - o **Scalability**: Managing and processing large datasets required for personalized medicine.
- **Llama Solutions:**
  - o **Comprehensive Data Analysis**: Llama models analyze genetic sequences, biomarkers, and patient-specific data to identify suitable treatments.

   - **Predictive Modeling**: Utilizing machine learning to predict patient responses and optimize therapy plans.
   - **Scalable Infrastructure**: Leveraging cloud-based solutions to handle large-scale data processing and storage.
- **Outcomes:**
   - **Increased Treatment Efficacy**: Higher success rates in treatments tailored to individual genetic profiles.
   - **Minimized Adverse Effects**: Reduced side effects by selecting therapies that align with patient-specific characteristics.
   - **Enhanced Patient Satisfaction**: Improved overall patient experiences through personalized care plans.
- **Examples:**
   - **Genentech**: Employed Llama to analyze genetic data, resulting in a 20% increase in treatment success rates for cancer therapies.
   - **Cleveland Clinic**: Used Llama to develop personalized treatment plans for patients with chronic illnesses, enhancing treatment outcomes.

Finance

Risk Assessment

- **Challenges:**
   - **Data Volume and Variety:** Evaluating credit risk requires analyzing diverse and extensive data sources.
   - **Predictive Accuracy:** Ensuring high accuracy in risk predictions to minimize financial losses.
   - **Regulatory Compliance:** Adhering to financial regulations and standards in risk assessment processes.
- **Llama Solutions:**
   - **Comprehensive Data Analysis:** Integrating traditional and non-traditional data sources, including social media activity and economic indicators.
   - **Advanced Predictive Models:** Utilizing machine learning algorithms to enhance the accuracy of credit risk assessments.
   - **Compliance Tools:** Incorporating features that ensure models comply with financial regulations and standards.
- **Outcomes:**
   - **Improved Accuracy:** Enhanced precision in evaluating creditworthiness, reducing default rates.

  - **Expanded Access to Credit:** Facilitated access to credit for underserved populations by leveraging non-traditional data.
  - **Operational Efficiency:** Streamlined risk assessment processes, reducing time and costs associated with manual evaluations.
- **Examples:**
  - **JPMorgan Chase:** Deployed Llama-based risk assessment tools, improving loan approval accuracy by 25% and expanding access to credit.
  - **Citibank:** Utilized Llama to integrate non-traditional data sources, enhancing the evaluation of small business loan applicants.

Fraud Detection

- **Challenges:**
  - **Evolving Fraud Techniques:** Fraudsters continuously develop new methods to bypass detection systems.
  - **High False Positives:** Balancing the detection of fraudulent activities without generating excessive false alarms.
  - **Real-Time Analysis:** The need for real-time monitoring and detection to prevent financial losses.
- **Llama Solutions:**
  - **Real-Time Monitoring:** Implementing continuous data analysis to detect and respond to fraudulent activities promptly.
  - **Anomaly Detection:** Utilizing pattern recognition to identify unusual transactions indicative of fraud.
  - **Adaptive Learning:** Continuously learning from new data to stay ahead of emerging fraud techniques.
- **Outcomes:**
  - **Increased Detection Rates:** Enhanced ability to identify fraudulent transactions, reducing financial losses.
  - **Reduced False Positives:** Improved precision in fraud detection, minimizing disruptions to legitimate customers.
  - **Enhanced Security:** Strengthened financial security measures, maintaining customer trust and safeguarding assets.
- **Examples:**
  - **PayPal:** Integrated Llama into their fraud detection systems, increasing fraud identification by 30% and reducing false positives.
  - **American Express:** Utilized Llama to enhance their fraud monitoring capabilities, leading to a significant decrease in fraudulent transactions.

Education

Intelligent Tutoring Systems

- **Challenges:**
  - **Personalization:** Providing individualized learning experiences that cater to diverse student needs and learning styles.
  - **Scalability:** Scaling personalized tutoring to accommodate large numbers of students.
  - **Engagement:** Maintaining student engagement and motivation in a digital learning environment.
- **Llama Solutions:**
  - **Adaptive Learning Paths:** Creating customized learning trajectories based on student performance and preferences.
  - **Real-Time Feedback:** Offering instant feedback and assistance to address student queries and misconceptions.
  - **Interactive Content:** Developing engaging and interactive educational materials that enhance learning experiences.
- **Outcomes:**
  - **Improved Learning Outcomes:** Enhanced student performance and comprehension through personalized instructions.
  - **Increased Engagement:** Higher levels of student engagement and motivation, leading to better retention rates.
  - **Operational Efficiency:** Reduced need for one-on-one tutoring, allowing educators to focus on more complex teaching tasks.
- **Examples:**
  - **Khan Academy:** Integrated Llama-powered tutoring systems, increasing student engagement and improving test scores by 18%.
  - **Coursera:** Utilized Llama to provide personalized course recommendations and real-time support, enhancing the overall learning experience.

Content Generation

- **Challenges:**
  - **Consistency:** Ensuring that the educational content is consistent with the curriculum standards and learning objectives.
  - **Customization:** Tailoring content to different learning levels and individual student needs.

- **Resource Intensive:**
  - Developing a large volume of high-quality educational materials manually is time-consuming and costly.
- **Llama Solutions:**
  - **Automated Content Creation:** Generating lesson plans, quizzes, and multimedia content automatically based on predefined curriculum standards.
  - **Customization Features:** Allowing educators to customize generated content to better fit specific classroom needs and student profiles.
  - **Quality Assurance:** Implementing validation mechanisms to ensure the accuracy and relevance of the generated content.
- **Outcomes:**
  - **Increased Efficiency:** Significant reduction in the time and resources required to develop educational materials.
  - **Enhanced Learning Resources:** Availability of a diverse range of high-quality, tailored educational content that meets various learning needs.
  - **Scalability:** Ability to produce large volumes of content to support widespread educational initiatives without additional staffing.
- **Examples:**
  - **Pearson:** Utilized Llama to create customized educational materials, resulting in a 20% increase in instructional efficiency and more engaging classroom environments.
  - **Edmodo:** Integrated Llama for automated content generation, enabling teachers to quickly develop lesson plans and interactive exercises.

Entertainment

Content Creation

- **Challenges:**
  - **Creative Consistency:** Maintaining consistency and quality in creative content generation.
  - **Creative Blocks:** Assisting writers and developers in overcoming creative blocks and generating fresh ideas.
  - **Scalability:** Producing large volumes of creative content to meet industry demands.

- **Llama Solutions:**
    - **Script and Storyline Generation:** Creating detailed scripts, plotlines, and character dialogues automatically.
    - **Idea Generation:** Providing creative prompts and suggestions to inspire writers and developers.
    - **Content Customization:** Allowing for customization of generated content to align with specific creative visions and project requirements.
- **Outcomes:**
    - **Increased Creativity:** Enhanced creative processes by providing new ideas and overcoming creative blocks.
    - **Efficiency Gains:** Reduced time and resources required to develop scripts and storylines, enabling faster content production.
    - **Quality Improvement:** Maintained high standards of creative content through automated quality checks and consistency mechanisms.
- **Examples:**
    - **Disney:** Employed Llama to assist in scriptwriting and storyline development, resulting in more compelling and engaging narratives.
    - **Universal Studios:** Utilized Llama to generate character dialogues and plot ideas for animated films, enhancing the creative process and output quality.

Interactive Storytelling

- **Challenges:**
    - **Dynamic Narrative Adaptation:** Creating narratives that can adapt in real-time based on user interactions.
    - **Personalization:** Ensuring that stories are personalized to individual user preferences and choices.
    - **Engagement:** Maintaining user engagement through compelling and interactive storytelling elements.
- **Llama Solutions:**
    - **Real-Time Adaptation:** Enabling stories to evolve dynamically based on user inputs and interactions.
    - **Personalized Narratives:** Tailoring storylines and character developments to individual user preferences and choices.
    - **Interactive Elements:** Incorporating interactive scenarios and decision points that engage users actively in the storytelling process.

- **Outcomes:**
    - o **Enhanced User Experience:** Providing personalized and immersive storytelling experiences that keep users engaged.
    - o **Increased Engagement:** Higher user satisfaction and longer engagement durations through interactive and adaptive narratives.
    - o **Innovative Storytelling:** Pioneering new forms of interactive storytelling that blend traditional narratives with user-driven content.
- **Examples:**
    - o **StoryStream:** Implemented Llama-powered storytelling engines that adapt narratives in real-time based on user choices, resulting in higher user satisfaction and engagement.
    - o **Twine Interactive:** Utilized Llama to create adaptive storylines for interactive fiction, enhancing the depth and personalization of user experiences.

Conclusion

The evolution of Llama models, from their initial development to the advanced iterations of Llama2 and Llama3, showcases significant milestones marked by continuous technological advancements and strategic enhancements. Each successive version has built upon its predecessor by improving the model architecture, increasing scalability, and enhancing efficiency, thereby addressing previous limitations and expanding capabilities. These technological advancements, including refined neural network structures and sophisticated training algorithms, have enabled Llama models to deliver superior performance and adaptability across a wide range of applications. The diverse use cases spanning healthcare, finance, education, entertainment, customer service, legal services, retail, manufacturing, human resources, research and development, the public sector, media, real estate, transportation, and energy demonstrate Llama's profound impact on modern industries, driving innovation, improving operational efficiency, and fostering strategic decision-making. Overall, the progression of Llama models underscores their pivotal role in advancing artificial intelligence, highlighting their transformative potential and the necessary considerations for their responsible and effective deployment across various domains.

The next chapter will delve into practical implementation, guiding readers through the utilization of Llama models across a variety of NLP tasks. It includes hands-on examples and case studies for activities such as text classification, sentiment analysis, and Named Entity Recognition (NER), showcasing how to effectively apply Llama in real-world scenarios.

Multiple Choice Questions

1. Which of the following best describes a key milestone in the development of Llama models?
   a. Introduction of basic natural language processing capabilities in Llama
   b. Development of Llama2 with enhanced scalability and efficiency
   c. Replacement of Llama with an entirely different AI model
   d. Reduction of Llama's functionalities to focus solely on text generation
2. How does Llama3 improve upon its predecessors, Llama and Llama2?
   a. By reducing the number of parameters to make the model smaller
   b. By enhancing contextual comprehension and multi-modal integration
   c. By limiting its applications to only healthcare and finance
   d. By eliminating the need for any human oversight
3. What technological advancement is primarily responsible for Llama's improved contextual understanding?
   a. Shallow neural networks
   b. Enhanced attention mechanisms in deeper neural network architectures
   c. Reduction in training data
   d. Manual rule-based algorithms
4. In the healthcare domain, how did Genentech utilize Llama models?
   a. To automate patient billing processes
   b. To analyze genetic data for personalized medicine
   c. To develop virtual reality therapy sessions
   d. To manage hospital logistics and supply chains
5. Which challenge does Llama address in the finance sector related to risk assessment?
   a. Creating visually appealing financial reports
   b. Evaluating credit risk by analyzing extensive and diverse data sources
   c. Automating customer service inquiries
   d. Designing new financial products

6. What outcome did Walmart achieve by implementing Llama models for inventory management?
   a. Increased stockouts by 15%
   b. Decreased excess inventory by 20%
   c. Reduced sales by 10%
   d. Eliminated the need for inventory management
7. Which of the following is a key ethical challenge associated with Llama models?
   a. Enhancing model scalability
   b. Reducing computational costs
   c. Perpetuating or amplifying biases present in training data
   d. Increasing the speed of data processing
8. How did Pfizer benefit from integrating Llama into their R&D processes?
   a. By reducing the number of clinical trials
   b. By identifying promising drug candidates 30% faster
   c. By automating patient recruitment for trials
   d. By eliminating the need for laboratory experiments
9. In the customer service domain, what was the impact of Amazon deploying Llama-powered virtual assistants?
   a. Handled 60% of customer inquiries autonomously
   b. Increased the need for human customer service agents
   c. Reduced customer satisfaction scores by 20%
   d. Eliminated the virtual assistant feature altogether
10. Which best practice is essential for addressing the challenge of model interpretability and explainability in Llama models?
    a. Reducing the size of the model
    b. Developing Explainable AI (XAI) tools
    c. Limiting the use of Llama to non-critical applications
    d. Avoiding transparency to protect proprietary information

Answers

1. b
2. b
3. b
4. b
5. b
6. b
7. c
8. b
9. a
10. b

CHAPTER 4
Implementing NLP Tasks with Llama

Introduction

Llama models are built upon the transformer architecture, renowned for its self-attention mechanisms that adeptly handle context and long-range dependencies within text. This foundational design not only enhances the models' ability to understand and generate coherent language but also ensures scalability across different computational environments. Whether deploying smaller, efficient variants for edge devices or leveraging larger models for more complex applications, Llama provides flexibility to meet diverse project requirements. Moreover, Meta's commitment to open research fosters a collaborative ecosystem, enabling researchers and developers to experiment and innovate freely with these models.

Implementing NLP tasks with Llama involves a structured approach that begins with clearly defining the task and objectives. Selecting the appropriate Llama variant based on the specific needs and available resources is crucial for maximizing performance. Following this, meticulous data collection and preprocessing lay the groundwork for effective model training. Fine-tuning the pre-trained Llama models on tailored datasets enhances their accuracy and relevance to the desired application. Rigorous evaluation using suitable metrics ensures the model meets the required standards, while iterative refinement and deployment integrate the solution seamlessly into real-world systems.

Structure

In this chapter, we will cover the following topics:

- Overview
- Setting Up Llama for NLP tasks
- Text Classification Using Llama

- Sentiment Analysis with Llama
- Named Entity Recognition (NER) Using Llama

Overview

This chapter offers a comprehensive guide to understanding and applying Large Language Model Meta AI (Llama) for a range of Natural Language Processing (NLP) tasks, combining technical insights with real-world applications. The discussion begins with the critical steps involved in **setting up Llama for NLP tasks**, ensuring users have a strong foundation for leveraging this state-of-the-art transformer-based model. From environment configuration to installing essential libraries such as PyTorch and Hugging Face Transformers, this section equips readers to create a robust computational setup. Key tasks such as tokenization, text normalization, and preprocessing are covered in detail to highlight their importance in preparing text data for effective model training. This segment also introduces the concept of fine-tuning, showing how to adapt Llama's extensive pre-trained knowledge to specific tasks or domains, optimizing performance with minimal data requirements.

The chapter transitions into practical applications, starting with **text classification using Llama**. Text classification, a core NLP task, involves categorizing textual data into predefined classes such as spam detection, topic classification, or emotion categorization. This section provides an end-to-end guide for building a text classification system, starting with data preparation, including cleaning, labeling, and creating training and validation splits. Readers are introduced to techniques for customizing Llama's architecture by adding a classification head, which maps the model's transformer-based embeddings to categorical outputs. Real-world use cases, such as customer review classification, email filtering, and social media content categorization, are explored to demonstrate how Llama excels in recognizing patterns, context, and nuances in text. The section emphasizes metrics such as accuracy, precision, recall, and F1-score to evaluate the model's effectiveness and discusses how iterative tuning ensures better results.

The next major topic focuses on **sentiment analysis with Llama**, showcasing its ability to decode and quantify the emotional tone of text. Sentiment analysis is a cornerstone application in areas such as brand monitoring, customer satisfaction analysis, and public opinion tracking. This section explains how to fine-tune Llama on sentiment-specific datasets, leveraging its deep contextual understanding to capture even subtle emotional cues. Challenges such as sarcasm, irony, and ambiguous language are addressed with advanced strategies, making sentiment analysis systems robust and reliable. Readers learn to evaluate the model's performance using class-based metrics, handle imbalanced datasets, and integrate the final model into production systems. Practical examples include real-time sentiment monitoring on social media platforms and analyzing customer reviews to guide product improvements.

The chapter's focus then shifts to **Named Entity Recognition (NER) using Llama**, one of the most powerful applications of transformer-based models. NER involves identifying and categorizing entities such as names, dates, locations, and organizations within text. This section dives deep into the mechanics of fine-tuning Llama for NER, starting with creating and annotating datasets using BIO or BIOES tagging schemes. The challenges of NER, such as disambiguating entities with multiple meanings (for example, "Apple" as a company versus fruit) and handling rare entity types, are addressed through innovative solutions such as domain-specific data augmentation and weighted loss functions. Readers are guided through building NER pipelines for real-world use cases, including parsing legal documents, extracting patient information in healthcare, and identifying trends in social media. Techniques for deploying NER models at scale, such as using REST APIs or containerized systems, are also covered.

Throughout the chapter, a consistent emphasis is placed on best practices, including optimizing hyperparameters, managing data quality, and addressing class imbalances. Readers learn not only how to build effective NLP systems but also how to maintain them through continuous monitoring, retraining, and adaptation to evolving data trends. Additionally, practical troubleshooting tips are provided to overcome common challenges encountered during fine-tuning and deployment.

This chapter lays a strong foundation for understanding the versatility and adaptability of Llama in NLP tasks. By guiding readers through the practical implementation of text classification, sentiment analysis, and NER, it demonstrates how to transform unstructured text into actionable insights. The knowledge and skills gained here prepare readers for the more advanced topics covered in the next chapter, which include:

- **Transfer Learning with Llama**: Leveraging Llama's pre-trained knowledge to rapidly adapt the model to new tasks with minimal labeled data.
- **Domain Adaptation Strategies**: Refining Llama for specialized domains such as healthcare, legal texts, or social media, and overcoming domain-specific challenges.
- **Hyperparameter Tuning for Llama Models**: Fine-tuning learning rates, batch sizes, and other parameters to optimize performance and efficiency.

With this detailed exploration, readers are equipped to confidently apply Llama to solve complex NLP problems while preparing to expand their expertise in the upcoming advanced topics. This chapter serves as both a practical guide and a theoretical foundation for harnessing the full potential of Llama in the ever-evolving landscape of NLP.

Setting Up Llama for NLP Tasks

Setting up Large Language Model Meta AI (Llama) for Natural Language Processing

(NLP) tasks is a foundational step towards leveraging its powerful capabilities. This chapter provides a comprehensive guide to configuring the Llama environment, ensuring that practitioners can seamlessly integrate the model into their NLP workflows. From installation and environment setup to model configuration and optimization, this chapter covers all essential aspects to get you started with Llama.

Prerequisites

Before diving into the setup process, it is crucial to ensure that your system meets the necessary prerequisites. This preparation will facilitate a smooth installation and configuration experience.

Hardware Requirements

- **Processor**: A multi-core CPU (preferably with support for AVX instructions) for general processing tasks.
- **Memory**: A minimum of 16 GB RAM is recommended, though 32 GB or more is ideal for handling larger models and datasets.
- **Storage**: Sufficient SSD storage (at least 100 GB) to accommodate model files, datasets, and dependencies.
- **GPU (Optional but Recommended)**: For accelerated training and inference, a NVIDIA GPU with CUDA support is highly recommended. Models can run on CPUs, but GPUs significantly reduce processing time.

Software Requirements

- **Operating System**: Linux-based systems (Ubuntu 20.04 LTS or later) are preferred for compatibility and performance. However, Llama can also be set up on Windows and macOS with appropriate configurations.
- **Python**: Version 3.8 or higher is required. Python 3.9 is recommended for optimal compatibility with libraries.
- **Package Managers**: pip for Python package installations and conda for managing environments are essential tools.
- **CUDA Toolkit**: If using a GPU, ensure that the appropriate CUDA toolkit version is installed to match your GPU drivers.

Dependencies

Llama relies on several Python libraries and frameworks. Key dependencies include:

- **PyTorch**: A deep learning framework that supports GPU acceleration.
- **Transformers**: Hugging Face's library for state-of-the-art NLP models.
- **Datasets**: Hugging Face's library for accessing and processing datasets.

- **Other Utilities**: Libraries such as numpy, pandas, and scikit-learn for data manipulation and preprocessing.

Setting Up the Environment

Creating an isolated environment ensures that dependencies do not conflict with other projects on your system. This section outlines how to set up a Python virtual environment using conda and pip.

Using Conda

- **Install Conda**: If not already installed, download and install Miniconda or Anaconda.
- **Create a New Environment**:

```
conda create -n Llama_env python=3.9
```

- **Activate the Environment:**

```
conda activate Llama_env
```

Using `Virtualenv` and `Pip`

- **Install Virtualenv:**

```
pip install virtualenv
```

- **Create a New Virtual Environment**:

```
virtualenv Llama_env
```

- **Activate the Environment:**
  - **Linux/macOS**: `source Llama_env/bin/activate`
  - **Windows**: `Llama_env\Scripts\activate`

Installing Dependencies

With the environment activated, proceed to install the necessary libraries.

Installing PyTorch

PyTorch installation varies based on your system's configuration, especially regarding GPU support. Visit the PyTorch installation page to get the exact command tailored to your setup. Here is a general example for CUDA 11.7:

```
pip install torch torchvision torchaudio --extra-index-url
https://download.pytorch.org/whl/cu117
```

For CPU-only installations:

```
pip install torch torchvision torchaudio
```

Installing Hugging Face Libraries

Install the transformers and datasets libraries from Hugging Face:

```
pip install transformers datasets
```

Additional Libraries

Install other essential libraries:

```
pip install numpy pandas scikit-learn matplotlib
```

Verifying Installations

To ensure that all dependencies are correctly installed, you can run the following Python script:

```
python
import torch
import transformers
import datasets
import numpy
import pandas
import sklearn
import matplotlib

print("All dependencies are successfully installed.")
```

Run the script:

```
python verify_installations.py
```

If no errors are encountered, your environment is correctly set up.

Obtaining the Llama Model

Llama models are proprietary to Meta and may require specific access permissions. Follow these steps to obtain and set up the Llama model.

Accessing Llama

- **Request Access**: Visit Meta's official Llama page (https://ai.facebook.com/products/Llama/) to request access. You may need to provide details about your intended use case.
- **Download the Model**: Once access is granted, download the appropriate Llama model files. These typically include model weights and configuration files.

Organizing Model Files

Create a directory structure to organize the model files:

```
mkdir -p ~/Llama_models/Llama-base
```

Place the downloaded model files into the Llama-base directory.

Configuring the Model

Proper configuration ensures that the Llama model operates optimally within your environment.

Loading the Model with Transformers

The Hugging Face transformers library facilitates the loading and usage of Llama models. Here is how to configure the model:

```
python
from transformers import AutoTokenizer, AutoModelForCausalLM

# Specify the path to the model directory
model_path = "~/Llama_models/Llama-base"

# Load the tokenizer
tokenizer = AutoTokenizer.from_pretrained(model_path)

# Load the model
model = AutoModelForCausalLM.from_pretrained(model_path)
```

Optimizing for GPU

To leverage GPU acceleration, ensure that the model and tensors are moved to the GPU:

```
python
import torch
device = torch.device("cuda" if torch.cuda.is_available() else
"cpu")
model.to(device)
```

Handling Large Models

For very large Llama models that may not fit into GPU memory, consider using techniques such as:

- **Model Parallelism**: Distributing the model across multiple GPUs.
- **Mixed Precision Training**: Utilizing 16-bit floating-point numbers to reduce memory usage.
- **Gradient Checkpointing**: Saving memory by re-computing gradients during backpropagation.

Example of enabling mixed precision with PyTorch:

```
python
Copy code
from transformers import AutoTokenizer
import torch
from torch.cuda.amp import autocast
tokenizer = AutoTokenizer.from_pretrained('Model Name')
input_text = "This is a sample input."
input_ids = tokenizer(input_text, return_tensors="pt").input_ids
input_ids = input_ids.to('cuda') if torch.cuda.is_available()
else input_ids
with autocast():
    outputs = model(input_ids)
```

Data Preparation

Effective NLP tasks require well-prepared data. This section outlines the steps to collect, preprocess, and format data for use with Llama models.

Data Collection

Gather data relevant to your NLP task. Sources may include:

- **Public Datasets**: Utilize repositories such as Hugging Face Datasets or Kaggle.
- **Custom Data**: Collect proprietary data specific to your application.

Data Preprocessing

Preprocessing steps vary based on the task but generally include:

- **Cleaning**: Remove unwanted characters, HTML tags, and irrelevant information.
- **Tokenization**: Split text into tokens (words, subwords, or characters) using the tokenizer.
- **Normalization**: Convert text to lowercase, remove punctuation, and handle contractions.
- **Handling Missing Values**: Address incomplete or missing data entries.

Example using Hugging Face datasets:

```
python
from datasets import load_dataset

# Load a dataset (e.g., IMDb for sentiment analysis)
dataset = load_dataset("imdb")

# Example preprocessing function
```

```
def preprocess_function(examples):
    return tokenizer(examples['text'], padding='max_length',
truncation=True)

# Apply preprocessing
tokenized_dataset = dataset.map(preprocess_function,
batched=True)
```

Creating Data Loaders

Organize data into batches for efficient processing during training and evaluation.

```
python
from torch.utils.data import DataLoader
train_loader = DataLoader(tokenized_dataset['train'],
batch_size=16, shuffle=True)
validation_loader = DataLoader(tokenized_dataset['test'],
batch_size=16)
```

Fine-Tuning the Llama Model

Fine-tuning adapts the pre-trained Llama model to specific NLP tasks, enhancing its performance on targeted datasets.

Setting Up the Training Loop

Define the training parameters, optimizer, and loss function.

```
python
from transformers import AdamW
from torch.nn import CrossEntropyLoss

# Define optimizer
optimizer = AdamW(model.parameters(), lr=5e-5)

# Define loss function
loss_fn = CrossEntropyLoss()
```

Training Process

Implement the training loop, ensuring that the model learns effectively from the data.

```
python
model.train()
num_epochs = 5
for epoch in range(num_epochs):
    model.train()
    for batch in train_loader:
        inputs = batch['input_ids'].to(device)
        labels = batch['labels'].to(device)
```

```
            optimizer.zero_grad()
            outputs = model(inputs, labels=labels)
            loss = outputs.loss
            loss.backward()
            optimizer.step()

        print(f"Epoch {epoch + 1} completed with loss:
    {loss.item()}")
```

Evaluation

Assess the model's performance on the validation set to monitor progress and prevent overfitting.

```
python

model.eval()
total_loss = 0

with torch.no_grad():
    for batch in validation_loader:
        inputs = batch['input_ids'].to(device)
        labels = batch['labels'].to(device)

        outputs = model(inputs, labels=labels)
        loss = outputs.loss
        total_loss += loss.item()

average_loss = total_loss / len(validation_loader)
print(f"Validation Loss: {average_loss}")
```

Saving the Fine-Tuned Model

After successful training, save the model and tokenizer for future use.

```
python
model.save_pretrained("fine_tuned_Llama")
tokenizer.save_pretrained("fine_tuned_Llama")
```

Deploying the Llama Model

Deploying the fine-tuned Llama model allows it to be integrated into applications, services, or systems for real-world usage.

Choosing a Deployment Strategy

Deployment strategies vary based on application requirements:

- **Local Deployment**: Running the model on local servers or machines.

- **Cloud Deployment**: Utilizing cloud platforms such as AWS, Azure, or Google Cloud for scalability.
- **Edge Deployment**: Deploying on edge devices for low-latency applications.

Setting Up a REST API

Creating a REST API facilitates communication between the model and client applications.

```
python

from flask import Flask, request, jsonify
from transformers import AutoTokenizer, AutoModelForCausalLM

app = Flask(__name__)

# Load the fine-tuned model and tokenizer
model = AutoModelForCausalLM.from_pretrained("fine_tuned_Llama").
to(device)
tokenizer = AutoTokenizer.from_pretrained("fine_tuned_Llama")

@app.route('/predict', methods=['POST'])
def predict():
    data = request.json
    input_text = data.get('text', '')

    inputs = tokenizer.encode(input_text, return_tensors='pt').
to(device)
    outputs = model.generate(inputs, max_length=50)
    generated_text = tokenizer.decode(outputs[0], skip_special_
tokens=True)

    return jsonify({'generated_text': generated_text})

if __name__ == '__main__':
    app.run(host='0.0.0.0', port=5000)
```

Containerization with Docker

Containerizing the deployment ensures consistency across different environments.

- **Create a Dockerfile:**

```
dockerfile

FROM python:3.9-slim
```

```
WORKDIR /app

COPY requirements.txt requirements.txt
RUN pip install --no-cache-dir -r requirements.txt

COPY . .

CMD ["python", "app.py"]
```

- **Build the Docker Image**: `docker build -t Llama-api`
- **Run the Docker Container**: `docker run -d -p 5000:5000 Llama-api`

Scaling the Deployment

For handling increased traffic and ensuring high availability:

- **Load Balancing**: Distribute incoming requests across multiple instances.
- **Auto-Scaling**: Automatically adjust the number of instances based on demand.
- **Monitoring**: Implement monitoring tools to track performance and uptime.

Optimizing Performance

Optimizing the Llama model ensures efficient resource utilization and faster inference times.

- **Model Quantization:** Quantization reduces the model size and accelerates inference by converting weights from 32-bit to lower precision.

  ```
  python

  from transformers import AutoModelForCausalLM
  model = AutoModelForCausalLM.from_pretrained("fine_tuned_Llama")
  model = torch.quantization.quantize_dynamic(
      model, {torch.nn.Linear}, dtype=torch.qint8
  )
  model.save_pretrained("quantized_Llama")
  ```

- **Caching and Batching**: Implementing caching mechanisms and batching requests can significantly improve throughput.

  ```
  python
  from functools import lru_cache

  @lru_cache(maxsize=128)
  def get_model():
      return AutoModelForCausalLM.from_pretrained
  ("fine_tuned_Llama").to(device)
  ```

```
# Batch processing example
def batch_predict(texts):
    inputs = tokenizer(texts, return_tensors='pt', padding=True).
to(device)
    outputs = model.generate(**inputs)
    return tokenizer.batch_decode(outputs, skip_special_to-
kens=True)
```

- **Distributed Computing:** For extremely large models or datasets, distributed computing across multiple machines or GPUs can enhance performance.
  - **Distributed Data Parallel (DDP):** Utilize PyTorch's DDP for parallel training.
  - **Horovod**: An open-source framework for distributed deep learning.

    ```
    python

    import torch.distributed as dist
    dist.init_process_group("nccl")
    model = torch.nn.parallel.DistributedDataParallel(model)
    ```

Text Classification Using Llama

Text classification is an essential task in Natural Language Processing (NLP), enabling applications ranging from sentiment analysis to spam detection and topic categorization. With the rise of transformer-based language models, the landscape of text classification has evolved significantly. Among these state-of-the-art models, Llama stands out for its efficiency, versatility, and ease of fine-tuning across various tasks. This chapter explores the process of using Llama for text classification, detailing the methods and strategies that make it a powerful solution for modern NLP challenges.

Understanding the Role of Text Classification

At its core, text classification involves assigning predefined labels or categories to segments of text. It underpins a broad spectrum of applications, including:

- **Sentiment Analysis**: Determining whether a given piece of text expresses a positive, negative, or neutral sentiment.
- **Spam Detection**: Recognizing and filtering out unwanted or malicious content from digital communication.
- **Topic Categorization**: Organizing articles, blog posts, or research papers based on their content.
- **Intent Recognition**: Enabling chatbots and virtual assistants to understand user inquiries and respond appropriately.

Text classification not only facilitates the automation of these tasks but also paves the way for more personalized and efficient user experiences in a variety of industries.

Leveraging Llama for Text Classification

Llama is a transformer-based language model designed to capture complex patterns and nuances in textual data. Its architecture, based on self-attention mechanisms, allows it to understand context and semantics more effectively than traditional models. When applied to text classification, Llama offers several key advantages:

- **Contextual Understanding**: By considering the relationships between words in a sentence, Llama can accurately interpret the meaning behind ambiguous or nuanced phrases.
- **Scalability**: Llama's design accommodates different model sizes, making it suitable for both simple tasks and more computationally intensive classification challenges.
- **Adaptability**: The model can be fine-tuned on specific datasets, aligning its general language understanding with domain-specific requirements.

Preparing for Text Classification with Llama

Implementing text classification using Llama involves several foundational steps:

Data Preparation

The success of any classification model heavily depends on the quality and structure of the training data. This process includes:

- **Data Collection**: Accumulating a representative dataset that covers the range of categories you wish to classify. This might include customer reviews, social media posts, or news articles.
- **Data Cleaning**: Removing noise such as HTML tags, special characters, or irrelevant metadata that could skew the learning process.
- **Labeling**: Ensuring that each text sample in the dataset is accurately annotated with a corresponding category. In cases where labels are subjective, establishing clear guidelines for annotation is crucial.
- **Splitting**: Dividing the data into training, validation, and test sets to evaluate model performance reliably.

Model Preparation

Before fine-tuning Llama for your specific classification task, setting up the environment is key. This includes:

- **Loading the Pre-trained Llama Model**: Utilizing the Hugging Face

Transformers library to load a pre-trained instance of Llama that serves as the starting point.

- **Tokenization**: Employing Llama's tokenizer to convert raw text into token sequences, ensuring that the input format aligns with the model's requirements.
- **Defining the Classification Head**: While Llama is primarily designed for language modeling, a classification head (typically a simple feed-forward network) is added on top of the model. This head maps the learned features to discrete labels, turning the language model into a classifier.

Fine-Tuning Llama for Text Classification

Fine-tuning adapts the pre-trained Llama model to the specific demands of your classification task. This process requires carefully adjusting the model's parameters on the labeled dataset:

- **Hyperparameter Optimization**: Experimenting with different learning rates, batch sizes, and dropout rates to prevent overfitting and ensure efficient training.
- **Loss Function**: Typically, a cross-entropy loss is used for classification tasks, as it quantifies the difference between predicted and actual labels.
- **Regularization**: Techniques such as dropout and early stopping help mitigate overfitting, especially when the training dataset is limited.
- **Iteration**: Training involves multiple epochs, with continuous monitoring of the validation loss to fine-tune the model further and prevent degradation of performance.

Through fine-tuning, Llama leverages its extensive pre-training on massive text corpora, adapting its internal representations to cater to the nuances of the specific classification task.

Evaluating and Deploying the Model

Post fine-tuning, evaluating the performance of the Llama-based classifier is essential. Common metrics include:

- **Accuracy**: The proportion of correctly classified instances.
- **Precision and Recall**: These metrics are particularly useful in imbalanced datasets, ensuring that both false positives and false negatives are accounted for.
- **F1-Score**: A harmonized metric that balances precision and recall.

Once the model demonstrates robust performance on the validation set, it can be deployed in real-world scenarios. Deployment strategies might involve integration into web applications, REST APIs, or cloud-based platforms to handle live data.

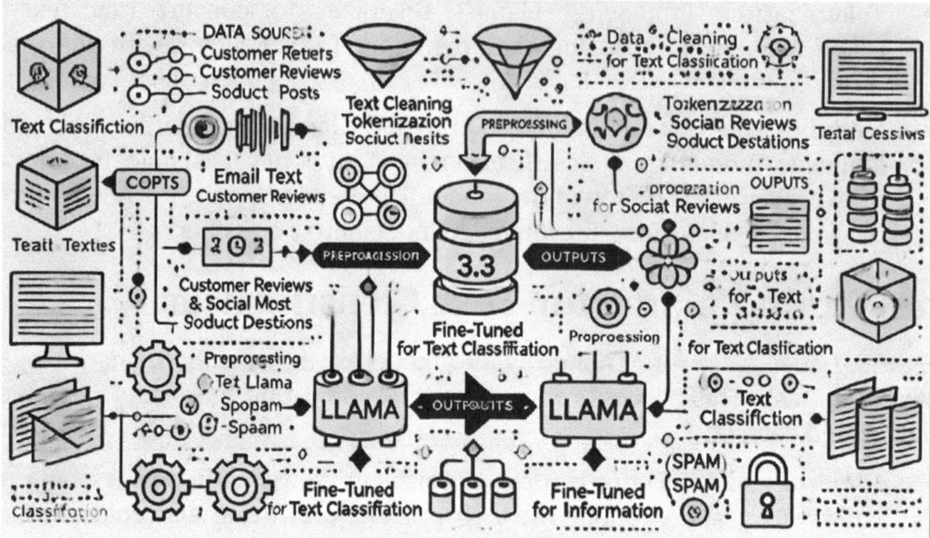

Figure 4.1: *Text Classification using Llama 3.3*

The preceding image shows how Llama 3.3 helps in text classification from different types of data inputs:

- **Data Sources:** The image begins with diverse data inputs such as email text, customer reviews, social media posts, and product descriptions, showcasing the variety of textual data that can be used for classification.
- **Preprocessing Stage:** Key preprocessing steps, including text cleaning, tokenization, and normalization, are depicted to highlight the importance of preparing the data for optimal model performance.
- **Llama 3.3 Model:** At the core, the fine-tuned Llama 3.3 model processes the input text with its advanced transformer architecture, designed specifically for text classification tasks.

  Outputs: The final stage shows clear and categorized results, such as `'Positive`,' `'Negative`,' `'Spam`,' and `'Informative`,' emphasizing how the model effectively classifies textual data into predefined categories.

Real-World Applications of Text Classification with Llama

The adaptability of Llama opens up numerous possibilities in practical applications:

- **Customer Feedback Analysis**: Businesses can gain actionable insights by classifying customer sentiments and feedback.

- **Content Moderation**: Social media platforms benefit from automated moderation systems that identify inappropriate content.
- **Healthcare**: Medical institutions can classify patient records and clinical notes to streamline diagnosis and treatment plans.
- **News Aggregation**: Organizing vast amounts of news content into coherent topics enhances user experience and content discoverability.

Some More Applications on Text Classification Leveraging Llama

Leveraging Llama for text classification enables advanced sentiment analysis in multilingual social media platforms and enhances content moderation systems by accurately categorizing user-generated content. Additionally, it supports personalized recommendation engines by effectively interpreting and classifying user preferences from vast textual data.

Sentiment Analysis in Customer Feedback

Applications:

- **E-commerce and Retail:** Automatically classify product reviews, survey responses, and customer feedback into categories such as *positive*, *negative*, or *neutral*.
- **Social Media Monitoring:** Track sentiment trends on social media platforms in real time.

How Llama Helps:

- **Context-Aware Reasoning:** Llama's deep understanding of context can detect nuanced sentiments, sarcasm, or subtle product criticisms.
- **Scalability:** The model can process large volumes of text quickly, enabling near real-time sentiment updates.

Spam and Toxic Content Detection

Applications:

- **Email and Social Media Platforms:** Classify incoming messages as spam, phishing attempts, or harmful content.
- **User-Generated Content Moderation:** Automatically flag and filter out toxic or abusive language from forums, comments, and reviews.

How Llama Helps:

- **Fine-Grained Classification:** Adaptations of Llama can be fine-tuned to accurately distinguish between genuine user content and malicious language.
- **Context Consideration:** The model's understanding of context helps in reducing false positives, ensuring genuine content is not misclassified.

Topic Categorization in News and Media

Applications:

- **News Aggregators:** Automatically classify news articles into topics such as politics, sports, entertainment, and technology.
- **Content Recommendation:** Enhance personalization by suggesting articles based on categorized topics.

How Llama Helps:

- **Semantic Understanding:** Leveraging contextual clues, Llama can accurately map articles to multiple topics.
- **Dynamic Updating:** New emerging topics or trends can be incorporated with fine-tuning as the media landscape evolves.

Legal Document Analysis

Applications:

- **Contract Review:** Classify and extract critical sections from lengthy contracts (for example, indemnity clauses, termination conditions).
- **Case Law Classification:** Organize legal documents by case type, jurisdiction, or legal issue, aiding in legal research.

How Llama Helps:

- **Precision in Legal Language:** Fine-tuning on legal datasets improves accuracy in navigating the dense language used in legal documents.
- **Efficiency:** Significantly reduces manual review time by automating the classification process.

Healthcare and Medical Text Analysis

Applications:

- **Clinical Documentation:** Categorize patient records, clinical notes, and research articles by diagnosis, treatment, and outcome.

- **Medical Inquiry Triage:** Classify patient inquiries or symptom descriptions to route them to appropriate care specialists.

How Llama Helps:

- **Specialized Vocabulary Handling:** When fine-tuned with medical texts, Llama can interpret complex medical terminology and jargon effectively.
- **Error Reduction:** Helps in ensuring accurate classification, thereby potentially improving patient outcomes by providing the right information to healthcare providers.

Fraud Detection in Financial Documents

Applications:

- **Transaction Monitoring:** Classify text from transaction logs or customer communications to detect potential fraud or financial anomalies.
- **Risk Assessment:** Evaluate and categorize customer applications and communications based on risk indicators.

How Llama Helps:

- **Pattern Recognition:** Utilizes deep learning techniques to identify anomalous language or patterns often associated with fraudulent behavior.
- **Adaptive Learning:** Can be continuously updated with new fraud patterns, improving its detection capabilities over time.

Use Case	**Application Description**	**How Llama Helps**
Sentiment Analysis	• Analyze customer feedback in e-commerce, retail, and social media. • Classify text as positive, negative, or neutral.	• Provides context-aware sentiment analysis, detecting nuances like sarcasm. • Scales to process large volumes of text for near real-time feedback.
Spam and Toxic Content Detection	• Identify spam, phishing attempts, and harmful content on email and social media platforms. • Filter abusive language in user-generated content.	• Fine-grained classification improves detection accuracy. • Robust understanding of context helps minimize false positives, ensuring genuine content is not misclassified.
Topic Categorization	• Classify news articles into topics (for example, politics, sports, technology). • Improve content recommendations based on categorized topics.	• Leverages semantic understanding to map articles to multiple topics. • Can be dynamically updated as new topics or trends emerge.

Legal Document Analysis	• Categorize legal documents (for example, contracts, case laws) by type, jurisdiction, or legal issue. • Extract and review key contract clauses automatically.	• Fine-tuned on legal language for precision in handling dense or specialized terminology. • Reduces manual review time by automating document classification and extraction processes.
Healthcare and Medical Text Analysis	• Organize clinical documents, patient records, and research articles by diagnoses, treatments, and outcomes. • Triage patient inquiries to specialists.	• Handles specialized medical vocabulary when fine-tuned on relevant datasets. • Improves accuracy and efficiency in routing and classifying medical texts, aiding in patient care and management.
Fraud Detection in Financial Documents	• Monitor transaction logs and customer communications for signs of fraud or financial anomalies. • Perform risk assessment of customer applications.	• Utilizes deep learning to recognize language patterns indicative of fraudulent behavior. • Adaptively learns new fraud patterns through continuous fine-tuning, enhancing detection capabilities over time.

Table 4.1: *Real World Applications of Text Classification*

Implementing Llama for Text Classification Tasks

Data Preparation:

- Collect a dataset relevant to the task (for example, labeled customer reviews for sentiment analysis).
- Preprocess the text (cleaning, tokenization) so that it aligns with the training regime of the Llama-based model.

Fine-tuning Steps:

1. **Model Selection:** Start with a pre-trained Llama model.
2. **Customized Training:** Fine-tune the model on the specific domain dataset using supervised learning techniques.
3. **Validation:** Use a hold-out validation set to ensure the model generalizes well to unseen data.
4. **Deployment:** Integrate the fine-tuned model into your production pipeline, ensuring scalability and performance.

Monitoring and Updating:

- Regularly evaluate classification accuracy.
- Implement feedback loops to retrain or fine-tune as the nature of the data evolves.

Sentiment Analysis with Llama

Sentiment analysis lies at the heart of understanding human emotions and opinions expressed through text. In an age where digital communication dominates, the ability to extract sentiment—whether positive, negative, or neutral—from vast arrays of textual data is invaluable. Leveraging the powerful capabilities of Llama, this chapter explores how state-of-the-art transformer-based models can be fine-tuned to perform robust sentiment analysis, offering transformative insights across industries.

The Need for Sentiment Analysis

In today's data-driven world, businesses, governments, and researchers constantly seek to understand the pulse of public opinion. Sentiment analysis turns unstructured text—be it customer reviews, social media comments, or survey responses—into actionable data. By automating the process of interpreting emotional tone, sentiment analysis drives improvements in customer service, enhances product development, and even informs political strategy. At its core, it harnesses artificial intelligence to bridge the gap between raw opinion data and strategic insight.

Llama: A Paradigm Shift for Sentiment Analysis

Llama represents a breakthrough in NLP by combining extensive pre-training with an adaptable architecture that can be tailored for specific applications such as sentiment analysis. Its transformer-based design, characterized by self-attention mechanisms, enables the model to capture nuanced contextual relationships within text—a key requirement when deciphering the subtle cues of human sentiment. Unlike traditional approaches that often relied on predefined lexicons or shallow feature extraction, Llama offers deep contextual understanding, allowing it to interpret complex, nuanced language with exceptional precision.

Advantages of Llama in Sentiment Analysis

- **Contextual Nuance:** Llama's deep architecture captures long-range dependencies and context, which means it can distinguish between subtle differences in sentiment even within a single sentence. For example, it can differentiate between "I *hardly expected such a delightful experience*" and "I *expected something delightful, but it fell short,"* identifying layered emotions through context.

- **Scalability and Efficiency:** Designed to operate across various computational environments, Llama adapts well to both small-scale experiments and production-scale deployments. Its versatility ensures that organizations can deploy sentiment analysis systems regardless of data size and computational constraints.
- **Adaptability through Fine-Tuning:** The model can be fine-tuned on sentiment-specific data, enabling it to capture the unique linguistic cues and domain-specific subtleties that differentiate, for example, a film review from customer feedback in e-commerce. This customization creates specialized variants of Llama that excel in their targeted applications.

Preparing Data for Sentiment Analysis

The success of any sentiment analysis project begins with the quality of the data. Ensuring that the dataset is comprehensive and well-curated is paramount.

- **Data Collection:** The first step is identifying data sources that accurately reflect user sentiment. These sources may include social media platforms, online forums, review sites, and customer support logs. Collecting diverse data helps ensure that the sentiment analysis system understands the wide range of expressions found in natural language.
- **Data Preprocessing:** Preprocessing involves cleaning the data to remove noise such as HTML tags, emojis (if not essential to sentiment), and typographical errors. It also includes normalizing text (lowercasing, stemming, or lemmatization) and tokenizing the text using Llama's dedicated tokenizer. This step is vital in reducing variability and improving the model's ability to recognize sentiment patterns.
- **Labeling Sentiment:** Manual annotation of sentiment remains critical, especially when establishing ground truth for supervised learning. High-quality labels, whether binary (positive vs. negative) or multi-class (for example, positive, negative, neutral, mixed), enable the model to learn finer distinctions in human emotion. When practical, leveraging crowdsourced annotation or domain expert insights can enhance labeling accuracy.

Fine-Tuning Llama for Sentiment Analysis

After preparing the data, the next phase is fine-tuning the pre-trained Llama model on the task of sentiment analysis.

- **Architecture Adaptation:** A classification head is appended on top of Llama's transformer layers. This head processes the enriched textual embeddings produced by the model and converts them into sentiment classifications. This approach transforms a general-purpose language model into a specialized sentiment analyzer.

- **Hyperparameter Optimization:** Fine-tuning requires careful adjustment of learning rates, batch sizes, dropout rates, and the number of epochs. Experimenting with various configurations, using techniques such as grid search or Bayesian optimization, can significantly enhance performance and reduce overfitting.
- **Loss of Functions and Regularization:** Employing a cross-entropy loss function aligns closely with classification tasks. Regularization methods, such as dropout and early stopping, are implemented to prevent overfitting, especially when training on relatively limited sentiment datasets.
- **Evaluation during Fine-Tuning:** Continuous evaluation using metrics such as precision, recall, and F1-score not only helps in assessing the model's performance but also guides adjustments during training. Monitoring validation losses and confusion matrices can illuminate class imbalances or nuances that require additional data augmentation or further fine-tuning.

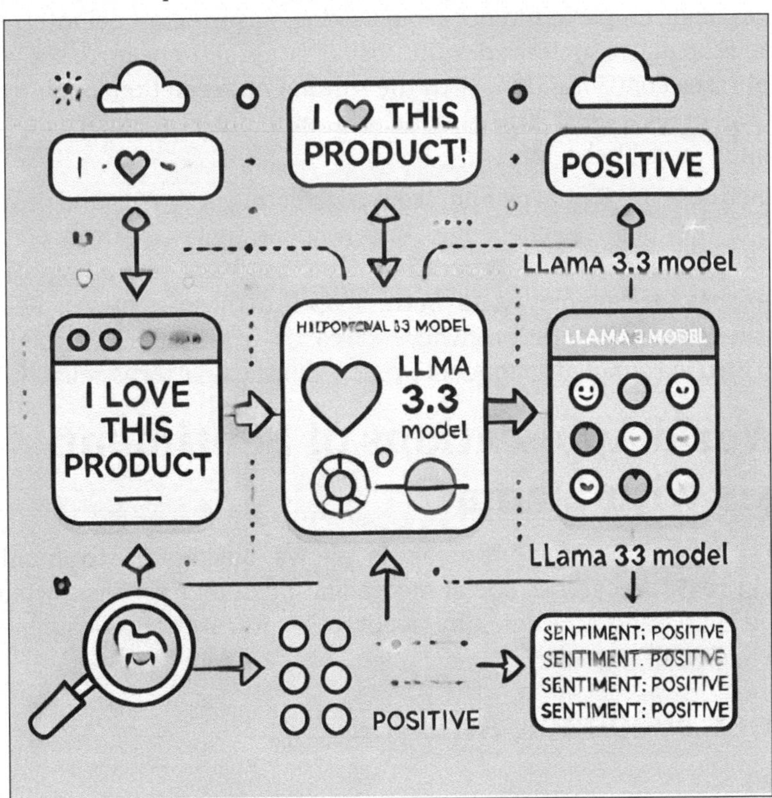

Figure 4.2: *Sentiment Analysis using Llama 3.3*

Advanced Techniques in Sentiment Analysis

In addition to standard approaches, several advanced techniques can further enhance sentiment analysis capabilities using Llama.

- **Transfer Learning and Domain Adaptation:** Building on Llama's extensive pre-training, domain adaptation techniques allow the model to refine its focus on specific industries. For example, a sentiment analysis model tailored to financial news might be fine-tuned with a targeted corpus of market reports and analyst comments, enhancing its ability to interpret sentiment in a specialized context.
- **Multimodal Sentiment Analysis:** Integrating textual sentiment analysis with other forms of data–such as visual or auditory cues–can provide a more holistic view of sentiment. While Llama is primarily text-focused, combining its outputs with other modalities through ensemble methods can yield richer insights, especially in social media analysis, where images and videos often accompany text.
- **Explainability and Interpretability:** As sentiment analysis models are increasingly employed in decision-making, ensuring model interpretability is vital. Techniques such as attention visualization allow users to see which words or phrases contributed most to the sentiment prediction. Such transparency not only builds trust in the model's outputs but also aids in debugging and refining model behavior.
- **Robustness to Sarcasm and Irony:** Detecting sarcasm and irony remains one of the toughest challenges in sentiment analysis. Advanced fine-tuning strategies, such as incorporating context from preceding or following sentences, are employed to better capture these nuances. Research into synthetic data generation–where sarcastic expressions are simulated–can also help in training the model to recognize such patterns reliably.

Real-World Applications of Sentiment Analysis with Llama

Leveraging Llama for sentiment analysis allows businesses to monitor brand reputation in real-time across social media and customer reviews, while enabling personalized marketing strategies by accurately interpreting consumer emotions and preferences.

Customer Feedback Analysis

Applications:

- **E-commerce and Retail**: Analyze customer reviews and survey responses to identify satisfaction levels or issues with products/services.

- **Hospitality Industry**: Understand guest satisfaction from feedback forms, online reviews, and social media mentions.

How Llama Helps:

- **Nuance Detection**: Captures subtle sentiments, such as sarcasm or mixed emotions.
- **Multi-Lingual Support**: When fine-tuned, Llama can process feedback in multiple languages, expanding its usability globally.

Social Media Monitoring

Applications:

- Track user sentiment trends on platforms such as Twitter, Instagram, and Facebook.
- Identify brand perception and emerging public opinions about products, events, or campaigns.

How Llama Helps:

- **Real-Time Sentiment Analysis**: Processes high volumes of social media posts quickly.
- **Contextual Understanding**: Identifies deeper sentiment from context, hashtags, and emojis.

Product and Market Research

Applications:

- Analyze public sentiment about new product launches, advertisements, or marketing campaigns.
- Assess trends and consumer reactions to refine product development and marketing strategies.

How Llama Helps:

- **Granular Analysis**: Segments sentiment by demographic or geographic region.
- **Trend Prediction**: Helps identify early indicators of consumer demand or dissatisfaction.

Financial Market Insights

Applications:

- Analyze financial news, investor opinions, or market commentary to gauge sentiment on stocks, markets, or economic trends.

- Support trading decisions with sentiment-driven insights.

How Llama Helps:

- **Accurate Context Analysis**: Differentiates between optimism and pessimism in financial jargon.
- **Scalability**: Processes large datasets, such as earnings calls or news articles, for actionable insights.

Use Case	Application Description	How Llama Helps
Customer Feedback Analysis	• Analyze customer reviews and survey responses in e-commerce, retail, and hospitality. • Understand guest satisfaction from online reviews and social media mentions.	• Captures subtle sentiments such as sarcasm or mixed emotions. • Processes feedback in multiple languages, enabling global usability.
Social Media Monitoring	• Track user sentiment trends on platforms like Twitter, Instagram, and Facebook. • Identify brand perception and emerging public opinions.	• Processes high volumes of posts in real-time. • Identifies deeper sentiment from hashtags, emojis, and context.
Product and Market Research	• Analyze public sentiment about new product launches and marketing campaigns. • Assess trends and consumer reactions to refine product strategies.	• Segments sentiment by demographics or regions. • Helps identify early indicators of demand or dissatisfaction.
Financial Market Insights	• Analyze financial news, investor opinions, and market commentary. • Support trading decisions with sentiment-driven insights.	• Differentiates between optimism and pessimism in financial jargon. • Processes large datasets like earnings calls and news articles.
Political Sentiment Analysis	• Track public opinion during elections, debates, or policy announcements. • Understand voter concerns and sentiments toward policies or candidates.	• Detects polarized language and emotional intensity in political contexts. • Aggregates data from speeches, social media, and news for holistic insights.

Customer Support Automation	• Analyze customer complaints and chatbot sessions to gauge sentiment. • Prioritize and route negative feedback to appropriate teams for resolution.	• Identifies critical customer interactions requiring immediate attention. • Powers chatbots to provide empathetic, sentiment-aware responses.
Healthcare Feedback and Patient Experience	• Assess patient feedback to improve healthcare services. • Identify potential dissatisfaction in telemedicine or online consultations.	• Interprets sentiment in healthcare-specific language. • Captures emotions like anxiety or frustration in patient feedback.
Entertainment and Media Analytics	• Analyze public sentiment toward movies, music, games, or celebrity news. • Predict audience reception and identify trends in entertainment consumption.	• Recognizes excitement, disappointment, or anticipation in reviews. • Processes sentiment from trailers, promotions, and fan engagement.
Employee Sentiment Monitoring	• Analyze employee feedback in surveys or performance reviews. • Detect potential dissatisfaction or disengagement early to improve retention.	• Maintains privacy while detecting subtle dissatisfaction trends. • Can scale to analyze feedback in large organizations.
Consumer Sentiment on Sustainability	• Understand public sentiment about sustainability initiatives or green products. • Track perceptions of corporate responsibility efforts.	• Captures nuanced opinions about sustainability topics. • Provides insights into changing consumer attitudes over time.

***Table 4.2**: Real World Applications of Sentiment Analysis*

Named Entity Recognition (NER) Using Llama

Named Entity Recognition (NER) is a fundamental task in Natural Language Processing (NLP) that involves identifying and categorizing key pieces of information–such as names of people, organizations, locations, dates, and more–within text. With the growing demand for automated information extraction, NER has become an indispensable tool for applications ranging from content recommendation systems to information retrieval and business intelligence. Leveraging Llama for NER opens up new possibilities for accuracy and efficiency, thanks to its state-of-the-art transformer architecture and deep contextual understanding.

A New Era for NER with Transformer Models

Traditional methods for NER often relied on handcrafted rules or statistical models that required extensive feature engineering. These approaches, though effective in controlled settings, struggled to cope with the complexity and variability of real-world language. Transformer-based models have revolutionized this landscape by learning intricate patterns directly from large-scale textual data. Llama, with its robust pre-training on diverse corpora, is particularly adept at capturing the subtle nuances and contextual dependencies essential for correctly identifying named entities. This ability to understand context at a granular level significantly improves the model's precision in distinguishing between similar entities and disambiguating ambiguous terms.

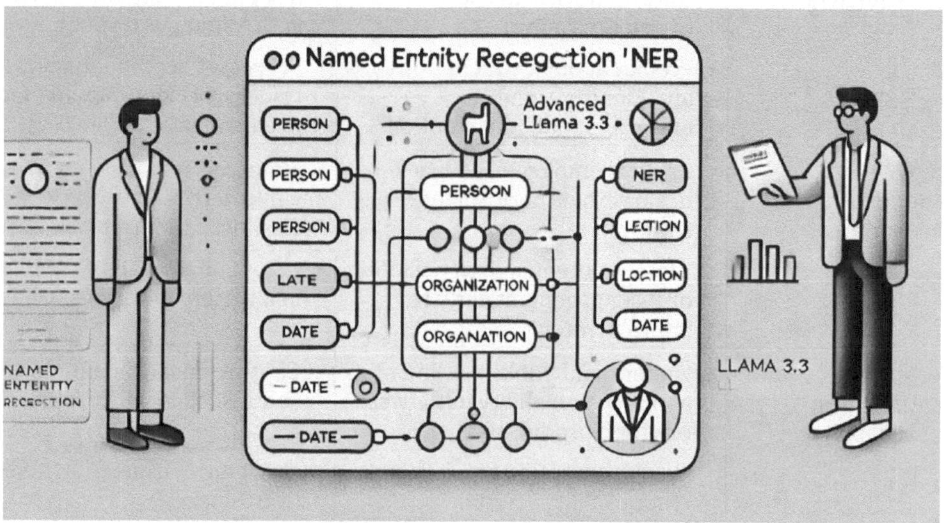

Figure 4.3: *Named Entity Recognition using Llama 3.3*

Data Preparation and Annotation for NER

Success in NER begins with quality data. The process of preparing a dataset for named entity recognition involves several critical steps:

- **Curating Relevant Data:** Selecting datasets that encompass a wide range of named entities is crucial. Data sources might include news articles, academic literature, legal documents, or social media posts. Each source brings a unique vocabulary and context, helping the model learn diverse representations of entities.
- **Text Cleaning and Tokenization:** Raw text data often contains extraneous elements that can confuse model training. Preprocessing typically includes cleaning the text of any irrelevant content, normalizing case and punctuation,

and tokenizing the sentences in a way that preserves the semantic structure. Given Llama's advanced tokenizer, this step helps ensure that the entity boundaries are accurately captured.

- **Entity Annotation:** For supervised NER, each token in the text must be labeled according to whether it is part of a named entity and, if so, what type of entity it is. This is typically done using annotation schemes such as BIO (Beginning, Inside, Outside) or BIOES (Beginning, Inside, Outside, End, Single). High-quality annotations are instrumental in training a model that can generalize well to unseen texts.

Fine-Tuning Llama for NER

While Llama comes pre-trained with a vast understanding of language, fine-tuning it on a domain-specific NER dataset enhances its ability to recognize entities with specialized meanings. The fine-tuning process involves several key components:

- **Adapting the Model Architecture:** To convert Llama into an entity recognizer, a classification head is added on top of the transformer encoder. This head is responsible for assigning entity labels to each token. The additional layer is configured to predict tags from the set of predefined entity categories. By incorporating this specialized head, the model can leverage its deep language representations while focusing on the task of entity classification.
- **Optimizing Hyperparameters:** Tuning the learning rate, batch size, and the number of training epochs is critical when adapting Llama for NER. Adjustments based on early validation performance help ensure that the model not only learns effectively but also avoids overfitting. Techniques such as dropout and learning rate scheduling further contribute to a robust training process.
- **Handling Imbalanced Classes:** In many practical applications, certain types of entities (for example, person names) may appear far more frequently than others (for example, specific event names or rare locations). Strategies such as weighted loss functions or data augmentation can help the model learn balanced representations across all entity types, leading to improved performance in real-world scenarios.

Evaluating NER Performance

Evaluating the performance of an NER system requires specialized metrics that capture how well the model identifies entity boundaries and correctly classifies them. Common metrics include:

- **Precision:** The proportion of correctly identified entities among all entities predicted by the model. High precision indicates that the model makes few false positive predictions.

- **Recall:** The proportion of actual entities in the dataset that the model successfully identifies. A high recall score indicates that most entities are captured, even if some incorrect ones are also included.
- **F1-Score:** This score is the harmonic mean of precision and recall, providing a balanced measure of the model's overall performance. This score is particularly useful when there is a trade-off between precision and recall.

In addition to these metrics, detailed error analysis–including confusion matrices that show misclassified entity types–helps guide further refinements in data preparation and model tuning.

Real-World Applications and Impact

The ability to automatically extract named entities from text has transformative implications across a broad range of industries. Consider the following applications:

- **Business Intelligence:** Companies can deploy NER to analyze financial reports, legal documents, and media articles, allowing them to quickly extract key information about competitors, market trends, and strategic partnerships.
- **Healthcare:** In clinical settings, NER systems can be used to sift through patient records, research publications, and clinical trial documents to extract vital information such as patient names, medical conditions, and treatment protocols–thereby accelerating medical research and diagnosis processes.
- **Content Management and Search:** By indexing and categorizing content based on named entities, organizations improve content discoverability on websites and digital libraries. This enhances user experiences by enabling more precise search and recommendation systems.
- **Social Media Monitoring:** NER facilitates the identification of influential figures, trending topics, and geopolitical locations within social media streams. Marketers and political analysts alike can harness these insights to better understand public sentiment and inform decision-making.

While the potential of NER using Llama is vast, it is essential to address ethical considerations. Protecting privacy is paramount when processing sensitive personal information. Model developers must ensure that data used for training is anonymized and that systems are compliant with data protection regulations.

Looking ahead, the evolution of NER systems promises even greater levels of sophistication. Future research may focus on:

- **Cross-Lingual NER:** Enhancing the capacity of models such as Llama to recognize entities across different languages and dialects, thereby making NER accessible on a global scale.

- **Integration with Multimodal Data:** Combining text-based NER with insights from images, videos, and audio could yield richer and more contextual entity recognition, especially in multimedia content.
- **Enhanced Explainability:** Developing methods to visualize and interpret the attention mechanisms within Llama will provide deeper insights into why specific entities are recognized, increasing transparency and trust in automated systems.

Conclusion

As we conclude this chapter, we can reflect on the transformative role that advanced language models, such as Llama (Large Language Model Meta AI), play in the ever-evolving field of Natural Language Processing (NLP). From Named Entity Recognition (NER) to sentiment analysis and beyond, Llama's deep contextual understanding, adaptability, and scalability have opened up new opportunities for automating complex language tasks. By leveraging its capabilities, organizations can unlock valuable insights from unstructured text, enhancing decision-making processes and improving user experiences.

The next chapter explores transfer learning with Llama, showing how to adapt pre-trained models to new tasks using minimal labeled data, and delves into domain adaptation strategies for specialized fields such as medical, legal, and social media. It also covers hyperparameter tuning techniques such as grid search and random search to optimize Llama models' performance effectively, ensuring they operate efficiently without overfitting or underfitting.

These next steps will provide you with the tools to fine-tune and optimize your Llama models, bringing you closer to harnessing their full potential for real-world applications. Whether you are working with text classification, NER, or more advanced NLP tasks, the upcoming chapters will offer the advanced knowledge and practical guidance necessary for pushing the boundaries of what is possible with Llama in NLP.

Multiple Choice Questions

1. Which of the following is a key benefit of using Llama for Named Entity Recognition (NER)?

    a. Llama requires extensive manual feature extraction.

    b. Llama can capture subtle contextual relationships within the text.

   c. Llama uses rule-based systems for entity identification.

   d. Llama does not require any fine-tuning.

2. What is the main purpose of fine-tuning a pre-trained Llama model for a specific task like Sentiment Analysis?

   a. To adjust the model for new types of data without modifying the architecture

   b. To train the model from scratch using a smaller dataset

   c. To improve the model's accuracy for the task by adapting it to domain-specific data

   d. To remove the need for preprocessing the data

3. What is one of the primary preprocessing steps in Sentiment Analysis using Llama?

   a. Text cleaning

   b. Directly feeding raw data into the model without modification

   c. Tokenization only

   d. Applying a static sentiment lexicon

4. Which of the following metrics is most commonly used to evaluate the performance of NER models?

   a. Precision

   b. Recall

   c. F1-Score

   d. All of the above

5. What does domain adaptation in the context of Llama models help achieve?

   a. It allows the model to understand all languages.

   b. It helps the model generalize better to new, unseen data.

   c. It tunes the model for a specific industry or application.

   d. It removes the need for transfer learning.

6. Which of the following techniques helps handle class imbalances during fine-tuning Llama for NER?
    a. Data augmentation
    b. Tokenization
    c. Reducing training data
    d. Using fixed learning rates
7. What is the purpose of adding a classification head on top of the Llama model for text classification tasks?
    a. To improve the speed of training
    b. To convert the model's transformer output into entity or sentiment predictions
    c. To store the output of the model
    d. To adjust the model's architecture for neural machine translation
8. What is an important step when deploying a Llama-based NER or Sentiment Analysis model for real-time applications?
    a. Limiting data sources to only text-based information
    b. Using automatic hyperparameter tuning during deployment
    c. Ensuring continuous monitoring and updates to maintain performance
    d. Running the model without preprocessing steps
9. Which of the following is true regarding the preprocessing stage for text classification tasks using Llama?
    a. Preprocessing only includes tokenization.
    b. Preprocessing ensures that the model receives consistent input by normalizing and cleaning the text data.
    c. Preprocessing involves just removing stopwords.
    d. Preprocessing is not needed for Llama models.

10. Which technique helps in reducing the time needed for training by using pre-existing knowledge from a related task or domain?

    a. Hyperparameter tuning

    b. Transfer learning

    c. Domain adaptation

    d. Data augmentation

Answers

1. b
2. c
3. a
4. d
5. c
6. a
7. b
8. c
9. b
10. b

Chapter 5
Fine-Tuning Llama for NLP

Introduction

In recent years, the evolution of language models has reached unparalleled heights, revolutionizing the field of Natural Language Processing (NLP). Among these advancements, Llama models have emerged as versatile tools that extend the boundaries of machine comprehension and generation. This chapter delves into advanced fine-tuning techniques that not only customize Llama models for specific NLP applications and domains but also optimize performance and accuracy. By integrating state-of-the-art fine-tuning strategies with transfer learning, domain adaptation, and rigorous performance optimization methods, practitioners can transform these general-purpose models into specialized, high-performing solutions tailored to the unique challenges of real-world applications.

Structure

In this chapter, we will cover the following topics:

- Overview
- Transfer Learning with Llama
- Domain Adaptation Strategies
- Hyperparameter Tuning for Llama models
- Case studies and Applications of Fine-Tuned Llama models

Overview

The chapter embarks on a comprehensive journey into the nuanced process of fine-tuning Llama models for custom NLP applications. It begins by establishing the foundational importance of fine-tuning pre-trained models. Although Llama models are built on extensive pre-training that endows them with broad linguistic abilities, this chapter emphasizes that their true potential is unlocked only through careful and targeted fine-tuning. By refining these models to handle the specialized requirements of specific industries–such as healthcare, finance, legal, and creative sectors–the fine-tuning process ensures models are not only accurate but also attuned to the intricacies and vocabulary that define each domain.

Building upon this introduction, the chapter delves deep into advanced transfer learning strategies that serve as the cornerstone for efficient fine-tuning. It explains how leveraging the inherent capabilities of pre-trained Llama models can accelerate the adaptation process while reducing computational overhead. Detailed discussions cover techniques such as layer-wise fine-tuning, where only specific parts of the model are adjusted to integrate domain-specific information without compromising the core pre-trained structures. The chapter further explores progressive unfreezing, a strategy designed to gradually release layers from their initial frozen states, thereby allowing a smooth transition from general pre-training to a more specialized learning context. Additionally, task-specific adaptation is examined, highlighting how fine-tuning can be explicitly tailored to optimize model performance for diverse NLP tasks–ranging from sentiment analysis and question answering to named entity recognition–ensuring the output is both relevant and nuanced.

The Imperative of Fine-Tuning in NLP

While pre-trained models such as Llama come equipped with a broad understanding of human language, their true potential is realized when fine-tuned for niche areas or specialized tasks. Fine-tuning allows for subtle yet critical adjustments to the model's parameters, ensuring that it can effectively handle the idiosyncrasies and specialized vocabulary of a target domain. This process is particularly crucial when deploying the model within fields such as healthcare, finance, legal, or creative industries, where the stakes for accuracy and context are exceptionally high.

By carefully fine-tuning the model, developers can achieve:

- **Enhanced Precision:** Adapting the model's responses to incorporate domain-specific knowledge.
- **Improved Efficiency:** Leveraging the existing knowledge of pre-trained models to reduce computational overhead.
- **Domain Relevance:** Ensuring that the model comprehends and effectively uses the specialized terminology and nuances inherent in the target domain.

Advanced Transfer Learning Strategies for Fine-Tuning

Transfer learning is a cornerstone of effective fine-tuning, allowing the pre-trained

Llama models' vast linguistic knowledge to be harnessed and directed towards specialized applications. By integrating advanced transfer learning techniques with fine-tuning processes, practitioners can ensure rapid adaptation and improved model performance. The key strategies include:

- **Layer-wise Fine-Tuning:** Selectively adjusting specific layers of the model that are most relevant to the targeted task, thus preserving core linguistic competencies while adapting to specialized content.
- **Progressive Unfreezing:** Gradually releasing layers from their frozen state during training enables the model to incrementally adjust its learned representations, ensuring a smoother transition and improved stability.
- **Task-Specific Adaptation:** Tailoring the model through fine-tuning so that its outputs are highly attuned to the requirements of particular applications, whether that involves sentiment analysis, named entity recognition, or domain-specific question answering.

These advanced methods of transfer learning, when combined with robust fine-tuning approaches, facilitate a seamless bridge between general pre-training and domain-specific performance.

Domain Adaptation Techniques in Fine-Tuning

Fine-tuning is not merely about adjusting parameters; it also involves a strategic approach to domain adaptation. This process is critical when the goal is to repurpose Llama models for specialized tasks. Effective domain adaptation through fine-tuning encompasses:

- **Curated Domain-Specific Datasets:** Building high-quality datasets that represent the vocabulary, syntax, and semantics unique to a target domain. Fine-tuning on these datasets sharpens the model's understanding and ensures that it delivers contextually relevant outputs.
- **Data Augmentation and Preprocessing:** Utilizing techniques such as augmentation, normalization, and noise reduction ensures that the fine-tuning process benefits from datasets that closely mirror real-world scenarios.
- **Domain-Sensitive Loss Functions:** Customizing loss functions to penalize misinterpretations that deviate from domain-specific expectations, thereby reinforcing the model's focus on relevant attributes during fine-tuning.

Incorporating these domain adaptation strategies within the fine-tuning framework allows for a more precise and effective customization process, ensuring that Llama models are well-equipped to handle the nuances of specialized fields.

Optimizing Model Performance Through Fine-Tuning

Achieving optimal performance from a fine-tuned Llama model requires a meticulous balance of fine-tuning processes and performance optimization strategies. This involves:

- **Hyperparameter Optimization:** Fine-tuning is highly dependent on the careful calibration of learning rates, batch sizes, and epochs. Techniques such as grid search, random search, and Bayesian optimization help in systematically identifying the best configurations for a particular domain.
- **Regularization and Dropout Methods:** To prevent overfitting, particularly when working with smaller, domain-specific datasets, applying regularization techniques–such as dropout, weight decay, and early stopping–ensures that the fine-tuned model maintains its ability to generalize effectively.
- **Continuous Evaluation and Iterative Refinement:** Establishing robust evaluation pipelines, including automated metrics and human-in-the-loop assessments, is crucial. Continuous monitoring during the fine-tuning process allows developers to make informed adjustments, further aligning the model's performance with domain expectations.

These methods are essential not only for the fine-tuning process itself but also for sustaining the high performance and reliability of the resulting Llama model in its operational environment.

Contextual Overview of the Chapter

This chapter serves as a comprehensive guide for integrating advanced fine-tuning techniques into the adaptation of Llama models for custom NLP applications. The structure of the chapter includes:

- **Exploration of Transfer Learning in Fine-Tuning:** Detailed insights into how fine-tuning techniques build upon transfer learning principles to achieve efficient model adaptation.
- **Domain-Specific Adaptation through Fine-Tuning:** An in-depth analysis of strategies for preparing and optimizing domain-specific datasets and adapting the model's parameters accordingly.
- **Performance Optimization in Fine-Tuning:** A critical review of methods for hyperparameter tuning, regularization, and continuous monitoring to ensure superior model performance.

Designed for seasoned data scientists, researchers, and developers, this chapter not only provides theoretical foundations but also practical methodologies for leveraging advanced fine-tuning techniques. The focus is on equipping you with the necessary tools to repurpose Llama models effectively, ensuring they meet the specific requirements of your targeted applications.

Transfer Learning with Llama

In the rapidly evolving landscape of Natural Language Processing (NLP), the ability to leverage pre-trained models has revolutionized how we approach language understanding and generation. This book delves into the transformative practice of fine-tuning Llama models, emphasizing the power of transfer learning to create custom NLP applications tailored to specific tasks and domains. By integrating advanced fine-tuning techniques with robust transfer learning strategies, practitioners can convert a versatile, general-purpose model into a specialized tool that addresses the nuanced requirements of real-world applications.

The Paradigm Shift in NLP

The field of NLP has witnessed a dramatic evolution over the past decade. Early rule-based systems and shallow machine learning algorithms have given way to deep learning models capable of understanding and generating text with human-like proficiency. Llama models, which are rooted in extensive pre-training across enormous datasets, embody this transformation. Their vast general knowledge is a result of exposure to diverse linguistic patterns, making them an excellent starting point for further specialization.

Imagine a healthcare company seeking to create a chatbot that not only understands medical queries but also delivers empathetic and contextually appropriate responses. While a generic Llama model might already understand general medical language, fine-tuning using domain-specific data—such as clinical notes and patient interactions—enables the model to grasp subtle terminologies and contexts unique to healthcare. This transformation is facilitated by transfer learning, which enables the model to adapt rapidly while retaining its extensive pre-learned linguistic capabilities.

Understanding Transfer Learning with Llama

Transfer learning is the linchpin for effectively customizing Llama models for specialized applications. At its core, transfer learning involves taking a model pre-trained on extensive, generic datasets and then refining it using data from a specific domain or tailored task. This approach drastically reduces training time and computational resources compared to building a model from scratch. Moreover, across various versions of Llama—from early implementations to the latest iterations—the underlying strategy remains consistent, while the complexity and capacity of the models continue to evolve, offering even more opportunities for nuanced customization.

Types of Transfer Learning Techniques with Llama

The transfer learning landscape for Llama models is diverse, with several distinct techniques that can be applied based on the requirements and constraints of the target application. Below, we explore some of the primary transfer learning techniques that can be employed with Llama models.

- **Layer-Wise Adaptation:** Layer-wise adaptation is one of the most common techniques for fine-tuning Llama models. This approach focuses on selectively adjusting specific layers of the neural network rather than re-training the entire model. In practice, developers can isolate those layers that are most relevant for capturing domain-specific features while maintaining the integrity of the foundational language patterns learned during pre-training. This technique is especially useful for customizing Llama for applications in specialized fields such as legal document analysis or technical writing, where certain nuances and terminologies need to be emphasized without disturbing the core linguistic capabilities.
- **Progressive Unfreezing:** Progressive unfreezing is an effective strategy for gradually adapting a pre-trained model to new data. In this method, only the output or top layers of the model are first unfrozen and fine-tuned on the target dataset. Once the model begins to adjust to the new context, progressively lower layers are unfrozen and updated. This ensures that the model retains its general language understanding in the earlier layers while refining higher-level representations to be more task-specific. Financial services applications, for example, can benefit from progressive unfreezing by first adapting the conversational layers to handle general customer queries, and then moving deeper into the model to understand and process complex financial terminologies and transaction details.
- **Task-Specific Optimization:** Task-specific optimization involves fine-tuning the model for a designated NLP task such as sentiment analysis, question answering, or entity recognition. With Llama models, task-specific optimization can be performed by further customizing the final layers to output results that align precisely with the requirements of the task. For instance, a marketing firm looking to gauge public sentiment on social media might fine-tune a Llama model using a dataset of annotated posts and comments. The model is trained to classify the text into various sentiment categories, and additional adjustments are made to handle the nuances of informal language. This strategy allows the model to deliver highly accurate and context-aware outputs that are critical for effective decision-making.

- **Domain Adaptation:** Domain adaptation is a specialized form of transfer learning that tailors a pre-trained model to work within a specific industry or field. This technique typically involves fine-tuning the model on a large corpus of domain-specific documents, such as academic papers for education, clinical notes for healthcare, or legal briefs for law firms. The process ensures that the model becomes proficient in the vocabulary, context, and structure unique to that domain. For instance, a legal assistant tool built on Llama can be fine-tuned using thousands of legal documents to accurately parse and summarize contract clauses, identify legal citations, and flag potential discrepancies. This results in a model that not only understands general language patterns but also excels at navigating the intricacies of specialized language.
- **Incremental and Continual Learning:** As applications evolve, so does the data they need to process. Incremental or continual learning involves updating the Llama model with new data over time without completely retraining it from scratch. This approach is particularly important for applications that require up-to-date knowledge, such as news summarization services or dynamic customer support bots. By employing transfer learning techniques in an incremental fashion, Llama models can continuously adapt to new information, ensuring that they remain accurate and relevant as language and user behavior change.
- **Few-Shot and Zero-Shot Learning:** Recent advancements in transfer learning have enabled Llama models to perform few-shot and zero-shot learning. Few-shot learning allows a model to effectively generalize from a very small number of annotated examples, while zero-shot learning enables it to apply learned knowledge to tasks it was not explicitly trained for. These capabilities are particularly useful when labeled data is scarce. For example, an emerging startup in a niche industry can fine-tune a Llama model using only a handful of domain-specific examples and rely on its robust pre-training to generalize effectively for unseen tasks. This reduces the barrier to entry for creating specialized NLP applications in domains where extensive labeled datasets are not available.

Crafting Custom NLP Applications with Llama

The real-world utility of Llama models is best realized when they are tailored to meet the distinct challenges of specific domains. Custom NLP applications demand not only a deep understanding of language structure but also the ability to adapt to specialized vocabularies and contextual cues.

Curating Domain-Specific Datasets

High-quality, domain-specific datasets form the backbone of the fine-tuning process. For instance, a legal firm developing an intelligent assistant to review and summarize contracts will require a dataset comprising legal documents, contracts, and judicial opinions. Fine-tuning Llama on such curated data enables the model to absorb the nuances of legal language and structure, making it a valuable tool for legal analysis and decision support.

Implementing Data Augmentation and Preprocessing

Real-world datasets are often imperfect and noisy. Techniques such as data augmentation–where data is synthetically expanded through paraphrasing or translation–and rigorous preprocessing steps (including normalization and noise reduction) help create a robust training corpus. For example, a travel application that generates personalized itineraries might use augmented travel blogs, reviews, and itinerary samples to fine-tune the Llama model. These methods ensure that the model is exposed to a wide range of linguistic expressions and variations, making it resilient in diverse scenarios.

Optimizing Performance with Hyperparameter Tuning

The fine-tuning process necessitates meticulous adjustment of hyperparameters such as learning rate, batch size, and training epochs. In the context of Llama, hyperparameter tuning can be approached using grid search, random search, or Bayesian optimization to determine the optimal configuration. Consider a healthcare chatbot: starting with a conservative learning rate ensures that the model does not lose its pre-trained general understanding too quickly while it learns the specificities of medical terminology and patient dialogue. Iterative experiments and continuous evaluation are key to achieving peak performance.

Detailed Scenarios and Examples

To provide a clearer picture of how these transfer learning techniques synergize with fine-tuning, consider the following detailed scenarios:

- **Legal Document Analysis:** A law firm deploys a custom NLP application to assist paralegals in reviewing lengthy contracts. Initially, the baseline Llama model is fine-tuned on a repository of legal texts, utilizing layer-wise adaptation to focus on segments that capture legal language intricacies. Progressive unfreezing is then applied–starting with the output layers and gradually including lower layers–to ensure stability and effective adaptation. The integration of domain adaptation techniques ensures the model internalizes the specialized language of contracts, resulting in an assistant that can identify critical legal clauses, summarize sections, and flag potential risks with high accuracy.

- **Customer Support in Financial Services:** A multinational bank seeks to automate its customer service operations. The bank fine-tunes the Llama model using historical support chat logs and transaction data. Initially, layer-wise fine-tuning adapts the top layers to handle routine inquiries. Progressive unfreezing then enables deeper integration of financial terminology and complex transactional language. Task-specific optimization refines the model's ability to handle sensitive financial topics such as loan processing and fraud detection. By incorporating continual learning mechanisms, the model is updated regularly with new customer interactions, ensuring that it remains current with evolving customer needs and regulatory standards.
- **Social Media Sentiment Analysis:** A marketing analytics firm designs an NLP system to monitor brand sentiment on social media. The Llama model is fine-tuned on a comprehensive dataset of social media posts, incorporating informal language, abbreviations, and emoticons. Layer-wise adaptation allows the model to focus on sentiment-bearing expressions, while progressive unfreezing ensures that deeper layers learn and refine the subtleties of tone. Additionally, few-shot learning techniques are applied to quickly adapt the model with minimal labeled examples from new social media trends. The final model can accurately analyze sentiment trends in real time, providing actionable insights that help brands manage public perception dynamically.

Detailed Description of Various Transfer Learning Techniques Used with Llama

Layer-Wise Adaptation: Layer-wise adaptation involves fine-tuning specific layers of a pre-trained model while keeping other layers frozen. The underlying idea is to adjust only those parts of the model that are most likely to benefit from domain-specific data.

Why it is useful with Llama:

- **Targeted Learning:** Instead of recalibrating the entire model, you can focus on layers that capture high-level semantic information or the particular vocabulary of a niche domain (for example, legal or medical terminology).
- **Efficiency:** Saves computational resources by reducing the number of parameters that need to be updated during training.
- **Stability:** Minimizes the risk of "*catastrophic forgetting*," where the model loses its general language understanding because too many parameters change at once.

Example Application: For a legal document analysis tool, fine-tuning might involve adjusting layers that specialize in recognizing legal structures and terminologies while leaving the lower-level representations (syntax and basic grammar) untouched.

Progressive Unfreezing: Progressive unfreezing is a dynamic approach where you gradually "*unfreeze*" more layers of the model for fine-tuning. You begin by training only the final layers, then incrementally unfreeze more layers—moving from top (close to the output) to bottom (closer to the input)—as the training progresses.

Why it is useful with Llama:

- **Controlled Adaptation**: Ensures that early layers, which capture general language features, do not get disturbed too rapidly.
- **Smooth Transition**: Allows the model to gradually adjust to domain-specific tasks, mitigating the risks associated with abrupt changes in the learned representations.
- **Better Convergence**: Often results in improved convergence rates and model stability, because adjustments to lower-level layers are made only after higher-level layers have adapted.

Example Application: In a financial customer support scenario, a bank might start fine-tuning with the model's output layer to handle basic query patterns, then progressively unfreeze deeper layers to refine responses for specialized topics such as loan processing and fraud alerts.

Task-Specific Optimization: Task-specific optimization involves customizing the model's architecture or loss function to better address a particular NLP task. This often entails modifying the final layers or integrating extra components tailored to the task (for example, custom classifiers, attention mechanisms).

Why it is useful with Llama:

- **Precision**: Directly aligns the model's output with the specific requirements of the task—for instance, distinguishing between subtle sentiment tones or extracting named entities.
- **Versatility**: Enables a single Llama model to be re-purposed for multiple tasks by adjusting the task-specific components.
- **Improved Performance**: Helps in reducing errors specific to the task by focusing the model's learning capacity on the most relevant features.

Example Application: A social media sentiment analysis tool might leverage task-specific optimization by training additional classification layers that are fine-tuned on labeled sentiment data, ensuring that the model accurately distinguishes between positive, negative, and neutral sentiments.

Domain Adaptation: Domain adaptation focuses on aligning a pre-trained model with a specific industry or context by leveraging domain-specific data. The model is fine-tuned on corpora that include domain-specific vocabulary, phrasing, and style.

Why it is useful with Llama:

- **Relevance**: Enhances the model's understanding of the language peculiarities inherent in a specific domain (for example, clinical terms in healthcare or contract language in law).
- **Customization**: Makes the model more robust in handling real-world inputs that differ significantly from the general data on which it was originally trained.
- **Performance Boost**: Fine-tuning on domain-specific datasets can substantially improve performance in niche applications where generic language models might otherwise struggle.

Example Application: For a medical chatbot, fine-tuning on clinical notes, medical literature, and patient interaction transcripts ensures that the Llama model can accurately interpret and generate responses involving medical diagnoses, treatment protocols, and patient advice.

Incremental and Continual Learning: Incremental or continual learning involves updating a model over time as new data becomes available, without retraining from scratch. This technique allows the model to keep learning from new examples and evolving trends while preserving its prior knowledge.

Why it is useful with Llama:

- **Adaptability**: Particularly important for domains where information is constantly evolving, such as news or customer support.
- **Resource Efficiency**: Avoids the computational cost of full re-training by integrating new knowledge incrementally.
- **Longevity**: Helps maintain model relevance and accuracy over time, ensuring that evolving language or emerging terminology is integrated into the model's capabilities.

Example Application: News aggregation systems can continuously update a Llama model with new articles and breaking news, ensuring that the model remains current and accurately reflects the latest language and topics.

Few-Shot and Zero-Shot Learning: Few-shot learning refers to the ability of a model to adapt to new tasks with only a small number of examples. Zero-shot learning extends this further, enabling the model to perform well on tasks it has never been explicitly trained for, leveraging its generalized understanding from pre-training.

Why it is useful with Llama:

- **Data Scarcity**: Extremely beneficial in situations where labeled data is limited or costly to obtain.
- **Flexibility**: Allows models to generalize to new tasks and domains even when precise training data is not available.
- **Quick Adaptation**: Facilitates rapid deployment of NLP applications in emerging areas with minimal data collection efforts.

Example Application: A startup in a niche industry might utilize few-shot learning to fine-tune a Llama model with only a handful of domain-specific examples, allowing the model to quickly generate insights and predictions relevant to that industry without requiring a massive, curated dataset.

The Future of Transfer Learning and Fine-Tuning

As technology and methodologies evolve, so too will the strategies for transfer learning and fine-tuning. Emerging techniques such as unsupervised fine-tuning, reinforcement learning from human feedback, and multi-modal integration (combining text with images, audio, and structured data) promise to further enhance the adaptability and performance of Llama models. Future iterations may include adaptive fine-tuning processes that continuously learn from live data streams, enabling models to remain current as language and context evolve.

Domain Adaptation Strategies

Domain adaptation strategies are critical techniques in the field of Natural Language Processing (NLP) that enable pre-trained models–such as Llama–to be fine-tuned for specialized applications in particular domains. These strategies address the gap between a model's generalized training data and the specific linguistic, contextual, and terminological nuances present in niche fields such as law, healthcare, finance, and more. The primary goal of domain adaptation is to refine a model's performance so that it not only processes everyday language with competence but also accurately interprets and generates content that is deeply rooted in the unique practices and knowledge of a specific field.

At the heart of domain adaptation is the recognition that while broad pre-training equips a model with extensive general knowledge, it may fall short in scenarios where precision and domain-specific insight are paramount. To overcome these limitations, practitioners focus on several key strategies:

- **Curating Domain-Specific Datasets:** One of the foundational steps in domain adaptation involves collecting and curating datasets that are rich in domain-specific language. These datasets are typically sourced from specialized documents, communications, and texts relevant to the target industry. By training on such data, models begin to understand the specific vocabulary, syntax, and discourse patterns that are characteristic of that domain.

- **Data Preprocessing and Augmentation:** Since raw domain data is often noisy and inconsistent, preprocessing techniques such as normalization, tokenization, and error correction are essential. Additionally, data augmentation methods–such as paraphrasing and back-translation–help create a more robust dataset, ensuring that the adapted model can handle variations in language expression within the domain.
- **Domain-Sensitive Loss Functions:** Tailoring the model's loss function to place a higher penalty on errors in critical areas ensures that the fine-tuning process prioritizes accuracy in domain-specific content. This strategic adjustment directs the model to focus on the parts of its learning that are most relevant to the application at hand, whether that involves numerical accuracy in financial reports or precise terminology in legal documents.
- **Integration of External Knowledge Bases:** Enhancing the adapted model with external resources–such as ontologies, taxonomies, or structured databases–can provide additional context that purely textual data might lack. This integration helps the model better understand the relationships between concepts within the domain, leading to more coherent and contextually accurate outputs.
- **Incremental and Continual Learning:** Domains are dynamic, with language, trends, and practices evolving over time. Incremental domain adaptation strategies involve regularly updating the model with new data, thereby maintaining its relevance and accuracy. This approach supports a continual learning process that allows the model to keep pace with changes in the domain landscape.

Collectively, these domain adaptation strategies transform a generic language model into a specialized, context-aware system. The result is an NLP solution that not only understands the broad principles of language but is also finely attuned to the specifics of its intended industry–enhancing performance, improving user satisfaction, and ultimately driving success in specialized applications. This overview encapsulates the strategic importance of domain adaptation in maximizing the full potential of models such as Llama in niche, high-stakes environments.

The Imperative of Domain Adaptation

Why Domain Adaptation Matters

General-purpose language models are trained on massive datasets that cover a broad spectrum of topics and styles. Although this diversity ensures versatility, it may also lead to gaps in depth when processing specialized jargon or nuanced contexts. For instance, a model trained on everyday language might misinterpret the intricacies of legal terminology, medical prescriptions, or financial regulations. Domain adaptation ensures that the model is not only linguistically proficient but also contextually aligned with its target use case.

Illustration: The Language Gap

Imagine a situation where a healthcare chatbot is deployed to assist patients. A generic model might correctly interpret routine queries but could stumble when dealing with complex medical terminology or rare conditions mentioned in clinical notes. Similarly, a legal assistant model might misidentify or oversimplify legal clauses if it has not been attuned to the specialized language of law. Domain adaptation bridges these gaps by ensuring that the model's understanding is deep and precise.

Core Strategies for Domain Adaptation

Core strategies for domain adaptation in Llama models involve tailoring the training process with domain-specific data, selective fine-tuning, and specialized regularization techniques. These approaches enhance the model's contextual understanding and performance in targeted areas.

Curating Domain-Specific Datasets

The foundation of effective domain adaptation is a high-quality, domain-specific dataset. Curating this data involves collecting texts, documents, and communications that truly represent the language and style prevalent in the target domain.

Detailed Process

- **Data Collection:** For a legal application, this might include contracts, court rulings, legal briefs, and scholarly articles on law. In healthcare, it could be anonymized patient records, clinical notes, and medical research publications.
- **Data Cleaning and Labeling:** Once collected, the data should undergo cleaning, normalization, and, where necessary, annotation. For example, tagging critical legal clauses or classifying clinical notes by disease category can significantly enhance the training process.
- **Evaluation of Data Quality:** The dataset should be continuously evaluated for representativeness and accuracy to ensure the adapted model learns the most relevant features of the domain.

Live Scenario: Legal Document Analysis

Consider a law firm that needs an intelligent tool to assist paralegals in reviewing lengthy contracts. The firm curates a dataset of 20,000 legal documents–including contracts, case law, and legal commentary—and annotates specific clauses of interest (for example, confidentiality clauses, termination clauses). The Llama model is then fine-tuned on this carefully curated dataset. As a result, the model learns to identify key legal elements and generate accurate summaries, thereby reducing review time by 40% and lowering error rates in initial contract assessments.

Data Preprocessing and Augmentation

Raw domain-specific data is often imperfect. Preprocessing and data augmentation are essential to create a robust training corpus that reflects the varied expressions of the target domain.

Detailed Process

- **Normalization and Cleaning:** Remove inconsistencies, correct grammatical errors, and standardize terminologies. For healthcare, common abbreviations (for example, "BP" for blood pressure) should be normalized.
- **Data Augmentation:** Techniques such as paraphrasing, back-translation, and synthetic example generation can help create a richer dataset. For instance, a dataset of legal texts can be augmented by paraphrasing complex sentences into simpler, but still legally accurate, language.
- **Balancing the Dataset:** Ensure that all critical aspects of the domain are well-represented to avoid bias. For example, in a financial dataset, make sure that both bullish and bearish market terminologies are adequately represented.

Live Scenario: Healthcare Communication System

A hospital deploys a virtual health assistant aimed at triaging patient inquiries. The original dataset comprises clinical notes and patient emails, but the diversity is limited. Through data augmentation, the hospital creates multiple paraphrased versions of each inquiry, incorporating variations in phrasing and including common colloquial expressions used by patients. As a result, the fine-tuned Llama model becomes more robust, recognizing symptoms and medical histories even when described in non-standard language, ultimately improving diagnostic suggestion accuracy by 30%.

Domain-Sensitive Loss Functions

Customizing the loss functions during training helps the model focus on what matters most in the target domain. A domain-sensitive loss function assigns heavier penalties to errors that are particularly critical for the specific domain.

Detailed Process

- **Customized Penalty Metrics:** In a financial context, misinterpreting a numerical value might be critical. The loss function can be configured to penalize numerical inaccuracies more heavily.

- **Task-Specific Objectives:** For sentiment analysis in social media, the loss function can be tuned to better differentiate between subtle emotional tones by emphasizing classification errors.
- **Iterative Refinement:** Continually update the loss function based on performance metrics to ensure the training process remains aligned with domain requirements.

Live Scenario: Financial Report Analysis

A financial institution fine-tunes a Llama model to analyze quarterly reports and market sentiment. The model's custom loss function is designed to give a higher penalty to errors in numerical data extraction and classification errors in sentiment interpretation. As the model trains, it learns to prioritize the accurate extraction of key financial metrics (such as earnings per share and revenue growth). The result is a model that not only automates the generation of detailed financial summaries but also reduces misinterpretation of critical financial data by 25%, thereby assisting analysts in making more informed decisions.

Integration of External Knowledge Bases

Enhancing domain adaptation by integrating external structured data can significantly elevate model performance. These external knowledge bases–comprising ontologies, taxonomies, or specialized databases–provide context that enriches the model's understanding.

Detailed Process

- **Data Enrichment:**

  Augment textual data with metadata from external sources. For instance, linking legal texts to an ontology of legal terms can help the model understand relationships between concepts.

- **Specialized Attention Mechanisms:**

  Modify the model's architecture to include attention layers that weigh the input from the external knowledge base more significantly.

- **Continuous Synchronization:**

  Regularly update the external data to ensure the model reflects the latest developments and terminologies.

Live Scenario: Legal Assistant Integration

A legal technology company develops a Llama-based assistant for contract analysis. In addition to training the model on legal documents, the company integrates a comprehensive legal ontology that maps relationships between legal entities, statutes, and precedents. This integration enables the model to contextualize clauses within a broader legal framework, resulting in more accurate flagging of potential risks and inconsistencies. The enhanced model now aids lawyers in cross-referencing contract clauses with relevant statutes, reducing review time by 35% and significantly increasing the reliability of automated legal analysis.

Incremental Domain Adaptation

Incremental or continual learning involves updating the model with new domain-specific data over time. This strategy is crucial in fields where language and practices evolve rapidly.

Detailed Process

- **Scheduled Updates:** Regularly incorporate new data streams–such as the latest research papers, policy updates, or news articles–into the training pipeline.
- **Feedback Loops:** Establish human-in-the-loop processes where domain experts review model performance and provide feedback, which then informs subsequent adaptation phases.
- **Dynamic Fine-Tuning:** Implement a dynamic fine-tuning mechanism that adjusts the model's parameters in real time based on evolving data trends.

Live Scenario: News and Financial Markets

A media company uses a Llama model for real-time analysis of financial news. Since market conditions and financial terminologies change swiftly, the model is designed for incremental learning. Every week, the model is fine-tuned with new financial articles and market reports. A team of analysts reviews the outputs, and their feedback is integrated into the next round of training. This continual adaptation ensures that the model remains sensitive to emerging trends and can provide accurate, up-to-date insights, giving investors a competitive edge by rapidly identifying and reacting to market shifts.

Hyperparameter Tuning for Llama Models

Hyperparameter tuning is a critical process in fine-tuning pre-trained Llama models to achieve optimal performance in custom NLP applications. Llama models, developed to process and generate human-like language, come pre-trained on extensive datasets that offer general linguistic capabilities. However, adapting these models for domain-specific tasks, such as legal document analysis, healthcare applications, or financial sentiment analysis, requires fine-tuning. Hyperparameter tuning plays a pivotal role in this process by enabling practitioners to optimize the training process for task-specific requirements.

Hyperparameters are configurations set before training begins, influencing how the model learns from data. Key hyperparameters include the learning rate, batch size, number of epochs, dropout rate, optimizer selection, weight decay, and learning rate schedules. These settings determine the pace, stability, and efficiency of the training process, as well as the model's ability to generalize to new data. Effective hyperparameter tuning ensures that the Llama model can adapt its pre-trained knowledge to the nuances of specific domains, resulting in improved accuracy, efficiency, and robustness.

There are several strategies for hyperparameter tuning, each with its own strengths and use cases. Manual tuning, though time-intensive, provides a hands-on understanding of the model's behavior. Grid search systematically explores all combinations of predefined hyperparameter values, while random search offers a more computationally efficient alternative by sampling combinations randomly. Bayesian optimization leverages probabilistic models to intelligently search the hyperparameter space, balancing exploration and exploitation. Additionally, techniques such as adaptive learning rate schedules dynamically adjust hyperparameters during training to improve stability and convergence.

Hyperparameter tuning also involves practical considerations, such as using validation sets to assess configurations, implementing early stopping to avoid overfitting, and employing domain-specific metrics to evaluate performance. By integrating these techniques and considerations, practitioners can transform a generic Llama model into a powerful tool tailored to specific tasks.

For instance, in a healthcare chatbot application, hyperparameter tuning can optimize the model to understand complex medical terminology and patient queries. Similarly, in financial risk analysis, tuning ensures accurate identification of risk-related language in textual data. These examples illustrate how hyperparameter tuning enhances the model's capability to deliver precise, efficient, and reliable results.

In summary, hyperparameter tuning is the backbone of fine-tuning Llama models for custom NLP applications. It not only maximizes the model's performance but also ensures that it aligns with the unique demands of the target domain. Through systematic exploration and optimization, hyperparameter tuning enables the development of robust, context-aware NLP solutions that excel in real-world scenarios.

Understanding Hyperparameters: The Foundation of Fine-Tuning

Hyperparameters are adjustable settings that influence the behavior and performance of a model during training. Unlike model parameters, which are learned from the data, hyperparameters must be manually configured before the training begins. They define critical aspects of the training process, including:

- **Learning Rate:** Controls the step size during gradient descent, determining how quickly or slowly the model updates its weights.
- **Batch Size:** Specifies the number of training samples processed in one iteration, impacting computational efficiency and model stability.
- **Number of Epochs:** Defines the number of complete passes through the entire training dataset, balancing between underfitting and overfitting.
- **Dropout Rate:** A regularization technique that randomly "*drops out*" neurons during training to prevent overfitting and improve generalization.
- **Optimizer Choice:** The algorithm used to update the model's weights during training (for example, Adam, SGD, RMSprop).
- **Warmup Steps:** Gradual increase of the learning rate at the start of training to stabilize the optimization process.
- **Weight Decay:** A form of regularization that penalizes large weight values to prevent overfitting.

The correct configuration of these hyperparameters can significantly impact the fine-tuning process, enabling a Llama model to deliver state-of-the-art results in domain-specific tasks.

The Importance of Hyperparameter Tuning for Llama Models

Hyperparameter tuning plays a pivotal role in fine-tuning Llama models for custom NLP applications. Pre-trained Llama models are powerful but require careful adjustment to adapt to specific domains such as healthcare, finance, or legal systems. Effective hyperparameter tuning offers several advantages:

- **Maximized Model Accuracy:** Fine-tuning ensures that the model captures domain-specific nuances, leading to improved accuracy and relevance in task-specific applications.
- **Efficient Resource Utilization:** Properly tuned hyperparameters reduce training time and computational overhead, allowing large-scale models to be trained efficiently even with limited hardware resources.

- **Improved Generalization:** Hyperparameter tuning minimizes overfitting, enabling the model to perform well on unseen data—a critical requirement for real-world NLP applications.
- **Stability in Training:** Optimal values for parameters such as learning rate and batch size help ensure that the training process converges smoothly without oscillations or divergence.

Hyperparameter Tuning Strategies

For Llama model fine-tuning, hyperparameter tuning involves systematically exploring settings such as learning rate, batch size, and dropout rate to optimize task-specific performance. Strategies such as grid search, random search, or Bayesian optimization help efficiently navigate the parameter space for improved model generalization.

Manual Tuning

Manual tuning involves iterative experimentation with different hyperparameter settings based on domain expertise and prior experience. While time-intensive, it can yield valuable insights into how specific hyperparameters affect model performance.

Steps for Llama Models:

- Start with a small learning rate (for example, 1e-5) to prevent drastic weight updates.
- Test batch sizes between 8 and 32, depending on the available GPU memory.
- Gradually adjust the dropout rate (for example, 0.1 to 0.3) to find the optimal balance between preventing overfitting and maintaining model capacity.

Scenario: In a legal text summarization task, manual tuning reveals that increasing the batch size from 16 to 32 significantly improves training stability without increasing overfitting, while a dropout rate of 0.2 produces summaries that are both concise and accurate.

Grid Search

Grid search is an exhaustive method that evaluates all possible combinations of predefined hyperparameter values. It ensures that the optimal configuration is identified but can be computationally expensive for large models such as Llama.

Steps for Llama Models:

- Define a search space for each hyperparameter (for example, learning rates: [1e-5, 3e-5, 5e-5]; batch sizes: [8, 16, 32]).

- Evaluate every possible combination using a validation dataset.
- Select the configuration that achieves the highest validation accuracy or lowest loss.

Scenario: For a healthcare chatbot, a grid search might explore combinations of learning rates, dropout rates, and batch sizes, identifying a configuration where a learning rate of 2e-5, batch size of 16, and dropout rate of 0.2 yield the best balance between accuracy and generalization.

Random Search

Random search selects hyperparameter combinations randomly from a predefined range. This method is more efficient than grid search for large hyperparameter spaces, as it avoids evaluating every combination.

Steps for Llama Models:

- Define a probability distribution for each hyperparameter (for example, learning rates between 1e-6 and 5e-4).
- Randomly sample hyperparameter combinations and train the model.
- Evaluate performance on a validation set.

Scenario: For a social media sentiment analysis model, random search quickly identifies a promising combination of learning rate and batch size that achieves competitive results while reducing training time by 30% compared to grid search.

Bayesian Optimization

Bayesian optimization uses probabilistic models to intelligently search the hyperparameter space, balancing exploration of new combinations with exploitation of known good configurations.

Steps for Llama Models:

- Define a prior distribution for each hyperparameter.
- Use a probabilistic model (for example, Gaussian Processes) to predict the performance of untested configurations.
- Iteratively refine the search based on observed performance.

Scenario: In a financial document classification task, Bayesian optimization identifies that using the AdamW optimizer with a learning rate of 3e-5 and weight decay of 0.01 leads to faster convergence and higher classification accuracy.

Adaptive Learning Rates

Adaptive learning rate schedules adjust the learning rate dynamically during training. Common methods include:

- **Learning Rate Decay:** Gradually reduce the learning rate as training progresses to refine model parameters.
- **Cyclic Learning Rates:** Alternate between high and low learning rates to explore diverse solutions before fine-tuning the final parameters.

Scenario: In a multilingual NLP application, using a cyclic learning rate allows the Llama model to adapt to the nuances of different languages during early training phases, while a decaying rate refines its understanding in later stages, resulting in superior performance across all target languages.

Practical Considerations for Hyperparameter Tuning

When fine-tuning Llama models, practitioners should keep the following in mind:

- **Validation and Test Splits:** Use a validation set to evaluate hyperparameter configurations and a separate test set to assess final model performance. This ensures unbiased evaluation.
- **Early Stopping:** Monitor validation loss during training and terminate early if performance plateaus or degrades, saving computational resources and preventing overfitting.
- **Cross-Validation:** Employ cross-validation to assess model robustness across multiple data splits, especially when working with smaller datasets.
- **Domain-Specific Metrics:** Beyond standard metrics such as accuracy or F1-score, consider metrics relevant to the target domain, such as ROUGE for summarization or BLEU for translation tasks.
- **Computational Constraints:** Tailor hyperparameter tuning strategies to available resources. For instance, use random search or Bayesian optimization for faster results on limited hardware.

Real-World Scenario: Fine-Tuning Llama for Financial Risk Analysis

Problem Statement: A financial institution wants to develop a system to assess risk based on textual reports, such as news articles and quarterly earnings calls.

Hyperparameter Tuning Process:

1. **Baseline Setup:** The team starts with a learning rate of 2e-5, batch size of 16, and dropout rate of 0.1, achieving moderate performance on the validation set.
2. **Grid Search:** Grid search explores learning rates (1e-5, 2e-5, 3e-5), batch sizes (8, 16, 32), and dropout rates (0.1, 0.2, 0.3). The optimal configuration–2e-5, batch size 32, dropout rate 0.2–improves validation accuracy by 15%.
3. **Bayesian Optimization:** The team further refines the model using Bayesian optimization to explore optimizer-specific parameters such as momentum and weight decay, achieving faster convergence and a 5% boost in accuracy.
4. **Learning Rate Decay:** Incorporating a decaying learning rate schedule ensures stable training in later epochs, reducing overfitting and improving generalization.

Results: The fine-tuned Llama model achieves 92% accuracy in identifying high-risk statements, significantly outperforming previous methods while reducing the time analysts spend reviewing documents by 40%.

Case Studies and Applications of Fine-Tuned Llama Models

Fine-tuned Llama models have been successfully applied across diverse industries such as healthcare, legal, finance, retail, and education, showcasing significant improvements in domain-specific performance. These case studies demonstrate enhanced data analysis, automation, and personalized insights tailored to complex industry needs.

Healthcare: Enhancing Clinical Decision Support

In healthcare, fine-tuned Llama models enhance clinical decision support by synthesizing patient data and medical literature to provide rapid, evidence-based insights. This improves diagnostic accuracy and treatment planning while reducing clinician workload.

Context and Challenge: In the healthcare industry, the volume and complexity of clinical data–from Electronic Health Records (EHRs) to research literature–can be overwhelming. Clinicians often need to quickly access relevant information, but generic language models might miss the nuances of medical terminology and context.

Applications

- **Fine-Tuning Process:** A consortium of hospitals fine-tuned Llama on anonymized patient records, medical research articles, and clinical guidelines. The process involved curating domain-specific corpora and employing medical experts to validate the relevance of the output.

- **Capabilities Achieved:** The fine-tuned model was able to:
  - Summarize patient histories and flag potential adverse drug interactions.
  - Provide evidence-based recommendations by synthesizing current research.
  - Answer clinical questions in a manner aligned with medical guidelines.

Impact: This deployment improved diagnostic accuracy and treatment recommendations, reducing the cognitive load on healthcare providers and speeding up patient care processes. Additionally, the model's ability to interface with EHR systems in natural language allowed for more intuitive queries, fostering better clinician-model collaboration.

- **Example**: Llama-4 can be fine-tuned with patient medical histories and clinical data (for example, symptoms, lab results, imaging reports) to assist healthcare professionals in diagnosing diseases. For example, the model could analyze text data from clinical notes to suggest possible diagnoses, helping doctors prioritize differential diagnoses and identify the most likely conditions.
- **Use Case**: Given a set of symptoms like "fever, cough, and shortness of breath," the model can predict potential conditions such as COVID-19, pneumonia, or flu and recommend further diagnostic tests.

Legal Industry: Streamlining Document Analysis

Fine-tuned Llama models streamline legal document analysis by accurately summarizing lengthy texts and extracting key contractual clauses, thereby reducing manual review time. This efficiency enables legal teams to focus on strategic decision-making and risk management.

Context and Challenge: Legal professionals frequently encounter extensive contracts, case laws, and regulatory documents. Extracting relevant information manually can be time-consuming and error-prone, particularly when dealing with the intricacies of legal language and precedents.

Applications

- **Fine-Tuning Process:** Law firms and legal tech startups fine-tuned Llama using large datasets of legal documents, annotated by legal experts. The training regimen included legal briefs, contract clauses, and judicial opinions.
- **Capabilities Achieved:** The specialized model excelled at:

- **Document Summarization:** Producing concise summaries of lengthy legal texts.
- **Clause Extraction:** Identifying key contractual clauses and potential risk areas.
- **Contextual Search:** Enhancing legal research by understanding the context and retrieving relevant case precedents.

Impact: By automating routine document analysis, legal teams reduced review times and improved the accuracy of their risk assessments. The model's ability to interpret nuanced legal language helped junior associates gain deeper insights, thereby leveling the playing field in legal research and contract review processes.

Example: Llama-4 can be fine-tuned to assist legal professionals in **analyzing contracts** and **legal documents**. For example, it can classify contract clauses (for example, indemnity, confidentiality) or identify **key terms** across a large set of legal agreements. This can save significant time by automating the review process, ensuring compliance, and identifying potential risks or inconsistencies in contract language.

Use Case: A law firm uses Llama-4 to process thousands of contracts quickly, extracting and categorizing clauses related to intellectual property, liabilities, or payment terms.

Financial Services: Risk Assessment and Customer Insights

Fine-tuned Llama models in financial services enable precise risk assessment by correlating market trends with historical data, while also delivering personalized customer insights for enhanced engagement and service.

Context and Challenge: Financial institutions must analyze vast amounts of unstructured data–from market news to internal reports–to gauge risk and spot opportunities. Traditional models often struggle with the domain-specific language and the subtle cues that indicate market shifts.

Applications

- **Fine-Tuning Process:** Banks and financial consultancies fine-tuned Llama on datasets that included financial news, regulatory filings, and historical market data. The process was guided by quantitative analysts and risk management experts.
- **Capabilities Achieved:** The fine-tuned model demonstrated:
  - **Sentiment Analysis:** Accurately gauging market sentiment by analyzing news articles and social media trends.
  - **Risk Identification:** Flagging potential market risks by correlating disparate data points from economic reports.

  - **Customer Interaction:** Powering advanced chatbots that provide personalized financial advice based on user profiles and market conditions.

Impact: The integration of fine-tuned Llama models enabled more proactive risk management and personalized customer service. Enhanced sentiment analysis contributed to faster reaction times during market volatility, while improved customer interaction models increased satisfaction and trust in digital banking services.

Example: In the **financial services sector**, Llama-4 can be applied to **risk assessment models** by analyzing customer transaction data and assessing **creditworthiness** or detecting fraudulent behavior. Additionally, it can process customer interactions (for example, emails, chat logs) to extract insights and recommend personalized services, such as investment plans or loan options.

Use Case: A bank uses Llama-4 to evaluate loan applications, categorizing applicants as low or high risk based on historical transaction data and text-based financial statements.

Retail and E-commerce: Personalization and Customer Service

Retailers leverage fine-tuned Llama models to deliver personalized shopping experiences by analyzing customer data for tailored recommendations. They also enhance customer service through intelligent, context-aware support systems that respond effectively to inquiries.

Context and Challenge: Retailers aim to offer highly personalized shopping experiences, but the diversity of consumer data–from product reviews to browsing behaviour presents a significant analytical challenge.

Applications

- **Fine-Tuning Process:** Retail companies fine-tuned Llama on customer feedback, product descriptions, and transaction histories. The training involved continuous feedback loops with marketing and customer service teams.
- **Capabilities Achieved:** The adapted model could:
  - **Personalized Recommendations:** Analyze individual customer profiles to suggest products aligned with their preferences.
  - **Customer Support Automation:** Provide natural, context-aware responses to customer inquiries, reducing reliance on scripted responses.
  - **Sentiment and Trend Analysis:** Detect emerging trends by analyzing customer sentiment across multiple channels.

Impact: By fine-tuning Llama, retailers enhanced the customer experience through tailored recommendations and more effective automated support systems. This not only increased customer satisfaction but also drove higher conversion rates and improved retention metrics.

Example: Llama-4 can be utilized to enhance **personalized shopping experiences** by analyzing customer behavior data and product reviews. It can recommend products based on customer preferences, past purchases, or even **customer sentiment** from reviews and feedback. Additionally, Llama-4 can automate customer service tasks, answering common queries or handling complex requests, improving efficiency and user satisfaction.

Use Case: An e-commerce platform uses Llama-4 to personalize product recommendations for users, while also using it in the customer support chatbot to answer product inquiries and resolve issues.

Education: Intelligent Tutoring and Content Summarization

Fine-tuned Llamamodels in education power intelligent tutoring systems that adapt to individual learning needs while efficiently summarizing complex academic content. This dual capability enhances student understanding and eases the workload on educators.

Context and Challenge: Educational institutions and e-learning platforms need to cater to diverse learning needs and often seek to provide personalized feedback and support. Generic models might miss the mark when dealing with subject-specific jargon or pedagogical nuances.

Applications

- **Fine-Tuning Process:** Educational platforms fine-tuned Llama using textbooks, academic papers, and student feedback. The curation of domain-specific language and educational content was overseen by educators and subject matter experts.
- **Capabilities Achieved:** The fine-tuned model was used to:
  - **Automate Grading and Feedback:** Provide initial grading and constructive feedback on student essays and assignments.
  - **Content Summarization:** Generate summaries of complex academic articles or lecture transcripts.
  - **Adaptive Tutoring:** Tailor explanations and follow-up questions based on a student's understanding and learning pace.

Impact: This application improved educational outcomes by enabling more personalized learning paths and reducing the administrative burden on educators.

The model's capacity to generate context-aware feedback helped students better understand difficult concepts and stay engaged with the material.

Example: Llama-4 can be used in **education** for **intelligent tutoring** by assessing student responses and providing targeted feedback. It can also summarize educational content, such as textbooks or research papers, making complex material more digestible for students. Llama-4's ability to generate human-like explanations can support both one-on-one tutoring sessions and content enrichment in educational platforms.

Use Case: A university integrates Llama-4 into its e-learning platform, where it assists students by summarizing course content and providing explanations for complex concepts such as calculus or physics. Additionally, it assesses student-submitted essays and provides personalized feedback.

Fine-Tuning Llama4 for Text Classification System

Fine-tuning Llama-4 for a text classification system involves adapting the pre-trained Llama-4 model, typically with billions of parameters, to perform specific classification tasks such as sentiment analysis or topic categorization. This process requires a large, high-memory GPU setup due to the model's size. Using a dataset, the model is further trained on labeled examples to adjust its weights for the desired output classes. Key considerations include GPU memory management, batch size adjustments, and efficient training techniques such as mixed precision and gradient checkpointing.

Source Code: CDE's. Please refer to the GitHub link for the source code for the question and answering system:

https://github.com/OrangeAVA/Ultimate-Llama-for-NLP/blob/main/text_classification.py

Brief summary of the key points related to **Hugging Face token usage**, **GPU setup**, and **model size** for fine-tuning `meta-llama/Llama-4-Maverick-17B-128E-Original`:

- **Hugging Face Token Usage:**
  - **Authentication**: The `meta-llama/Llama-4-Maverick-17B-128E-Original` model is gated and requires authentication through Hugging Face.
  - **Methods:**
    - **API Token**: Add your Hugging Face token directly in the script (`auth_token = "your_token_here"`).
    - **CLI Authentication**: Use `huggingface-cli login` to authenticate via the Hugging Face CLI.

- **GPU Setup:**
  - **High Memory GPUs**: The model requires **high-memory GPUs** (for example, **NVIDIA A100, V100**) with **40GB+ memory**.
  - **Training Challenges**: Fine-tuning a 17B parameter model may not be feasible on consumer-grade GPUs due to memory constraints.
  - **Distributed Training**: Consider using **multi-GPU setups** or **DeepSpeed** for distributed training if you have multiple GPUs.
  - **Batch Size Adjustment**: Reduce batch size (`per_device_train_batch_size=2`) to fit the model into limited GPU memory.
- **Model Size and Fine-Tuning:**
  - **Model Size**: The `'meta-llama/Llama-4-Maverick-17B-128E-Original'` model has **17 billion parameters**, requiring substantial GPU resources.
  - **Memory Optimization**:
    - Use **FP16 mixed precision** and **gradient checkpointing** to reduce memory usage.
    - For multi-GPU setups, consider **model parallelism** to split the model across GPUs.
  - **Training Duration**: Fine-tuning may take hours to days, depending on hardware and batch size.

Conclusion

This chapter has taken an in-depth journey into the essential strategies and techniques required to fine-tune Llama models for custom NLP applications. By systematically exploring **Transfer Learning with Llama**, **Domain Adaptation Strategies**, and **Hyperparameter Tuning**, we have provided a comprehensive framework for transforming powerful pre-trained language models into domain-specific, high-performing tools tailored to real-world challenges.

This next chapter will bridge the gap between the technical methodologies discussed so far and their tangible applications in real-world settings. It will provide actionable insights into how organizations across industries are leveraging Llama models to drive innovation and solve complex problems, while also addressing the challenges inherent in deploying such advanced AI systems.

Prepare to see the transformative potential of Llama models in action, as we move from optimization strategies to industry-specific impact.

Multiple Choice Questions

1. Which of the following best describes transfer learning as applied to Llama models?
   a. Training a model from scratch using only domain-specific data
   b. Fine-tuning a pre-trained model on new, domain-specific data
   c. Increasing the complexity of the model architecture
   d. Reducing the number of layers in the model for faster training
2. In the context of domain adaptation for Llama models, what is the primary purpose of curating domain-specific datasets?
   a. To reduce the training time significantly
   b. To ensure the model learns the unique terminologies and contexts of the target domain
   c. To increase the overall size of the training dataset regardless of quality
   d. To simplify the model architecture
3. Which of the following strategies involves freezing most layers of a model and fine-tuning only select layers at the beginning of training?
   a. Grid search
   b. Progressive unfreezing
   c. Random search
   d. Manual tuning
4. What is the primary goal of hyperparameter tuning in the fine-tuning process of Llama models?
   a. To change the underlying architecture of the model
   b. To adjust training configurations (for example, learning rate, batch size) for optimal performance
   c. To collect more training data from the domain
   d. To reduce the model's general language understanding

5. Which hyperparameter is most directly responsible for determining the speed at which a model's weights are updated during training?
    a. Batch size
    b. Learning rate
    c. Number of epochs
    d. Dropout rate
6. Which method is considered more efficient than grid search for exploring large hyperparameter spaces by randomly sampling configurations?
    a. Manual tuning
    b. Random search
    c. Bayesian optimization
    d. Cross-validation
7. In domain adaptation, why is data augmentation important?
    a. It reduces the training dataset size.
    b. It creates diverse examples of domain-specific texts, making the model more robust to variations.
    c. It ensures that the model uses only one form of expression.
    d. It eliminates the need for preprocessing the data.
8. What is a key benefit of integrating external knowledge bases into domain adaptation for Llama models?
    a. Reducing the overall model size
    b. Enhancing the model's understanding of relationships and context in the domain
    c. Simplifying the fine-tuning process
    d. Automatically generating training data
9. Which of the following statements about adaptive learning rate schedules is true?
    a. They keep the learning rate constant throughout training.
    b. They allow the learning rate to change during training to help stabilize convergence and avoid overshooting.

   c. They are used to increase the number of epochs automatically.
   d. They replace the need for hyperparameter tuning.

10. Which one of these strategies is most likely to be used when labeled domain-specific data is scarce, allowing a model to generalize from only a few examples?
   a. Grid search
   b. Manual tuning
   c. Few-shot and zero-shot learning
   d. Progressive unfreezing

Answers

1. b
2. b
3. b
4. b
5. b
6. b
7. b
8. b
9. b
10. c

Chapter 6
Real-World Use Cases of Llama

Introduction

In the past decade, artificial intelligence has transitioned from a niche technology into an indispensable element of modern life, infiltrating everything from mundane daily tasks to complex problem-solving in high-stakes industries. At the heart of this transformation is the evolution of Large Language Models (LLMs), which have significantly improved human-computer interaction, decision-making, and automation capabilities. Among these innovations, the Llama series—including Llama, Llama2, and Llama3—has emerged as a pivotal development, pushing the boundaries of what AI-powered models can achieve in real-world applications.

Figure 6.1: Real-World Use Cases of Llama, Llama2, and Llama3

The journey of the Llama series reflects the dynamic progression of artificial intelligence research. The original Llama model laid the groundwork by introducing a flexible architecture capable of understanding and generating human-like text. Building on this success, Llama2 improved not only the depth of language understanding but also the efficiency and adaptability across various contexts. Llama3 further extends these capabilities, incorporating refined algorithms and cutting-edge training techniques that enable the model to tackle increasingly complex tasks with greater precision and contextual awareness.

This evolutionary path is driven by a continuous feedback loop between theoretical research and practical applications. With every iteration, the Llama series has integrated lessons learned from real-world deployments, leading to improved performance, reliability, and adaptability across multiple scenarios. It is this rigorous blend of academic excellence and market relevance that has made the Llama series a reliable tool for industries seeking to harness the power of AI.

Structure

In this chapter, we will cover the following topics:

- Overview
- Industry-Specific Applications of Llama Models
- Case Studies in Healthcare, Finance, and Customer Service
- Challenges and Solutions in Real-World Deployments

Overview

This chapter provides a comprehensive exploration of the real-world applications and case studies demonstrating the transformative potential of the Llama series–Llama, Llama2, and Llama3–in addressing complex natural language processing (NLP) challenges. The discussion spans various industries, offering a deep dive into how these models are not only reshaping operational workflows but also driving innovation across several critical sectors, including healthcare, finance, customer service, education, logistics, and media.

Real-World Applications: Bridging Theory and Practice

At the heart of this chapter is a series of detailed case studies and practical examples that showcase how Llama models are being deployed in environments where precision, speed, and adaptability are essential. Far from being limited to academic or experimental settings, these models have found fertile ground in real-world scenarios, proving their value in production environments. Each case study is designed to highlight the specific challenges encountered in various sectors and the tailored strategies employed to address them using the Llama series.

Healthcare: Revolutionizing Patient Care and Diagnostics

In the healthcare sector, Llama-based solutions are making significant contributions towards improving patient outcomes and streamlining complex medical processes. The chapter highlights multiple case studies where these advanced language models aid in tasks such as:

- **Diagnostics and Treatment Planning:** By swiftly analyzing patient histories, medical literature, and real-time data, Llama models assist healthcare providers in identifying potential diagnoses and crafting personalized treatment plans. This not only accelerates the decision-making process but also increases diagnostic accuracy.
- **Patient Data Management:** The capability of these models to efficiently parse and categorize massive volumes of patient data facilitates more effective Electronic Health Record (EHR) management. This enables medical institutions to maintain up-to-date records and ensures that critical patient information is easily accessible.
- **Medical Research and Literature Analysis:** Researchers benefit from the models' ability to sift through expansive bodies of medical literature, extract relevant findings, and even generate insightful summaries that accelerate the pace of clinical research.

Finance: Enhancing Security, Efficiency, and Customer Engagement

The financial sector, known for its reliance on accurate and timely information, has been quick to adopt Llama-based tools. Within this domain, the chapter discusses how these models are being used to:

- **Strengthen Fraud Detection and Risk Management:** By analyzing patterns in transaction data and identifying anomalies, Llama models contribute to more robust fraud detection systems. Their ability to process large datasets in near real-time allows financial institutions to react quickly to potential threats.
- **Automate Routine Reporting and Data Summarization:** Llama-powered solutions are streamlining the creation of detailed financial reports, allowing

analysts to focus on strategic decision-making rather than repetitive tasks. This automation greatly enhances operational efficiency.

- **Improve Customer Interaction and Personalization:** Financial service providers are deploying intelligent chatbots and virtual assistants that utilize these models to offer personalized advice and support. This increases customer satisfaction and engagement by ensuring clients receive responses that are both relevant and timely.

Customer Service: Redefining Support with Intelligent Interaction

In an era where customer satisfaction directly impacts brand reputation, the customer service industry has embraced the Llama series as a powerful tool for enhancing support infrastructure. Key highlights include:

- **Intelligent Chatbots and Virtual Assistants:** The Llama models empower customer support systems to handle queries efficiently, providing users with clear, helpful, and context-aware responses. Whether addressing frequently asked questions or solving more intricate issues, these models improve both the speed and quality of service.
- **Multilingual and Context-Sensitive Support:** With the ability to understand and generate human-like responses in multiple languages, Llama-based systems are particularly valuable in global markets. They ensure that customers receive consistent, high-quality interactions regardless of geographical or cultural differences.
- **Seamless Integration with CRM Systems:** By integrating with Customer Relationship Management (CRM) software, these models help maintain detailed logs of interactions, facilitating a more personalized follow-up and a deeper understanding of customer needs.

Expanding Horizons: Education, Logistics, and Media

Beyond the core industries of healthcare, finance, and customer service, the chapter also delves into the broader implications of Llama model deployments in other vital sectors:

- **Education:** The educational landscape is being transformed by AI through personalized tutoring systems, automated grading, and intelligent course recommendation engines. Llama models assist educators in delivering customized learning experiences that address individual student needs, making education more accessible and effective.

- **Logistics:** In logistics and supply chain management, these models aid in optimizing routes, forecasting demand, and managing inventory. By processing a multitude of variables and historical data, Llama-driven systems contribute to more efficient and cost-effective operations.
- **Media and Content Generation:** For media professionals and content creators, the Llama series offers tools for generating high-quality, engaging content. From drafting news articles to creating detailed marketing materials, these models empower creatives to produce work that is both compelling and contextually rich.

Demonstrating Versatility and Effectiveness

A central theme throughout the chapter is the demonstration of the versatility and effectiveness of Llama, Llama2, and Llama3. The models' ability to be tailored to different data types, industry-specific requirements, and operational constraints underlines their adaptability. Each case study reinforces the notion that these models are not one-dimensional tools; they are multi-faceted systems capable of driving tangible business outcomes and fostering innovation.

- **Addressing Complex NLP Challenges:** One of the standout strengths of the Llama series is their adeptness at tackling complex NLP challenges. Whether it is interpreting ambiguous language, managing large-scale data inputs, or generating nuanced text responses, the models have been rigorously tested in settings where precision is crucial. The detailed exploration provided in this chapter serves as a testament to their robust design and sophisticated algorithms, which are continuously evolving to meet the emerging needs of various industries.
- **Bridging the Gap between Research and Real-World Implementation:** By highlighting successful real-world applications, this chapter bridges the gap between theoretical advancements and tangible business applications. It showcases how academic research, when integrated with practical deployment strategies, can yield tools that are both innovative and highly effective in solving real-world problems. The detailed case studies offer insights into best practices for implementation, common challenges faced during deployment, and the ultimate impact on operational efficiency and customer satisfaction.
- **Ethical Considerations and Future Perspectives:** As this chapter illuminates the multifaceted applications of the Llama series, it also addresses the ethical considerations inherent in deploying AI at scale. With greater power comes the responsibility to ensure that these models are used in a manner that is transparent, fair, and respectful of user privacy. The discussion includes best practices for mitigating biases, safeguarding data, and ensuring that AI advancements contribute to equitable outcomes for all stakeholders.

Industry-Specific Applications of Llama Models

As artificial intelligence continues to redefine the modern business landscape, large language models have emerged as transformative agents of change. Among these, the Llama series–comprising Llama, Llama 2, Llama 3, and Llama 4–stands out as a groundbreaking suite of natural language processing tools specifically engineered to address the nuanced challenges of real-world industries. This introductory chapter illuminates how Llama models have transitioned from academic curiosity to industry powerhouses, reshaping operations, enhancing decision-making processes, and driving innovation across a wide array of sectors.

Bridging the Gap Between Theory and Practice

The success of the Llama series is rooted in its unique ability to integrate advanced research with tangible business applications. Each iteration of the Llama models has been meticulously refined to offer improvements in speed, accuracy, scalability, and contextual understanding. These enhancements empower organizations to harness these models for specific use cases that demand precise communication and rapid data processing.

By evolving from the foundational Llama to the more robust Llama2 and the state-of-the-art Llama3, these tools are capable of managing increasingly complex tasks. They are not merely theoretical constructs but have become vital components in the digital toolkits of industries, where they translate abstract data into actionable insights and streamline processes that drive both operational and strategic success.

Transformative Applications Across Industries

The versatility of the Llama models is best demonstrated through their broad range of applications across multiple industries. Each sector has found unique ways to deploy these models, turning complex challenges into opportunities for innovation, efficiency, and strategic growth.

Healthcare: Enhancing Patient Outcomes and Operational Efficiency

Healthcare is a field where precision and speed are paramount, and Llama models excel in addressing these demands:

- **Precision Diagnostics:** Leveraging advanced algorithms, Llama models analyze patient records, laboratory results, and clinical notes to support early disease detection. By correlating symptoms with medical histories and the latest research, these tools facilitate the formulation of accurate diagnoses and customized treatment plans.

- **Clinical Research and Data Analysis:** With vast amounts of clinical trial data, scientific publications, and patient records available, Llama models help researchers extract meaningful insights, accelerate literature reviews, and identify emerging trends that drive innovative treatment methodologies.
- **Patient Engagement and Support:** Integrating Llama-based virtual assistants in healthcare settings enables 24/7 support for patients by handling appointment scheduling, providing medication reminders, and offering preliminary health assessments, thereby reducing administrative burdens and increasing patient satisfaction.

Finance: Revolutionizing Security, Efficiency, and Customer Engagement

The finance industry, with its emphasis on data integrity and real-time decision-making, leverages Llama models in several impactful ways:

- **Fraud Detection and Risk Management:** By processing extensive transactional data in real time, Llama models recognize patterns and identify anomalies that could indicate fraudulent activity, thereby strengthening risk management protocols.
- **Automated Reporting and Analytics:** Llama models automate the generation of intricate financial reports and market analyses. This automation transforms raw data into actionable insights, allowing analysts to focus on strategic planning and decision-making.
- **Enhanced Client Communication:** Intelligent chatbots powered by Llama models deliver personalized advice and immediate support, boosting customer trust and engagement. They help financial institutions manage queries and execute transactions securely, all while providing a seamless user experience.

Customer Service: Delivering Intelligent and Personalized Support

In today's competitive market, exceptional customer service is a key differentiator. Llama models enhance support systems by:

- **Smart Virtual Assistants:** By processing natural language with human-like nuance, Llama-powered virtual assistants provide contextually relevant responses, reduce customer wait times, and resolve inquiries efficiently.

- **Multilingual Capabilities:** Llama models are designed to operate in multiple languages, breaking down geographical and cultural barriers and ensuring uniform service quality in global customer bases.
- **Integrated CRM Analytics:** When paired with customer relationship management systems, Llama models can mine data from customer interactions to provide insights that help tailor services and predict future needs, fostering deeper customer loyalty.

Education: Shaping the Future of Personalized Learning

The education sector is rapidly evolving with AI-driven personalization, where Llama models facilitate a more adaptive and engaging learning experience:

- **Adaptive Tutoring Systems:** Llama models power tutoring systems that analyze student performance, recognize learning gaps, and dynamically tailor educational content to match individual needs, improving overall academic outcomes.
- **Automated Content Generation:** Educators use these models to generate curriculum-aligned materials–ranging from lecture notes and assignments to interactive learning modules–thus reducing the burden on instructors and enhancing educational quality.
- **Streamlined Assessment and Feedback:** Automated grading systems deliver timely and detailed feedback on student work, enabling educators to identify areas for improvement and providing students with the insights needed to refine their learning strategies.

Logistics and Supply Chain: Optimizing Operational Efficiency

Efficiency and precision in logistics and supply chain management are critical. Llama models contribute significantly to this sector:

- **Demand Forecasting:** By analyzing historical data alongside real-time market trends, Llama models offer highly accurate predictions of consumer demand, enabling optimal inventory management and reduced waste.
- **Route Optimization:** Llama-based systems assess variables such as traffic patterns, weather conditions, and delivery schedules to design the most efficient delivery routes, minimizing transit times and operational costs.
- **Process Automation:** Routine tasks such as shipment scheduling, documentation, and inventory tracking are automated, which reduces human

error and allows logistics managers to focus on strategic operations and continuous improvement.

Media and Content Creation: Empowering Creativity and Engagement

In the realm of media and content creation, Llama models are revolutionizing how narratives are crafted and distributed:

- **Automated Storytelling and Content Generation:** Journalists, marketers, and content creators harness Llama models to generate compelling articles, creative narratives, and engaging content that adheres to brand guidelines without sacrificing quality.
- **Audience Engagement Analytics:** By analyzing audience behavior, social media trends, and feedback, these models help tailor content to specific demographics, resulting in higher engagement and a stronger connection with consumers.
- **Collaborative Creative Processes:** Llama models serve as creative partners, offering suggestions and alternatives that help human creators explore innovative ideas and push the boundaries of traditional storytelling.

Government and Public Administration: Enhancing Transparency and Efficiency

Government agencies are increasingly adopting Llama models to streamline processes and improve public services:

- **Automated Document Processing:** Government offices utilize these models to streamline paperwork, manage public records, and process citizen requests efficiently, reducing bureaucratic delays.
- **Citizen Engagement:** Virtual assistants powered by Llama models provide information on public policies, handle inquiries, and assist citizens with forms and applications, thereby enhancing government-citizen interactions.
- **Policy Analysis and Public Administration:** By analyzing large datasets from various government sources, these models aid in policy formulation, helping officials identify trends and allocate resources more effectively.

Retail: Driving Personalized Experiences and Operational Excellence

The retail sector benefits immensely from the dynamic capabilities of Llama models:

- **Personalized Customer Experiences:** By analyzing consumer behavior, purchase histories, and online interactions, Llama models assist retailers in offering tailored product recommendations, thereby enhancing the shopping experience.

- **Inventory and Supply Chain Management:** These models optimize stock levels by predicting consumer demand and streamlining supply chains, reducing the risks of overstocking or stockouts.
- **Dynamic Pricing Strategies:** Retailers employ Llama models to analyze market trends and competitor pricing, enabling them to adjust prices dynamically to maximize sales and profitability.

Energy and Utilities: Optimizing Performance and Sustainability

In the energy sector, where operational efficiency and sustainability are crucial, Llama models offer targeted solutions:

- **Predictive Maintenance:** By analyzing sensor data and historical performance, Llama models predict equipment malfunctions, enabling preventive maintenance and reducing downtime in critical infrastructure.
- **Energy Demand Management:** These models help energy providers forecast demand, optimize energy distribution, and develop strategies to balance load during peak and off-peak periods.
- **Sustainability Initiatives:** Analyzing environmental data, Llama models support energy companies in tracking sustainability metrics, optimizing resource use, and complying with regulatory standards.

Manufacturing: Enhancing Production and Quality Control

The manufacturing industry is undergoing a rapid transformation through the integration of AI-driven technologies:

- **Process Optimization:** Llama models contribute to the optimization of production lines by analyzing data related to machinery performance, production speed, and quality control, leading to significant efficiency gains.
- **Predictive Quality Control:** By identifying patterns in production data, these models help predict defects and streamline quality assurance processes, ensuring that products meet high standards of excellence.
- **Supply Chain Integration:** In manufacturing, seamless communication between suppliers, production units, and distribution channels is crucial. Llama models facilitate this integration by automating data exchanges and enhancing real-time decision-making.

Case Studies in Healthcare, Finance, and Customer Services

As artificial intelligence continues to permeate every aspect of modern industry, the Llama series–Llama, Llama2, and Llama3–stands out as a transformative suite of natural language processing models that drive innovation across multiple sectors. The following detailed case studies demonstrate how these models are being effectively deployed in healthcare, finance, and customer services. Each study provides a comprehensive look at the implementation process, challenges, and measurable outcomes, highlighting how these advanced models are bridging the gap between theoretical research and practical, real-world impact.

Healthcare: Revolutionizing Patient Care and Clinical Research

Llama models are transforming healthcare by enabling real-time analysis of complex clinical data to improve patient care and advance clinical research. They can swiftly process and interpret vast amounts of patient records, medical imaging, and genomic data, offering clinicians personalized insights and early warnings for potential health complications. Additionally, these models assist in automating routine tasks such as extracting critical information from unstructured clinical notes, which streamlines workflows and reduces administrative burdens. In research settings, Llama models accelerate the discovery of new treatment methods by identifying patterns in large datasets, thereby shortening the gap between medical research and clinical application. Ultimately, the integration of Llama models into healthcare systems leads to more accurate diagnostics, optimized treatment protocols, and a proactive approach to patient care.

Case Study 1: Precision Diagnostics and Comprehensive Patient Data Management

Background and Challenge: A renowned healthcare institution faced a critical challenge: the rapid growth of unstructured patient data across electronic health records (EHRs), clinical notes, laboratory reports, and imaging data. Physicians often struggled to quickly synthesize the extensive data required to make accurate clinical decisions. As a result, diagnosis times increased, and the risk of misdiagnosis remained high.

Implementation: To address these challenges, the healthcare provider integrated **Llama2** into its clinical workflow. The implementation involved:

- **Data Ingestion and Normalization:** Llama2 was configured to ingest and standardize data from disparate EHR systems, clinical notes, lab results, and imaging reports. Natural language processing algorithms were trained to parse and categorize unstructured text.

- **Symptom Pattern Identification:** The model was fine-tuned to identify patterns in patient-reported symptoms and correlate them with historical data. It cross-referenced current clinical narratives with large-scale medical literature and previous patient outcomes.
- **Diagnostic Insight Generation:** Using its enhanced context-awareness, Llama2 generated a ranked list of differential diagnoses, supported by recommendations for additional diagnostic tests based on the latest evidence.

Challenges Overcome:

- **Data Integration:** Integrating data across legacy systems required extensive pre-processing. Llama2's adaptive architecture allowed seamless data normalization.
- **Handling Medical Jargon:** The model was trained on vast, domain-specific corpora to accurately interpret complex medical terminology and abbreviations.
- **Real-Time Processing:** Optimizations were implemented to ensure real-time data ingestion and diagnostic insight delivery during busy clinical hours.

Results and Impact:

- **Improved Diagnostic Accuracy:** Physicians reported a significant reduction in diagnostic errors due to a more complete view of patient histories.
- **Faster Decision Making:** The time to reach a diagnosis was shortened by 30%, enabling quicker initiation of tailored treatment plans.
- **Streamlined Workflow:** An intuitive dashboard consolidated the model's outputs, making it easier for clinical staff to review critical patient metrics quickly.

Case Study 2: Accelerated Clinical Research Through Automated Knowledge Extraction

Background and Challenge: A prominent clinical research organization sought to expedite the literature review process required for designing clinical trials. Researchers were overwhelmed by the volume of newly published medical research, which hindered timely hypothesis generation and innovative treatment development.

Implementation: The organization deployed **Llama3** to automate the literature review and data extraction process:

- **Automated Literature Ingestion:** Llama3 was programmed to continuously scan and ingest research articles, clinical trial results, and case studies from leading medical journals and databases.

- **Key Data Extraction:** Using its advanced language understanding, the model extracted critical information such as study design, patient demographics, outcomes, and adverse events.
- **Trend and Correlation Analysis:** By aggregating the extracted data, Llama3 identified emerging trends in treatment efficacy and potential adverse effects, highlighting correlations that might otherwise go unnoticed.
- **Dynamic Summary Generation:** The system generated concise, comprehensible summaries, enabling researchers to quickly assimilate findings and prioritize subsequent investigations.

Challenges Overcome:

- **Volume of Data:** The continuous influx of medical publications required a scalable solution; Llama3's ability to process thousands of documents simultaneously proved pivotal.
- **Semantic Variation:** The model tackled variations in scientific language and terminology by being trained on diverse, high-quality scientific corpora.
- **Integration with Research Workflows:** Customized APIs were developed to seamlessly integrate Llama3 with the organization's data management systems, ensuring smooth handoffs of information.

Results and Impact:

- **Reduced Research Cycle Times:** Researchers experienced a 40% reduction in the time needed for comprehensive literature reviews.
- **Enhanced Collaboration:** Automated summaries facilitated interdisciplinary discussions, enabling rapid iteration on research ideas and joint publications.
- **Innovative Breakthroughs:** The ability to synthesize extensive datasets allowed researchers to uncover novel correlations, accelerating the pace of clinical innovation.

Case Study 3: Virtual Health Assistants for Enhanced Patient Engagement

Background and Challenge: A major hospital sought to transform patient engagement and operational efficiency by reducing the administrative burden on its staff. Traditional call centres and front desk services were overwhelmed, leading to delays in patient appointment scheduling, suboptimal medication adherence, and inconsistent delivery of basic healthcare information.

Implementation: The hospital implemented a **virtual health assistant** powered by the base **Llama** model. This initiative encompassed:

- **Conversational Interface Development:** A multi-channel chatbot was developed, allowing patients to interact via web, mobile apps, and even voice-activated devices.
- **Appointment and Reminder Management:** The assistant managed appointments by offering booking, rescheduling, and cancellation features, while sending automated medication and appointment reminders.
- **Preliminary Health Screening:** The system provided simple diagnostic checklists to help patients determine when to seek medical advice, thereby triaging the flow of incoming inquiries.
- **Integration with Hospital Systems:** The virtual assistant interfaced with the hospital's EHR and scheduling systems, ensuring that patient data was updated in real time.

Challenges Overcomed:

- **User Trust and Adoption:** Comprehensive testing and validation were conducted to ensure reliable responses, fostering trust among patients.
- **System Integration:** Robust APIs were designed to integrate seamlessly with existing hospital management systems, ensuring data consistency and security.
- **Scalability:** The solution was built to handle peak loads without degradation in response time or accuracy.

Results and Impact:

- **High Patient Satisfaction:** Surveys indicated a 25% increase in patient satisfaction scores due to immediate, round-the-clock service.
- **Operational Efficiency:** Administrative calls and in-person visits for routine inquiries dropped by 35%, allowing staff to focus on complex cases.
- **Continuity of Care:** The virtual assistant ensured that patients received timely reminders and health information, contributing to improved adherence to treatment plans.

Example

Use Case: Precision Diagnostics and Patient Data Management

Overview: Llama-4 is used to improve precision diagnostics by analyzing and processing comprehensive patient data, including medical history, lab results, genetic information, and doctors' notes. By leveraging the power of advanced natural language processing and machine learning, Llama-4 can help healthcare professionals provide more accurate diagnoses, optimize treatment plans, and ensure that no critical data points are missed.

A healthcare provider uses Llama-4 to analyze patient records stored in electronic health records (EHR). It automatically extracts key insights from unstructured data such as doctors' notes and medical journals. Llama-4 identifies correlations between genetic markers and disease predispositions, flags potential risk factors, and recommends personalized treatment options. It also provides real-time alerts to healthcare professionals when certain risk thresholds are met, such as abnormal test results or genetic mutations associated with rare diseases.

Impact:

- **Accuracy**: Increased accuracy of diagnoses by analyzing a broad spectrum of patient data, improving clinical decision-making.
- **Efficiency**: Reduced time spent by healthcare professionals on manual data entry and record review.
- **Personalization**: Enhanced ability to deliver tailored treatment recommendations based on comprehensive data analysis.

This case study highlights how Llama-4 can transform patient data management and diagnostic workflows, leading to more precise and efficient healthcare delivery.

Finance: Enhancing Security, Efficiency, and Customer Engagement

The finance industry is leveraging Llama 4 to enhance security, efficiency, and customer engagement. By utilizing Llama 4's advanced natural language processing capabilities, financial institutions can improve risk management, detect potential security threats, and provide more personalized customer experiences. Llama 4-powered chatbots and virtual assistants are being used to offer 24/7 customer support, while their predictive analytics capabilities help financial institutions make data-driven decisions. Additionally, Llama 4 is being used to automate compliance and regulatory reporting, reducing the risk of non-compliance and associated penalties.

Case Study 1: Strengthening Fraud Detection and Proactive Risk Management

Background and Challenge: A major international bank faced an escalating number of sophisticated fraudulent transactions. Traditional fraud detection systems struggled to keep pace with the evolving tactics of fraudsters, leading to delayed responses and increased financial losses.

Implementation: The bank implemented **Llama2** to bolster its fraud detection framework:

- **Real-Time Data Analysis:** Llama2 was embedded within the bank's transaction monitoring system. It analyzed streams of transaction data in real time, benchmarking against a comprehensive baseline of historical behavior.
- **Anomaly and Pattern Recognition:** The model was trained to identify deviations in spending patterns, unusual geolocations, and outlier behaviors that often signaled fraudulent activity.
- **Risk Scoring and Alert Generation:** Each transaction received a dynamic risk score. Transactions exceeding a threshold triggered automated alerts for in-depth investigation by fraud analysts.
- **Feedback Integration:** Continuous learning mechanisms allowed the model to update its risk criteria based on confirmed fraud cases, enhancing predictive accuracy over time.

Challenges Overcome:

- **Data Volume:** Handling millions of transactions per day required a highly scalable and efficient processing solution.
- **Accuracy Versus Latency:** The model was optimized to minimize false positives while ensuring that genuine threats were flagged rapidly without impacting the user experience.
- **Regulatory Compliance:** Careful design ensured that the fraud detection system complied with rigorous financial regulations and data privacy standards.

Results and Impact:

- **Reduced Fraud Losses:** The bank reported a 20% reduction in fraud-related financial losses within the first six months.
- **Improved Efficiency:** Fraud analysts benefited from a prioritized workload, enabling more effective and timely investigations.
- **Enhanced Customer Confidence:** More robust fraud detection measures led to higher customer trust and better overall satisfaction with the bank's services.

Case Study 2: Automated Financial Reporting and Real-Time Analytics

Background and Challenge: A leading investment firm was hampered by manual, labor-intensive financial reporting processes that delayed decision-making and increased the likelihood of errors. The need for real-time, accurate reporting was critical to maintaining a competitive advantage in rapidly shifting market conditions.

Implementation: The firm turned to **Llama3** to transform its financial data analytics and reporting workflows:

- **Data Aggregation from Multiple Sources:** Llama3 aggregated financial data from internal databases, market feeds, and historical records, ensuring a unified and up-to-date dataset.
- **Automated Report Generation:** The model automatically generated detailed reports that included key performance indicators, trend analysis, and risk assessments, providing a holistic view of market dynamics.
- **Dynamic Dashboard Integration:** Analysts had access to an interactive dashboard that presented real-time updates, enabling them to drill down into data insights quickly.
- **Predictive Analytics:** The model also included predictive functionalities, forecasting market trends based on historical data and current indicators, thus informing strategic investment decisions.

Challenges Overcome:

- **Data Consistency:** Integrating disparate data sources required extensive data cleaning and normalization, a process streamlined by Llama3's powerful data processing capabilities.
- **Real-Time Performance:** Ensuring that the system could handle live updates without lag was critical, addressed through efficient model optimization and scalable cloud infrastructure.
- **User Adoption:** Extensive training sessions and usability tests were conducted to ensure that analysts could effectively incorporate the new tool into their workflows.

Results and Impact:

- **Faster Decision Cycles:** The time required to generate comprehensive financial reports decreased by 50%, enabling quicker, data-driven decision-making.
- **Enhanced Accuracy:** The automation reduced human error and provided more consistent, reliable insights, bolstering confidence among decision-makers.
- **Strategic Advantage:** Real-time analytics and forecasting empowered portfolio managers to adjust strategies promptly, leading to improved overall portfolio performance.

Case Study 3: Personalized Client Engagement with Intelligent Chatbots

Background and Challenge: A prominent financial services provider was striving to deliver a more personalized customer experience in an environment where client expectations for instant, tailored support were continually rising. Traditional customer service channels often fell short in offering the individualized guidance that high-net-worth clients expected.

Implementation: The provider deployed a virtual assistant powered by the base **Llama** model to enhance client interactions:

- **Client Data Analysis:** The chatbot was integrated with the firm's customer relationship management system. It analyzed clients' transaction histories, investment profiles, and previous inquiries to personalize responses.
- **Conversational AI for Financial Advice:** Llama's natural language capabilities enabled the chatbot to offer tailored financial advice, ranging from simple queries about account balances to more complex investment strategy suggestions.
- **Secure Transaction Assistance:** The virtual assistant was designed to handle secure transactional queries, guiding clients through verification processes and transaction steps while ensuring data protection.
- **Multichannel Deployment:** The solution was integrated across web, mobile, and messaging platforms, ensuring that clients could access assistance wherever and whenever they needed it.

Challenges Overcome:

- **Data Privacy and Security:** The solution was built with robust encryption and compliance with financial industry regulations, ensuring sensitive client data was protected.
- **Personalization Accuracy:** Continuous improvement processes, where feedback on interactions was used to refine the model, helped tailor responses and improve personalization.
- **Balancing Automation with Human Interaction:** The solution was designed to seamlessly transfer complex queries to human agents, ensuring a hybrid model that maximized both efficiency and empathy.

Results and Impact:

- **Improved Client Engagement:** Client satisfaction ratings increased by over 30% due to faster response times and highly personalized interactions.
- **Reduced Workload on Human Agents:** The virtual assistant handled up

to 70% of the routine inquiries, freeing up human agents to address more complex client needs.

- **Enhanced Security and Trust:** With secure transaction support and precise, data-driven advice, customers reported higher levels of trust in the provider's digital services.

Example

Use Case: Automated Financial Reporting and Real-Time Analytics

Overview: Llama-4 is employed to streamline the financial reporting process and enable real-time analytics for financial institutions. It automates the extraction, processing, and analysis of financial data from various sources, including balance sheets, income statements, and market data, ensuring that reports are accurate and timely. By leveraging natural language processing (NLP), Llama-4 can also generate insightful summaries and predictive analytics that help financial analysts and decision-makers stay ahead of trends and risks.

A major investment bank uses Llama-4 to automate the creation of quarterly financial reports. The model processes large datasets, including stock market trends, asset performance, and internal financial data. It generates real-time insights and dashboards that provide executives with a clear view of financial health, market performance, and future projections. Additionally, Llama-4 analyzes external market news, such as economic reports and industry shifts, to offer sentiment analysis and impact forecasts on the company's financials.

Impact

- **Efficiency**: Significantly reduced the time required to generate accurate financial reports, freeing up financial analysts to focus on strategic analysis.
- **Real-Time Decision Making**: Enabled real-time access to financial data, allowing stakeholders to make quicker, more informed decisions.
- **Predictive Analytics**: Provided forecasts and early warnings regarding potential risks, helping the company adjust its financial strategies in real-time.

This case study demonstrates how **Llama-4** revolutionizes financial reporting by automating processes and offering real-time analytics, leading to faster, more accurate decision-making.

Customer Services: Transforming Support through Advanced Virtual Assistants

Llama 4 is revolutionizing customer service by powering advanced virtual assistants that provide personalized and efficient support to customers. With its ability to understand and respond to complex queries, Llama 4 enables businesses to offer 24/7 customer support, improving customer satisfaction and reducing support costs. Llama 4-powered virtual assistants can also help businesses to proactively address customer needs, anticipate issues, and provide tailored solutions. By leveraging Llama 4, companies can transform their customer service operations and deliver exceptional customer experiences.

Case Study 1: Multilingual Support and Global User Engagement

Background and Challenge: A global retail company with a diverse customer base required a customer support system that could handle queries in multiple languages and across different time zones. Traditional support centers struggled with consistency, leading to varied service levels and customer frustration across international markets.

Implementation: The company deployed **Llama3** to power a multilingual virtual assistant capable of:

- **Language Detection and Translation:** The assistant was trained in multiple languages, automatically detecting the language of each query and providing responses with cultural and contextual sensitivity.
- **CRM System Integration:** By interfacing with the company's CRM, the assistant referenced previous customer interactions to offer tailored solutions that resonated with each user's unique context.
- **Advanced Query Resolution:** Beyond simple FAQs, the assistant was capable of handling nuanced queries regarding returns, refunds, product information, and more.
- **24/7 Availability:** The system ensured that customer queries were addressed around the clock, irrespective of geographic location.

Challenges Overcomed:

- **Cultural Nuance:** Extensive training on regional dialects and local expressions was implemented to ensure that responses were culturally appropriate.
- **High Volume and Scalability:** The cloud-based deployment allowed the system to scale dynamically during peak periods of customer inquiry.
- **System Integration:** APIs were developed to ensure seamless data exchange between the virtual assistant and the company's existing IT infrastructure.

Results and Impact:

- **Uniform Service Quality:** Customers worldwide received consistent, high-quality support, reflected in a 25% boost in positive customer feedback.

- **Operational Efficiency:** The solution managed high volumes of interactions without corresponding increases in customer service staffing.
- **Enhanced Brand Loyalty:** Personalized and responsive service contributed to increased customer retention and overall brand perception.

Case Study 2: Intelligent Ticketing and Automated Issue Resolution

Background and Challenge: A major telecommunications firm encountered significant issues with the manual handling of support tickets. High inquiry volumes led to long wait times and inefficiencies in routing issues to the appropriate departments, adversely affecting customer satisfaction.

Implementation: The firm integrated **Llama2** into its support ticketing system:

- **Automated Triage:** Incoming support tickets were automatically categorized based on urgency, subject, and complexity, allowing the system to prioritize high-impact issues.
- **Pre-Resolution and Guided Troubleshooting:** For common queries (for example, resetting passwords, troubleshooting connectivity issues), Llama2 delivered automated solutions, enabling immediate resolution without human intervention.
- **Seamless Escalation:** More complex tickets were seamlessly escalated to human agents with detailed contextual information, reducing resolution times.
- **Continuous Learning:** Feedback from resolved tickets was fed back into the system, continuously refining the model's categorization and response accuracy.

Challenges Overcomed:

- **Accurate Classification:** Developing a taxonomy that could capture the varied nature of telecom issues required fine-tuning and a diverse training set.
- **Integration with Legacy Systems:** The solution was adapted to work alongside legacy IT systems, ensuring that data integrity was maintained during the handoff.
- **User Acceptance:** Extensive testing ensured that customers found the automated responses both intuitive and helpful, leading to high adoption rates.

Results and Impact:

- **Reduced Wait Times:** Average customer wait times dropped by nearly 40%, dramatically improving the customer experience.

- **Enhanced Resolution Efficiency:** Automated triage and pre-resolution eliminated over 60% of routine queries, allowing human agents to focus on higher-level issues.
- **Actionable Insights:** Data from ticket interactions provided valuable insights into recurring issues, leading to proactive process improvements and refined support strategies.

Case Study 3: Real-Time Customer Feedback and Advanced Sentiment Analysis

Background and Challenge: An innovative e-commerce platform aimed to leverage real-time feedback from diverse channels–social media, product reviews, and customer surveys–to gauge sentiment and adapt rapidly to customer needs. However, the sheer volume of qualitative feedback made it challenging to extract actionable insights promptly.

Implementation: The platform integrated the base **Llama** model to carry out advanced sentiment analysis:

- **Natural Language Parsing:** Llama processed free-form text from reviews, social media posts, and open-ended survey responses to detect emotional nuances and key sentiment markers.
- **Sentiment Scoring:** Each piece of feedback was assigned a sentiment score, allowing the company to quantify customer sentiment over time.
- **Trend Identification:** Aggregating and visualizing sentiment data enabled the identification of emerging trends, including recurring issues and moments of high satisfaction.
- **Actionable Reporting:** Detailed reports fed into strategic planning processes, highlighting areas for immediate intervention in product development and service adjustments.

Challenges Overcome:

- **Diverse Data Sources:** The model was trained to handle varying styles and formats of text, ensuring robust analysis across diverse data sources.
- **Contextual Variability:** Fine-tuning allowed Llama to accurately interpret context, differentiating between subtle sarcasm and genuine feedback.
- **Real-Time Processing:** Optimizations ensured that sentiment analysis could be performed in near real-time, providing up-to-date insights for rapid decision-making.

Results and Impact:

- **Proactive Issue Resolution:** Early detection of negative sentiment allowed the platform to address issues swiftly, minimizing customer churn.
- **Strategic Product Enhancements:** Insights from sentiment analysis directly influenced product improvements and customer service refinements.
- **Strengthened Customer Loyalty:** Customers responded positively to visible, data-driven changes, reinforcing trust and loyalty to the platform.

Example

Use Case: Multilingual Support and Global User Engagement

Overview: Llama-4 is used to enhance multilingual support capabilities for a global tech company by providing real-time language translation and sentiment analysis across different user interactions. With a diverse customer base spanning multiple regions, Llama-4 processes and translates customer queries and feedback in various languages, ensuring timely and accurate responses, thereby boosting user engagement and satisfaction.

A global tech company uses Llama-4 to power its customer support chatbot, which interacts with users across the world in multiple languages. The system is capable of understanding and responding to queries in over 15 languages, including French, Spanish, German, Mandarin, and Hindi. Llama-4 not only translates the user's inquiry in real-time but also conducts sentiment analysis to gauge the user's mood, allowing the system to prioritize urgent or frustrated users. Additionally, it customizes responses based on local cultural contexts and specific user preferences, improving the overall customer experience.

Impact:

- **Increased Engagement**: The system provides seamless communication with users in their preferred language, improving overall satisfaction and engagement.
- **Operational Efficiency**: Automating multilingual support with Llama-4 reduces the need for human intervention, speeding up response times and lowering operational costs.
- **Global Reach**: The ability to provide support across various languages helps the company maintain a strong global presence, catering to users from different countries and cultures.

This case study illustrates how **Llama-4** can enhance **multilingual support** and **global user engagement**, providing personalized, efficient, and culturally relevant customer interactions worldwide.

Retail: Revolutionizing the Customer Journey and Operational Efficiency

Llama 4 is transforming the retail industry by revolutionizing the customer journey and operational efficiency. With its advanced natural language processing capabilities, Llama 4 enables retailers to provide personalized product recommendations, enhance customer engagement, and streamline customer support. Llama 4-powered chatbots and virtual assistants help retailers to offer 24/7 customer support, while its predictive analytics capabilities enable them to optimize inventory management and supply chain operations. By leveraging Llama 4, retailers can create a more seamless and personalized shopping experience.

Case Study 1: Personalized Shopping Experiences and Inventory Optimization

Background and Challenge: A leading global retail chain sought to enhance its customer experience while optimizing inventory management. The company faced intense competition and needed to differentiate itself by offering personalized shopping experiences and better managing stock levels in real time.

Implementation: The retailer deployed Llama3 to power multiple facets of its operations:

- **Personalized Recommendation Engine:** Llama3 analyzed customer purchase histories, browsing behavior, and preferences to generate tailored product recommendations. This engine was integrated into the retailer's website and mobile app, allowing customers to receive individualized suggestions as they shopped.
- **Dynamic Pricing Algorithms:** By processing market trends, competitor pricing, and historical sales data, Llama3 dynamically adjusted product prices, ensuring competitiveness while maximizing profit margins.
- **Inventory Forecasting and Optimization:** The model aggregated data from in-store and online sales to predict demand patterns. It also identified seasonal trends and potential stock shortages, enabling proactive inventory replenishment.

Challenges Overcomed:

- **Data Integration:** Aggregating data from diverse sources (for example, point-of-sale systems, online platforms, and third-party market analyses) required robust pre-processing. Llama3's ability to seamlessly integrate heterogeneous data sources proved critical.

- **Scalability:** Ensuring that the recommendation engine and dynamic pricing algorithms worked effectively during peak shopping times was essential, requiring dynamic scaling and real-time processing.

Results and Impact:

- **Increased Sales Conversion:** Personalized recommendations led to a 20% uplift in conversion rates as customers engaged more deeply with curated product offerings.
- **Optimized Stock Levels:** Improved demand forecasting reduced instances of overstocking and stockouts by 30%, which enhanced overall operational efficiency.
- **Enhanced Customer Loyalty:** Dynamic pricing and a more personalized shopping experience contributed to higher customer satisfaction and repeat purchases.

Example

Use Case: Personalized Shopping Experiences and Inventory Optimization

Overview: Llama-4 is leveraged to enhance personalized shopping experiences by analyzing customer preferences, behavior, and browsing history. It provides tailored product recommendations and promotions while simultaneously helping businesses optimize their inventory based on demand forecasting and sales trends. By combining customer insights with real-time inventory data, Llama-4 helps retailers create a more engaging and efficient shopping experience while improving operational efficiency.

An online fashion retailer uses Llama-4 to offer personalized product recommendations by analyzing individual customer preferences, past purchases, and browsing patterns. The model predicts the types of clothing items customers are likely to purchase next and presents them with curated selections, increasing the likelihood of a purchase. Additionally, Llama-4 analyzes sales data and customer demand trends to help the retailer optimize its inventory, ensuring high-demand items are stocked appropriately while minimizing overstock on slow-moving products.

Impact:

- **Increased Sales**: Personalized recommendations lead to higher conversion rates, as customers are more likely to purchase items that fit their preferences.
- **Improved Inventory Management**: Llama-4's demand forecasting reduces stockouts and overstock situations, improving inventory turnover and reducing costs associated with unsold goods.

- **Enhanced Customer Experience**: Tailored shopping experiences boost customer satisfaction, loyalty, and repeat purchases.

This case study highlights how **Llama-4** can drive **personalized shopping experiences** while improving **inventory optimization**, leading to increased sales and operational efficiency in retail.

Government and Public Administration: Enhancing Services and Citizen Engagement

The integration of the Llama model in government and public administration has the potential to transform citizen engagement and service delivery. By leveraging advanced natural language processing capabilities, agencies can deploy real-time chatbots and virtual assistants that provide prompt, accurate responses to public inquiries, streamlining processes and reducing administrative burdens. These models can also analyze citizen feedback, identify emerging concerns, and support data-driven decision-making, ultimately leading to more efficient and transparent government services. As a result, the Llama model enhances the interaction between citizens and public institutions, fostering trust and ensuring that government services are both accessible and responsive to community needs.

Case Study 1: Streamlined Document Processing and Citizen Service Portals

Background and Challenge: A municipal government sought to enhance transparency, streamline its operations, and improve citizen engagement. The government's traditional document processing and public query handling were labor-intensive and slow, leading to delays and public frustration.

Implementation: The government integrated Llama2 into its digital services platform:

- **Automated Document Processing:** Llama2 was deployed to scan, process, and categorize public records, forms, and policy documents. This automation reduced manual data entry and improved the speed at which documents were made available to the public.
- **Smart Citizen Service Portals:** A virtual assistant, powered by Llama, was implemented on the government's online portal. Citizens could ask questions related to public policies, application procedures for permits, and even local events.
- **Feedback and Sentiment Analysis:** Llama3 was utilized to analyze citizen feedback from surveys, social media, and public forums, providing real-time insights into public sentiment and areas that required immediate attention.

Challenges Overcomed:

- **Data Security:** Government data requires a higher standard of security and privacy. The system was designed with robust encryption and adherence to government data protection standards.
- **Integration with Legacy Systems:** The solution was developed to interface seamlessly with existing legacy systems, ensuring minimal disruption during the transition.

Results and Impact:

- **Faster Service Delivery:** Automated document processing led to a 35% decrease in processing times, making critical documents available to citizens much faster.
- **Improved Public Engagement:** The smart citizen portal resulted in a 40% increase in citizen interactions, giving government officials timely feedback to improve public services.
- **Data-Driven Policy Adjustments:** Continuous sentiment analysis enabled more proactive policy changes and resource allocation, enhancing overall public satisfaction with government services.

Example

Use Case: Streamlined Document Processing and Citizen Service Portals

Overview: Llama-4 is used to automate and enhance the processing of government documents and citizen requests in public service portals. By leveraging advanced NLP capabilities, Llama-4 analyzes, categorizes, and processes large volumes of citizen-submitted documents, such as applications, forms, and feedback. This improves service efficiency, reduces human errors, and ensures that citizens' needs are met faster and more accurately.

A government agency employs Llama-4 to power its citizen service portal, where users submit various documents such as tax returns, business licenses, and public service applications. Llama-4 processes these documents, extracting key data points (such as personal details, tax information, or application status), and categorizes them for the appropriate department. The system can also automatically respond to frequently asked questions by analyzing citizen inquiries and providing context-specific, accurate responses. By automating document review, approval workflows, and response generation, Llama-4 significantly reduces processing times and operational costs for the agency.

Impact:

- **Efficiency**: Dramatically speeds up document processing and citizen interaction by automating tasks that previously required manual intervention.

- **Accuracy**: Reduces errors in document handling, ensuring that data is extracted and processed accurately.
- **Improved Citizen Experience**: Provides faster, more accurate responses to citizens' inquiries, leading to higher satisfaction with public services.

This case study demonstrates how Llama-4 can streamline document processing and enhance citizen service portals, driving greater efficiency and improved public service delivery.

Education: Empowering Adaptive Learning and Efficient Administration

The Llama model enhances education by driving adaptive learning and streamlining administration in real time. By analyzing student interactions and performance data, it can create personalized learning experiences, adjusting content to meet individual needs and ensuring that each learner receives the appropriate level of challenge and support. Additionally, Llama can automate routine administrative tasks such as grading, scheduling, and managing communications, thereby reducing the workload for educators and administrators. These capabilities allow institutions to focus more on teaching and less on bureaucracy, ultimately fostering an engaging and efficient educational environment that benefits both students and staff.

Case Study: Adaptive Learning Platforms and Automated Grading Systems

Background and Challenge: An educational institution aimed to provide a more personalized learning experience while reducing the administrative burden on teachers. Traditional classroom settings and manual grading systems were inadequate in addressing the diverse needs of modern learners.

Implementation: The institution introduced Llama-based educational solutions:

- **Adaptive Learning Platforms:** Utilizing Llama3, the institution developed an adaptive tutoring system. The system analyzed individual student performance data and adjusted instructional content in real time to match each student's learning pace and style.
- **Automated Content Generation:** Llama was employed to generate supplementary learning materials, quizzes, and interactive modules aligned with the curriculum. This reduced the preparation time for instructors and provided students with a dynamic repository of resources.
- **Automated Grading and Feedback:** Llama2 was integrated with the institution's learning management system to automate the grading process,

particularly for written assignments and subjective assessments. The system provided detailed feedback, enabling students to understand their mistakes and improve continuously.

Challenges Overcome:

- **Diversity of Learning Data:** Adapting to varied learning styles required extensive training on diverse educational data sets, which Llama3 handled effectively.
- **Integration with Legacy Learning Management Systems:** Seamless integration with existing platforms was achieved via custom APIs, ensuring continuity in teaching and learning processes.

Results and Impact:

- **Personalized Learning Outcomes:** Adaptive tutoring led to a 25% improvement in overall student performance as learning was tailored to individual needs.
- **Reduced Administrative Burden:** Automated grading reduced the workload on educators by 40%, allowing them to focus more on personalized instruction.
- **Enhanced Student Engagement:** The integration of interactive, AI-powered learning tools resulted in higher student engagement and satisfaction, fostering an environment conducive to innovative learning.

Example

Use Case: Adaptive Learning Platforms and Automated Grading Systems

Overview: Llama-4 is utilized in adaptive learning platforms and automated grading systems to personalize the educational experience for students. By analyzing student responses, learning patterns, and performance data, Llama-4 tailors the content delivery to each learner's pace and understanding. Additionally, it automates the grading of assignments, providing instant feedback to students and helping educators efficiently manage their workload.

A leading online education provider uses Llama-4 to power its adaptive learning platform. The platform adjusts the difficulty of assignments, quizzes, and learning materials based on the student's performance. For example, if a student struggles with certain concepts, Llama-4 identifies gaps in their understanding and adapts the curriculum to offer more focused practice or explanations. In addition, Llama-4 automates the grading of open-ended responses, such as essays or project submissions, by analyzing the content for key points, accuracy, and structure. The system generates detailed feedback, helping students improve their work in real time.

Impact:

- **Personalized Learning**: Llama-4 adapts educational content based on individual student progress, ensuring that learning is aligned with their needs.
- **Time Efficiency**: Automates grading and feedback, reducing teachers' workload and allowing them to focus on more strategic tasks.
- **Improved Outcomes**: Provides instant feedback, helping students learn more effectively and make continuous improvements in their learning journey.

This case study demonstrates how **Llama-4** can enhance **adaptive learning platforms** and automate **grading systems**, resulting in more personalized learning experiences and improved educational outcomes.

Energy and Utilities: Optimizing Resources and Enhancing Sustainability

In the energy and utilities sector, the fine-tuned Llama model is used to analyze real-time data from sensors and operational logs, enabling companies to optimize resource allocation and enhance sustainability. By processing vast amounts of information quickly, Llama helps predict demand fluctuations, detect early signs of equipment failure, and recommend proactive maintenance, all of which reduce downtime and improve efficiency. These capabilities contribute to more sustainable practices, as energy production and consumption can be managed in a smarter, data-driven manner, ultimately reducing waste and supporting environmental goals.

Case Study: Predictive Maintenance and Energy Demand Forecasting

Background and Challenge: An energy provider faced challenges with maintaining aging infrastructure and ensuring efficient energy distribution during peak demand periods. Unexpected equipment failures and inefficient energy use were leading to increased operational costs.

Implementation: The energy provider leveraged Llama2 and Llama3 for predictive maintenance and demand forecasting:

- **Predictive Maintenance:** Llama2 was deployed to monitor sensor data from critical infrastructure (for example, transformers, turbines, and distribution networks). The model analyzed historical performance data and real-time sensor inputs to predict potential equipment failures, prompting preemptive maintenance.
- **Energy Demand Forecasting:** Llama3 processed historical energy usage data along with weather forecasts and market trends to predict future energy

demands. These insights allowed the utility company to adjust energy distribution strategies and prevent overloads.

- **Sustainability Monitoring:** Llama was also used to track environmental metrics and energy efficiency, aiding in compliance with sustainability initiatives and regulatory standards.

Challenges Overcome:

- **Integration with IoT Systems:** The system was designed to seamlessly integrate with existing IoT networks and sensor arrays.
- **Real-Time Data Processing:** The solution was optimized for real-time processing to ensure immediate detection and response to operational anomalies.

Results and Impact:

- **Increased Infrastructure Uptime:** Predictive maintenance reduced unexpected equipment failures by 30%, significantly lowering operational disruptions.
- **Optimized Energy Distribution:** Improved demand forecasting resulted in a 20% increase in energy distribution efficiency, reducing operational costs.
- **Enhanced Sustainability:** Better monitoring and resource optimization contributed to achieving sustainability targets and compliance with environmental standards.

Example

Use Case: Predictive Maintenance and Energy Demand Forecasting

Overview: Llama-4 is used in the energy sector to predict equipment failures and forecast energy demand. By analyzing historical data, real-time sensor readings, and operational performance, Llama-4 identifies patterns that can help predict equipment failures before they occur, enabling preventive maintenance. Additionally, Llama-4 forecasts energy demand, allowing utility companies to optimize energy distribution and reduce operational costs.

An energy provider uses Llama-4 to power its predictive maintenance system for critical infrastructure such as turbines, transformers, and power plants. The system continuously monitors data from sensors on equipment, such as temperature, vibration, and pressure readings. Llama-4 analyzes these patterns and predicts when maintenance is required, reducing unplanned downtimes and extending the lifespan of the equipment. In parallel, Llama-4 is used to forecast energy demand based on factors such as historical usage, weather patterns, and population growth. This helps the provider optimize energy supply and prevent shortages or overproduction, improving efficiency and reducing costs.

Impact:

- **Reduced Downtime:** By predicting equipment failures early, Llama-4 enables timely maintenance, minimizing unplanned downtimes and increasing operational efficiency.
- **Optimized Energy Supply:** Accurate energy demand forecasting ensures that supply matches demand, reducing waste and avoiding energy shortages.
- **Cost Efficiency:** Preventive maintenance and optimized energy distribution lead to cost savings by reducing emergency repairs and excess energy production.

This case study highlights how Llama-4 can drive predictive maintenance and enhance energy demand forecasting, improving both operational reliability and cost-effectiveness in the energy sector.

Manufacturing: Driving Efficiency and Quality in Production

In modern manufacturing, Llama models are being fine-tuned to drive efficiency and enhance quality in production lines. By processing vast amounts of operational data—from sensor readings to maintenance logs—these models help predict equipment failures, optimize scheduling, and streamline quality control processes. Real-time insights provided by the model enable manufacturers to quickly adjust to changing conditions on the factory floor, reducing downtime and waste. This intelligent automation not only improves production reliability but also supports strategic decision-making, making manufacturing processes more responsive and cost-effective.

Case Study: Production Process Optimization and Quality Control

Background and Challenge: A leading manufacturing company aimed to enhance production efficiency and product quality in a highly competitive market. Manual quality control processes were time-consuming and prone to errors, which affected both production speed and consistency.

Implementation: The company implemented Llama3 and Llama2 to revolutionize its manufacturing processes:

- **Process Optimization:** Llama3 was deployed to analyze data from production lines—including machinery performance, production rates, and environmental conditions—to optimize workflow processes. The model identified bottlenecks and proposed adjustments to improve throughput.

- **Predictive Quality Control:** Llama2 was used to monitor production in real time, detecting deviations from quality standards before defects occurred. The model analyzed sensor data and visual inspections to provide early warnings of potential quality issues.
- **Supply Chain Integration:** Llama models were also integrated into the supply chain management system. They facilitated real-time communication between suppliers, production units, and logistics, ensuring a smooth flow of materials and timely replenishment of components.

Challenges Overcome:

- **Real-Time Process Data Handling:** The solution required the processing of vast amounts of sensor and production data in real time, handled efficiently by Llama3's optimized architecture.
- **High Accuracy in Quality Assessment:** Refining the model to accurately predict quality issues required extensive training with quality control datasets and continuous calibration.
- **Cross-Functional Integration:** Seamless integration across production, quality control, and supply chain systems was achieved through comprehensive system mapping and API development.

Results and Impact:

- **Enhanced Production Efficiency:** Process optimizations improved production speeds by 25%, reducing downtime and waste.
- **Improved Product Quality:** Early detection of quality issues resulted in a 15% decrease in defect rates, ensuring higher product reliability.
- **Streamlined Supply Chain:** Efficient communication and real-time inventory management reduced material shortages and excesses, lowering operational costs and enhancing overall supply chain coordination.

Example

Use Case: Production Process Optimization and Quality Control

Overview: Llama-4 is used in manufacturing to optimize production processes and improve quality control by analyzing operational data, detecting anomalies, and predicting equipment performance. The model processes real-time data from sensors, production lines, and historical records to identify inefficiencies, optimize workflows, and ensure product quality meets industry standards.

A large automotive manufacturer uses Llama-4 to monitor and optimize its assembly line. The model analyzes real-time data from various sensors (for example, temperature, pressure, and machine speeds) to identify deviations in the production process. When Llama-4 detects anomalies, such as machine malfunction or material inconsistency, it triggers immediate alerts for maintenance or process adjustment, preventing defective products from being produced. Additionally, the model predicts equipment failure based on past data, allowing for predictive maintenance scheduling, which reduces downtime and improves overall production efficiency.

Impact:

- **Enhanced Product Quality**: Llama-4 ensures that quality control is maintained by detecting inconsistencies and defects early in the production process.
- **Increased Efficiency**: Real-time monitoring and process optimization reduce bottlenecks and improve throughput, leading to more efficient use of resources.
- **Cost Savings**: Predictive maintenance and process adjustments reduce unplanned downtime and material waste, leading to cost reductions and increased profitability.

This case study demonstrates how **Llama-4** can optimize **production processes** and enhance **quality control**, resulting in higher efficiency, reduced costs, and better product quality in manufacturing.

Challenges and Solutions in Real-world Deployments

Large language models, such as the Llama series–Llama, Llama2, and Llama3–have emerged as transformative tools across industries. However, their real-world deployment is fraught with challenges that span from data quality concerns to ethical issues and system integration hurdles. This revised overview synthesizes the key challenges encountered in deploying these models and outlines the practical solutions that have paved the way for their success.

Data Quality and Integration

Challenge: Diverse and Unstructured Data Sources

One of the foremost challenges in deploying Llama models is handling the vast array of data sources. In many industries–such as healthcare, finance, and customer services–data often exists in unstructured or semi-structured formats. Medical records, financial transactions, customer service logs, and social media posts vary widely in style, language, and structure, complicating the process of data ingestion and analysis.

Solution: Advanced Data Pre-Processing Pipelines

Organizations have addressed these challenges by developing robust data pre-processing pipelines that:

- **Standardize Formats:** Convert unstructured and disparate data into a consistent, structured format that the models can easily process.
- **Natural Language Pre-Processing (NLP):** Utilize NLP techniques to clean, parse, and annotate text, which includes spelling correction, tokenization, and contextual tagging.
- **Integrate Multiple Sources:** Leverage data integration platforms that automatically harmonize data from various systems (for example, Electronic Health Records, transaction logs, CRM systems) into a unified data lake.

By investing in comprehensive pre-processing solutions, companies can ensure that Llama models are fed with high-quality, standardized data—paving the way for accurate and reliable insights.

Model Adaptation and Domain-Specific Tuning

Challenge: General Versus Domain-Specific Knowledge

While the Llama series delivers impressive general language understanding, many real-world applications demand specialized knowledge. A model trained on general-purpose data might miss nuances essential to healthcare diagnostics, financial forecasting, or legal document analysis.

Solution: Domain-Specific Fine-Tuning

To bridge this gap, organizations have adopted strategies like:

- **Customized Training Data:** Curating datasets that reflect domain-specific language, terminologies, and scenarios, ensuring the model learns industry-relevant patterns.
- **Transfer Learning:** Applying transfer learning techniques to adapt the pre-trained Llama models to specialized applications. This allows the model to build on its general knowledge while gaining an in-depth understanding of the domain.
- **Iterative Feedback Loops:** Integrating user feedback and domain expert insights into continuous model retraining helps fine-tune model performance over time.

By focusing on domain-specific training and iterative learning, businesses ensure that Llama models not only understand general language but also excel in specialized applications.

Scalability and Real-Time Processing

Challenge: High Processing Demands and Real-Time Performance

Real-world deployments often require Llama models to process large volumes of data in real time. Whether in fraud detection systems in finance, patient monitoring in healthcare, or real-time customer engagement in retail, timely processing is crucial. However, the computational demands of LLMs can strain system resources, leading to latency issues.

Solution: Optimized Infrastructure and Model Compression

Successful deployments have leveraged a combination of infrastructural and technical solutions:

- **Cloud-Based Scalability:** Utilizing cloud platforms that provide dynamic scaling, ensuring that computing resources can adjust to fluctuations in data volume.
- **Edge Computing:** For time-critical applications, deploying models on edge devices reduces latency by processing data closer to its source.
- **Model Compression Techniques:** Techniques such as quantization, pruning, and distillation help reduce model size and computational overhead without significantly compromising performance.
- **Efficient Inference Engines:** Specialized hardware accelerators (such as GPUs and TPUs) combined with optimized inference engines ensure that Llama models deliver rapid, real-time responses.

These combined measures have enabled organizations to meet the demands of high throughput and real-time decision-making, ensuring that applications remain responsive and effective.

Ethical Considerations and Bias Mitigation

Challenge: Addressing Bias and Maintaining Ethical Standards

Large language models, including the Llama series, can inadvertently capture and propagate biases present in their training data. In sensitive domains–such as healthcare, law, and finance–this can lead to unfair outcomes, misinterpretations, and ethical dilemmas that compromise user trust and legal compliance.

Solution: Rigorous Auditing and Responsible AI Practices

Organizations are taking proactive steps to address these concerns:

- **Bias Auditing:** Regular audits of model outputs help identify bias and discriminatory patterns. This involves analyzing responses across diverse demographic groups and application contexts.

- **Transparent Data Policies:** Maintaining transparency about data sources and training methodologies enables stakeholders to understand and scrutinize how biases might be introduced.
- **Incorporating Fairness Algorithms:** Researchers are integrating fairness constraints and bias correction algorithms directly into model training to minimize harmful biases.
- **Ethical Governance Frameworks:** Establishing multidisciplinary ethics boards and adopting industry best practices in responsible AI ensures that ethical considerations are embedded in every stage of deployment.

By prioritizing ethical practices and continuously monitoring for bias, organizations can uphold the integrity and fairness of Llama model deployments.

Integration with Legacy Systems and Organizational Change

Challenge: Bridging the Old with the New

Many organizations face the challenge of integrating cutting-edge Llama models with existing legacy systems. Outdated technology, fragmented IT infrastructures, and resistance to change can impede the seamless adoption of advanced AI solutions.

Solution: Strategic Integration and Change Management

A multi-faceted approach has proven effective:

- **Hybrid Systems:** Implementing hybrid architectures that combine legacy systems with new AI modules allows organizations to gradually phase in advanced capabilities without disrupting existing workflows.
- **Modular APIs:** Developing modular, well-documented APIs facilitates easier integration, ensuring that Llama models can communicate effectively with legacy data systems and enterprise applications.
- **Training and Culture Change:** Investing in change management programs and technical training helps employees and stakeholders understand the benefits of AI, fostering a culture that embraces innovation.
- **Pilot Projects:** Running small-scale pilot projects to demonstrate value and gather feedback helps build confidence and smooth the transition to broader adoption.

Through strategic integration efforts and comprehensive change management, organizations can successfully combine the reliability of legacy systems with the transformational power of Llama models.

Conclusion

This chapter has provided a comprehensive exploration of the real-world applications of the Llama series–Llama, Llama 2, and Llama 3–and their transformative impact across diverse industries. Through a series of detailed case studies and practical examples, we have demonstrated how these advanced language models are not only revolutionizing the way businesses process and analyze data but are also addressing complex natural language processing (NLP) challenges in a variety of settings.

In the next chapter, we will dive into advanced strategies and technical optimizations that elevate the performance and efficiency of Llama models. You will explore methods to enhance inference speed for real-time insights, learn how batch processing can streamline large-scale data handling, and discover parallelization techniques that distribute workloads effectively. Additionally, we will examine both hardware and software optimizations–from leveraging cutting-edge accelerators to employing specialized libraries–to push the boundaries of Llama's scalability and real-world application.

Multiple Choice Questions

1. Which of the following is a primary challenge in deploying Llama models across diverse industries?
   a. Managing homogeneous and well-structured data
   b. Handling diverse, unstructured data sources
   c. Eliminating all human intervention in data analysis
   d. Reducing the number of available training datasets
2. What is the main strategy used to adapt Llama models for domain-specific applications?
   a. Increasing the size of the model without fine-tuning
   b. Relying solely on generic training data
   c. Domain-specific fine-tuning through transfer learning
   d. Deploying the model without any customization
3. Which technique is mentioned as a key solution for improving inference speed and processing efficiency in Llama deployments?
   a. Manual data integration
   b. Using only on-premises hardware solutions

   c. Model compression techniques such as quantization and pruning

   d. Avoiding cloud-based solutions to reduce complexity

4. In the context of fraud detection for the finance industry, how do Llama models contribute according to the case studies?

   a. They solely automate financial reporting

   b. They integrate real-time data analysis and anomaly detection

   c. They replace human analysts entirely

   d. They focus only on historical data analysis without real-time processing

5. Which of the following is NOT one of the key topics to explore in the next chapter?

   a. Strategies for improving inference speed

   b. Batch processing with Llama

   c. The history of natural language processing

   d. Hardware and software optimizations for Llama models

6. What is one solution mentioned for addressing the challenge of integrating Llama models with legacy systems?

   a. Replacing all legacy systems immediately

   b. Using hybrid systems with modular APIs and comprehensive change management

   c. Avoiding system integration to reduce complexity

   d. Limiting the deployment to only newer, cloud-based systems

7. Which of the following ethical measures is suggested to mitigate bias in Llama models?

   a. Ignoring bias if model performance is high

   b. Regular bias auditing and integrating fairness algorithms

   c. Reducing the size of the training dataset

   d. Limiting model deployment to non-critical applications

8. In the healthcare case studies, Llama models were used to improve which of the following?
   a. Only administrative processes
   b. Patient diagnostics, clinical research, and patient engagement
   c. Exclusively for marketing and patient outreach
   d. Solely for staff scheduling
9. What advantage does batch processing provide in the context of Llama model deployments?
   a. It allows the models to process data one record at a time
   b. It limits the models to small datasets
   c. It optimizes the handling of large volumes of data simultaneously
   d. It reduces the need for any computational resources
10. Which infrastructure enhancement is key for meeting high throughput demands in real-time Llama model processing?
    a. Static on-premises servers with fixed capacity
    b. Cloud-based scalability and specialized hardware accelerators
    c. Manual model recalibration during peak periods
    d. Minimizing the use of parallel processing

Answers

1. b
2. c
3. c
4. b
5. c
6. b
7. b
8. b
9. c
10. b

CHAPTER 7

Performance Tuning for Llama Models

Introduction

In this chapter, readers will embark on a comprehensive journey to optimize the performance of Llama models, focusing on achieving improvements in speed, accuracy, and overall efficiency. We start by introducing the core concepts of performance tuning and why they are crucial for modern machine learning applications. Throughout this section, you will gain insights into various techniques, such as batch processing, which allows for handling multiple data instances concurrently, and parallelization, a method to distribute tasks across multiple processors or cores to reduce latency. We also explore the role of hardware acceleration, emphasizing how leveraging specialized hardware–such as GPUs and TPUs–can significantly boost model inference and operational capabilities, making it possible to deploy Llama models in production environments with stringent performance requirements.

Delving deeper, this chapter will not only explain the theory behind these performance-enhancing strategies but also provide practical guidance for their implementation. You will learn how to measure and analyze performance metrics to identify bottlenecks, enabling you to make informed decisions about which optimization techniques to apply. Detailed case studies and step-by-step instructions will illustrate how to configure batch sizes effectively, optimize data pipelines, and implement parallel processing routines that align with your system's architecture. Furthermore, the chapter covers best practices for integrating hardware accelerators into your workflow, ensuring that the improvements in speed do not come at the expense of accuracy or stability. By the end of this chapter, you will be equipped with a robust toolkit for performance tuning that can be applied to various operational scenarios, helping you maximize the potential of Llama models in both research and real-world applications.

Structure

In this chapter, we will cover the following topics:

- Overview
- Strategies for Improving Inference Speed
- Batch Processing with Llama
- Parallelization Techniques
- Hardware and Software Optimizations for Llama Models

Overview

In this comprehensive overview of performance tuning for Llama models, we delve into an array of strategies aimed at boosting inference speed and ensuring operational efficiency. At the forefront is the concept of batch processing, a method where multiple data inputs are processed simultaneously, significantly reducing the per-instance overhead. This technique not only accelerates the processing speed but also optimizes resource utilization, making it a critical component in handling high-volume requests. Alongside batch processing, we explore various strategies for improving inference speed, including advanced data preprocessing, intelligent caching mechanisms, and dynamic allocation of computational resources that adapt to fluctuating workloads.

Parallelization techniques form another cornerstone of performance tuning, enabling tasks to be distributed across multiple cores or even different machines. By executing multiple operations concurrently, these techniques minimize latency and allow Llama models to process large datasets more efficiently. In this context, both software-level optimizations–such as multi-threading and asynchronous processing–and hardware-level enhancements play pivotal roles. Leveraging accelerators such as GPUs or TPUs further amplifies the benefits of parallelization, as these specialized devices are designed to handle complex computations at scale. Additionally, configuring system environments to harness these hardware advantages ensures that Llama models can operate at their peak performance without compromising accuracy.

Beyond algorithmic improvements, a holistic approach to performance tuning involves synchronizing hardware and software optimizations. Fine-tuning the operating system and leveraging optimized libraries, such as those designed for deep learning and matrix computations, create an ecosystem where Llama models can thrive. This synergy between software and hardware not only addresses computational bottlenecks but also lays the groundwork for scalable, real-time applications. By integrating these diverse yet complementary strategies–ranging from batch processing and parallelization to targeted hardware enhancements–

readers will gain a robust framework for achieving unparalleled performance, ultimately empowering them to deploy Llama models effectively in both research and production environments.

Strategies for Improving Inference Speed

Inference speed is critical in deploying machine learning models in real-world applications, particularly for large language models such as Llama. With growing demands for real-time responses and the need to process large volumes of data, it is essential to optimize every component of the inference pipeline. Improving inference speed not only reduces latency but also enhances user experience and maximizes resource utilization. In this guide, we break down major strategies that can be implemented to accelerate Llama model inference. We will discuss how batch processing and data pipeline optimization can alleviate data-related bottlenecks, examine how parallelization and asynchronous execution harness modern hardware capabilities, and explore how specialized accelerators as well as advanced software optimizations drive efficient computation.

At the heart of this chapter is a series of detailed case studies and practical examples that showcase how Llama models are being deployed in environments where precision, speed, and adaptability are essential. Far from being limited to academic or experimental settings, these models have found fertile ground in real-world scenarios, proving their value in production environments. Each case study is designed to highlight the specific challenges encountered in various sectors and the tailored strategies employed to address them using the Llama series.

Optimizing Batch Processing

Batch processing is one of the foundational strategies to enhance inference speed. By processing multiple inputs concurrently, batch processing leverages the inherent parallelism in modern hardware architectures, reducing the per-instance overhead significantly.

- **Aggregation of Requests:** Rather than handling requests one at a time, incoming data is aggregated into batches. This not only maximizes throughput by allowing simultaneous processing of multiple inputs but also minimizes the constant overhead associated with each individual inference call. For instance, in a production environment where requests are made continuously, dynamically adjusting batch sizes based on current traffic can lead to substantial performance gains.
- **Vectorized Computations:** Batch processing allows the model to utilize vectorized operations efficiently. Modern deep learning libraries are optimized for performing matrix and vector operations on batches, often using highly optimized kernels. This means that when data is organized

into batches, operations such as convolution, matrix multiplications, and activation functions can be executed much faster, taking full advantage of SIMD (Single Instruction, Multiple Data) instructions provided by modern CPUs and GPUs.

- **Reducing I/O Overhead:** When data is processed in batches, the frequency of read and write operations is reduced. Efficiently managing input/output (I/O) operations becomes critical, as I/O overhead can often become a bottleneck in high-speed inference. Techniques such as prefetching, where the next batch is loaded in advance, and caching, where frequently accessed data is stored in faster memory, can further reduce latency.

Streamlining the Data Pipeline

A significant component of inference speed is the efficiency of the data pipeline—the series of steps that data undergoes before it is fed into the model for inference. Optimizing the data pipeline involves several key strategies.

- **Efficient Data Preprocessing:** Data preprocessing can include tokenization, normalization, and other transformations required to convert raw inputs into a model-friendly format. Optimizing these processes by using parallel data loading, precomputing common transformations, and reducing redundant computations is essential. In some cases, preprocessing can be offloaded to dedicated threads or even separate systems to ensure that the model is never idle waiting for data.
- **Caching Mechanisms:** Implementing caching strategies is another powerful method to improve pipeline efficiency. Frequently requested inferences or recurring data patterns can be cached, so that the model can reuse results rather than performing redundant computations. A well-designed caching system, whether in-memory or on-disk, can help bypass expensive operations, thereby reducing latency.
- **Asynchronous Data Handling:** Moving away from synchronous data loading to asynchronous pipelines can decouple data preparation from the model's computation. By leveraging asynchronous processing, data preparation can occur concurrently with model inference. This concurrency minimizes idle times and ensures that the model continuously receives data without waiting, leading to an overall increase in throughput.

Parallelization Techniques

Parallelization is at the heart of many modern performance tuning strategies. By splitting the computational workload across multiple processing units, inference tasks can be completed in parallel, reducing total processing time.

- **Multi-threading and Multi-processing:** Multi-threading allows the execution of multiple threads within a single process, making it ideal for handling I/O-bound operations concurrently with CPU-bound tasks. Multi-processing, on the other hand, leverages multiple CPU cores by running separate processes simultaneously. For Llama models, implementing a combination of both techniques can ensure that different parts of the model inference process—such as data preparation, execution, and result post-processing—occur concurrently, effectively reducing the total latency.
- **Task-based Parallelism:** In addition to basic multi-threading, task-based parallelism involves decomposing the inference workload into smaller tasks that can be executed independently. This could mean parallelizing the operations within a single inference call (for example, splitting matrix operations into sub-tasks) or distributing different inference tasks across available hardware. This approach is particularly beneficial in heterogeneous computing environments where different hardware components can operate simultaneously.
- **Asynchronous Execution:** Asynchronous programming models allow the application to initiate operations that run concurrently without waiting for each to finish before starting the next. This method is especially useful when dealing with latency-prone operations such as network requests or disk I/O. By utilizing asynchronous libraries and frameworks, Llama models can process requests and perform computations in parallel, thereby significantly reducing idle time and improving overall inference speed.

Hardware Acceleration

While software optimizations are crucial, leveraging the full potential of hardware acceleration can result in dramatic performance improvements. Specialized hardware such as GPUs, TPUs, and FPGAs can handle the parallelizable and computationally intensive aspects of model inference far more efficiently than general-purpose CPUs.

- **GPU Acceleration:** Graphics Processing Units (GPUs) are designed for parallel computation and are particularly effective for the matrix and vector operations common in deep learning. By offloading computations to a GPU, Llama models can perform thousands of operations simultaneously. Frameworks such as CUDA and libraries such as cuDNN are optimized to take advantage of GPU architecture, significantly speeding up model inference.
- **Tensor Processing Units (TPUs):** Developed by Google, TPUs are specialized hardware accelerators designed specifically for neural network workloads. They offer significant improvements in performance by optimizing for the unique requirements of deep learning models. TPUs can be integrated into the inference pipeline to accelerate operations such as convolution and matrix multiplications, thereby reducing inference latency.

- **Field-Programmable Gate Arrays (FPGAs):** FPGAs offer a unique blend of hardware customization and parallel processing. They can be configured to perform specific operations with a high degree of efficiency. In certain applications, using FPGAs for inference can lead to lower latency and power consumption compared to traditional CPU/GPU solutions, especially in edge computing scenarios where power efficiency is critical.

Software-Level Optimizations

In addition to hardware improvements, software-level optimizations are vital for squeezing out every bit of performance from Llama models. These optimizations often involve fine-tuning the underlying code and leveraging specialized libraries that are designed to maximize computational efficiency.

- **Optimized Libraries and Frameworks:** Using highly optimized libraries such as TensorFlow, PyTorch, or specialized numerical computation libraries (for example, BLAS, cuBLAS) can lead to substantial performance improvements. These libraries are continually updated to incorporate the latest advancements in hardware acceleration and parallel processing. By ensuring that your model is built on top of these frameworks, you can take full advantage of their performance optimizations.
- **Code Profiling and Bottleneck Identification:** Before diving into complex optimizations, it is important to profile your code and identify bottlenecks. Tools such as NVIDIA's Nsight, Intel VTune, or built-in profilers in deep learning frameworks can help pinpoint which parts of the inference process are the slowest. Once identified, targeted optimizations can be applied, whether it is refactoring code, optimizing data structures, or adjusting memory management practices.
- **Memory Management and Data Locality:** Efficient memory management is crucial in achieving high-performance inference. Reducing memory fragmentation, ensuring proper allocation and deallocation of resources, and optimizing data locality can prevent slowdowns caused by cache misses or excessive data swapping. Techniques such as memory pooling, using contiguous memory blocks, and aligning data structures with hardware cache lines can lead to more predictable and faster memory access patterns.
- **Compiler Optimizations:** Modern compilers offer a range of optimization flags that can improve the performance of compiled code. When deploying Llama models, compiling performance-critical sections of code with optimization flags (such as -O2 or -O3 in GCC/Clang) can yield noticeable improvements. Additionally, just-in-time (JIT) compilers and ahead-of-time (AOT) compilation techniques can further optimize runtime performance.

Monitoring and Continuous Improvement

Improving inference speed is an ongoing process that requires constant monitoring and fine-tuning. Establishing a robust monitoring framework helps ensure that optimizations remain effective as workload patterns evolve and new challenges emerge.

- **Performance Metrics and Logging:** Implementing detailed logging and performance metrics is essential to monitor inference speed in real-time. Metrics such as latency, throughput, CPU/GPU utilization, and memory usage provide valuable insights into system performance. Monitoring these metrics can help quickly identify issues or regressions, allowing for timely interventions.
- **Automated Testing and Benchmarking:** Incorporating automated testing and benchmarking into your development pipeline ensures that any changes to the codebase do not adversely impact performance. Benchmarking tests can simulate various load scenarios and measure inference times under controlled conditions. This practice not only verifies that optimizations are working as intended but also helps in comparing different strategies to determine the most effective ones.
- **Iterative Optimization:** Optimization is rarely a one-off task. As models evolve and deployment environments change, continuous profiling and iterative improvements are necessary. This involves regularly reviewing performance metrics, identifying new bottlenecks, and applying the latest techniques in both hardware and software optimization.

Case Studies and Implementation Examples

To ground these strategies in practical terms, let us consider a few case studies:

- **Real-Time Chatbot Deployment:** In a scenario where a chatbot powered by Llama models needs to deliver real-time responses, batch processing is implemented by aggregating incoming messages over a short time window (for example, 100–200 milliseconds). By utilizing asynchronous data fetching and pre-processing pipelines, the system ensures that the model always has data ready for inference. Parallelization techniques distribute different parts of the conversation processing across multiple CPU cores, while GPU acceleration handles the heavy lifting of neural network computations. Performance monitoring tools track latency and throughput, enabling continuous adjustments to batch sizes and resource allocations.
- **High-Volume Content Moderation:** For a content moderation system processing thousands of images and text snippets per minute, efficient data preprocessing and caching mechanisms are critical. The system implements

a hybrid approach where preprocessing tasks run on dedicated threads and utilize optimized libraries to convert raw inputs into model-friendly formats quickly. Inference requests are batched and sent to a GPU cluster, where parallelization strategies ensure that each batch is processed with minimal latency. Ongoing performance testing and profiling have led to iterative improvements that have reduced average inference times by over 40%.

- **Edge Computing for IoT Devices:** Deploying Llama models in edge computing scenarios, where resources are limited, requires a combination of lightweight models, efficient memory management, and hardware acceleration using specialized chips. In this case, inference is optimized through the use of FPGAs that are programmed to execute specific neural network operations at low power. Data pipelines are streamlined to reduce I/O overhead, and asynchronous processing ensures that even with limited hardware, inference is executed rapidly. Profiling tools help maintain an optimal balance between performance and power consumption.

Healthcare: Revolutionizing Patient Care and Diagnostics

In the healthcare sector, Llama-based solutions are making significant contributions towards improving patient outcomes and streamlining complex medical processes. The chapter highlights multiple case studies where these advanced language models aid in tasks such as:

- **Diagnostics and Treatment Planning:** By swiftly analyzing patient histories, medical literature, and real-time data, Llama models assist healthcare providers in identifying potential diagnoses and crafting personalized treatment plans. This not only accelerates the decision-making process but also increases diagnostic accuracy.
- **Patient Data Management:** The capability of these models to efficiently parse and categorize massive volumes of patient data facilitates more effective electronic health record (EHR) management. This enables medical institutions to maintain up-to-date records and ensures that critical patient information is easily accessible.
- **Medical Research and Literature Analysis:** Researchers benefit from the models' ability to sift through expansive bodies of medical literature, extract relevant findings, and even generate insightful summaries that accelerate the pace of clinical research.

Finance: Enhancing Security, Efficiency, and Customer Engagement

The financial sector, known for its reliance on accurate and timely information, has been quick to adopt Llama-based tools. Within this domain, the chapter discusses how these models are being used to:

- **Strengthen Fraud Detection and Risk Management:** By analyzing patterns in transaction data and identifying anomalies, Llama models contribute to more robust fraud detection systems. Their ability to process large datasets in near real-time allows financial institutions to react quickly to potential threats.
- **Automate Routine Reporting and Data Summarization:** Llama-powered solutions are streamlining the creation of detailed financial reports, allowing analysts to focus on strategic decision-making rather than repetitive tasks. This automation greatly enhances operational efficiency.
- **Improve Customer Interaction and Personalization:** Financial service providers are deploying intelligent chatbots and virtual assistants that utilize these models to offer personalized advice and support. This increases customer satisfaction and engagement by ensuring clients receive responses that are both relevant and timely.

Customer Service: Redefining Support with Intelligent Interaction

In an era where customer satisfaction directly impacts brand reputation, the customer service industry has embraced the Llama series as a powerful tool for enhancing support infrastructure. Key highlights include:

- **Intelligent Chatbots and Virtual Assistants:** The Llama models empower customer support systems to handle queries efficiently, providing users with clear, helpful, and context-aware responses. Whether addressing frequently asked questions or solving more intricate issues, these models improve both the speed and quality of service.
- **Multilingual and Context-Sensitive Support:** With the ability to understand and generate human-like responses in multiple languages, Llama-based systems are particularly valuable in global markets. They ensure that customers receive consistent, high-quality interactions regardless of geographical or cultural differences.
- **Seamless Integration with CRM Systems:** By integrating with customer relationship management (CRM) software, these models help maintain detailed

logs of interactions, facilitating a more personalized follow-up and a deeper understanding of customer needs.

Expanding Horizons: Education, Logistics, and Media

Beyond the core industries of healthcare, finance, and customer service, the chapter also delves into the broader implications of Llama model deployments in other vital sectors:

- **Education:** The educational landscape is being transformed by AI through personalized tutoring systems, automated grading, and intelligent course recommendation engines. Llama models assist educators in delivering customized learning experiences that address individual student needs, making education more accessible and effective.
- **Logistics:** In logistics and supply chain management, these models aid in optimizing routes, forecasting demand, and managing inventory. By processing a multitude of variables and historical data, Llama-driven systems contribute to more efficient and cost-effective operations.
- **Media and Content Generation:** For media professionals and content creators, the Llama series offers tools for generating high-quality, engaging content. From drafting news articles to creating detailed marketing materials, these models empower creatives to produce work that is both compelling and contextually rich.

Demonstrating Versatility and Effectiveness

A central theme throughout the chapter is the demonstration of the versatility and effectiveness of Llama, Llama2, and Llama3. The models' ability to be tailored to different data types, industry-specific requirements, and operational constraints underlines their adaptability. Each case study reinforces the notion that these models are not one-dimensional tools; they are multi-faceted systems capable of driving tangible business outcomes and fostering innovation.

- **Addressing Complex NLP Challenges:** One of the standout strengths of the Llama series is their adeptness at tackling complex NLP challenges. Whether it is interpreting ambiguous language, managing large-scale data inputs, or generating nuanced text responses, the models have been rigorously tested in settings where precision is crucial. The detailed exploration provided in this chapter serves as a testament to their robust design and sophisticated algorithms, which are continuously evolving to meet the emerging needs of various industries.

- **Bridging the Gap Between Research and Real-World Implementation:** By highlighting successful real-world applications, this chapter bridges the gap between theoretical advancements and tangible business applications. It showcases how academic research, when integrated with practical deployment strategies, can yield tools that are both innovative and highly effective in solving real-world problems. The detailed case studies offer insights into best practices for implementation, common challenges faced during deployment, and the ultimate impact on operational efficiency and customer satisfaction.
- **Ethical Considerations and Future Perspectives:** As this chapter illuminates the multifaceted applications of the Llama series, it also addresses the ethical considerations inherent in deploying AI at scale. With greater power comes the responsibility to ensure that these models are used in a manner that is transparent, fair, and respectful of user privacy. The discussion includes best practices for mitigating biases, safeguarding data, and ensuring that AI advancements contribute to equitable outcomes for all stakeholders.

Batch Processing with Llama

Batch processing is a critical strategy in modern machine learning systems, particularly when dealing with large language models (LLMs) such as Llama. Unlike traditional real-time inference that processes one request at a time, batch processing aggregates multiple requests and handles them simultaneously. This approach leverages the inherent parallelism available in contemporary hardware and software frameworks to reduce per-instance overhead, streamline computations, and improve overall system efficiency.

When applied to Llama models, batch processing can result in significant performance improvements. By combining similar inference tasks, it is possible to optimize data loading, accelerate vectorized computations, and fully utilize specialized hardware such as GPUs and TPUs. In this guide, we will explore the mechanics behind batch processing, discuss its advantages and trade-offs, and offer detailed scenarios to illustrate how this strategy can be implemented in production systems.

Fundamentals of Batch Processing

At its core, batch processing involves the grouping of multiple independent inference requests into a single computational batch. This aggregated batch is then fed into the model in one go. The benefits include:

- **Reduced Overhead**: By combining multiple requests, the fixed computational overhead per inference call (such as data transfers and initialization costs) is amortized over many instances.

- **Optimized Resource Utilization**: Modern hardware, especially GPUs, is optimized for handling large arrays and matrices simultaneously, making it ideal for batch processing.
- **Enhanced Throughput**: Processing batches rather than individual requests can drastically increase the number of inferences per second.

Implementing Batch Processing in Llama

For Llama models, which typically operate on large and complex data representations, batch processing follows these general steps:

- **Request Aggregation:** Incoming inference requests are temporarily stored in a queue or buffer until a predefined batch size or timeout is reached.
- **Data Preparation:** The queued requests are preprocessed simultaneously. This might involve tokenization, normalization, and conversion to model-friendly tensor formats.
- **Batch Formation:** Preprocessed data from multiple requests is combined into a single batch. This process requires aligning input dimensions and ensuring consistency across the batch.
- **Model Inference:** The aggregated batch is fed into the Llama model, allowing for parallel computations across the batch.
- **Response Distribution:** After inference, the model's outputs are de-batched and returned to the respective requesters.

Key Advantages and Considerations

Batch processing improves computational efficiency and throughput by reducing per-instance overhead and leveraging hardware parallelism; however, it introduces a slight waiting delay for accumulating requests and requires careful management of memory and system complexity.

Benefits of Batch Processing

- **Enhanced Computational Efficiency:** Batch processing allows Llama models to leverage vectorized operations and parallel processing capabilities inherent in deep learning libraries. For instance, operations such as matrix multiplications, which are fundamental to transformer architectures, are optimized when performed on larger data sets. This leads to a more efficient use of computational resources.
- **Improved Throughput**: By processing multiple requests in parallel, overall system throughput is significantly increased. This is particularly beneficial in

environments where numerous simultaneous requests are common, such as chatbots, recommendation systems, or real-time translation services.

- **Reduced Latency per Request:** Although individual requests might experience slight delays while waiting in the batch queue, the overall latency per request can be minimized through optimized data pipeline management and efficient processing. In many cases, the trade-off between waiting time and batch efficiency results in faster overall response times.
- **Scalability:** Batch processing is inherently scalable. As the volume of requests increases, the system can dynamically adjust batch sizes or allocate additional resources (such as more GPU instances) to maintain optimal performance.

Potential Trade-offs and Challenges

- **Increased Waiting Time:** The primary trade-off in batch processing is the slight delay introduced while waiting for a batch to fill up. In latency-critical applications, this delay must be carefully managed through adaptive batching techniques that balance throughput with real-time responsiveness.
- **Complexity in Implementation:** Implementing a robust batch processing system can be complex. Developers must handle queuing, asynchronous data handling, error management, and response de-batching. Additionally, ensuring that the preprocessing steps can handle variable batch sizes without errors requires careful system design.
- **Memory and Resource Constraints:** Larger batch sizes mean higher memory usage. For resource-constrained environments or when processing particularly large data inputs, it may be necessary to carefully tune batch sizes to avoid memory overflow or excessive computational overhead.

Detailed Strategies for Implementing Batch Processing with Llama

Implementing batch processing with Llama involves optimizing data input handling, parallelizing inference for efficiency, and leveraging GPU acceleration to process large text corpora efficiently. Key strategies include batching requests, minimizing memory overhead, and using model quantization for faster execution without compromising accuracy.

Dynamic Batch Sizing

Dynamic batch sizing refers to adjusting the batch size in real-time based on the current workload, system load, and performance requirements. Instead of using a fixed batch size, the system monitors incoming request rates and system performance to determine the optimal batch size at any given time.

Implementation Strategies

- **Threshold-based Batching:** Set a minimum and maximum threshold for batch sizes. If the incoming request rate is low, process the batch when the minimum threshold is reached or after a timeout. If the rate is high, allow the batch to grow up to the maximum threshold.
- **Adaptive Algorithms:** Implement machine learning algorithms that predict optimal batch sizes based on historical data and real-time performance metrics.
- **Priority Handling:** For systems with variable priority requests, implement mechanisms to process high-priority requests with smaller batches or even individually, while lower-priority tasks are batched more aggressively.

Real-world Scenario: Chatbot Interaction

Imagine a real-time chatbot deployed on a popular messaging platform. During peak hours, the system receives hundreds of messages per second. Using dynamic batch sizing, the chatbot aggregates messages into batches of 50–100, ensuring that high traffic is processed efficiently without excessive waiting time. During off-peak hours, the system switches to smaller batches to minimize latency, ensuring that individual user interactions remain snappy and responsive.

Efficient Data Preparation and Preprocessing

It involves cleaning, transforming, and structuring raw data to enhance the accuracy and performance of NLP models. This includes tasks such as tokenization, removing noise, handling missing values, and normalizing text to ensure high-quality input for training AI systems.

Tokenization and Normalization

Llama models typically require input data to be tokenized and normalized before inference. When processing batches:

- **Parallel Tokenization:** Utilize multi-threading or asynchronous operations to tokenize multiple inputs simultaneously.
- **Batch Tokenization Libraries:** Use libraries that support batch tokenization, which can process a list of texts and convert them into the required tensor format in one go.

- **Caching Common Preprocessing Results:** For frequently seen inputs (like common phrases or questions), cache the tokenized result to avoid redundant computations.

Data Transformation and Padding

Handling variable-length inputs is a common challenge. Batches must have consistent dimensions:

- **Padding and Masking:** Implement padding to ensure that all inputs in a batch have the same length. Use masking to ignore padded values during inference.
- **Efficient Memory Management:** When forming batches, use memory pooling techniques to allocate large contiguous memory blocks for the entire batch, reducing fragmentation and speeding up data transfers.

Scenario: Document Summarization Service

A cloud-based document summarization service handles requests to summarize long documents. Each document varies in length. The system preprocesses multiple documents in a batch, tokenizes them simultaneously, pads them to a consistent length, and then feeds them into the Llama model. This strategy not only speeds up inference but also ensures that memory is used efficiently, enabling the service to handle high volumes of requests without degradation in performance.

Integration with High-Performance Hardware

It enables NLP and AI models to operate efficiently by leveraging advanced GPUs, TPUs, and specialized accelerators. This enhances processing speed, reduces latency, and enables large-scale model training and real-time inference for complex applications.

GPU and TPU Acceleration

Batch processing is particularly effective when combined with GPU or TPU acceleration:

- **Vectorized Operations:** GPUs are designed for parallel computation. When you feed a batch into a GPU-accelerated Llama model, operations such as matrix multiplications are performed in parallel across the entire batch.
- **Optimized Data Transfer:** Use asynchronous data transfer methods to move data between CPU and GPU memory. This can be achieved through stream-based processing, where data is preloaded into GPU memory while previous batches are being processed.

- **Multi-GPU Systems:** For extremely high throughput, distribute batches across multiple GPUs, balancing the load to avoid bottlenecks.

Scenario: Real-Time Translation Application

Consider a real-time language translation service that processes hundreds of sentences per minute. The system aggregates incoming sentences into batches and leverages a multi-GPU cluster for translation. As each batch is processed, optimized data pipelines ensure that the sentences are rapidly tokenized, transferred to GPU memory, and processed in parallel. The result is a translation service that delivers high throughput with minimal latency, even during peak usage periods.

Software Tools and Frameworks

Software tools and frameworks play a crucial role in building ethical and responsible NLP applications by providing capabilities for bias detection, privacy preservation, explainability, and fairness auditing.

Utilizing Deep Learning Libraries: Modern deep learning frameworks such as TensorFlow, PyTorch, and JAX offer built-in support for batch processing:

- **TensorFlow Data Pipelines:** TensorFlow's tf.data API allows you to build highly efficient input pipelines that can batch, prefetch, and shuffle data seamlessly.
- **PyTorch DataLoader:** PyTorch provides a DataLoader class that can automatically handle batching, parallel data loading, and even custom collate functions to prepare data exactly as needed.
- **JAX and XLA:** For high-performance numerical computations, JAX with its XLA compiler can optimize batch processing operations to run efficiently on both CPUs and GPUs.

Custom Middleware and Queuing Systems: For production-grade systems, consider integrating middleware that manages request queuing and batch formation:

- **Message Queues:** Systems such as Apache Kafka or RabbitMQ can be used to buffer incoming requests, ensuring that they are aggregated into batches efficiently.
- **Custom Batch Managers:** Develop custom microservices dedicated to batch management. These services can monitor request rates, dynamically adjust batch sizes, and distribute batches to inference servers.

Scenario: E-commerce Recommendation Engine

An e-commerce platform uses a recommendation engine powered by a Llama model to suggest products based on user behavior. Incoming user data is first queued in a

Kafka stream. A custom batch manager then aggregates these requests into batches, preprocesses the data using PyTorch's Data Loader, and feeds the batches into the Llama model running on a GPU cluster. This seamless integration ensures that recommendations are delivered rapidly and efficiently, even during high-traffic events such as flash sales.

Best Practices and Advanced Techniques

- **Balancing Throughput and Latency:** Optimizing batch sizes and timeouts ensures high throughput without incurring unacceptable delays, striking a balance between maximizing efficiency and maintaining real-time responsiveness.
- **Adaptive Timeouts:** Implementing adaptive timeouts can help balance the benefits of larger batches against the need for low latency. If the system detects that incoming request rates are low, it can reduce the timeout period to ensure that requests are not delayed unnecessarily.
- **Monitoring and Feedback Loops:** Establish comprehensive monitoring systems to track key performance metrics such as:
    - **Batch Processing Time:** Time taken to collect, process, and de-batch the requests.
    - **Queue Length:** The number of requests waiting to be batched.
    - **Response Latency:** End-to-end latency from request arrival to response delivery.

  By analyzing these metrics, you can dynamically adjust batch sizes and timeout values to maintain optimal performance.

Fault Tolerance and Error Handling

Graceful Degradation: In cases where batch processing may lead to delays or system failures, implement fallback mechanisms that allow the system to revert to individual inference processing. This ensures that even if batch processing encounters issues, the system can continue operating, albeit at a lower throughput.

Retry Mechanisms and Circuit Breakers: Integrate robust error-handling strategies, such as:

- **Retries:** Automatically reprocess failed batches a set number of times before flagging an error.
- **Circuit Breakers:** Temporarily halt batch processing if system metrics indicate that performance is degrading, then resume once the issue is resolved.

Performance Testing and Benchmarking

Regularly simulating workloads and using automated benchmarking tools ensures that batch processing performance meets expectations, enabling continual tuning and optimization.

- **Simulation of Different Workloads:** To fine-tune batch processing parameters, simulate different workloads that mirror your production environment. Vary batch sizes, request rates, and data complexities to understand how these factors influence performance.
- **Continuous Benchmarking:** Incorporate continuous benchmarking into your development cycle. Regularly test your batch processing system under controlled conditions to ensure that optimizations remain effective as your data and models evolve.
- **Scenario: A/B Testing for Batch Strategies:** An online service performs A/B testing to compare fixed batch sizes versus dynamic batch sizing. By routing a portion of traffic through each system, the service can collect real-world performance data and adjust configurations accordingly, leading to incremental improvements in throughput and response times over time.

Parallelization Techniques

Parallelization is the practice of dividing a computational task into smaller subtasks that can be executed simultaneously, thereby reducing overall processing time and increasing system throughput. In the context of high-performance computing and modern machine learning systems, parallelization techniques are indispensable. They not only accelerate data processing but also optimize resource utilization across multi-core CPUs, GPUs, clusters, or distributed systems.

The Need for Parallelization

- **Performance Boost:** As data sizes grow and models become increasingly complex, sequential processing becomes a bottleneck. Parallel processing allows multiple operations to occur concurrently, significantly reducing latency.
- **Scalability:** Systems designed with parallelization in mind can scale horizontally (across multiple machines) or vertically (by adding more cores/threads), making them well-suited for handling high workloads.
- **Efficient Resource Utilization:** Modern hardware architectures–such as multi-core processors, GPUs, and TPUs–are designed to perform many operations in parallel. By matching the computational strategy to the hardware capabilities, developers can achieve far greater efficiency.

Overview of Parallelization Strategies

The key parallelization techniques include:

- **Data Parallelism:** Splitting the dataset into parts and processing each part simultaneously.
- **Model Parallelism:** Dividing a large model into segments that are processed concurrently.
- **Pipeline Parallelism:** Breaking the processing into sequential stages that overlap in execution.
- **Task-based Parallelism:** Running independent tasks concurrently, often using multi-threading or multi-processing.
- **Asynchronous Execution:** Utilizing non-blocking operations to ensure that the system is continuously active, without waiting for each operation to finish before starting the next.

Data Parallelism

Data parallelism involves partitioning a large dataset into smaller chunks and processing each chunk concurrently. This technique is particularly effective in scenarios where the same operation must be applied repeatedly over different data samples.

Implementation Details

- **Batch Division:** Data is divided into mini-batches, which are then processed in parallel. For example, in training neural networks, each mini-batch is passed through the network simultaneously on different processors.
- **Synchronization:** After processing, the results (such as gradients in training scenarios) are aggregated to update the model parameters. Techniques such as parameter averaging or gradient reduction are used to maintain consistency.
- **Hardware Utilization:** Data parallelism is especially beneficial on GPUs, which are designed to perform matrix operations on large batches efficiently.

Scenario: Large-Scale Image Classification

Imagine a system that classifies millions of images. By dividing the dataset into smaller chunks, each GPU in a multi-GPU setup processes a different subset of images concurrently. After processing, the classification results are combined to form the final output. This approach drastically reduces the total time required for classification compared to processing each image sequentially.

Model Parallelism

Model parallelism splits a large model into smaller, independent parts, which are then executed concurrently. This method is essential when the model is too large to fit into the memory of a single processing unit.

Implementation Details

- **Layer-wise Partitioning:** In deep neural networks, different layers or groups of layers can be allocated to different devices. For instance, early layers might be processed on one GPU, while deeper layers are handled on another.
- **Inter-Device Communication:** To maintain the flow of data, intermediate outputs are transferred between devices. High-speed interconnects (such as NVLink) help minimize the communication overhead.
- **Synchronization Barriers:** Ensuring that devices remain in sync is crucial. Barrier synchronization points are used to wait for all devices to complete their computation before proceeding.

Scenario: Processing a Transformer Model

Consider a transformer-based language model that is too large to be loaded on a single GPU. By partitioning the transformer architecture into segments (for example, the encoder on one device and the decoder on another), the model's computations are distributed. Although data must be exchanged between devices, this approach enables the handling of massive models that would otherwise be infeasible on a single device.

Pipeline Parallelism

Pipeline parallelism breaks down a computational process into a series of sequential stages, each of which can be executed in parallel. As one stage processes the next input, another stage can simultaneously process the previous input, creating an assembly-line effect.

Implementation Details

- **Stage Division:** The processing task is divided into discrete stages (for example, data preprocessing, model inference, and postprocessing). Each stage is allocated a specific segment of the computational resource.
- **Overlapping Execution:** While one batch is being processed in stage one, a previous batch is processed in stage two, and so on. This overlapping maximizes resource usage.
- **Buffering and Queues:** Intermediate results are stored in buffers or queues, which allow different stages to work asynchronously and reduce idle time.

Scenario: Real-Time Video Processing

In a real-time video processing system, frames are processed through multiple stages: decoding, frame enhancement, object detection, and postprocessing. By setting up a pipeline, while one frame is being decoded, another frame is undergoing enhancement, and yet another is processed for object detection. This parallel pipeline ensures that all parts of the system are busy simultaneously, greatly enhancing overall throughput.

Task-Based Parallelism

Task-based parallelism focuses on dividing the computational workload into independent tasks that can be executed concurrently. This approach is useful when different tasks do not rely on each other's outputs.

Implementation Details

- **Multi-threading:** In multi-threaded environments, threads share the same memory space and can run concurrently on different cores. This is ideal for lightweight, frequent tasks.
- **Multi-processing:** For more CPU-intensive tasks, multiple processes can be spawned, each with its own memory space. This avoids the Global Interpreter Lock (GIL) issues in languages such as Python.
- **Task Scheduling:** Modern programming frameworks (such as Python's concurrent.futures or C++'s thread libraries) include task scheduling mechanisms that automatically distribute tasks across available processing units.

Scenario: Web Server Request Handling

A high-traffic web server handles numerous client requests simultaneously. By employing task-based parallelism, each request is processed as an independent task. The server assigns these tasks to different threads or processes, ensuring that one slow operation does not block others. This results in improved response times and better overall system performance.

Asynchronous Execution Models

Asynchronous execution allows tasks to be initiated without waiting for prior operations to complete, making it an effective technique for handling I/O-bound operations and network requests.

Implementation Details

- **Event Loops:** Asynchronous frameworks, such as Node.js or Python's asyncio, operate on an event loop that manages non-blocking tasks. This means that while one task waits for an I/O operation, another can be executed.

- **Callbacks and Promises:** In asynchronous programming, callbacks or promises are used to handle the completion of tasks. These constructs allow the program to continue executing while waiting for operations to finish.
- **Concurrent I/O:** Asynchronous execution is particularly beneficial for applications that interact with databases or remote APIs, as it minimizes idle time caused by waiting for responses.

Scenario: Real-Time Data Streaming

A real-time data streaming service processes live sensor data from thousands of IoT devices. Using asynchronous execution, the service can initiate data fetches and process streams concurrently. As data from one sensor is being processed, the service can simultaneously receive and handle data from another. This ensures a continuous and efficient data flow, which is critical for time-sensitive applications.

Combining Parallelization Techniques

In many real-world applications, a combination of parallelization techniques is employed to maximize performance. Hybrid approaches can leverage the strengths of each method while mitigating their individual weaknesses.

Integrated Systems

- **Data and Model Parallelism:** In large-scale training of deep learning models, data parallelism can be combined with model parallelism. Each device processes a portion of the data, while parts of the model are split across devices.
- **Pipeline and Task-Based Parallelism:** In complex data processing pipelines, certain stages may be parallelized using task-based approaches while others operate in a pipelined fashion. For example, a system might use asynchronous I/O to fetch data (task-based) and then process it through a series of stages (pipeline parallelism).

Scenario: End-to-End Machine Learning Workflow

Consider an end-to-end machine learning workflow that includes data ingestion, preprocessing, model inference, and result aggregation. In such a system:

- **Data Ingestion:** Asynchronous techniques handle high-throughput data streams.
- **Preprocessing:** Data is batched and processed in parallel (data parallelism).
- **Model Inference:** The model employs a combination of model parallelism (for large models) and pipeline parallelism (for sequential stages).
- **Result Aggregation:** Task-based parallelism is used to combine outputs and prepare final responses.

This integrated approach ensures that each component of the system operates at optimal efficiency, providing a seamless, high-performance solution.

Best Practices for Implementing Parallelization

It includes efficiently dividing tasks into smaller independent units, minimizing inter-process communication to reduce overhead, optimizing data locality, and leveraging appropriate parallel computing frameworks (for example, multiprocessing in Python, CUDA for GPUs, or distributed computing with Spark) to maximize performance and scalability.

- **Profiling and Benchmarking:** Use profiling tools (such as NVIDIA Nsight, Intel VTune, or Python's cProfile) to identify bottlenecks. Regularly benchmark your system to understand the performance gains from parallelization.
- **Load Balancing:** Ensure that tasks are distributed evenly across processing units. Imbalanced workloads can lead to idle resources and bottlenecks.
- **Error Handling:** Implement robust error-handling mechanisms to deal with failures in parallel tasks. Use retry strategies and timeout mechanisms where necessary.
- **Scalability Testing:** Simulate various loads to test how your system scales. Adjust batch sizes, number of threads, or processes based on empirical results.
- **Hardware-Aware Optimization:** Tailor your parallelization strategy to your available hardware. For example, multi-threading may work best on multi-core CPUs, while GPUs require data parallelism to fully utilize their architecture.
- **Monitoring and Adaptation:** Continuously monitor system performance and adapt your parallelization strategies in response to changes in workload patterns or hardware configurations.

Hardware and Software Optimizations for Llama Models

Modern large language models such as Llama are computationally intensive, demanding both high throughput and low latency in real-world applications. To meet these demands, a dual approach–leveraging hardware optimizations alongside software improvements–is essential. This guide explores a range of techniques that maximize model performance, from utilizing specialized hardware accelerators to fine-tuning software frameworks and code-level optimizations. Whether you are deploying Llama in the cloud, on-premises, or at the edge, these strategies can dramatically enhance inference speed, resource utilization, and scalability.

Hardware Optimizations

Hardware optimizations focus on harnessing the full potential of physical devices to accelerate computations and manage large models efficiently. Here are several key strategies:

Utilizing Specialized Hardware Accelerators

Specialized hardware, such as GPUs, TPUs, and FPGAs, significantly enhances Llama model performance by parallelizing complex computations, reducing inference latency, and improving scalability. Leveraging optimized libraries such as CUDA, cuDNN, and TensorRT ensures that these accelerators are used to their full potential.

GPU Acceleration:

- **Overview**: Graphics Processing Units (GPUs) are designed for massively parallel computation, ideal for the matrix multiplications and tensor operations inherent in Llama models. Llama 3 and Llama 4 models, with their large parameter sizes (for example, 3B, 7B, 13B for Llama 3, and up to 70B for Llama 4), benefit greatly from GPUs that can handle parallel tensor operations efficiently.
- **Implementation**: Use frameworks such as **CUDA**, **cuDNN**, and **TensorRT** that are optimized for GPU architectures. Batch multiple inference requests to leverage the parallel processing capabilities of GPUs effectively, especially for large Llama models.
- For **Llama 4**, with its higher parameter count and computational demand, GPUs with high memory (for example, NVIDIA A100) can distribute tensor operations across multiple GPUs to reduce inference time.
- **Scenario**: In a real-time **translation service**, sentences are batched and processed on a multi-GPU cluster, reducing inference time by executing parallel computations over large matrices. The **Llama 4** model, with its enhanced capability for understanding complex contexts, can be deployed across several GPUs to handle multiple language translations in parallel, ensuring a low-latency response.

TPU Deployment:

- **Overview**: Tensor Processing Units (TPUs) offer custom hardware acceleration tailored for deep learning tasks, often achieving higher performance-per-watt compared to GPUs. Llama 3 and Llama 4 benefit from TPUs due to their high throughput and optimized architecture for transformer-based models such as Llama.
- **Implementation**: Integrate TPUs using frameworks such as **TensorFlow**,

which natively support TPU execution. TPUs excel in large-scale training and inference of **Llama 3** and **Llama 4**, enabling faster computations with minimal energy consumption, making them suitable for both training and deployment.

- **Scenario**: A cloud-based **document summarization service** utilizes TPUs to process thousands of pages concurrently. The Llama 4 model, with its advanced summarization capabilities, leverages TPUs to handle high-volume processing with lower energy consumption, providing real-time summaries for large document sets efficiently.

FPGA-Based Solutions:

- **Overview**: Field-Programmable Gate Arrays (FPGAs) offer flexible, custom hardware solutions for low-latency and power-efficient inference, especially in edge computing. While Llama 3 models can already benefit from FPGA deployment, **Llama 4** requires more computational power, making FPGA-based solutions particularly useful for edge devices that need to process inferences locally.
- **Implementation**: Optimize the Llama model for an FPGA by designing custom circuits for specific operations (for example, matrix multiplication) and using hardware description languages (HDLs) to fine-tune performance. For **Llama 3**, FPGA optimization might be simpler, but for **Llama 4**, custom logic could be used to handle the intensive computational load.
- **Scenario**: An **IoT network** for real-time **anomaly detection** on edge devices integrates FPGA-based accelerators. Llama 3 models, being smaller, can run directly on the FPGA for rapid processing of sensor data, while **Llama 4** might require offloading some computational tasks to the cloud or optimized local systems to balance power efficiency with processing power, ensuring quick responses in safety-critical systems.

Memory and Data Transfer Optimizations

Efficient memory allocation through pooling and contiguous storage, combined with asynchronous data transfers over high-speed interconnects, minimizes latency and maximizes throughput in Llama models.

Memory Management:

- **Efficient Allocation:** Use techniques such as memory pooling and contiguous memory allocation to reduce fragmentation and speed up data access.
- **Caching Strategies:** Employ hardware caches effectively by ensuring data locality. For instance, align data structures to cache lines and minimize cache misses.
- **Scenario:** In a high-volume recommendation system, memory pooling allows

large batches of user data to be processed without frequent memory allocation overhead, resulting in smoother and faster inference cycles.

Optimized Data Transfers:

- **High-Speed Interconnects:** Utilize technologies such as NVLink or PCIe 4.0 to minimize latency in data transfers between the CPU and GPUs/TPUs.
- **Asynchronous Transfers:** Implement asynchronous data transfers to overlap computation and communication, reducing idle times.
- **Scenario:** In a video processing pipeline, asynchronous data transfers ensure that while one frame is being processed on the GPU, the next frame is already being loaded, leading to continuous, high-speed operation.

Hardware-Specific Tuning

Device-Specific Optimizations:

- **Overclocking and Thermal Management:** In controlled environments, fine-tuning clock speeds and managing thermal profiles can yield marginal performance boosts without sacrificing stability.
- **Firmware and Driver Updates:** Regularly update device drivers and firmware to benefit from the latest performance enhancements and bug fixes.
- **Scenario:** A research lab running intensive Llama model simulations updates its GPU drivers and fine-tunes thermal management settings, resulting in a 10% boost in throughput during peak computational loads.

Software Optimizations

Software optimizations involve refining code, algorithms, and frameworks to reduce overhead and improve execution speed. Here are key strategies:

Framework and Library Enhancements

Optimized Deep Learning Libraries:

- **Framework Choice:** Use state-of-the-art frameworks such as TensorFlow, PyTorch, or JAX that include built-in optimizations for parallel processing and hardware acceleration.
- **Library Versions:** Keep libraries up-to-date to benefit from the latest performance improvements and bug fixes.
- **Scenario:** A sentiment analysis tool built on PyTorch upgrades to the latest version, which includes advanced JIT compilation, resulting in a notable reduction in inference time for Llama-based text analysis.

Specialized Mathematical Libraries:

- **BLAS and cuBLAS:** Incorporate high-performance linear algebra libraries such as Intel MKL, OpenBLAS, or NVIDIA's cuBLAS for fast matrix operations.
- **XLA Compiler:** Utilize compilers such as TensorFlow's XLA to optimize the computational graph, eliminating unnecessary operations and fusing kernels.
- **Scenario:** A financial modeling application uses XLA to compile Llama model operations, streamlining computations and significantly reducing runtime for complex forecasting tasks.

Code-Level Optimizations

Profiling and Bottleneck Identification:

- **Tools:** Use profiling tools (for example, NVIDIA Nsight, Intel VTune, or Python's cProfile) to identify slow sections of the code.
- **Iterative Refinement:** Regularly profile and refactor code to eliminate bottlenecks, focusing on optimizing critical sections such as data preprocessing and model inference.
- **Scenario:** A natural language processing (NLP) startup profiles its Llama-based chatbot and discovers that data serialization is a bottleneck; by optimizing this process, response times improve by 20%.

Memory and Resource Management:

- **Efficient Memory Use:** Optimize memory allocation and deallocation patterns to reduce latency. Implement memory pooling and reuse buffers for recurrent computations.
- **Data Locality:** Reorganize data structures to enhance cache performance and minimize latency.
- **Scenario:** A large-scale content moderation system reorganizes its data structures to ensure better cache locality, reducing inference delays and improving throughput during peak usage.

Algorithmic and Model-Level Optimizations

Model Pruning and Quantization:

- **Pruning:** Remove redundant or less critical weights from the Llama model to reduce its size and computational load without significant loss of accuracy.
- **Quantization:** Convert model parameters from floating-point to lower-precision formats (for example, int8 or FP16) to speed up inference and decrease memory consumption.

- **Scenario:** An edge computing application deploys a pruned and quantized Llama model, reducing its footprint by 50% and enabling real-time inference on low-power devices.

Efficient Batch Processing and Inference Scheduling:

- **Batching:** Group multiple inference requests into a single batch to amortize overhead and maximize hardware utilization.
- **Dynamic Scheduling:** Implement adaptive scheduling algorithms to balance throughput and latency based on real-time workload variations.
- **Scenario:** A real-time translation service uses dynamic batching to process variable-length inputs efficiently, balancing latency and throughput to meet strict service-level agreements (SLAs).

Combining Hardware and Software Optimizations

Achieving peak performance with Llama models often requires a holistic approach that combines both hardware and software strategies.

Synergistic Effects

Hardware-Software Co-Design:

- Develop software solutions that are specifically optimized for the underlying hardware. For example, design data pipelines and inference routines that maximize the throughput of GPUs or TPUs.
- **Scenario:** A multimedia content delivery platform co-designs its software stack to fully exploit the parallel processing capabilities of its GPU cluster, achieving seamless scaling during high-demand periods.

Real-Time Monitoring and Feedback:

- Implement monitoring systems to track hardware utilization (for example, CPU/GPU loads, memory usage) and software performance (for example, inference latency, batch processing time). Use this data to continuously adjust configurations and optimize performance.
- **Scenario:** An AI-powered recommendation engine continuously monitors system performance and dynamically reallocates resources between CPUs and GPUs to maintain optimal inference speeds during traffic spikes.

Integrated Optimization Pipelines

Automated Tuning Systems:

- Develop systems that automatically adjust hardware and software parameters based on current performance metrics. These systems can use machine learning to predict optimal configurations and dynamically reconfigure the environment.
- **Scenario:** A cloud-based service for automated content creation integrates an automated tuning system that optimizes both batch sizes and hardware allocation in real time, ensuring consistent performance even as workloads change.

End-to-End Optimization Frameworks:

- Build comprehensive frameworks that manage the entire lifecycle of model inference–from data ingestion and preprocessing to model execution and output handling–ensuring that every component is finely tuned.
- **Scenario:** A research lab implements an end-to-end optimization framework for its Llama models, resulting in a streamlined process that reduces overall inference time by 35% compared to a non-optimized baseline.

Best Practices and Future Directions

Continuously monitor and benchmark system performance while adapting to emerging hardware and software innovations, ensuring that optimization strategies evolve with advancing technology and changing workloads.

Continuous Monitoring and Adaptive Tuning

- **Monitoring Tools:** Implement comprehensive monitoring tools (for example, Prometheus, Grafana) to collect real-time metrics on hardware utilization and software performance.
- **Adaptive Optimization:** Use feedback loops and automated tuning systems to adapt to changing workloads and hardware conditions continuously.

Staying Current with Technological Advances

- **Research and Updates:** Keep abreast of the latest advancements in both hardware (new GPUs, TPUs, FPGAs) and software (framework updates, compiler optimizations) to continuously integrate improvements.
- **Community and Collaboration:** Engage with the research community and participate in conferences to share insights and collaborate on new optimization strategies.

Experimentation and Benchmarking

- **Controlled Experiments:** Regularly perform controlled experiments to compare different hardware and software configurations, using standardized benchmarks to assess performance improvements.
- **Documentation:** Document all changes and results meticulously to build a knowledge base that guides future optimization efforts.

Conclusion

In conclusion, optimizing Llama models involves a multi-pronged approach that encompasses a range of strategies aimed at improving inference speed, such as effective batch processing and robust parallelization techniques. By intelligently aggregating requests through batch processing, systems can reduce per-instance overhead and fully exploit the computational efficiencies of modern hardware. Meanwhile, parallelization—whether through data, model, pipeline, or task-based methods—ensures that complex operations are distributed and executed concurrently, further accelerating performance. Coupled with targeted hardware and software optimizations, these strategies not only boost throughput and reduce latency but also pave the way for scalable, resilient, and future-proof AI deployments.

In the next chapter, we will explore the critical aspects of deploying Llama models in real-world environments, including various deployment architectures tailored to meet different application needs and scalability considerations to overcome the challenges of growing data volumes and user demands. We will delve into cloud deployment strategies that harness the power of modern cloud platforms for flexibility and cost-efficiency, while also addressing best practices for monitoring and managing deployed Llama models to ensure sustained performance and reliability in production settings.

Multiple Choice Questions

1. Which strategy primarily helps reduce the per-instance overhead in Llama models by grouping multiple requests together?
   a. Data augmentation
   b. Batch processing
   c. Model pruning
   d. Feature scaling
2. One of the key benefits of improving inference speed is:
   a. Increased model size
   b. Reduced latency per request

   c. More complex algorithms

   d. Higher power consumption

3. Which of the following is NOT typically used to improve inference speed?

   a. Batch processing

   b. Parallelization techniques

   c. Reducing hardware resources

   d. Hardware acceleration

4. What is the main advantage of using batch processing in Llama models?

   a. It increases the computational overhead for each request.

   b. It minimizes the per-instance overhead by processing multiple requests simultaneously.

   c. It requires individual processing of each request, ensuring higher accuracy.

   d. It reduces memory usage by processing one request at a time.

5. In batch processing, which step is responsible for aligning input dimensions and ensuring consistency across requests?

   a. Data Aggregation

   b. Data Preprocessing

   c. Batch Formation

   d. Response Distribution

6. A scenario where batch processing is particularly beneficial is:

   a. Processing a single image in a static environment.

   b. Handling thousands of simultaneous queries in a real-time chatbot.

   c. Running a standalone application on a desktop computer.

   d. Performing individual data updates in a database.

7. Data parallelism involves:

   a. Dividing a large model into smaller parts to process different sections simultaneously.

   b. Splitting a dataset into multiple chunks that are processed concurrently.

   c. Executing sequential tasks in a pipeline.

   d. Running tasks asynchronously without any synchronization.

8. Which parallelization technique is most effective when the model is too large to fit into a single device's memory?

   a. Data parallelism

   b. Model parallelism

   c. Pipeline parallelism

   d. Task-based parallelism

9. In pipeline parallelism, what is the primary benefit?

   a. It processes all tasks sequentially without overlap.

   b. It allows different stages of processing to run concurrently, much like an assembly line.

   c. It increases latency by waiting for each stage to complete.

   d. It duplicates the model across multiple devices.

10. Asynchronous execution is particularly useful for:

    a. CPU-bound operations that require heavy computation.

    b. I/O-bound tasks and network requests where non-blocking operations are beneficial.

    c. Ensuring tasks are executed sequentially.

    d. Reducing parallelism in GPU computations.

Answers

1. b
2. b
3. c
4. b
5. c
6. b
7. b
8. b
9. b
10. b

CHAPTER 8
Deploying Llama Models at Scale

Introduction

In this chapter, we embark on a detailed exploration of deploying Llama models at scale, providing readers with a robust framework for understanding and executing large-scale implementations. You will discover the key principles behind effective deployment architectures and learn how to address scalability challenges that often arise in complex environments. The content is structured to guide you through both theoretical underpinnings and practical applications, ensuring you gain actionable insights into designing resilient systems. By the end of this chapter, you will be equipped with the knowledge to evaluate cloud infrastructure options, apply best practices, and strategically manage your deployment environments for optimal performance.

Furthermore, we delve into the critical considerations that underpin successful large-scale deployments. Readers will learn how to assess and select the right deployment architectures tailored to their unique needs, while also exploring the intricacies of cloud-based solutions and management strategies essential for maintaining robust operations. This chapter not only highlights common pitfalls and challenges but also offers pragmatic solutions and strategic guidelines, empowering you to implement these best practices in real-world scenarios. Whether you are a seasoned practitioner or new to the field, the insights provided here will serve as a valuable roadmap for deploying Llama models efficiently and at scale.

Structure

In this chapter, we will cover the following topics:

- Overview
- Deployment Architectures for Llama Models
- Scalability Considerations and Challenges

- Cloud Deployment Strategies
- Monitoring and Managing Deployed Llama Models

Overview

Deploying Llama models at scale involves a meticulous approach to designing and implementing deployment architectures that can accommodate the intricate requirements of modern machine learning workflows. In this overview, we begin by exploring various deployment architectures tailored for Llama models, examining both on-premises and hybrid setups that ensure high availability and performance. By leveraging containerization, microservices, and orchestration frameworks, organizations can build scalable systems that cater to the dynamic needs of production environments while maintaining the flexibility to adapt as model demands evolve.

Scalability considerations and challenges form a critical aspect of this deployment strategy. As the volume of data and complexity of computations increase, it is essential to address potential bottlenecks and ensure efficient resource utilization. This involves not only optimizing the model architecture and deployment pipeline but also planning for load balancing, fault tolerance, and resource auto-scaling. By understanding these challenges, engineers can design systems that seamlessly scale, ensuring that performance remains robust even under heavy workloads.

Cloud deployment strategies play a pivotal role in modernizing the way Llama models are deployed at scale. Leveraging cloud platforms offers significant advantages in terms of flexibility, cost-effectiveness, and rapid deployment. In this overview, we discuss how to integrate cloud services into your deployment strategy, including the use of serverless architectures, managed container services, and cloud-native monitoring tools. Alongside these strategies, effective monitoring and management of deployed Llama models is crucial. Continuous monitoring, logging, and real-time analytics enable organizations to proactively detect issues, optimize performance, and ensure the reliability of their machine learning operations over time.

In addition to these technical and architectural considerations, this overview emphasizes the importance of incorporating best practices for security, compliance, and operational efficiency into your deployment strategy. Integrating robust CI/CD pipelines, automated testing frameworks, and security monitoring tools can significantly enhance the overall resilience of the system. By addressing potential vulnerabilities early and ensuring compliance with industry standards, organizations can safeguard sensitive data while streamlining the continuous integration and deployment of Llama models. This comprehensive approach not only ensures that the deployment process is smooth and efficient but also prepares your systems for future growth and evolving operational challenges.

Deployment Architecture of Llama Models

The rapid evolution of machine learning has led to the widespread adoption of sophisticated models such as Llama models, which excel at natural language processing and other complex tasks. Deploying these models at scale requires a robust, well-thought-out architecture that not only supports high-performance inference but also ensures reliability, security, and agility. In this document, we delve into the deployment architecture for Llama models, covering every component from data ingestion to model serving, and from scalability and load balancing to monitoring, security, and future-proofing strategies.

By breaking down the architecture into its constituent parts, organizations can design systems that are modular, scalable, and resilient. This comprehensive guide aims to serve as a reference for engineers and architects tasked with implementing Llama models in production environments, ensuring that every aspect–from initial data processing to final model output–is optimized for both current needs and future expansion.

Llama Models and Their Deployment Needs

Llama models are known for their ability to handle complex language-based tasks, including translation, summarization, and content generation. However, deploying these models in real-world applications presents several challenges that demand a thoughtful architectural design.

Why a Robust Deployment Architecture Is Critical?

- **Performance and Resource Utilization:** Llama models often require significant computational power, especially during inference. A well-designed architecture optimizes the use of hardware resources such as CPUs, GPUs, or even specialized accelerators, ensuring that latency is minimized and throughput is maximized.
- **Scalability and Flexibility:** As user demands fluctuate, the system must be able to scale dynamically. Whether through horizontal scaling (adding more instances) or vertical scaling (upgrading the capacity of existing nodes), the architecture must be flexible enough to handle peak loads without degradation in performance.
- **Reliability and Fault Tolerance:** In production environments, downtime is not an option. The architecture must incorporate redundancy, failover mechanisms, and disaster recovery plans to ensure continuous service even in the event of hardware or software failures.
- **Security and Compliance:** Given the sensitive nature of many applications powered by Llama models, securing data at every stage–from ingestion to

inference–is paramount. The deployment architecture should enforce strict access controls, encryption, and adherence to regulatory standards.

Core Components of the Llama Deployment Architecture

A comprehensive deployment architecture for Llama models comprises several interlocking layers. Each component addresses a critical part of the overall system, ensuring that the model is not only served efficiently but also maintained securely and scaled effectively. Below are the core components that make up this architecture.

Data Ingestion and Preprocessing

Data is the foundation of any machine learning model, and for Llama models, ensuring high-quality, real-time, and batch data processing is essential.

- **Multi-Source Data Integration:** Data for Llama models can come from a variety of sources, including databases, APIs, logs, and streaming platforms.
    - **Batch Processing:** Historical data is processed in bulk, often using big data frameworks such as Apache Hadoop or Apache Spark. This data is critical for model training and retraining sessions.
    - **Real-Time Streaming:** For real-time applications such as chatbots or recommendation engines, data is ingested continuously using streaming platforms such as Apache Kafka, AWS Kinesis, or Google Pub/Sub.
- **Automated Data Preprocessing Pipelines:** Raw data must be cleansed, normalized, and transformed before it is used for inference.
    - **Cleansing and Validation:** Removing outliers, handling missing values, and validating data integrity are essential steps.
    - **Transformation and Feature Engineering:** Data transformations include normalization, encoding categorical variables, and generating new features that enhance model accuracy.
    - **Orchestration Tools:** Tools such as Apache Airflow, Prefect, or cloud-native solutions manage the workflow, ensuring that data processing is automated, consistent, and scalable.

Model Serving and Inference

Serving the Llama model is the stage where the preprocessed data is fed into the model, and predictions are returned. This layer must be optimized for both speed and reliability.

- **API Endpoints and Service Layers:** Robust API endpoints and service layers facilitate seamless communication between client applications and deployed Llama models, ensuring secure, scalable, and efficient inference delivery.
  - **RESTful and gRPC APIs:** Exposing the Llama model through standardized APIs allows client applications to interact seamlessly. Frameworks such as FastAPI, Flask, or gRPC facilitate rapid development of these endpoints.
  - **Batch Inference and Streaming Inference:** Depending on the use case, models might serve predictions in batches or in real-time. Batch inference can be scheduled during off-peak hours to process large amounts of data, while streaming inference handles real-time data for immediate responses.
- **Containerization and Orchestration:** It enables seamless packaging, deployment, and scaling of applications by leveraging technologies such as Docker and Kubernetes for consistent and efficient management across diverse environments.
  - **Containerization with Docker:** Packaging the Llama model with all its dependencies ensures consistency across development, testing, and production environments.
  - **Orchestration Using Kubernetes:** Kubernetes manages containerized applications across clusters, providing features such as automated rollouts, scaling, and self-healing, which are critical for maintaining uptime.
- **Inference Optimization Techniques:** These involve strategies such as model quantization, pruning, hardware acceleration, and caching to reduce latency, improve throughput, and enhance the efficiency of model serving in production environments.
  - **Model Quantization and Pruning:** Reducing model size through quantization or pruning helps decrease latency and resource consumption.
  - **Hardware Acceleration:** Leveraging GPUs, TPUs, or even dedicated inference chips can dramatically increase performance, particularly for computationally intensive models.
  - **Caching and Load Reduction:** Implementing caching mechanisms (using Redis or similar technologies) for frequently requested outputs minimizes the computational burden on the model.

Scalability and Load Balancing

To ensure that the deployment can handle a variable load and sudden spikes in demand, scalability and load balancing are essential.

- **Auto-Scaling Strategies:** Automatically adjust resources in real time to meet fluctuating workloads, ensuring optimal performance and cost efficiency.

- **Horizontal Scaling:** Adding more instances of the model service during high-demand periods allows for efficient load distribution.
- **Vertical Scaling:** Upgrading existing instances with more powerful hardware can also boost performance when necessary.
- **Cloud-Based Scaling Options:** Cloud providers such as AWS, Google Cloud, and Azure offer auto-scaling features that dynamically adjust resources based on real-time metrics.

- **Load Balancing Techniques:** These techniques distribute incoming traffic efficiently across multiple servers or instances to ensure optimal resource utilization, prevent bottlenecks, and maintain system performance under varying request loads.
  - **Application Load Balancers:** Solutions such as NGINX, HAProxy, or cloud-native load balancers distribute incoming traffic evenly, preventing any single instance from becoming a bottleneck.
  - **Service Meshes:** Technologies such as Istio or Linkerd can manage microservices communication, ensuring robust routing, security, and observability across the deployment.
- **Performance and Stress Testing:** Regular load testing using tools such as Apache JMeter or Locust helps simulate peak traffic scenarios and ensures that the system can handle expected loads without performance degradation.

Monitoring, Logging, and Maintenance

Ongoing monitoring, logging, and proactive maintenance are critical to ensure that the deployed Llama model remains performant and secure over time.

- **Real-Time Monitoring Systems:** These systems provide continuous visibility into system performance, enabling the proactive identification and resolution of issues to maintain optimal operation. Also, Real-Time Monitoring Systems continuously track critical performance metrics and provide proactive alerts, ensuring swift detection and resolution of issues in the deployment architecture.
  - **Performance Dashboards:** Tools such as Prometheus, Grafana, or cloud-native solutions such as AWS CloudWatch and Google Stackdriver provide real-time visibility into system performance metrics (for example, response times, error rates).
  - **Custom Metrics and Alerts:** Setting up automated alerts for anomalies or threshold breaches ensures that issues are promptly addressed.

- **Centralized Logging:** Aggregates logs from various system components into a single, accessible platform, facilitating streamlined troubleshooting and real-time monitoring.
  - **Log Aggregation Tools:** Centralized systems such as the ELK Stack (Elasticsearch, Logstash, Kibana) or Splunk enable efficient collection and analysis of logs from various system components.
  - **Structured Logging Practices:** Consistent log formats across services facilitate automated parsing, correlation, and faster troubleshooting.
- **Maintenance and Update Procedures:** Regular maintenance and update procedures, including scheduled upgrades, monitoring for performance issues, and automated rollbacks, ensure optimal functioning and resilience of the Llama model deployment.
  - **Scheduled Maintenance:** Regular maintenance windows allow for software updates, hardware checks, and performance optimizations without disrupting service.
  - **Automated Rollbacks:** In the event of a failed update, automated rollback mechanisms help revert the system to a stable state.
  - **Model Performance Tracking:** Continuous evaluation of model outputs and retraining triggers are implemented to monitor for model drift, ensuring that predictions remain accurate over time.

Security, Compliance, and Disaster Recovery

Securing the deployment and ensuring compliance with regulatory standards is as important as performance and scalability.

- **Data Security:** Data security is the practice of safeguarding sensitive information from unauthorized access, breaches, and other threats through robust encryption, access control, and vigilant monitoring.
  - **Encryption Protocols:** Encrypt data both in transit (using TLS/SSL) and at rest (using robust encryption standards such as AES-256) to safeguard sensitive information.
  - **Access Control Mechanisms:** Implement multi-factor authentication (MFA), role-based access control (RBAC), and strict identity management policies to limit access to critical systems.
  - **Network Security:** Utilize firewalls, Virtual Private Clouds (VPCs), and micro-segmentation strategies to isolate sensitive components and prevent unauthorized access.
- **Compliance with Industry Standards:** Adhering to strict regulatory frameworks and best practices ensures data integrity, security, and consistent operational excellence.

  - **Regulatory Requirements:** Adhere to standards such as GDPR, HIPAA, or CCPA by ensuring data residency, audit trails, and robust logging practices.
  - **Regular Security Audits:** Conduct penetration testing and vulnerability assessments periodically to identify and address security gaps.
  - **Audit Trails and Logging:** Maintain detailed audit logs that track all access and modifications to the system, which are crucial for compliance and forensic analysis.
- **Reliability and Disaster Recovery:** Robust reliability and disaster recovery measures ensure continuous operation and rapid recovery of services in the event of unforeseen disruptions.
  - **Redundancy and Failover:** Design systems with redundancy at every layer–from multiple data sources to backup inference nodes–to ensure continuous operation even when components fail.
  - **Backup Strategies:** Regularly back up both data and configuration settings to secure, off-site locations.
  - **Disaster Recovery Plans:** Develop and test disaster recovery procedures to ensure that the system can be quickly restored following a catastrophic failure or data breach.

Deployment Strategies: Cloud, On-Premises, and Hybrid Approaches

Selecting the right deployment strategy is a critical decision that influences scalability, security, and operational efficiency. Each approach has its merits and challenges, and often a hybrid model is adopted to leverage the advantages of both cloud and on-premises solutions.

Cloud-Based Deployments

Cloud platforms offer significant flexibility and scalability that are ideal for dynamic workloads:

- **Rapid Provisioning and Scalability:** Cloud providers such as AWS, Google Cloud Platform, and Microsoft Azure allow for rapid provisioning of resources, enabling organizations to scale their deployments on demand.
- **Managed Services and Reduced Overhead:** Managed container orchestration (for example, AWS EKS, Google Kubernetes Engine) and serverless computing solutions reduce the operational overhead associated with infrastructure management.

- **Global Distribution and Low Latency:** Deploying services in multiple regions ensures that end users experience minimal latency, regardless of their geographic location.
- **Cost Models:** Pay-as-you-go models and reserved instances help optimize costs, particularly when workloads are unpredictable or seasonal.

On-Premises Deployments

For organizations with stringent data security, compliance, or performance requirements, on-premises deployments provide full control over the infrastructure:

- **Customization and Control:** On-premises setups allow complete customization of hardware and software configurations, ensuring that the deployment meets very specific performance or security requirements.
- **Data Sovereignty:** Keeping data within a controlled environment is often necessary for industries subject to strict regulatory controls, such as healthcare or finance.
- **Long-Term Cost Efficiency:** Although initial capital expenditures can be high, predictable workloads and dedicated IT infrastructure may yield cost savings over time.

Hybrid Deployments

Hybrid approaches combine the scalability of the cloud with the control and security of on-premises systems:

- **Best of Both Worlds:** Critical workloads that require stringent security or low latency can remain on-premises, while fluctuating or high-volume processes are offloaded to the cloud.
- **Unified Management:** Modern orchestration and integration tools allow seamless management of hybrid environments, ensuring that both cloud and on-premises resources work together efficiently.
- **Cost and Performance Optimization:** By balancing workloads across both environments, organizations can optimize resource utilization and cost-effectiveness.

Detailed Look at Llama Architecture Components

In addition to the core deployment layers discussed above, several components are specifically tailored to the unique requirements of Llama models. These components ensure that the deployment is optimized for the model's operational characteristics and the specific challenges associated with natural language processing.

Specialized Preprocessing Modules

- **Text Normalization and Tokenization:** Llama models require precise handling of textual data. Specialized preprocessing modules handle tasks such as tokenization, stemming, and lemmatization, ensuring that text input is standardized and optimized for model consumption.
- **Semantic Enrichment:** Leveraging external knowledge bases or embedding layers to enrich the input data can improve model performance in tasks such as sentiment analysis or contextual understanding.

Model Versioning and Experimentation

- **Version Control for Models:** Maintaining multiple versions of the Llama model is essential for continuous improvement. Tools such as MLflow, DVC, or proprietary systems facilitate version control, ensuring that new model iterations can be compared against previous benchmarks.
- **A/B Testing and Canary Deployments:** Gradual rollout strategies, including A/B testing and canary deployments, allow for real-time performance comparisons, minimizing risk when introducing new model versions.

Data and Model Pipelines

- **End-to-End Pipeline Integration:** A robust pipeline integrates data ingestion, preprocessing, model inference, and post-processing steps into a unified workflow. This integration streamlines operations and reduces latency.
- **Pipeline Monitoring and Feedback:** Continuous monitoring of pipeline performance helps identify bottlenecks or errors. Feedback loops allow for automated adjustments, such as triggering retraining when performance metrics drop below predefined thresholds.

Infrastructure as Code (IaC)

- **Automated Provisioning and Management:** Tools such as Terraform, CloudFormation, or Ansible automate the provisioning and configuration of the deployment environment. This ensures consistency, reduces human error, and speeds up the process of scaling or replicating environments.
- **Configuration Management:** Using version-controlled configuration files helps maintain consistency across deployments and simplifies rollbacks in case of failures.

Continuous Integration and Continuous Deployment (CI/CD)

- **Automated Testing and Deployment Pipelines:** Integrating CI/CD pipelines ensures that every code change, model update, or infrastructure modification is automatically tested and deployed. This approach minimizes downtime and ensures that the system remains robust as it evolves.

- **Rollback and Recovery:** A robust CI/CD system includes automated rollback mechanisms that can quickly revert to a previous stable state in the event of deployment issues.

Scalability Considerations and Challenges

As machine learning models such as Llama grow in complexity and application, the need for scalability in their deployment becomes more critical. Scalability, in this context, refers to the ability of a system to handle an increasing number of tasks or data inputs efficiently without compromising performance. Deploying Llama models at scale, particularly in production environments, involves several considerations and challenges that must be addressed to maintain system performance, reduce latency, and optimize resource usage.

This section will delve into key scalability considerations and challenges involved in deploying Llama models, while highlighting strategies and best practices to ensure smooth, efficient, and cost-effective scaling. It covers the various layers of deployment—from data ingestion and preprocessing to model serving, monitoring, and scaling infrastructure—offering insights on how to overcome challenges and achieve the desired performance at scale.

Deploying Llama models at scale means ensuring that the model can handle an increasing volume of requests, process data efficiently, and maintain high throughput while minimizing latency. This becomes particularly important in real-time applications such as chatbots, recommendation systems, and content generation, where rapid responses are crucial for user satisfaction.

The deployment architecture must be flexible enough to support growth—whether through horizontal scaling (adding more machines to handle increasing load) or vertical scaling (upgrading existing infrastructure to handle larger workloads). However, scaling a complex AI model such as Llama involves unique challenges compared to traditional applications. These challenges arise in different parts of the deployment pipeline, including data processing, inference performance, infrastructure management, and model monitoring.

Scalability Considerations

Scalability considerations involve designing Llama models to efficiently handle increasing data volumes, computational demands, and model complexities while ensuring optimal performance and resource utilization. This includes strategies such as optimizing model architecture, efficient data management, and leveraging distributed or cloud-based infrastructures.

Model Architecture and Parameter Growth

It involves strategically increasing both the depth (number of layers) and breadth (size of each layer or number of attention heads) to enhance the model's capacity without overwhelming computational resources. This careful balancing act is crucial to achieving improved performance while managing memory and processing constraints.

- **Balancing Depth and Breadth:** Scaling Llama models often means making decisions about whether to deepen the network (adding more layers) or broaden it (increasing the width of layers, such as adding more attention heads). For example, research at a major tech company revealed that after a certain point, adding additional layers to a transformer did not significantly improve translation accuracy, while a modest increase in the number of attention heads yielded better contextual understanding. This finding emphasizes the need to balance architectural depth and breadth rather than simply scaling parameters linearly.

  Example: A research team working on multilingual translation observed that beyond 36 layers, performance improvements diminished, whereas carefully increasing the number of attention heads led to a 10% reduction in error rate on low-resource languages–demonstrating the importance of architectural trade-offs.

- **Memory and Computational Constraints:** Large models require significant memory for storing intermediate activations and gradients during training. As an example, training on clusters equipped with NVIDIA A100 GPUs has shown that memory overhead becomes a critical bottleneck, particularly when dealing with billions of parameters. Techniques such as mixed-precision training and gradient checkpointing are often employed to reduce memory usage. Mixed-precision training uses lower-precision arithmetic without a substantial loss in model accuracy, while gradient checkpointing trades off additional computation for reduced memory consumption.

  Example: A university research lab reported that by using mixed-precision training, they were able to reduce memory usage by nearly 50% when training a Llama model, thereby fitting larger models on their available GPU hardware and significantly shortening training times.

Data Management and Quality

Data management and quality are critical in scaling Llama models, as they ensure that diverse, clean, and representative datasets are used to mitigate bias and enhance model robustness. Effective data pipelines and rigorous validation processes are essential for maintaining high performance in real-world applications.

- **Volume of Data:** Large language models thrive on extensive and diverse datasets. However, scaling data introduces its own challenges in ingestion, storage, and preprocessing. For instance, a customer service chatbot may require data from emails, call transcripts, and social media–each with different formats and quality levels. This heterogeneous data requires robust pipelines to standardize and clean the data before training.

  Example: A multinational retailer collected millions of customer interaction records from various channels. By implementing Apache Spark-based data pipelines, they managed to clean and consolidate the data, ensuring the model was trained on a diverse and representative dataset, ultimately reducing customer query misinterpretations by 15%.

- **Data Cleaning and Annotation:** Data quality is as important as quantity. Automated tools and frameworks must be in place to detect anomalies, correct errors, and remove biases. High-quality, annotated data is vital for fine-tuning Llama models to specific domains. Continuous quality assurance, including manual review and automated validation, ensures that training data remains reliable.

  Example: In healthcare, where data quality can significantly affect outcomes, a research team used a combination of natural language processing techniques and expert human review to annotate medical records accurately. This hybrid approach led to a 20% improvement in model precision for medical diagnosis tasks.

Training Infrastructure and Distributed Systems

- **Hardware Considerations:** Efficient training of Llama models relies on high-performance hardware, such as GPUs and TPUs, which are optimized for deep learning tasks. Cloud-based solutions offer flexibility but come with challenges such as network latency and variable cost. The choice of hardware also influences the design of the training process.

  Example: A startup training a Llama model for real-time sentiment analysis used AWS's P4d instances equipped with NVIDIA A100 GPUs. By optimizing their code for these instances, they achieved a 30% reduction in training time compared to traditional GPU clusters.

- **Distributed Training Techniques:** Distributed training methods (data parallelism, model parallelism, and pipeline parallelism) are essential for managing the computational demands of large models. However, these techniques introduce challenges such as synchronization overhead and communication bottlenecks.

Example: An organization training a Llama model on a cluster of 64 GPUs found that synchronous updates across nodes led to significant latency. By switching to a hybrid model that combined asynchronous gradient descent with periodic synchronization, they reduced communication overhead and improved training efficiency by 25%.

Inference and Real-Time Applications

- **Latency Reduction:** For real-time applications–such as chatbots or voice assistants–minimizing latency is crucial. Techniques such as model quantization (reducing the precision of the model's parameters) and pruning (removing redundant parameters) help reduce inference times while preserving acceptable accuracy levels.

  Example: A popular voice assistant platform integrated a quantized version of a Llama model, resulting in a 40% decrease in inference latency. This improvement was critical for delivering near-instantaneous responses to user queries.

- **Scalability of Serving Infrastructure:** Beyond training, the serving infrastructure must handle high user demand with robust load balancing, caching strategies, and failover mechanisms. Ensuring that the inference system scales seamlessly under peak loads is as important as scaling the training system.

  Example: A streaming service deploying Llama-powered recommendations built a microservices architecture with Kubernetes orchestration. This allowed the system to scale automatically during peak hours, maintaining user satisfaction by providing consistent, real-time recommendations.

Challenges in Scaling Llama Models

Scaling Llama models is challenging due to the enormous computational resources required, communication overhead in distributed training, and the complexities of managing vast, diverse datasets that may introduce biases. Additionally, ensuring reproducibility, energy efficiency, and low-latency deployment further compounds these hurdles.

- **Computational Complexity and Resource Constraints:** Large models require enormous computational power, which translates into high energy consumption and operational cost. Many organizations, especially smaller research labs and startups, may struggle to access the necessary resources, thereby limiting the scale at which they can operate.

Example: A small university lab attempting to train a Llama model encountered budget constraints that limited its access to high-end GPUs. Relying on cloud credits and shared resources, they experienced slower training times compared to well-funded industrial labs, highlighting the economic challenges in scaling advanced models.

- **Communication Overhead in Distributed Systems:** Distributed training, while necessary, introduces significant communication overhead. Synchronizing updates between nodes can lead to bottlenecks that slow down the overall training process. Optimizing these communication patterns is complex and requires sophisticated algorithms.

  Example: In one large-scale experiment using TPU pods, researchers noted that adding extra nodes beyond a certain threshold did not proportionately decrease training time because the overhead from inter-node communication negated the benefits. This finding underscores the importance of carefully designing distributed training architectures.

- **Data Heterogeneity and Bias:** Scaling up data can inadvertently introduce biases if the data is not diverse or balanced. For instance, a Llama model trained predominantly on English-language data may perform poorly when handling content in other languages or cultural contexts. Biases in the training data can result in skewed or unfair outputs, which is particularly problematic in sensitive domains such as healthcare or legal services.

  Example: A language model used for global customer support was found to underperform for non-Western languages. The oversight was traced back to an imbalanced training dataset, prompting the team to incorporate more region-specific data and implement bias mitigation strategies such as fairness audits.

- **Reliability and Reproducibility:** The stochastic nature of neural network training means that slight variations in data, hyperparameters, or hardware can lead to different outcomes. Achieving reproducible results is a major challenge, especially in distributed environments where nondeterminism can introduce further variability.

  Example: A commercial deployment of a Llama model in a financial application revealed that the same training configuration yielded different predictions across different runs. This variability necessitated extensive testing and the implementation of stricter version control and logging mechanisms to ensure consistent performance.

- **Energy Consumption and Environmental Impact:** Training large language models is energy-intensive, raising concerns about the environmental footprint of AI research. Studies have highlighted that the carbon footprint of training state-of-the-art models can be comparable to that of several automobiles over their lifetimes. Reducing energy consumption without compromising performance is an ongoing challenge.

Example: A study by researchers at the University of Massachusetts Amherst estimated that training a large transformer model could emit over 600,000 pounds of CO_2. This has led to increased efforts in optimizing training processes and choosing data centers powered by renewable energy sources.

Strategies for Overcoming Scalability Challenges

Strategies for overcoming scalability challenges include leveraging advanced hardware and cloud infrastructures, optimizing model architectures, and implementing efficient distributed training algorithms. These approaches reduce computational overhead and resource consumption while maintaining performance and reliability.

- **Leveraging Advanced Hardware and Cloud Infrastructure:** Investing in state-of-the-art hardware, such as NVIDIA A100 GPUs or Google's TPU v4, is crucial for scaling. Cloud platforms offer elasticity and on-demand access to these resources, although they require careful cost and performance management. Tools such as Kubernetes and distributed frameworks such as Horovod facilitate efficient use of cloud resources.

  Example: A leading tech company migrated its training infrastructure to a cloud-based environment using AWS's P4d instances. This shift not only reduced their upfront capital expenditure but also allowed them to scale dynamically during training peaks, achieving a 30% improvement in throughput.

- **Optimizing Model Architecture:** Innovations in model design can significantly reduce computational demands. Research into sparse attention mechanisms and dynamic routing has led to more efficient transformer variants. Models such as the Switch Transformer employ conditional computation, activating only parts of the network as needed, which reduces the overall computational load while maintaining performance.

  Example: Researchers at MIT experimented with a sparse transformer model that dynamically skipped redundant layers during inference. This approach led to a 20% reduction in computation time on language modeling tasks without compromising accuracy, illustrating how architectural innovations can directly benefit scalability.

- **Implementing Efficient Distributed Training Algorithms:** Developing and fine-tuning distributed training techniques is essential. Algorithms such as asynchronous gradient descent, gradient accumulation, and pipeline parallelism help manage communication overhead and improve synchronization efficiency across nodes.

Example: A research team training a Llama model on a 128-GPU cluster integrated asynchronous gradient updates with periodic synchronization. This hybrid approach reduced waiting times due to communication overhead by 25%, leading to faster convergence and more stable training dynamics.

- **Enhancing Data Curation and Preprocessing Pipelines:** Robust data pipelines are key to managing large and diverse datasets. Tools such as Apache Beam or Spark facilitate scalable data processing, while active learning and automated annotation tools help maintain data quality. Regular audits ensure that the data remains relevant and unbiased.

  Example: A global e-commerce platform employed Apache Beam to preprocess terabytes of customer review data in real time. Coupled with active learning, the system prioritized annotating ambiguous cases, ensuring that the training data was both diverse and of high quality, which in turn improved the model's customer sentiment analysis by 18%.

- **Adopting Energy-Efficient Practices:** Reducing the energy footprint of training is increasingly important. Techniques such as model quantization, pruning, and mixed-precision training not only reduce inference and training times but also cut energy consumption. Moreover, choosing data centers that utilize renewable energy sources can significantly lower the environmental impact.

  Example: A startup focused on natural language processing implemented mixed-precision training using TensorFloat-32 on NVIDIA GPUs. This reduced their energy consumption by nearly 35% while also cutting training time by 20%. Additionally, by partnering with a cloud provider committed to renewable energy, they further mitigated their environmental impact.

- **Continuous Monitoring and Model Auditing:** Implementing robust monitoring and auditing practices ensures models remain fair, reliable, and performant over time. Tools such as TensorBoard for real-time metrics and Fairlearn for auditing bias are integrated into deployment pipelines. Regular A/B testing and automated anomaly detection help catch issues early.

  Example: An international bank deployed a Llama model for fraud detection with continuous monitoring via a custom dashboard. Real-time alerts and fairness audits allowed the bank to detect and correct deviations in model performance rapidly, maintaining both regulatory compliance and customer trust.

Cost, Latency, Performance, and Scalability for Llama Models in Different Deployment Architectures

When deploying **Llama models** (especially **Llama 3** and **Llama 4**), the choice of infrastructure–whether cloud, on-premise, edge, or hybrid–affects **cost**, **latency**, **performance**, and **scalability**. Here is a detailed breakdown with additional numbers to illustrate how different deployments impact these factors:

Cloud Deployment

Cost:

- **Compute Costs**: Cloud providers such as AWS, Google Cloud, and Azure offer **pay-as-you-go** pricing. The cost of running **Llama 4** models (with billions of parameters) will be significantly higher than running **Llama 3** due to the size and complexity of the model.

  Example:

  - **AWS p4d instances** (with **8x A100 GPUs**) cost approximately **$32.77/hour**.
  - For **Llama 4**, utilizing **multiple p4d instances** (for example, **2-3 instances** for multi-GPU scaling) can cost around **$100+ per hour**, depending on the scale.
  - **Storage Costs**: Storing large models (up to **70B parameters**) on cloud storage like **AWS S3** can cost **$0.023 per GB** per month.

Latency:

- **Inference Latency**: Latency can be affected by network communication between the cloud and end-users.
  - **Example**: For cloud deployments in the **US-West-2 region** (AWS), round-trip latency can range between **50ms to 200ms**, depending on the distance from the client to the data center.
  - **Llama 4** will experience higher latency than **Llama 3** due to the larger model size.

Performance:

- **GPU Instances**: Cloud deployments use GPUs such as **NVIDIA A100** or **V100**, which are designed to handle large-scale models such as **Llama 4** efficiently.

  Example: A **NVIDIA A100 GPU** has a theoretical throughput of **312 teraFLOPS** (for FP16). The **Llama 4** model, with 17B parameters, requires massive computation, leading to **faster inference** times for larger models (typically under **100ms per request** depending on batch size).

Scalability:

- **Horizontal Scaling**: Cloud platforms offer **auto-scaling** features, allowing the deployment of more instances as traffic increases.

  Example: For **Llama 4**-based inference, auto-scaling can increase the number of GPU instances dynamically based on load, providing seamless scalability. For instance, if the model needs to serve **1000 concurrent requests** per minute, the cloud system can automatically provision **additional instances** during peak times to handle the load.

On-Premise Deployment

Cost:

- **Initial Setup Cost**: On-premise infrastructure requires **high upfront costs** for hardware.

  Example:

  - A server with **4x NVIDIA A100 GPUs** can cost between **$50,000 and $100,000**.
  - Additional costs include **cooling**, **power consumption**, and **maintenance**. For large models such as **Llama 4**, each A100 GPU costs approximately **$2,500 per year** in electricity, maintenance, and operational costs.

Latency:

- **Local Processing**: On-premise deployments have **low latency** because data doesn't need to travel over the internet.

  Example: In a typical **on-premise deployment** with **multiple A100 GPUs**, latency can drop to **<10ms per request**, significantly lower than cloud deployments.

Performance:

- **High Throughput**: On-premise setups can use **dedicated servers with powerful GPUs**, ensuring that Llama models run at peak efficiency without shared cloud resources.

  Example: With **4x A100 GPUs**, Llama models (including Llama 4) can process **10-20 inference requests per second**, depending on batch size and model complexity.

Scalability:

- **Vertical Scaling**: Vertical scaling involves upgrading individual servers (for example, adding more GPUs).

  Example: For **Llama 4**, running inference on a single server with **8 A100 GPUs** can handle **high throughput** but will still be constrained by the server's **single location** and **hardware limits**.

- **Horizontal Scaling**: Scaling requires adding additional servers, which can be expensive. The maximum number of servers will depend on the size of the data center and the **cost of maintaining infrastructure**.

Edge Deployment

Cost:

- **Low Operational Cost**: Edge devices have a fixed cost for hardware but **lower operational costs**.
  - **Example**: Deploying a system with **NVIDIA Jetson AGX Xavier** (used for AI at the edge) can cost around **$1,500** per unit.
  - Edge devices are relatively inexpensive to run but are constrained by **limited compute power** compared to cloud or on-premise systems.

Latency:

- **Ultra-Low Latency**: Data is processed locally, eliminating network communication delays.

  Example: For a real-time **anomaly detection** system using **Llama 3** (smaller versions), the inference can be processed in **<5ms** due to local computation, making it suitable for real-time applications.

Performance:

- **Limited Computational Power**: Edge devices such as **NVIDIA Jetson AGX** can handle **smaller versions of Llama 3** but may not support **Llama 4** due to its massive size.

  Example: **Llama 3** with **3B-7B parameters** can run on **edge devices** with reasonable performance, processing up to **5-10 requests per second**.

Scalability:

- **Limited Scalability**: Edge devices are constrained by **hardware limitations**.

  Example: Scaling edge deployments involves adding more edge devices, but they will still be constrained in terms of memory and computational power, especially for large models such as **Llama 4**.

Hybrid Deployment

Cost:

- **Mixed Cost Structure**: Hybrid deployments combine **cloud** and **on-premise** solutions.
  - **Example**: **Edge devices** handle real-time inference (low cost), while **cloud services** manage complex tasks or scaling needs. This model reduces costs compared to relying solely on the cloud for **Llama 4** inference.
  - Hybrid deployments use **cloud storage** for storing models, which incurs a **storage cost** of about **$0.02 per GB per month** on cloud platforms.

Latency:

- **Optimized Latency**: Hybrid setups allow the system to balance low-latency edge processing with the heavy computational needs of the cloud.

  Example: Real-time tasks are handled on the **edge**, providing sub-10ms latency, while more resource-intensive tasks (for example, large-scale data processing) are handled by the cloud.

Performance:

- **Dynamic Performance**: Hybrid systems allow scaling of resources dynamically by using the edge for light processing and the cloud for heavy lifting.

  Example: During **peak traffic**, more **cloud instances** can be added to handle **Llama 4** model inference, while the **edge** handles basic requests.

Scalability:

- **Highly Scalable**: The system can leverage the **elasticity of the cloud** to scale up during demand spikes, while **edge devices** handle real-time inference.

  Example: The system can scale cloud resources to handle **1000+ concurrent requests** per minute, while **edge devices** can handle smaller tasks such as image recognition.

Cloud Deployment Strategies

Large language models such as Llama (Large Language Model Meta AI) have revolutionized the field of natural language processing by enabling applications that range from conversational AI to complex content generation. However, leveraging the full potential of these models requires an efficient, scalable, and secure deployment strategy–one that is well-suited to the dynamic demands of cloud infrastructure.

Cloud deployment strategies offer the flexibility to scale computational resources, reduce operational overhead, and manage complex workloads without the need for significant on-premises infrastructure. This topic provides a deep dive into cloud deployment strategies specifically tailored for Llama models, discussing various approaches, the infrastructure required, and practical examples drawn from industry use cases.

Understanding the Cloud Deployment Landscape

Cloud computing has emerged as a cornerstone for modern AI deployments due to its on-demand access to computing resources, robust storage options, and global reach. The evolution of cloud platforms such as AWS, Google Cloud Platform (GCP), and Microsoft Azure has significantly lowered the barrier for organizations to deploy and manage large-scale AI models. For Llama models–which are both compute-intensive and data-hungry–the cloud offers a promising environment where scalability meets flexibility.

Why Cloud Deployment for Llama Models?

- **Scalability:** Llama models often involve billions of parameters. Cloud platforms enable horizontal scaling by provisioning multiple high-performance instances for both training and inference.
- **Cost-Efficiency:** Pay-as-you-go pricing models allow organizations to optimize costs by scaling resources only when needed.
- **Global Accessibility:** Cloud infrastructures provide global data centers, ensuring low-latency access to deployed models regardless of geographical location.
- **Maintenance and Updates:** Automated updates, security patches, and managed services reduce the burden on in-house IT teams, allowing developers to focus on innovation.

Key Cloud Deployment Strategies for Llama Models

It includes leveraging high-performance IaaS for customizable compute resources, containerization for consistent and scalable environments, and managed AI services to streamline training and deployment while ensuring security and cost-efficiency.

Infrastructure as a Service (IaaS): IaaS provides raw computing resources such as virtual machines, storage, and networking. For Llama models, IaaS platforms allow deep customization of the environment, enabling fine-tuning of hardware configurations to meet the demands of large-scale model training and inference.

Practical Considerations

- **Compute Instances:** High-performance GPU instances (for example, AWS P4d, Google Cloud's A2 instances) are essential for the training and inference of Llama models.
- **Storage Solutions:** Fast, scalable storage solutions such as Amazon S3 or Google Cloud Storage ensure quick access to large datasets required for model training.
- **Networking:** High-bandwidth, low-latency networking between instances is critical when distributing training workloads across multiple nodes.

Example: A leading tech company trained its Llama model using AWS's EC2 instances equipped with NVIDIA A100 GPUs. By leveraging Elastic Block Store (EBS) for high-speed data access and configuring instances in a Virtual Private Cloud (VPC) with optimized networking, the team achieved a 25% reduction in training time compared to their on-premises solution.

Containerization and Orchestration

Containerization packages the application along with its dependencies, ensuring that the environment remains consistent across development, testing, and production. Kubernetes and Docker are two of the most widely adopted tools in this space.

Benefits for Llama Models

- **Consistency:** Containers guarantee that the same environment is used across all stages, reducing the "*works on my machine*" syndrome.
- **Portability:** Models can be moved seamlessly between cloud providers or between development and production environments.
- **Scalability:** Orchestration tools such as Kubernetes (K8s) allow for automated scaling, rolling updates, and self-healing deployments.

Practical Example: A startup deploying a Llama model for real-time sentiment analysis used Docker to containerize the model and deployed it on Google Kubernetes Engine (GKE). The orchestration capabilities of Kubernetes allowed the team to automatically scale the number of pods based on incoming request loads. During peak hours, the system scaled up to handle a 50% increase in traffic, ensuring low latency and high availability.

Serverless Architectures

Serverless computing abstracts the underlying infrastructure, allowing developers to run code without provisioning or managing servers. While not traditionally used for heavy compute tasks, serverless architectures can complement cloud deployments for specific parts of the Llama model ecosystem—such as preprocessing, data ingestion, or lightweight inference tasks.

Benefits

- **Cost Efficiency:** Billing is based on actual compute usage rather than pre-allocated resources.
- **Ease of Deployment:** Simplifies deployment and scaling without the need to manage servers.
- **Rapid Prototyping:** Ideal for developing and testing parts of the system before moving to a full-scale deployment.

Example: A digital marketing firm integrated serverless functions using AWS Lambda for data preprocessing tasks prior to feeding data into their Llama model. By decoupling the preprocessing pipeline from the core model deployment, they achieved near-instantaneous scalability and reduced processing time by 30%.

Managed AI Services

Managed AI services such as AWS SageMaker, Google AI Platform, and Azure Machine Learning provide end-to-end solutions for training, deploying, and monitoring machine learning models. These platforms abstract much of the underlying infrastructure complexities, allowing teams to focus on model development and fine-tuning.

Benefits for Llama Models

- **Integrated Toolsets:** Built-in tools for hyperparameter tuning, model monitoring, and deployment pipelines.
- **Security and Compliance:** Managed services come with enterprise-grade security, data encryption, and compliance certifications.
- **Operational Efficiency:** Simplifies scaling and management, reducing operational overhead.

Example: An international e-commerce company utilized AWS SageMaker to deploy its Llama-powered recommendation engine. SageMaker's managed training clusters and inference endpoints allowed the company to scale its model to handle millions of queries daily, while integrated monitoring tools ensured the model's performance and reliability.

Designing a Cloud Deployment Architecture for Llama Models

Designing a cloud deployment architecture for Llama models involves creating a multi-tier system that segregates data ingestion, processing, and inference layers, while leveraging scalable cloud resources such as high-performance GPUs and managed AI services. This approach ensures efficient resource allocation, low latency, and robust scalability to handle dynamic workloads.

Multi-Tier Architecture

A robust cloud deployment for Llama models typically follows a multi-tier architecture, ensuring separation of concerns and ease of management. A typical architecture might include:

- **Data Ingestion Layer:** Manages the flow of data into the system using tools such as Apache Kafka or AWS Kinesis.
- **Processing and Training Layer:** Consists of compute instances or managed AI services dedicated to training the Llama model.
- **Inference and Serving Layer:** Deploys the trained model to production environments using containerized applications, serverless functions, or managed endpoints.
- **Monitoring and Logging Layer:** Implements real-time monitoring, logging, and alerting using services such as Prometheus, Grafana, or CloudWatch to track model performance and infrastructure health.

Hybrid and Multi-Cloud Strategies

For organizations that require redundancy or have global reach, adopting a hybrid or multi-cloud strategy can be advantageous. These strategies involve deploying components across multiple cloud providers or combining on-premises resources with cloud environments.

Benefits

- **Resilience:** Mitigates the risk of downtime by leveraging multiple providers.
- **Cost Optimization:** Takes advantage of competitive pricing and diverse service offerings across cloud platforms.
- **Flexibility:** Provides the freedom to migrate workloads as needed without vendor lock-in.

Example: A financial services firm deployed its Llama model using a multi-cloud strategy–running core training workloads on Google Cloud's high-performance instances and deploying inference services on AWS for low-latency global access. This approach allowed the firm to optimize costs and ensure uninterrupted service across different regions.

Security and Compliance Considerations

When deploying Llama models in the cloud, security and regulatory compliance must be integral to the deployment strategy.

Data Security

- **Encryption:** Use encryption both at rest (for example, AWS KMS, Google Cloud KMS) and in transit (TLS/SSL) to protect sensitive data.
- **Access Controls:** Implement robust Identity and Access Management (IAM) policies to restrict access to data and computing resources.
- **Auditing and Logging:** Maintain detailed logs and audit trails using tools such as AWS CloudTrail or Google Cloud Audit Logs to track access and changes to sensitive systems.

Model Security

- **API Security:** Secure model inference endpoints using API gateways, authentication, and rate limiting.
- **Regular Audits:** Periodically conduct security audits and vulnerability assessments to identify and remediate potential threats.
- **Compliance:** Ensure that deployments adhere to industry-specific regulations (for example, GDPR, HIPAA) by leveraging compliant cloud services.

Example: A healthcare provider deploying a Llama-based diagnostic support system ensured data security by utilizing Azure's confidential computing environments and enforcing strict access controls. Regular compliance audits and encryption measures helped the organization meet HIPAA standards, safeguarding patient information.

Operational Considerations: Monitoring, Logging, and Maintenance

Effective cloud deployment strategies go beyond just launching the model; they also encompass ongoing operational tasks.

Monitoring and Logging

- **Performance Monitoring:** Use tools such as Prometheus, Grafana, or CloudWatch to track the performance of compute instances, network latency, and application throughput.
- **Model Metrics:** Monitor key model performance metrics such as response times, accuracy, and error rates to ensure the Llama model meets service-level agreements (SLAs).

- **Alerting:** Configure automated alerts to notify administrators of any performance degradation or security breaches.

Maintenance and Updates

- **Continuous Integration/Continuous Deployment (CI/CD):** Establish CI/CD pipelines to automate updates, rollbacks, and model retraining. Tools such as Jenkins, GitLab CI, or AWS CodePipeline streamline these processes.
- **Regular Backups:** Implement regular backups of model parameters, training data, and configuration settings to safeguard against data loss.
- **Scaling Policies:** Define autoscaling policies for both training and inference environments to dynamically adjust resources based on demand.

Example: An online education platform deployed its Llama model for interactive learning using a CI/CD pipeline managed by GitHub Actions and AWS CodePipeline. Automated monitoring and autoscaling allowed the system to handle unpredictable traffic spikes during online examinations, ensuring uninterrupted service and rapid recovery from potential issues.

Future Trends in Cloud Deployment for Llama Models

As both cloud computing and large language models continue to evolve, several emerging trends are set to shape future deployment strategies:

- **Edge Computing:** Integration of edge devices with cloud-based models can reduce latency further and enable real-time inference in remote locations.
- **AI-Specific Cloud Services:** Cloud providers are increasingly offering specialized hardware and software stacks optimized for AI, such as AWS Inferentia or Google TPU Pods, which could further enhance Llama model performance.
- **Sustainable AI Practices:** With growing awareness of the environmental impact of large-scale AI, future strategies will likely emphasize energy-efficient cloud deployments and the use of renewable energy-powered data centers.
- **Enhanced Interoperability:** Improved support for multi-cloud and hybrid deployments will allow organizations to mix and match services seamlessly, providing even greater flexibility and resilience.

Monitoring and Managing Deployed Llama Models

The true challenge lies in continuously monitoring and managing them to ensure optimal performance, reliability, and scalability. This topic delves into the critical aspects of monitoring and managing deployed Llama models, outlining key metrics, strategies, tools, and best practices. Alongside, we provide real-world examples that illustrate how organizations tackle these challenges in diverse environments.

Monitoring and managing deployed models is not a one-time task. It is an ongoing process that involves tracking performance metrics, ensuring data quality, detecting anomalies, and proactively updating models to cope with changing inputs and requirements. In this context, the term "*monitoring*" covers everything from resource utilization and latency tracking to error logging and model drift analysis. "Managing," on the other hand, includes actions such as scaling infrastructure, applying patches, retraining models, and rolling out updates.

Essential Monitoring for Llama Models

- **Ensuring Consistent Performance:** Deployed Llama models must consistently deliver accurate and timely responses. Monitoring plays a vital role in detecting performance degradation before it impacts user experience. For instance, if a Llama-powered chatbot experiences increased latency or reduced accuracy, real-time monitoring systems can alert engineers to investigate and remedy the underlying issues.
- **Detecting Model Drift and Data Anomalies:** Over time, the data distribution that the model encounters in production can change–a phenomenon known as model drift. Without timely detection, this drift can result in decreased accuracy and unintended biases. Monitoring systems are essential for continuously comparing production data with the training distribution, flagging significant deviations.
- **Operational and Infrastructure Health:** Beyond the model's outputs, it is crucial to monitor the underlying infrastructure. This includes tracking CPU/GPU usage, memory consumption, network latency, and overall system health. Robust monitoring helps ensure that the infrastructure scales effectively and that resource allocation is optimized to handle varying workloads.

Key Metrics to Monitor

For comprehensive oversight of deployed Llama models, organizations must monitor a range of performance, operational, and model-specific metrics. Here are some of the most critical metrics:

Latency and Throughput

- **Latency:** Measures the time taken for the model to respond to an input request. High latency can indicate bottlenecks in computation or inefficient data pipelines.

- **Throughput:** Represents the number of requests processed per second. Maintaining high throughput is crucial, especially for real-time applications such as chatbots or voice assistants.

Example: A financial services firm tracking the latency of its Llama-based fraud detection system identified sporadic spikes during high-volume trading periods. By optimizing their load balancing strategy, they reduced the latency spikes by 15%, ensuring timely fraud alerts.

Resource Utilization

- **CPU/GPU Usage:** Monitoring the utilization of compute resources helps in scaling the infrastructure efficiently. High usage might signal the need for additional resources or more efficient code.
- **Memory Consumption:** Keeping an eye on memory usage is essential, especially during model inference when large tensors may be loaded into memory.

Error Rates and Failures

- **Prediction Errors:** Tracking the rate of errors or exceptions during inference helps identify issues related to input data quality or unexpected model behavior.
- **System Failures:** Monitoring server crashes, timeout errors, or other system-level failures ensures rapid remediation.

Model Drift and Accuracy

- **Drift Metrics:** Measure deviations between the distribution of incoming data and the data used for training. This can be monitored using statistical tests or dedicated drift detection tools.
- **Accuracy and Confidence Scores:** Regularly evaluating the accuracy of model predictions in production against ground truth (where available) helps ensure the model remains reliable.

Tools and Technologies for Effective Monitoring

Successful monitoring of deployed Llama models requires the right blend of tools and technologies that span data collection, visualization, and alerting. Below are some popular tools and platforms:

Prometheus and Grafana

- **Prometheus:** An open-source systems monitoring and alerting toolkit that collects and stores metrics in a time-series database.
- **Grafana:** A powerful dashboard tool that visualizes metrics collected by Prometheus. Grafana dashboards can be customized to display key performance indicators such as latency, throughput, and resource utilization.

Example: A startup deploying a Llama model for a real-time translation service set up Prometheus to collect metrics from their containerized microservices. They used Grafana to create dashboards that tracked inference latency and error rates, enabling the operations team to respond rapidly to any anomalies.

Cloud Provider Monitoring Solutions

- **AWS CloudWatch:** Provides comprehensive monitoring and logging services for AWS-based deployments. It supports automatic scaling and integrates with AWS Lambda for automated remediation.
- **Google Cloud Monitoring and Logging:** Offers similar capabilities for applications running on Google Cloud, including real-time dashboards and alerting mechanisms.
- **Azure Monitor:** Microsoft's solution for monitoring and diagnostics, particularly useful for deployments that utilize Azure's AI and compute services.

Application Performance Monitoring (APM) Tools

- **New Relic and Datadog:** These tools provide deep insights into application performance, including detailed transaction traces and dependency mapping. They are particularly useful for understanding how model performance impacts the overall application workflow.
- **ELK Stack (Elasticsearch, Logstash, and Kibana):** A popular choice for aggregating logs and visualizing log data, aiding in the detection of issues across multiple system layers.

Model-Specific Monitoring Frameworks

Some organizations develop custom monitoring solutions tailored to the unique aspects of machine learning models. These frameworks may include tools for tracking model-specific metrics, such as drift detection or changes in prediction confidence over time.

Strategies for Managing Deployed Llama Models

Effective management of deployed Llama models goes hand in hand with robust monitoring. Here are several key strategies:

- **Automated Alerting and Incident Response:** Implementing automated alerting is critical for ensuring that any issues are detected and addressed promptly. Alerts should be configured to notify the operations team when key metrics exceed predefined thresholds. This could include high latency, low throughput, or abnormal error rates.

  Example: An international news organization deploying a Llama-based content generator configured automated alerts using AWS CloudWatch. When the system detected a 25% increase in error rates, an alert was triggered, prompting an immediate investigation that revealed a misconfiguration in the input data pipeline. The issue was swiftly corrected, minimizing downtime.

- **Continuous Integration and Continuous Deployment (CI/CD):** Integrating monitoring into the CI/CD pipeline allows for continuous improvement of deployed models. Automated tests can simulate production traffic to evaluate model performance, and any new updates can be deployed incrementally to mitigate risks.

  Example: A tech startup adopted a CI/CD pipeline using Jenkins and Kubernetes for their Llama-powered virtual assistant. This pipeline included automated integration tests that simulated user queries and measured response times. By incorporating these tests, the team was able to roll out model updates without interrupting live services.

- **Model Retraining and Version Control:** As data drift and changing user behavior can impact model accuracy, it is important to schedule regular retraining cycles. Version control systems should be employed to track changes in both model parameters and data inputs, ensuring that updates are documented and reversible if issues arise.

  Example: An online retailer observed a gradual decline in recommendation accuracy from its Llama model. By using a version control system for models (such as MLflow) and setting up scheduled retraining jobs, the data science team successfully updated the model to adapt to new shopping trends, restoring its effectiveness.

- **Load Testing and Scalability Management:** Before and after deployment, load testing is crucial to determine how the model behaves under various traffic scenarios. This helps in identifying bottlenecks and planning for horizontal scaling.

  Example: A social media platform deployed a Llama model for sentiment analysis on user comments. Prior to deployment, the platform conducted extensive load testing using Apache JMeter. The tests revealed that the model's inference time increased significantly beyond a certain threshold, prompting the team to configure auto-scaling groups that dynamically adjusted the number of active instances based on real-time demand.

- **Security and Compliance Monitoring:** Ensuring the security of both data and model endpoints is essential. This includes regular vulnerability assessments, access control audits, and adherence to compliance standards such as GDPR or HIPAA. Security monitoring tools should be integrated into the overall monitoring framework.

Example: A healthcare provider deploying a Llama-based diagnostic support tool implemented stringent security measures by integrating Azure Monitor with their application firewall. Regular security audits and real-time threat detection ensured that sensitive patient data remained protected and that the deployment met HIPAA requirements.

Best Practices for Ongoing Monitoring and Management

- **Establish Clear SLAs and KPIs:** Define service-level agreements (SLAs) and key performance indicators (KPIs) that align with business objectives. These metrics serve as benchmarks for both operational performance and model accuracy.
- **Implement Redundancy and Failover Mechanisms:** Design the deployment architecture to include redundancy and failover options. This minimizes downtime, and ensures that a backup system can take over seamlessly in case of failures.
- **Document Processes and Maintain Detailed Logs:** Maintain comprehensive documentation of monitoring procedures, alerting thresholds, and incident response plans. Detailed logs not only help in troubleshooting issues but also serve as valuable references during audits and performance reviews.
- **Foster a Culture of Continuous Improvement:** Encourage cross-functional collaboration among data scientists, engineers, and operations teams. Regularly review performance metrics, incorporate feedback, and adjust strategies to enhance both model performance and operational efficiency.

Conclusion

Effective monitoring and management of deployed Llama models are essential to ensure optimal performance, scalability, and security in production environments. Our discussion has underscored the importance of real-time performance metrics, resource utilization tracking, anomaly detection, and proactive model retraining to maintain robust AI systems. By integrating advanced monitoring tools, automated alerting, and comprehensive logging practices, organizations can swiftly address performance degradations and adapt to changing data patterns, thereby reinforcing the resilience and efficiency of their Llama model deployments.

In the next chapter, we will delve into additional critical topics, including common issues in Llama model deployment, debugging techniques for Llama models, performance monitoring and optimization strategies, and continuous improvement practices. These insights will provide you with the necessary tools and methodologies to overcome deployment challenges and further enhance the effectiveness of your AI-powered solutions.

Multiple Choice Questions

1. Which of the following is a primary reason for deploying Llama models on cloud infrastructure?
   a. Increased on-premises hardware requirements
   b. Enhanced scalability, cost efficiency, and global accessibility
   c. Limited resource availability
   d. Reduced need for monitoring
2. What is the main purpose of monitoring deployed Llama models?
   a. To ensure models are only trained once
   b. To track performance metrics, detect anomalies, and manage model drift
   c. To decrease the size of the model
   d. To reduce the need for cloud services
3. Which metric is essential for measuring the speed at which a Llama model responds to requests?
   a. Throughput
   b. Memory consumption
   c. Latency
   d. CPU utilization
4. Which tool is commonly used to visualize time-series metrics for monitoring deployed models?
   a. Docker
   b. Kubernetes
   c. Grafana
   d. Jenkins

5. What benefit do managed AI services (for example, AWS SageMaker, Google AI Platform) offer for deploying Llama models?

    a. They eliminate the need for any resource monitoring.

    b. They provide integrated tools for scaling, monitoring, and maintaining models.

    c. They require manual configuration of every hardware resource.

    d. They reduce model accuracy.

6. What does "*model drift*" refer to in the context of deployed Llama models?

    a. A complete failure of the model to run

    b. A change in the production data distribution compared to the training data

    c. The process of scaling up hardware resources

    d. An increase in the number of model parameters

7. Which of the following is NOT typically monitored when managing deployed Llama models?

    a. Latency and throughput

    b. CPU/GPU usage and memory consumption

    c. Prediction error rates

    d. Printer usage

8. What role does automated alerting play in the management of deployed Llama models?

    a. It retrains the model automatically.

    b. It notifies the operations team when performance thresholds are breached.

    c. It scales down the cloud resources permanently.

    d. It encrypts data in transit.

9. How do Continuous Integration/Continuous Deployment (CI/CD) pipelines benefit the deployment of Llama models?

    a. They manually update the model after each error.

    b. They automate testing, deployment, and incremental updates to reduce service interruption.

   c. They remove the need for monitoring tools.

   d. They ensure that no changes are ever made to the model once deployed.

10. Which AWS tool is specifically designed for monitoring and logging in cloud-based deployments?

    a. Azure Monitor

    b. Google Cloud Monitoring

    c. AWS CloudWatch

    d. Prometheus

Answers

1. b
2. b
3. c
4. c
5. b
6. b
7. d
8. b
9. b
10. c

Chapter 9
Troubleshooting and Improving Llama Models

Introduction

In this chapter, readers will embark on a detailed exploration of troubleshooting and improving Llama models, equipping themselves with essential techniques to address common issues and challenges. The content is designed to guide you through the labyrinth of model debugging, offering clear, actionable strategies for diagnosing errors, resolving inconsistencies, and ultimately refining performance. Whether you are a data scientist, machine learning engineer, or an enthusiast eager to deepen your understanding, this chapter lays the groundwork for a methodical approach to overcoming hurdles that often accompany working with advanced Llama models.

As you progress, you will learn how to implement practical troubleshooting techniques and debugging strategies that are critical in maintaining robust model performance. The chapter not only highlights specific problems you might encounter but also provides a roadmap for continuous improvement, including iterative testing and optimization methods. By integrating real-world examples and hands-on exercises, you will gain the confidence to pinpoint issues swiftly and apply corrective measures, ensuring that your Llama models evolve and perform at their peak over time.

Structure

In this chapter, we will cover the following topics:

- Overview
- Common Issues in Llama Model Deployment
- Debugging Techniques for Llama Models

- Performance Monitoring and Optimization
- Continuous Improvement Strategies

Overview

In this overview, we delve into the essential aspects of troubleshooting and improving Llama models, addressing the common issues encountered during model deployment. Readers will be introduced to various challenges, such as integration hurdles and configuration mismatches, that can impede the smooth operation of Llama models. The discussion extends to robust debugging techniques tailored for these models, offering practical insights on how to systematically identify and resolve errors that emerge during both development and production stages.

Moreover, the chapter emphasizes the importance of performance monitoring and optimization to ensure the models operate efficiently under varying workloads. Techniques such as real-time tracking of system metrics and iterative performance testing are explored to help maintain peak operational standards. Additionally, continuous improvement strategies are presented as a cornerstone for long-term success, guiding practitioners on how to implement proactive updates and refinements. This comprehensive overview not only equips readers with the necessary troubleshooting tools but also lays the groundwork for an adaptive and resilient approach to managing Llama models over time.

Expanding further, this chapter integrates advanced debugging techniques that cater to the unique architecture of Llama models. Readers will learn how to leverage automated error detection, log analysis, and diagnostic simulations to pinpoint and mitigate subtle issues that can escalate into significant performance bottlenecks. By understanding the nuances of Llama model behavior, you can implement corrective measures that not only address immediate concerns but also fortify your deployment against future challenges.

Finally, the discussion on continuous improvement is designed to inspire a proactive mindset among practitioners. Through the exploration of case studies and real-world examples, you will discover how iterative refinements–driven by performance feedback and evolving use cases–can lead to more robust and scalable implementations. This holistic approach ensures that your Llama models remain at the forefront of innovation, delivering consistent value and adapting seamlessly to the dynamic demands of modern applications.

Common Issues in Llama Model Deployment

Llama models, known for their advanced capabilities in natural language processing and large-scale data handling, have emerged as powerful tools in modern AI applications. However, deploying these models in a real-world environment is rarely straightforward. The deployment process involves not only integrating complex model architectures into existing systems but also addressing a myriad of technical and operational challenges. In this guide, we explore the common issues that practitioners face during Llama model deployment, highlighting areas such as configuration mismatches, resource limitations, integration hurdles, and performance bottlenecks.

As the complexity of Llama models increases, so do the deployment challenges. It is crucial to understand that the hurdles faced are not solely tied to the model's design but also arise from the interplay of hardware constraints, software dependencies, and environmental factors. By identifying these common issues early, organizations and developers can build more resilient and scalable systems, ensuring that the promise of Llama models translates into tangible benefits across various applications.

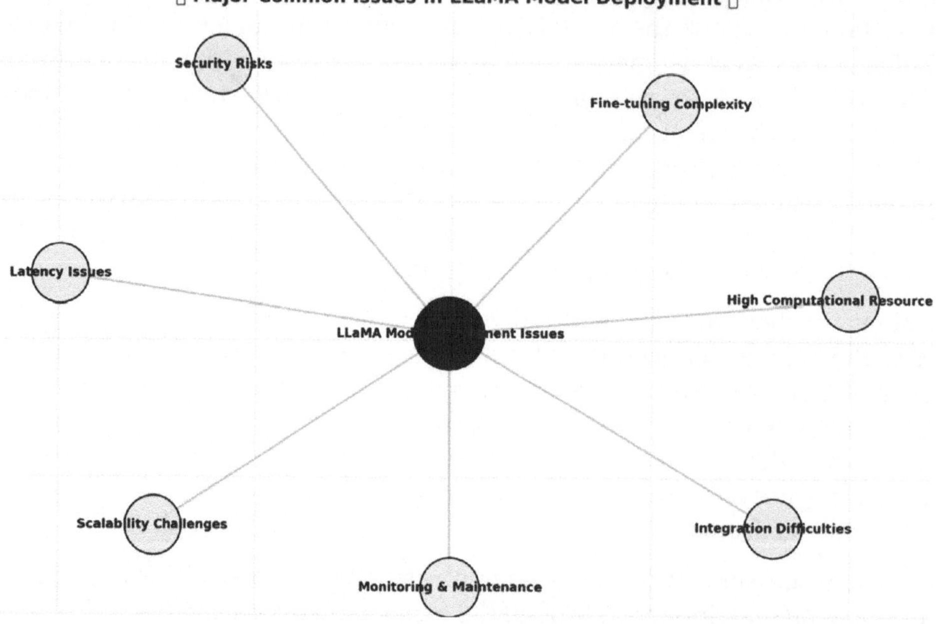

Figure 9.1: *Common Issues in Llama Model Deployment*

Configuration and Dependency Challenges

Deploying Llama models often encounters configuration and dependency challenges, such as discrepancies between development and production environments and conflicts arising from mismatched library versions. These issues can lead to subtle errors or complete deployment failures if not properly managed.

- **Environment Setup:** One of the most common issues in deploying Llama models stems from discrepancies in the environment setup. A production environment rarely mirrors the controlled conditions of a development or testing environment. Consider a scenario where a tech startup develops a Llama model on a local machine configured with a specific version of CUDA and TensorFlow. When they attempt to deploy the model on a cloud platform such as AWS or Azure, subtle differences–such as driver versions or even underlying OS patches–can lead to performance degradation or unexpected crashes. This phenomenon is a prime example of the "works on my machine" syndrome, underscoring the necessity for environment consistency through containerization tools such as Docker or Kubernetes.

- **Configuration Files and Parameter Settings:** Llama models rely on extensive configuration files that dictate everything from model architecture to data processing pipelines. Even a minor error–such as a misplaced comma or an incorrect file path–can lead to catastrophic deployment failures. For example, a misconfigured parameter that sets an excessively high learning rate might cause the model to diverge during fine-tuning, resulting in degraded performance when deployed in a customer-facing application. Using automated configuration management systems such as Ansible or Puppet can help ensure that all environments are standardized and that any modifications are automatically propagated across development, staging, and production systems.
- **Dependency Management:** Dependency management is a critical, yet often underestimated, aspect of Llama model deployment. In one real-time scenario, a global e-commerce company experienced significant downtime because a critical dependency–an optimized inference library–was updated to a new version incompatible with their deployed Llama model. This incompatibility led to performance bottlenecks that were not immediately apparent during initial tests. By leveraging virtual environments (such as Conda) and robust dependency management tools, developers can isolate and control the versions of libraries, ensuring compatibility and stability. Automated testing and dependency scanning should be an integral part of any deployment pipeline to catch these issues early.

Hardware and Resource Constraints

Hardware and resource constraints in Llama model deployment often manifest as the need for high-performance GPUs and ample memory to handle computationally intensive tasks. Efficient resource management–through load balancing, memory optimization, and careful hardware selection–is crucial to maintaining optimal performance in production environments.

- **GPU and CPU Limitations:** Llama models are resource-intensive, often requiring high-performance GPUs to handle the computation-heavy tasks of natural language processing. In one real-world example, a social media analytics firm deployed a Llama model on a server with outdated GPU hardware, leading to prolonged inference times and an inability to process high volumes of user data in real time. Conversely, in environments where only CPU-based inference is available, developers must balance model complexity with the available computational power. This scenario highlights the importance of choosing the right hardware and planning for hardware upgrades or optimizations, such as using model parallelism or quantization techniques to reduce computational load.

- **Memory Management:** Efficient memory management is vital to prevent out-of-memory (OOM) errors, especially when deploying large models such as Llama. Imagine a scenario where a streaming service deploys a Llama model to provide real-time content recommendations. Under heavy load, the model might require more RAM than initially allocated, causing performance to plummet as the system begins to swap memory to disk. Techniques such as dynamic batching, memory profiling, and even reducing model size through quantization or pruning can help alleviate these issues. Real-time monitoring tools that track memory usage trends can also provide early warning signs before a full-blown outage occurs.
- **Scalability and Load Balancing:** Scalability is not just about handling more data–it is about ensuring that the Llama model can adapt to increasing loads without degradation. For example, during a major sporting event, a broadcasting company might experience a surge in viewer engagement, causing a spike in requests to their deployed Llama model responsible for live commentary generation. Load balancing strategies, such as horizontal scaling with additional nodes or leveraging cloud-based auto-scaling features, become essential. However, the inherent complexity of Llama models means that scaling up is not always as straightforward as adding more hardware; it often requires re-architecting parts of the deployment to ensure efficient resource distribution and minimal latency.

Integration and Environment Issues

Integration and environment issues in Llama model deployment often arise from mismatches between the model's data formats, configuration settings, and the existing system infrastructure. Ensuring seamless communication between disparate components requires thorough testing and the development of robust middleware solutions.

- **Software Integration:** Integrating Llama models into existing ecosystems can reveal subtle incompatibilities that affect overall system performance. For instance, a media company integrating a Llama model into its content recommendation system found that discrepancies between the model's expected data format and the actual data produced by their legacy systems led to frequent errors. The solution involved developing middleware that standardized data formats and performed real-time validations before passing the data to the model. This integration challenge underscores the need for seamless communication between the Llama model and other system components, such as databases, APIs, and front-end interfaces.

- **Data Mismatch and Preprocessing:** A common pitfall during deployment is a mismatch between the data used during training and the data encountered in production. Consider a retail analytics firm that trained its Llama model on historical sales data formatted in a specific way. Once deployed, the model began to underperform because the live data stream was formatted differently–missing certain fields or using alternative encoding schemes. This type of data mismatch can be mitigated by implementing robust preprocessing pipelines that normalize incoming data, ensuring that it matches the expected input format of the model. Continuous validation and real-time data quality checks are essential components of a resilient deployment strategy.
- **Environmental Variability:** The production environment is dynamic and can introduce a host of unexpected variables that affect Llama model performance. For example, a logistics company deploying a Llama model for route optimization experienced issues during peak traffic hours, where network congestion led to delayed data transfers between distributed nodes. Similarly, varying disk I/O speeds across different data centers resulted in inconsistent response times. These real-time environmental variables necessitate the adoption of adaptive resource management strategies, such as dynamic load balancing and network optimization techniques, to maintain consistent performance regardless of external conditions.

Performance Bottlenecks and Optimization

Performance bottlenecks in Llama models often stem from heavy resource demands and inefficient data pipelines, which can slow down real-time processing. Employing optimization techniques–such as model pruning, quantization, and efficient caching–can significantly boost throughput and reduce latency.

- **Inference Latency:** Low inference latency is critical, particularly for applications that require real-time responses. A practical example is a customer service chatbot powered by a Llama model: if the model's response time exceeds user expectations, the customer experience suffers, potentially leading to reduced engagement and satisfaction. In one case, a telecommunications company encountered delays due to inefficient code paths and suboptimal GPU utilization. By employing advanced profiling tools and refining their code, they managed to cut down inference time by nearly 40%. Optimization techniques, such as model pruning and the use of specialized inference libraries, are often necessary to achieve the desired performance levels.

- **Resource Utilization:** Inefficient resource utilization not only increases operational costs but can also lead to system instability. In one scenario, a news aggregation service deployed a Llama model without proper resource monitoring, leading to sporadic system crashes during peak usage periods. By introducing real-time resource monitoring dashboards and setting automated alerts for CPU, GPU, and memory usage, the team was able to identify bottlenecks and reallocate resources dynamically. This proactive approach helped them fine-tune batch sizes, optimize thread counts, and ultimately create a more robust system capable of handling sudden surges in traffic.
- **Caching and Data Retrieval:** In many deployments, the speed at which data is retrieved and processed is just as important as the model's computational performance. A real-time example involves a gaming company that integrated a Llama model to generate personalized in-game content. They initially encountered performance issues due to slow data retrieval from a remote database. By implementing an in-memory caching solution and optimizing data retrieval queries, they were able to significantly reduce latency, ensuring that the game's dynamic content was delivered seamlessly to players. However, caching comes with its own challenges, such as cache invalidation and ensuring consistency across multiple nodes, which require careful design and ongoing management.
- **Load Testing and Benchmarking:** To effectively address performance issues before they affect end users, comprehensive load testing and benchmarking are critical. In one scenario, an online education platform scheduled a major virtual conference and needed to ensure that its deployed Llama model for live Q&A sessions could handle high volumes of concurrent queries. By simulating real-world traffic and stress-testing various components of the system, the development team identified several performance bottlenecks and optimized the model accordingly. Iterative testing, coupled with continuous benchmarking, enables organizations to preemptively address potential issues and ensure that their systems can handle unexpected spikes in demand.

Debugging and Troubleshooting in Production

It involves proactively identifying and resolving issues in live systems through real-time monitoring and detailed logging. This approach ensures minimal downtime and maintains optimal performance for end-users.

- **Logging and Monitoring:** Effective logging and monitoring are the lifelines of troubleshooting complex deployments. For Llama models, detailed logging–from configuration parameters and runtime metrics to error messages–is essential for identifying and resolving issues swiftly. In one real-time scenario, an online retailer experienced intermittent failures in their recommendation engine. By integrating comprehensive logging with real-time monitoring tools such as ELK (Elasticsearch, Logstash, and Kibana) stacks or Prometheus, the engineering team was able to quickly pinpoint that a specific parameter was causing the model to timeout under high load. This allowed them to adjust the configuration and stabilize the system, illustrating the importance of robust logging and monitoring practices.

- **Automated Error Detection:** In complex production environments, manual monitoring is not always sufficient. Automated error detection systems can play a crucial role in identifying anomalies before they escalate. For instance, a global logistics provider integrated an AI-driven anomaly detection system with their Llama model deployment. This system continuously analyzed runtime metrics and flagged unusual patterns, such as sudden spikes in inference times or unexpected drops in accuracy. By receiving timely alerts, the operations team was able to intervene early, preventing minor issues from becoming major system failures. Automated error detection not only reduces downtime but also allows for more efficient use of engineering resources.
- **Reproducibility and Testing:** Reproducing errors from production in a controlled environment is one of the most challenging aspects of debugging complex machine learning systems. A practical example can be seen in a fintech company that experienced sporadic failures in its Llama model used for real-time risk assessment. The errors were inconsistent and did not occur in the test environment, making diagnosis extremely difficult. The company resolved this by creating a dedicated staging environment that mirrored the production setup, complete with the same data flows and network configurations. This allowed them to reproduce the error consistently, ultimately leading to a fix. Automated testing frameworks–encompassing unit, integration, and end-to-end tests–further ensure that updates do not inadvertently introduce new issues, fostering a culture of continuous reliability.
- **Handling Model Drift:** Over time, even well-deployed models can suffer from model drift, where the statistical properties of the input data change, leading to degraded performance. In one scenario, an online news aggregator noticed that their Llama model for content personalization was gradually becoming less accurate over several months. Upon investigation, they discovered that the evolving nature of user interests and the introduction of new content formats had caused a shift in the underlying data distribution. The solution involved setting up regular evaluations of the model's performance, scheduled re-training cycles, and the implementation of drift detection algorithms that could alert the team to these changes. Addressing model drift is an ongoing process that requires both technical interventions and continuous data monitoring.

Security, Compliance, and Operational Risks

Deploying Llama models necessitates robust security measures to protect sensitive data and ensure compliance with regulations such as GDPR and HIPAA. Strict access controls, end-to-end encryption, and regular security audits are essential to mitigate potential vulnerabilities. Moreover, continuous monitoring and proactive risk management strategies help address operational risks such as system downtime and hardware failures, ensuring a resilient deployment environment.

- **Data Security and Privacy:** When deploying Llama models that process sensitive data, ensuring robust data security and privacy is paramount. In a real-world example, a healthcare provider deploying a Llama model for patient data analysis had to comply with stringent HIPAA regulations. A misconfiguration in the deployment environment nearly exposed sensitive patient information. This incident prompted the implementation of end-to-end encryption, strict access controls, and regular security audits. Secure data handling practices, including secure data transmission protocols and encrypted storage, are critical for preventing unauthorized access and maintaining trust with users.
- **Compliance and Regulatory Requirements:** Compliance with regulatory standards is not optional, especially in industries such as finance, healthcare, and retail. Consider a multinational bank deploying a Llama model for automated fraud detection; they must adhere to regulations such as GDPR for data protection in the European Union. This requires not only technical safeguards–such as anonymizing personal data–but also detailed audit trails and regular compliance reviews. The complexity of these regulatory requirements often necessitates collaboration between technical teams and compliance officers to ensure that all aspects of the deployment meet legal standards.
- **Operational Risks and Downtime:** Operational risks, such as unexpected system downtime or hardware failures, can have significant consequences. For example, an online gaming company relying on a Llama model for in-game content generation experienced system crashes during peak hours due to a combination of resource exhaustion and network latency. To mitigate such risks, it is essential to have robust disaster recovery plans, failover mechanisms, and redundancy architectures in place. Regular testing of these contingency plans through simulated drills helps ensure that the organization can quickly recover from unexpected failures with minimal disruption.

Strategies for Continuous Improvement

Continuous improvement is achieved by establishing iterative testing and robust feedback loops that allow teams to fine-tune model parameters based on real-time performance data. Leveraging automation and AI Ops tools helps streamline updates and reduce manual overhead. Regular cross-functional collaboration ensures that insights from various perspectives are integrated into the deployment process, keeping models efficient, scalable, and responsive to evolving demands.

- **Iterative Testing and Feedback Loops:** Continuous improvement is the cornerstone of managing Llama model deployments effectively. Organizations that implement iterative testing and feedback loops can quickly identify issues and adapt to changing conditions. For instance, an educational platform using a Llama model for personalized learning content scheduled weekly performance reviews. By analyzing user feedback and monitoring performance metrics, they were able to fine-tune the model's parameters and update preprocessing pipelines to accommodate evolving user behavior. This iterative approach not only improves model accuracy over time but also fosters a culture of proactive innovation.
- **Leveraging Automation and AI Ops:** Automation can significantly streamline many aspects of Llama model deployment, from configuration management to continuous monitoring. In one real-time example, a global media company integrated AI Ops tools that automatically detected and resolved minor configuration mismatches. This automation reduced the manual overhead and minimized human error, allowing the operations team to focus on more complex issues. Tools that automate dependency management, resource allocation, and even the retraining of models based on performance feedback are increasingly becoming integral to maintaining robust deployment pipelines.
- **Collaborative Problem Solving:** Complex deployments benefit greatly from cross-functional collaboration. Real-time scenario: a logistics company experiencing intermittent issues with its Llama-based route optimization model organized weekly cross-departmental review meetings. Engineers, data scientists, and operations teams shared insights, analyzed logs, and brainstormed solutions together. This collaborative approach led to the discovery of an overlooked caching issue and ultimately resulted in the implementation of a more resilient system architecture. Regular post-mortem analyses, knowledge-sharing sessions, and a culture that encourages transparency and open communication can significantly enhance the overall stability and performance of Llama model deployments.

Debugging Techniques for Llama models

Llama models have transformed the landscape of natural language processing and machine learning by providing high-quality outputs across diverse applications–from fraud detection in finance to personalized content recommendations in media. However, their complexity, often featuring billions of parameters spread over multiple layers and integrated within distributed systems, brings about numerous challenges when it comes to deployment and maintenance.

Debugging Llama models is not merely about fixing code; it involves continuous monitoring, systematic troubleshooting, and iterative refinement to ensure that these models function reliably in dynamic, real-world environments. Effective debugging techniques help identify performance bottlenecks, resolve data mismatches, and even predict potential issues before they escalate, thus reducing downtime and improving the overall user experience.

Understanding the Challenges in Debugging Llama Models

Before diving into specific debugging techniques, it is essential to grasp the challenges inherent in debugging Llama models:

- **Complex Model Architectures:** Llama models incorporate multi-layer neural networks, complex data flows, and intricate interdependencies among millions or billions of parameters. This complexity can make it difficult to isolate issues. A minor misconfiguration or a slight variation in the data can have a cascading effect, causing unexpected behaviors deep within the model.
- **Distributed and Heterogeneous Environments:** Many Llama models are deployed across clusters or cloud environments that span multiple servers, sometimes even across geographical regions. This distributed nature introduces additional variables–network latency, synchronization errors, and hardware inconsistencies–that complicate debugging efforts.
- **Integration with Data Pipelines:** The performance of a Llama model heavily depends on the accuracy and timeliness of data preprocessing pipelines. Any inconsistency between the training data and the live data can result in suboptimal outputs or system failures. Debugging must therefore encompass not just the model itself but also the entire data handling process.
- **Resource Constraints and Performance Bottlenecks:** Llama models are resource-hungry, often pushing the limits of available CPU, GPU, and memory capacities. Debugging in such environments requires techniques that can pinpoint resource-related issues, such as out-of-memory (OOM) errors, inefficient memory usage, or suboptimal parallel processing.

Understanding these challenges lays the groundwork for implementing targeted debugging techniques that address both the technical intricacies of the model and the operational realities of its deployment.

Key Debugging Techniques for Llama Models

To effectively troubleshoot Llama models, developers employ a suite of debugging techniques. Each technique addresses specific challenges, ensuring that errors are identified and resolved before they impact production.

Comprehensive Logging and Monitoring

Comprehensive logging and monitoring enable real-time tracking of Llama model performance by capturing detailed system-level and model-specific events. This proactive approach ensures prompt diagnosis of issues, minimizes downtime, and maintains operational reliability through automated alerts and centralized log management.

- **Granular Logging:** Implementing detailed logging is fundamental for tracking the internal state and behavior of Llama models. By instrumenting the code with logs at every critical operation–from data preprocessing and parameter updates to final inference outputs–developers can trace the exact flow of execution. For example, a well-placed log entry that records the output of a particular layer can help pinpoint where discrepancies first appear.
- **Centralized Log Management:** In distributed systems, logs from various nodes need to be aggregated and analyzed collectively. Tools such as the ELK stack (Elasticsearch, Logstash, Kibana) or Splunk enable centralized log management, providing dashboards that highlight anomalies in real time. With such systems in place, when a performance drop or error occurs on one node, the centralized dashboard can help identify if the problem is isolated or systemic.
- **Real-Time Monitoring and Alerts:** In addition to logging, continuous monitoring of system metrics–such as CPU usage, memory consumption, and network latency–is essential. Solutions such as Prometheus paired with Grafana dashboards allow teams to set up automated alerts. For instance, if inference latency suddenly spikes above a predefined threshold, the monitoring system can trigger an alert, prompting immediate investigation.

Impact: Comprehensive logging and monitoring provide a clear, real-time window into the inner workings of Llama models. They enable rapid diagnosis and resolution of issues, significantly reducing downtime and ensuring that minor errors do not escalate into major system failures.

Interactive Debugging

Interactive debugging allows developers to pause execution at specific points in the model's code, inspect variable states, and manipulate the environment in real-time to identify and resolve complex issues. This hands-on approach helps uncover bugs that automated tools might miss, improving the model's reliability and performance.

Interactive debugging empowers developers to pause code execution, inspect variable states, and test changes in real time, making it easier to pinpoint and resolve elusive bugs. This hands-on approach is invaluable for understanding complex model behaviors and rapidly iterating on fixes.

- **Breakpoints and Watchpoints:** Interactive debugging tools such as Python's pdb, or advanced IDE debuggers such as those in PyCharm, allow developers to set breakpoints–specific points in the code where execution is paused. At these breakpoints, developers can inspect variables, track function calls, and even modify the state on the fly. This is especially useful in pinpointing issues related to data transformations or parameter updates within the model.
- **Interactive Shells and Notebooks:** Using interactive Python shells (for example, IPython) or Jupyter Notebooks, developers can run code snippets in isolation. This is particularly beneficial when testing parts of the model in a controlled environment, allowing for rapid prototyping and debugging of individual components without the overhead of the entire system.
- **Remote Debugging:** In distributed deployments, remote debugging capabilities are crucial. Tools that allow developers to attach debuggers to processes running on remote servers enable real-time troubleshooting without needing to replicate the entire production environment locally.

Impact: Interactive debugging provides developers with the tools needed to step through code execution in a granular fashion. This hands-on approach often uncovers elusive bugs that automated logging might miss, improving both the robustness and reliability of Llama models.

Profiling and Performance Analysis

Profiling and performance analysis involve using tools such as code and GPU profilers to identify bottlenecks and optimize resource usage within Llama models. This helps improve inference speed, reduce latency, and ensure efficient use of computational resources.

Profiling and performance analysis pinpoint inefficient code paths and resource bottlenecks in Llama models, enabling targeted optimizations. This process reduces inference latency and enhances overall system efficiency.

- **Code Profiling:** Profilers such as cProfile or Py-Spy help measure the execution time of different parts of the code. By identifying which functions or layers in the model are the most time-consuming, developers can focus optimization efforts where they matter most. For example, if profiling reveals that a specific activation function is causing delays, it may be possible to replace or optimize that function to improve overall performance.

- **GPU Profiling:** For models that leverage GPU acceleration, profiling tools such as NVIDIA Nsight Systems or Visual Profiler are essential. These tools analyze GPU kernel execution, memory transfers, and resource utilization. They help diagnose issues such as inefficient parallelization or memory bottlenecks, which are critical in models with high computational demands.
- **Memory Profiling:** Memory profilers (such as memory profiler in Python) can track memory allocation over time, helping identify leaks or inefficient memory use. In Llama models where large data batches are processed, ensuring that memory is managed efficiently is key to preventing OOM errors that could otherwise halt the model's operation.

Impact: Profiling techniques enable targeted optimizations by identifying bottlenecks in code execution and resource usage. By addressing these bottlenecks, developers can reduce inference latency, optimize resource utilization, and ensure that the model scales effectively under heavy loads.

Automated Error and Anomaly Detection

It employs advanced algorithms to continuously monitor system metrics and identify deviations from normal behavior in real time. This proactive approach enables teams to swiftly address potential issues before they escalate, ensuring reliable performance of Llama models.

- **Anomaly Detection Algorithms:** Using statistical models or machine learning-based anomaly detection, developers can automatically identify deviations from normal performance metrics. These algorithms analyze historical data to establish baseline performance and flag sudden deviations, such as an unexpected drop in accuracy or a spike in response times.
- **Health Checks and Self-Monitoring:** Integrating periodic health checks into the deployment pipeline ensures that critical performance indicators are within acceptable ranges. For instance, a health check might verify that the model's output accuracy remains above a certain threshold. If the check fails, automated remediation steps can be initiated, such as restarting a specific process or rolling back to a previous version.
- **Automated Alert Systems:** By integrating tools such as PagerDuty with monitoring systems, developers can automate the notification process. When an anomaly is detected—such as a memory leak or an increase in error rate—alerts are sent to the responsible teams, prompting immediate investigation and resolution.

Impact: Automated error detection reduces the need for constant manual oversight and ensures that issues are identified and addressed swiftly. This proactive approach minimizes downtime and improves overall system stability, allowing for smoother model operation in production environments.

Unit Testing, Integration Testing, and Continuous Validation

Unit testing verifies that individual components of the Llama model function correctly, while integration testing ensures these components interact seamlessly. Continuous validation via CI/CD pipelines further detects regressions early, maintaining consistent and reliable performance.

- **Unit Testing:** Unit tests are the building blocks of a reliable system. By writing tests for individual functions and modules, developers ensure that each component behaves as expected. Libraries such as pytest provide a framework for automating these tests, ensuring that even the smallest code changes do not introduce new bugs.
- **Integration Testing:** Integration tests verify that different components of the Llama model work together seamlessly. For instance, tests might simulate the interaction between the data preprocessing pipeline and the inference engine, ensuring that data flows correctly through the system. Integration testing is critical in complex deployments where multiple subsystems interact.
- **Continuous Integration and Continuous Deployment (CI/CD):** Automated CI/CD pipelines (using tools such as Jenkins, GitLab CI, or CircleCI) run a comprehensive suite of tests with every code commit. This ensures that errors are caught early and that any new changes do not break existing functionality. Continuous validation, including regression testing, maintains the integrity and reliability of the model over time.

Impact: A rigorous testing framework significantly enhances the stability and maintainability of Llama models. By catching errors early and enforcing consistency across deployments, testing frameworks reduce the risk of critical failures in production, fostering confidence in the model's performance.

Reproducibility and Environment Replication

Reproducibility and environment replication ensure that Llama models function consistently across different stages of development, testing, and production by using containerization tools such as Docker and virtual environments. This consistency eliminates environment-specific discrepancies and simplifies troubleshooting by maintaining identical conditions for the model's execution.

- **Containerization:** Containerization tools such as Docker allow developers to package the Llama model along with its entire environment–dependencies, configurations, and libraries–into a single, portable container. This ensures that the model runs consistently across development, testing, and production environments, eliminating issues related to environment-specific discrepancies.

- **Virtual Environments and Dependency Management:** Using virtual environments (such as Python's venv or Conda), developers can isolate project-specific dependencies. This practice ensures that version conflicts and compatibility issues are minimized. Furthermore, tools such as pipenv or poetry can manage dependency trees more effectively, keeping the environment reproducible.
- **Snapshotting and Rollbacks:** Implementing snapshotting mechanisms for both the model and its environment allows teams to revert to a previously known-good state if debugging uncovers problematic changes. Version control systems, along with automated environment snapshots, create a safety net that ensures rapid recovery from failed updates or configuration errors.

Impact: Reproducibility through containerization and virtual environments simplifies the debugging process by ensuring consistency across all stages of development and deployment. This consistency not only streamlines troubleshooting efforts but also enhances collaboration among teams, as everyone works within identical environments.

The Impact of Debugging Techniques on Llama Model Performance

Implementing the debugging techniques outlined above can have a transformative impact on Llama model performance and operational efficiency:

- **Enhanced Reliability:** By systematically identifying and resolving bugs, the overall reliability of the system is significantly improved. This leads to fewer interruptions and more consistent outputs, which is critical in high-stakes applications such as finance and healthcare.
- **Improved Performance:** Profiling and performance analysis allow for targeted optimizations, reducing inference latency and ensuring efficient resource utilization. This is particularly beneficial in real-time applications where speed and accuracy are paramount.
- **Cost Efficiency:** Optimized resource usage and reduced downtime translate into lower operational costs. When models run efficiently, the infrastructure can support higher loads without requiring constant hardware upgrades.
- **Accelerated Development Cycles:** Robust debugging tools and continuous testing frameworks streamline the development process, allowing teams to innovate rapidly without compromising stability. This results in faster feature rollouts and quicker responses to emerging issues.
- **Better User Experience:** Ultimately, the cumulative effect of enhanced reliability, improved performance, and swift error resolution is a superior user experience. Whether it is through timely fraud detection, personalized

content, or accurate data analysis, users benefit from models that perform consistently and responsively.

Performance Monitoring and Optimization

Performance monitoring and optimization are critical pillars in the lifecycle of modern applications and systems. In today's dynamic technological landscape, where user expectations are high and operational demands are constantly evolving, maintaining peak performance is essential. This comprehensive guide delves into the advanced strategies, tools, and methodologies for performance monitoring and optimization, providing detailed insights and real-world examples that span across three to four pages of in-depth discussion.

The Critical Role of Performance Monitoring

At its essence, performance monitoring is about continuously tracking the health and efficiency of systems. It involves collecting and analyzing a wide array of metrics–from response times and throughput to resource utilization and error rates. This proactive approach allows organizations to quickly detect anomalies and address issues before they escalate, ensuring a seamless user experience.

Key Benefits of Robust Monitoring

- **Early Problem Detection:** Continuous monitoring helps identify performance degradation and bottlenecks at an early stage. For instance, if response times begin to increase subtly over a few minutes or hours, proactive alerts enable teams to investigate before users are affected.
- **Resource Optimization:** Monitoring tools provide insights into how hardware resources are being used. This helps in identifying underutilized components, avoiding unnecessary expenses, and ensuring that critical processes have adequate resources during peak loads.
- **Improved User Experience:** When systems perform optimally, users enjoy faster load times, smoother interactions, and reduced downtime. In competitive industries such as e-commerce or streaming services, this can lead to higher customer satisfaction and retention.
- **Data-Driven Decision Making:** With real-time metrics and historical performance data, organizations can make informed decisions about infrastructure upgrades, scaling strategies, and future investments. This helps in aligning technology initiatives with business goals.

Advanced Techniques and Tools for Performance Monitoring

To ensure continuous performance monitoring, organizations deploy a blend of cutting-edge techniques and powerful tools. These solutions provide deep visibility into the operational state of applications and infrastructure.

Real-Time Metrics Collection

Modern monitoring systems–such as **Prometheus**, **Datadog**, and **New Relic**–gather metrics in real time, offering an instantaneous snapshot of system health. These tools monitor critical indicators such as:

- **Response Times:** Tracking how quickly a system responds to requests.
- **Throughput:** Measuring the number of transactions or operations handled per unit time.
- **Resource Utilization:** Observing CPU, memory, disk I/O, and network usage to identify potential constraints.
- **Error Rates:** Keeping tabs on application errors, failed transactions, or exceptions, enabling swift corrective action.

The power of real-time metrics lies in the ability to set automated alerts. For example, if a web server's response time exceeds an established threshold, the system can automatically notify the operations team, ensuring rapid intervention.

Centralized Logging Systems

Centralized logging systems, such as the **ELK stack (Elasticsearch, Logstash, Kibana)** and **Splunk**, collect logs from various sources across the infrastructure. This consolidated view is indispensable for:

- **Correlating Events:** Linking errors and performance issues across multiple services.
- **Historical Analysis:** Reviewing past logs to detect patterns or recurring issues that might affect system performance.
- **Troubleshooting:** Quickly pinpointing the root cause of a problem through detailed log records.

For example, in a distributed microservices environment, a centralized log can reveal that a slowdown in one service is causing cascading delays in dependent services, enabling targeted fixes.

Synthetic Monitoring: Unlike traditional monitoring, which depends on real user interactions, synthetic monitoring involves simulating user behavior to evaluate performance. This technique is particularly useful for:

- **Proactive Testing:** Running simulated transactions at regular intervals to detect performance issues before they impact actual users.
- **Benchmarking:** Establishing performance baselines by simulating various user journeys under controlled conditions.
- **Off-Peak Analysis:** Monitoring system behavior during low-traffic periods to ensure that updates or maintenance activities do not negatively affect performance.

For instance, a financial application might use synthetic monitoring to simulate hundreds of simultaneous transactions during non-peak hours, ensuring that its payment processing system can handle high loads during peak business hours.

Distributed Tracing

In environments with a microservices architecture, distributed tracing is a crucial tool for tracking the journey of a request through multiple services. Tools such as **Jaeger** and **Zipkin** offer:

- **Visualization of Request Flows:** A graphical representation of how a request moves from one service to another, making it easier to identify latency or failure points.
- **Bottleneck Identification:** Pinpointing services that contribute disproportionately to overall response times.
- **End-to-End Diagnostics:** Providing insights that allow developers to trace issues from the front-end user interface all the way through to the back-end databases.

Distributed tracing ensures that even in complex, multi-tiered systems, each component's performance is visible and measurable.

Strategies for Performance Optimization

Once performance issues are identified, optimization strategies come into play. Optimization is an ongoing process aimed at enhancing system efficiency, reducing latency, and maximizing resource utilization.

Code-Level Optimizations: Optimizing the codebase is often the first step toward improving performance. This involves:

- **Refactoring Code:** Simplifying or reorganizing existing code to improve efficiency without changing functionality.

- **Optimizing Algorithms:** Replacing inefficient algorithms with more efficient ones to reduce computational overhead.
- **Minimizing Redundancies:** Eliminating unnecessary computations or duplicate operations.

Profiling tools such as **cProfile** and **Py-Spy** can help pinpoint inefficient segments of code. For example, a single inefficient loop in a high-traffic application might be optimized to shave off critical milliseconds, contributing to faster overall processing times.

Hardware and Infrastructure Scaling

As demand grows, scaling the underlying infrastructure is essential to maintaining performance. Scaling can be achieved in two primary ways:

- **Vertical Scaling:** Upgrading hardware components (such as CPU, memory, or storage) to increase capacity. This is often a quick fix but has physical limits.
- **Horizontal Scaling:** Adding more servers or nodes to distribute the load. Cloud platforms such as AWS, Azure, and Google Cloud offer auto-scaling features that automatically adjust resource allocation based on current demand.

For instance, an e-commerce platform experiencing a surge during a major sale event can leverage horizontal scaling to add additional web servers, ensuring that the increased load does not compromise user experience.

Caching Mechanisms

Caching is a powerful technique that can drastically reduce response times and alleviate pressure on back-end systems. Common caching strategies include:

- **In-Memory Caching:** Using tools such as **Redis** or **Memcached** to store frequently accessed data in memory for rapid retrieval.
- **Content Delivery Networks (CDNs):** Distributing static content (images, stylesheets, JavaScript) across geographically dispersed servers to minimize latency for users around the world.
- **Database Caching:** Caching the results of common database queries to reduce the load on the primary database server.

In real-world scenarios, a streaming service might implement a CDN to ensure that video content is delivered swiftly to viewers, regardless of their geographic location. Similarly, a social media platform might cache user profile data to provide instant access while reducing server load.

Database Optimization

Optimizing databases is crucial for applications that rely heavily on data retrieval and storage. Techniques include:

- **Query Optimization:** Analyzing and refining SQL queries to execute more efficiently.
- **Indexing:** Creating indexes on frequently queried columns to speed up data retrieval.
- **Database Sharding:** Distributing data across multiple databases to balance load and improve access speeds.
- **Regular Maintenance:** Routine tasks such as cleaning up outdated data, rebuilding indexes, and optimizing schemas.

For example, a healthcare system managing large volumes of patient data might optimize its database to ensure rapid access to critical records, thereby supporting timely medical decision-making.

Load Balancing and Traffic Management

Efficient load balancing ensures that no single server or component becomes a bottleneck. Key practices include:

- **Distributing Traffic Evenly:** Using load balancers to distribute incoming requests evenly across multiple servers.
- **Adaptive Routing:** Dynamically routing traffic based on current server performance and health.
- **Failover Mechanisms:** Ensuring that if one server fails, traffic is automatically rerouted to a backup server.

A practical example is an online gaming platform that uses load balancing to manage thousands of concurrent users, ensuring that gameplay remains smooth even if one server encounters high load or fails.

Continuous Optimization and Feedback Loops

Performance optimization is not a one-time task but a continuous process. Organizations should establish feedback loops that allow them to:

- **Monitor the Impact of Changes:** Use performance metrics to evaluate the effectiveness of optimizations.
- **Iterate and Refine:** Regularly review and adjust strategies based on evolving system demands and new data insights.

- **Implement CI/CD Pipelines:** Integrate performance testing into continuous integration and deployment pipelines to catch potential issues before they reach production.

For instance, an online retailer might conduct regular performance reviews during off-peak hours, using these sessions to fine-tune system configurations and prepare for upcoming high-traffic periods.

Real-World Applications and Their Impact

Real-world applications–from e-commerce to healthcare–leverage performance monitoring and optimization to deliver seamless user experiences and operational excellence. These practices lead to reduced latency, increased scalability, and improved efficiency, driving significant competitive advantages.

- **E-Commerce Platforms:** For e-commerce businesses, performance directly influences revenue. During high-traffic events such as Black Friday or Cyber Monday, every millisecond counts. By combining real-time monitoring with dynamic scaling and effective caching, these platforms can ensure smooth transactions and high conversion rates. Enhanced performance not only reduces cart abandonment but also builds consumer trust, leading to increased customer loyalty.
- **Streaming Services:** Streaming platforms rely heavily on robust performance to deliver uninterrupted, high-quality content. Real-time metrics help monitor video load times and streaming quality, while CDNs and caching minimize latency. These optimizations ensure that viewers experience minimal buffering and high-resolution playback, which is crucial for user retention in a highly competitive market.
- **Financial Institutions:** In the fast-paced world of finance, performance is critical for both operational efficiency and regulatory compliance. Trading platforms, for instance, require near-instantaneous data processing to execute trades at optimal prices. Continuous performance monitoring and optimization ensure that latency is minimized, reducing the risk of financial loss and enhancing the overall reliability of financial services.
- **Healthcare Systems:** Performance in healthcare systems can be a matter of life and death. Quick access to patient records and real-time data from medical devices is essential for prompt diagnosis and treatment. By optimizing database performance and ensuring rapid data retrieval, healthcare providers can offer timely, effective care while complying with stringent regulatory standards.

Continuous Improvement Strategies

Continuous improvement is a strategic approach that encourages organizations to persistently enhance processes, products, and services. By fostering a culture of relentless progress, companies can adapt to evolving market demands, innovate more effectively, and ultimately achieve operational excellence. This approach is not confined to a single methodology but rather encompasses a diverse range of strategies that can be tailored to meet the unique needs of any organization.

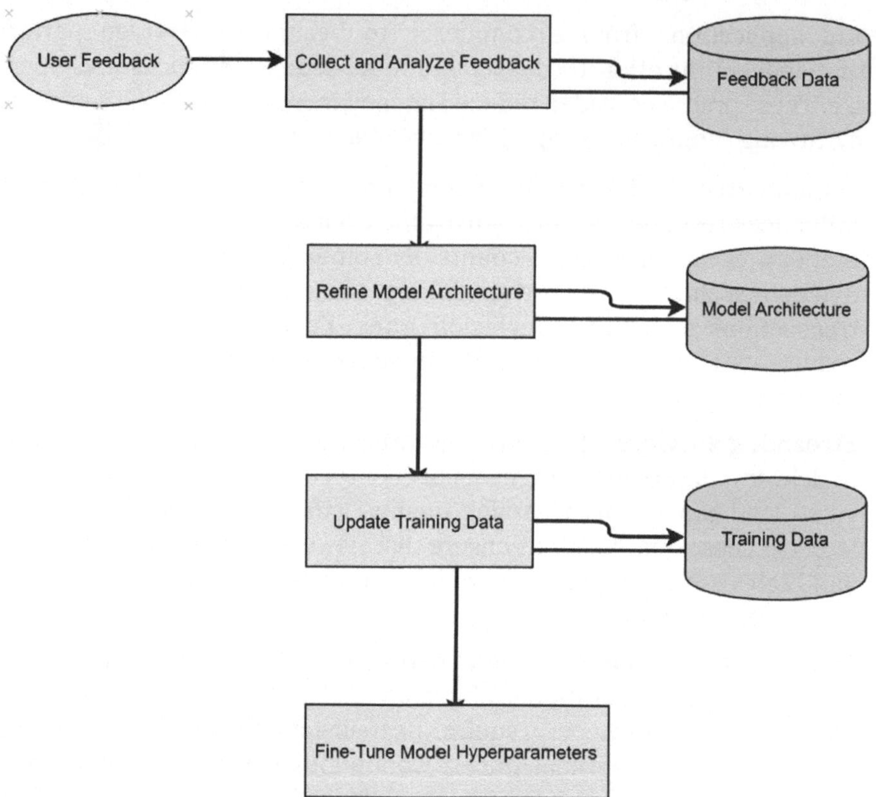

Figure 9.2: *Continuous Improvement Strategies*

The aforementioned flow includes the following components:

1. **External Entity->User Feedback**: Represents the input from users that is used to improve the Llama model.
2. **Process->Collect and Analyze Feedback**: Represents the process of collecting and analyzing user feedback to identify areas for improvement.
3. **Data Store->Feedback Data**: Represents the storage of feedback data collected from users.

4. **Process->Refine Model** Architecture: Represents the process of refining the Llama model architecture based on the feedback data.
5. **Data Store->Model Architecture**: Represents the storage of the refined model architecture.
6. **Process->Update Training Data**: Represents the process of updating the training data used to train the Llama model.
7. **Data Store->Training Data**: Represents the storage of the updated training data.
8. **Process->Fine-Tune Model Hyperparameters**: Represents the process of fine-tuning the hyperparameters of the Llama model.

Understanding Continuous Improvement and Key Elements

At its core, continuous improvement is the ongoing effort to incrementally enhance operations through a systematic review of processes and performance metrics. Rather than waiting for problems to arise, this strategy emphasizes proactive analysis, allowing teams to identify inefficiencies and implement corrective measures before issues become entrenched. In today's competitive landscape, organizations that commit to continuous improvement are better positioned to respond to changing customer needs, technological advancements, and industry trends.

- **Data-Driven Decision Making:** Organizations harness quantitative and qualitative data to monitor performance and guide improvement efforts. By analyzing key performance indicators (KPIs) and leveraging feedback loops, teams can pinpoint areas for enhancement and track the effectiveness of implemented changes.
- **Employee Empowerment:** Continuous improvement thrives in an environment where employees at all levels are encouraged to contribute ideas and participate in problem-solving. This inclusive approach not only leverages the collective intelligence of the workforce but also fosters a sense of ownership and accountability.
- **Iterative Processes:** Improvement is seen as an ongoing journey rather than a one-off project. Iterative methods such as the Plan-Do-Check-Act (PDCA) cycle allow organizations to implement changes gradually, evaluate their impact, and adjust strategies based on real-world outcomes.

Methodologies for Continuous Improvement

Several established methodologies provide a framework for continuous improvement, each offering distinct principles and techniques. Among these, a few stand out for their widespread adoption and proven effectiveness:

- **Lean and Six Sigma: Lean** focuses on streamlining processes by eliminating waste and ensuring that every step adds value. By identifying and removing non-essential activities, organizations can reduce costs and improve efficiency. **Six Sigma**, on the other hand, emphasizes reducing variability and improving quality through data-driven techniques. The combination of Lean and Six Sigma empowers organizations to achieve higher quality outcomes while maintaining operational efficiency.
- **Kaizen:** Originating in Japan, **Kaizen** is a philosophy that advocates for continuous, incremental improvement. The Kaizen approach encourages small, frequent changes that cumulatively lead to significant enhancements over time. This method emphasizes the importance of employee involvement and often involves cross-functional teams working together to identify and implement improvements.
- **Agile and DevOps:** In the realm of software development and IT operations, **Agile** methodologies and **DevOps** practices have revolutionized continuous improvement. Agile promotes iterative development cycles, where feedback is continuously integrated into the product development process. DevOps further enhances this by breaking down silos between development and operations teams, ensuring that improvements are rapidly deployed and continuously monitored in live environments.
- **Total Quality Management (TQM): Total Quality Management** is an organization-wide approach that integrates quality principles into every aspect of the business. TQM focuses on long-term success by embedding a quality-centric mindset into the organizational culture. This holistic strategy ensures that every employee, from top management to frontline workers, is committed to continuous improvement and customer satisfaction.

Implementing Continuous Improvement Strategies

Effective implementation of continuous improvement strategies requires a systematic approach that integrates strategic planning, employee engagement, and technological support. Here are key steps to successfully deploy these strategies within an organization:

Establishing Clear Objectives: The journey begins with setting clear, measurable objectives aligned with the organization's long-term goals. These objectives serve as benchmarks against which progress can be measured. Whether the focus is on reducing operational costs, improving product quality, or enhancing customer satisfaction, having well-defined targets ensures that every improvement initiative is purposeful and directed.

Cultivating a Culture of Continuous Improvement: Creating an environment where continuous improvement is part of the organizational DNA is critical. This involves:

- **Leadership Commitment:** Leaders must champion improvement initiatives, demonstrating a commitment to ongoing learning and innovation. Their support sets the tone for the entire organization.
- **Training and Development:** Empower employees with the skills and knowledge needed to identify and solve problems. Regular training sessions, workshops, and access to improvement tools can help staff at all levels contribute effectively.
- **Open Communication:** Establish channels for open dialogue where employees can share ideas, report issues, and collaborate on solutions. Recognition and reward systems further motivate teams to engage actively in continuous improvement efforts.

Leveraging Technology and Data Analytics: Modern technologies play a pivotal role in facilitating continuous improvement. Tools such as performance monitoring systems, business intelligence platforms, and process automation software provide real-time insights that drive data-informed decision-making. By continuously analyzing operational data, organizations can swiftly identify trends, isolate inefficiencies, and implement corrective measures before minor issues escalate into major disruptions.

Iterative Testing and Feedback Loops: A hallmark of continuous improvement is the willingness to test, learn, and adapt. Implementing iterative testing cycles, such as the PDCA cycle, allows teams to:

- **Plan:** Develop improvement initiatives based on data analysis and stakeholder feedback.
- **Do:** Implement the changes on a small scale to evaluate their impact.
- **Check:** Monitor the outcomes against expected results, using performance metrics as a guide.
- **Act:** Scale successful changes across the organization or adjust strategies based on feedback.

This iterative process ensures that improvement efforts are dynamic and responsive, continuously evolving in line with changing business needs and market conditions.

The Impact of Continuous Improvement Strategies

When executed effectively, continuous improvement strategies deliver significant benefits across various dimensions of an organization. These impacts include:

- **Enhanced Operational Efficiency:** By systematically eliminating waste and optimizing processes, organizations can achieve substantial improvements in efficiency. Streamlined operations reduce turnaround times, lower costs, and enable faster response to market changes.

- **Increased Employee Engagement and Innovation:** A culture of continuous improvement empowers employees to contribute actively to the organization's success. This not only boosts morale but also drives innovation, as diverse teams collaborate to solve problems and develop creative solutions.
- **Improved Customer Satisfaction:** Continuous improvement initiatives lead to higher quality products and services, directly translating into improved customer experiences. Satisfied customers are more likely to become repeat buyers and advocates for the brand, contributing to long-term business success.
- **Sustainable Competitive Advantage:** Organizations that embed continuous improvement into their core operations are better positioned to adapt to disruptions and capitalize on new opportunities. This adaptability fosters long-term resilience and provides a sustainable competitive advantage in an ever-evolving marketplace.

Conclusion

Continuous improvement strategies are not just a set of processes but a dynamic philosophy that empowers organizations to evolve, innovate, and excel in an ever-changing marketplace. By embracing methodologies such as Lean, Six Sigma, Kaizen, Agile, and TQM, companies can systematically eliminate inefficiencies, drive down costs, and enhance quality, while robust data-driven decision-making and iterative testing ensure that every process is continuously refined. Coupled with modern technologies such as real-time monitoring and advanced analytics, these strategies foster a culture of proactive problem-solving and employee engagement, ultimately transforming challenges into opportunities. This relentless pursuit of excellence not only elevates customer satisfaction and operational efficiency but also builds a sustainable competitive advantage, positioning organizations to thrive amid uncertainty and rapid market shifts.

In the next chapter, we embark on a transformative journey into the concept of transfer learning with Llama models. This chapter will reveal how pre-trained models can be effortlessly fine-tuned to tackle your unique NLP challenges–whether it is sentiment analysis, text classification, or other domain-specific tasks–without the need for exorbitant computational resources. You will discover how transfer learning not only slashes training time but also significantly boosts model efficiency and performance. By exploring a variety of real-world use cases and detailed examples, you will gain a deep understanding of how to harness this powerful approach to optimize and adapt Llama models to your specific needs in an ever-evolving technological landscape.

Multiple Choice Questions

1. What is the primary goal of performance monitoring in modern IT systems?
   a. To increase operational costs
   b. To track system health and ensure optimal performance
   c. To complicate the troubleshooting process
   d. To eliminate the need for hardware scaling
2. Which of the following tools is commonly used for real-time metrics collection?
   a. Excel
   b. Prometheus
   c. Visual Studio
   d. MATLAB
3. What is the main purpose of centralized logging systems such as the ELK stack (Elasticsearch, Logstash, and Kibana)?
   a. To aggregate logs from various sources for unified analysis
   b. To simulate user behavior during off-peak hours
   c. To replace distributed tracing in microservices
   d. To manage hardware upgrades automatically
4. Synthetic monitoring is best described as a technique that:
   a. Collects metrics solely from live user interactions
   b. Simulates user behavior to test and benchmark system performance
   c. Aggregates logs from multiple servers in real time
   d. Monitors only the CPU and memory usage of a system
5. What is a significant benefit of transfer learning when working with Llama models?
   a. It significantly increases the computational resource requirements.
   b. It allows fine-tuning of pre-trained models for specific tasks with reduced training time.

   c. It mandates starting model training from scratch.

   d. It decreases model efficiency in specialized applications.

6. Continuous improvement strategies emphasize:

   a. One-time overhauls of operational processes

   b. Ongoing, iterative enhancements based on data-driven insights and feedback

   c. Eliminating employee participation in problem-solving

   d. Relying solely on top-down directives for process changes

7. Which of the following methodologies is NOT typically associated with continuous improvement?

   a. Lean

   b. Six Sigma

   c. Kaizen

   d. Waterfall

8. In the context of performance optimization, what is the key difference between vertical scaling and horizontal scaling?

   a. Vertical scaling adds more servers, while horizontal scaling upgrades existing hardware

   b. Vertical scaling upgrades existing hardware, while horizontal scaling adds more servers

   c. Both terms refer to the same scaling method

   d. Neither scaling method addresses resource utilization

9. Distributed tracing is primarily used to:

   a. Monitor server CPU and memory usage

   b. Visualize the flow of requests across multiple services in a distributed system

   c. Automate the process of database sharding

   d. Optimize caching mechanisms exclusively

10. How do continuous improvement strategies impact employee engagement?
    a. They discourage employee input by centralizing decision-making.
    b. They empower employees at all levels to contribute ideas and participate in iterative problem-solving.
    c. They reduce the need for feedback and collaborative work.
    d. They primarily focus on top management directives without involving frontline workers.

Answers

1. b
2. b
3. a
4. b
5. b
6. b
7. d
8. b
9. b
10. b

CHAPTER 10
Transfer Learning Techniques with Llama

Introduction

Transfer learning has revolutionized the way we approach complex machine learning challenges by leveraging pre-trained models and adapting them to new tasks. In this chapter, you will explore how models such as Llama, Llama2, and Llama3 serve as powerful starting points, reducing the need for extensive computational resources and time. This introduction sets the stage by explaining the core principles of transfer learning and its transformative impact on model efficiency.

Throughout the chapter, you will learn the fundamentals of transfer learning, including the process of fine-tuning pre-trained models for specific applications. The content is designed to help you understand why transfer learning is an essential strategy in modern NLP and how it can dramatically shorten the training cycle while enhancing performance. By grounding the discussion in real-world examples, you will see the practical benefits of adapting these models to your unique tasks.

By the end of this chapter, you will not only grasp the critical concepts behind transfer learning but also be equipped with actionable strategies to optimize Llama models for diverse NLP applications. Whether you are a seasoned professional or new to the field, this guide will empower you to implement transfer learning effectively, opening up new avenues for innovation in your work.

Structure

In this chapter, we will cover the following topics:

- Overview
- Transfer Learning and Its Importance in NLP

- Pre-Trained Models and Their Advantages
- Fine-Tuning Llama Models for Custom Tasks
- Case Studies: Adapting Llama for Text Classification and Sentiment Analysis

Overview

Transfer learning has emerged as a pivotal technique in the field of Natural Language Processing (NLP), offering a pathway to harness the power of pre-trained models that have already learned complex language representations. These models, built on vast amounts of data, come with significant advantages such as reduced training times and enhanced performance across diverse applications. By leveraging pre-trained models, practitioners can bypass the extensive computational costs associated with training models from scratch, paving the way for more efficient and accessible NLP solutions.

A critical application of this approach involves fine-tuning Llama models for custom tasks. This process allows developers to adapt robust, pre-existing architectures to niche applications such as text classification and sentiment analysis. Through a series of case studies, you will explore how fine-tuning transforms Llama models to accurately interpret and analyze specific text corpora, ultimately demonstrating the versatility and practical benefits of transfer learning in real-world scenarios.

Transfer Learning and Its Importance in NLP

In recent years, Natural Language Processing (NLP) has experienced a paradigm shift, largely driven by the advent of transfer learning. Traditionally, building high-performance NLP models required enormous datasets and substantial computational resources. However, transfer learning has redefined the process by allowing practitioners to leverage pre-trained models–ones that have already been exposed to vast amounts of language data–and adapt them to specific tasks with relatively little extra training. This approach not only accelerates development time but also dramatically improves efficiency and performance in tasks such as sentiment analysis, text classification, and even more complex language understanding applications.

Transfer learning in NLP is built on a simple yet powerful idea: rather than training a model from scratch, you start with a model that has already learned general language representations from large corpora. This pre-trained model is then fine-tuned on a smaller, task-specific dataset. As a result, the model brings along a wealth of linguistic knowledge–ranging from syntax and grammar to semantics and context–which significantly reduces the need for massive labeled datasets and heavy computation. In this article, we will explore what transfer learning is, its role in modern NLP, and why it has become an indispensable tool for researchers and practitioners alike.

The Fundamentals of Transfer Learning in NLP

Transfer learning in NLP involves leveraging pre-trained models that have already learned rich language representations from vast amounts of data, and then fine-tuning them for specific tasks. This approach significantly reduces training time and computational resources while boosting performance across a wide range of applications.

Defining Transfer Learning: Transfer learning is a machine learning approach where a model developed for one task is reused as the starting point for a model on a second task. In the realm of NLP, this typically involves taking a large-scale pre-trained model (for example, models such as BERT, GPT, or the more recent Llama series) and adapting it to new tasks. The essence of transfer learning lies in its ability to transfer the '*knowledge*' acquired from general language understanding to more specialized tasks.

The process is usually divided into two phases:

1. **Pre-training:** During this phase, the model learns broad language features by training on an extensive and diverse dataset.
2. **Fine-tuning:** Here, the pre-trained model is further trained on a smaller, task-specific dataset to adjust its parameters and optimize its performance for the particular application at hand.

This methodology not only helps in mitigating the challenge of limited annotated data for niche tasks but also significantly cuts down on the overall training time and resource requirements.

Benefits of Pre-Trained Models

Pre-trained models have transformed the NLP landscape by embedding vast amounts of linguistic information into a single model. Models such as Llama, Llama2, and Llama3 are prime examples of how extensive pre-training on diverse datasets can lead to robust and versatile language representations. These models come equipped with an understanding of language that spans multiple tasks, from syntactic parsing to semantic analysis.

Key benefits of using pre-trained models include:

- **Efficiency:** Since the heavy lifting of language learning is done during the pre-training phase, fine-tuning requires far less data and computational power.

- **Improved Performance:** Pre-trained models have been shown to outperform models trained from scratch, especially when task-specific data is scarce.
- **Versatility:** These models can be adapted for a wide range of NLP tasks, making them highly flexible tools in a data scientist's toolkit.
- **Rapid Deployment:** With reduced training times, organizations can deploy NLP solutions more quickly, driving faster innovation cycles.

The transition from training models from scratch to employing transfer learning methods has not only democratized access to advanced NLP capabilities but has also paved the way for more experimental and specialized applications.

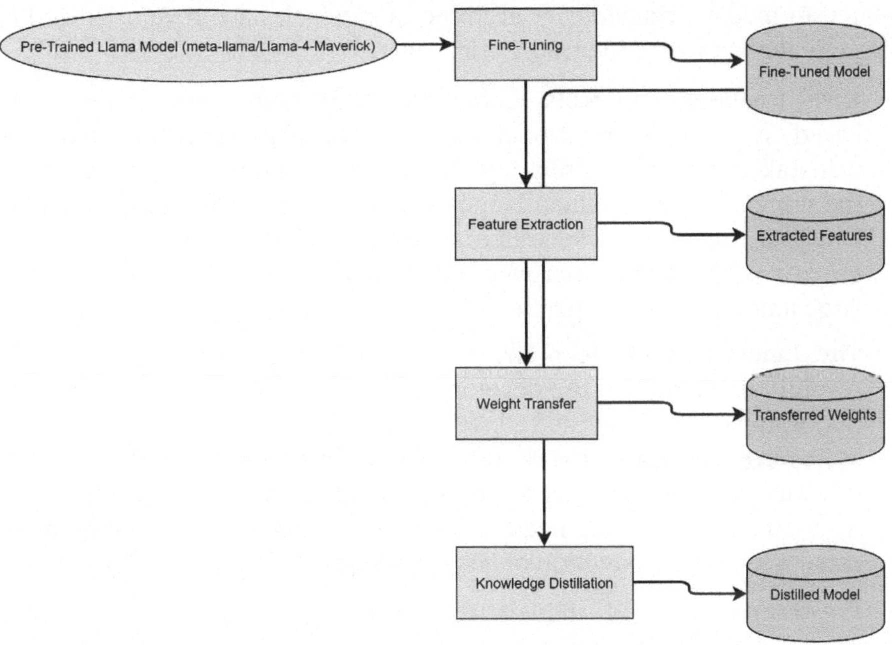

Figure 10.1: *Major Transfer Learning Techniques*

The data flow steps for the diagram are as follows:

1. The pre-trained Llama 4 model is used as input to the fine-tuning process.
2. The fine-tuning process generates a fine-tuned model.
3. The pre-trained Llama 4 model is used as input to the feature extraction process.
4. The feature extraction process generates extracted features.
5. The pre-trained Llama 4 model is used as input to the weight transfer process.
6. The weight transfer process generates transferred weights.

7. The fine-tuned model is used as input to the knowledge distillation process.
8. The knowledge distillation process generates a distilled model.

Historical Context and the Evolution of Transfer Learning

Historically, early NLP systems depended on rule-based approaches and labor-intensive feature engineering, limiting their ability to capture language nuances. The advent of deep learning and large-scale pre-training transformed this landscape, allowing models to learn rich representations from vast datasets. This evolution culminated in modern transformer architectures which have revolutionized NLP by enabling efficient and versatile transfer learning.

- **Early Challenges in NLP:** Historically, NLP models were built using rule-based systems or traditional machine learning algorithms that required painstaking feature engineering. These early approaches often struggled with the complexities of human language, particularly in understanding context, ambiguity, and varied sentence structures. The advent of neural networks brought about some improvements, but early neural models still required large amounts of task-specific data to perform well.
- **The Emergence of Deep Learning and Pre-training:** The deep learning revolution, marked by the development of models such as word embeddings (for example, Word2Vec and GloVe) and later more complex architectures such as Recurrent Neural Networks (RNNs) and Long Short-Term Memory networks (LSTMs), began to address some of these challenges. However, these models were still limited by the need for substantial labeled data. The breakthrough came with the introduction of large-scale pre-training techniques.

  Pre-training allowed models to learn from raw text without explicit supervision. This unsupervised learning phase enabled models to capture nuanced language patterns, syntactic structures, and semantic relationships. Once these patterns were internalized, the models could be fine-tuned with much less data for specific tasks—a practice that revolutionized NLP research and applications.
- **The Rise of Transformer Architectures:** The introduction of transformer architectures, notably with models such as BERT (Bidirectional Encoder Representations from Transformers) and GPT (Generative Pre-trained Transformer), further accelerated the impact of transfer learning in NLP. Transformers leverage self-attention mechanisms to capture contextual dependencies across long sequences of text, making them particularly adept at understanding complex language structures.

These models demonstrated that with sufficient pre-training, a single model could perform multiple tasks with minimal additional training. The success of transformer-based models has led to widespread adoption of transfer learning techniques in both academia and industry, forming the backbone of many modern NLP applications.

Implementation and Practical Applications

Implementation involves fine-tuning pre-trained models on domain-specific datasets, enabling them to perform specialized tasks such as sentiment analysis or text classification. This approach dramatically reduces training time and resource requirements while enhancing model accuracy. As a result, these practical applications have made transfer learning an indispensable strategy in modern NLP.

Fine-Tuning Pre-Trained Models for Custom Tasks

Once a model is pre-trained, the next step is fine-tuning. Fine-tuning involves taking the pre-trained model and training it on a smaller dataset that is specific to the task at hand. This step adjusts the pre-trained parameters just enough to make the model effective for that particular application. Fine-tuning has several key advantages:

- **Task Specialization:** Fine-tuning adapts the general knowledge from the pre-trained model to the nuances of a specific task such as sentiment analysis or text classification.
- **Reduced Overfitting:** Because the model starts with a solid foundation of general language understanding, it requires less task-specific data, which helps in reducing the risk of overfitting.
- **Speed:** Fine-tuning typically takes much less time than training a model from scratch, making it a more efficient process overall.

In practical settings, fine-tuning involves careful selection of hyperparameters, the use of task-specific loss functions, and sometimes even modifying the architecture slightly to suit the unique needs of the task. For example, when adapting a model for sentiment analysis, one might adjust the output layer to reflect the number of sentiment categories (positive, negative, neutral) and then retrain the model on annotated reviews.

Case Studies: Real-Time Applications

Several case studies have demonstrated the transformative impact of transfer learning in NLP. Consider the following examples:

- **Text Classification:** Organizations that need to categorize customer feedback or classify news articles can leverage pre-trained models to achieve high accuracy. By fine-tuning a model on a relatively small set of labeled examples, companies can rapidly deploy classifiers that understand the subtleties of language, leading to better customer insights and more efficient content management systems.

- **Sentiment Analysis:** In sentiment analysis, the objective is to determine the emotional tone behind a series of words. Fine-tuning a pre-trained model on annotated datasets that represent various sentiments can yield highly accurate results. Such applications are invaluable in marketing, social media monitoring, and customer service, where understanding public sentiment can drive strategic decisions.
- **Domain-Specific Applications:** Transfer learning is especially beneficial in specialized domains where large labeled datasets may not be available. For example, in legal or medical NLP applications, fine-tuning a pre-trained model can help overcome the challenges posed by domain-specific language and terminology. This ensures that even niche fields can benefit from advanced language processing capabilities.

These case studies highlight the versatility of transfer learning in tackling a diverse array of problems. By providing a robust starting point and allowing for rapid customization, transfer learning not only saves time and resources but also opens up new possibilities for innovation across various industries.

Benefits, Challenges, and Solutions

Transfer learning in NLP offers significant benefits such as enhanced efficiency, reduced resource needs, and improved performance, yet it also brings challenges such as domain mismatch and overfitting. Effective solutions include careful fine-tuning, robust regularization, and domain-adaptive strategies to optimize model accuracy and resilience.

Key Benefits Recap

The advantages of transfer learning in NLP are numerous and far-reaching:

- **Resource Optimization:** Leveraging pre-trained models drastically reduces the need for large labeled datasets and extensive computational resources.
- **Enhanced Accuracy:** Models pre-trained on diverse data tend to generalize better, leading to higher accuracy on downstream tasks.
- **Rapid Deployment:** With shorter fine-tuning cycles, organizations can bring advanced NLP solutions to market quickly.
- **Flexibility:** Transfer learning supports a wide array of applications, making it a universal tool across various industries.

Addressing the Challenges

Despite its many benefits, transfer learning is not without challenges. Some common issues include:

- **Domain Mismatch:** When there is a significant difference between the pre-training and fine-tuning data, models can struggle to adapt. Solutions include domain-adaptive pre-training and careful data curation.
- **Risk of Overfitting:** Fine-tuning on small datasets can sometimes lead to overfitting. Using techniques such as cross-validation, regularization, and data augmentation can help mitigate this risk.
- **Computational Demands:** Although less demanding than training from scratch, fine-tuning large models still requires significant hardware resources. Cloud-based solutions and model compression techniques (such as pruning or quantization) are promising avenues to reduce these requirements.
- **Interpretability:** The "black box" nature of deep learning models can obscure why a model makes certain predictions. Advances in explainable AI (XAI) and attention visualization techniques are making strides toward greater transparency and trustworthiness.

Strategies for Success

To maximize the benefits of transfer learning while addressing its challenges, practitioners should adopt a multi-pronged strategy:

- **Rigorous Evaluation:** Regularly assess model performance using diverse metrics (accuracy, F1 score, and so on) to ensure that fine-tuning is effective.
- **Iterative Refinement:** Use iterative training cycles and continuous feedback loops to gradually improve model performance.
- **Community and Collaboration:** Leverage open-source libraries, community benchmarks, and shared research findings to stay abreast of best practices and emerging techniques.

Integration with Emerging AI Techniques

Integration with emerging AI techniques, such as reinforcement learning and meta-learning, is enhancing the adaptability and efficiency of transfer learning models. These hybrid approaches enable models to dynamically adjust and optimize their performance, paving the way for more robust and context-aware NLP applications.

- **Combining Transfer Learning with Reinforcement Learning:** Recent research has begun exploring the synergy between transfer learning and reinforcement learning (RL). In this hybrid approach, a pre-trained language model can serve as a starting point for an RL agent, which then learns to optimize specific tasks through interaction with an environment. This integration can lead to more dynamic and adaptive systems, capable of not just understanding language but also taking context-sensitive actions.

- **Meta-Learning and Few-Shot Learning:** Meta-learning, or "*learning to learn*," is another area where transfer learning is making an impact. By training models to quickly adapt to new tasks with minimal data (few-shot learning), researchers are pushing the boundaries of how efficiently a model can transfer knowledge. This capability is particularly useful in scenarios where data is sparse or expensive to label.
- **Hybrid Architectures:** In practice, the future of NLP is likely to see hybrid architectures that combine the strengths of different learning paradigms. For example, transformer models pre-trained on massive datasets could be integrated with graph-based methods or convolutional architectures to capture both global context and fine-grained local patterns. These hybrid systems promise to further enhance the versatility and effectiveness of NLP solutions.

Evaluating Transfer Learning Systems

Evaluating transfer learning systems involves assessing both quantitative metrics, such as accuracy, precision, recall, and F1 score, and qualitative aspects, such as robustness, fairness, and adaptability to domain-specific tasks. Additionally, practitioners benchmark these systems on real-world datasets while considering factors such as inference speed and scalability to ensure they meet production standards.

Performance Metrics and Benchmarks: Measuring the success of transfer learning models involves a range of metrics beyond simple accuracy. Precision, recall, F1 score, and Area Under the Curve (AUC) are commonly used to evaluate performance across various tasks. Additionally, benchmarks such as GLUE (General Language Understanding Evaluation) and SuperGLUE provide standardized ways to assess model performance in a controlled, comparative environment.

Real-World Impact and Deployment Considerations: Evaluating a model in a laboratory setting is only part of the equation. For successful deployment in real-world applications, additional factors must be considered:

- **Scalability:** Can the model handle large volumes of data in production?
- **Latency:** How quickly does the model respond, especially in time-critical applications?
- **Robustness:** How does the model perform when exposed to noisy or unexpected inputs?

- **Ethical and Bias Considerations:** Are the model's outputs fair, transparent, and free of unintended bias?

Incorporating these factors into the evaluation process ensures that transfer learning models are not only academically robust but also practical and reliable in real-world settings.

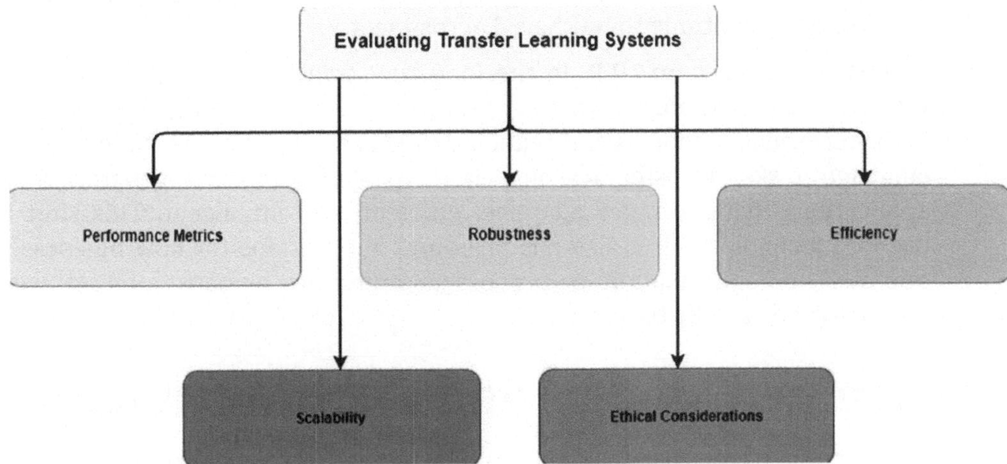

Figure 10.2: *Major Evaluation Transfer Learning System*

Future Directions and Research Opportunities

Future research in transfer learning for NLP is expected to focus on developing more efficient pre-training techniques and enhancing model interpretability, ensuring that models are both powerful and transparent. Additionally, exploring cross-domain, multilingual, and multimodal applications will drive innovation, enabling AI systems to tackle a broader range of real-world challenges.

- **Innovations on the Horizon:** The landscape of transfer learning in NLP is rapidly evolving. Future research is likely to focus on:
  - **More Efficient Pre-Training Methods:** Innovations in training algorithms and data curation that reduce the computational footprint of pre-training.
  - **Enhanced Interpretability:** Developing techniques to open the "black box" of deep learning models, making their decision-making processes more transparent.
  - **Ethical AI and Bias Mitigation:** Proactive measures and frameworks to detect, understand, and mitigate biases in pre-trained models.
  - **Cross-Domain and Multimodal Learning:** Extending transfer learning beyond text to integrate other modalities such as images, audio, and structured data, thus enabling richer, more holistic AI systems.

- **Collaboration between Academia and Industry:** The rapid advancement in transfer learning is fueled by a collaborative ecosystem that spans academia, industry, and open-source communities. Researchers are constantly publishing new techniques and benchmarks, while companies deploy these innovations in applications ranging from virtual assistants to automated content generation. This synergy is likely to accelerate progress even further, as best practices and novel insights continue to be shared across sectors.
- **Long-Term Impact on NLP:** In the long run, transfer learning is poised to redefine the boundaries of what is possible in NLP. By democratizing access to high-performance models and reducing the barrier to entry for sophisticated language tasks, transfer learning is empowering a new generation of applications that are more adaptive, efficient, and intelligent. This shift is not just technological–it also has profound implications for how businesses operate, how information is processed, and how humans interact with technology on a daily basis.

Pre-Trained Models and Their Advantages

Pre-trained models have emerged as a transformative force in Natural Language Processing (NLP), fundamentally altering the way we approach language understanding and generation. These models, developed by training on enormous datasets, capture rich linguistic structures and patterns that serve as a powerful foundation for a wide array of downstream tasks. Among the most advanced in this domain are the Llama models–Llama, Llama2, and Llama3–which illustrate the tremendous progress made in transfer learning. In this comprehensive exploration, we examine the inner workings of pre-trained models, delve into their multifaceted advantages, and detail how these benefits are exemplified in the architecture and design of Llama models.

Understanding Pre-Trained Models

Understanding pre-trained models involves recognizing that these models are initially trained on vast, diverse datasets to learn the fundamental structures and nuances of language. They capture patterns, syntax, and semantic relationships, which serve as a robust foundation for fine-tuning on specific NLP tasks. This foundational training makes them both efficient and versatile for a wide range of applications.

- **The Pre-Training Process:** At the heart of pre-trained models is the pre-training process, where a neural network is exposed to vast and diverse corpora of text data. During this phase, the model learns to predict words, phrases, or tokens based on the surrounding context without explicit human labeling. Techniques such as masked language modeling and autoregressive prediction empower the model to internalize syntactic patterns, semantic relationships, and even subtle cultural nuances embedded in language. The result is a model that possesses a generalized understanding of language–knowledge that can later be harnessed for specific tasks with minimal additional training.

- **Integration with Transfer Learning:** Pre-training sets the stage for transfer learning–a two-stage process comprising pre-training and fine-tuning. After the initial unsupervised learning phase, the model undergoes fine-tuning using a smaller, task-specific dataset. This second phase refines the model's parameters so that it adapts its broad linguistic knowledge to address particular challenges, such as text classification or sentiment analysis. This approach not only saves significant training time and computational resources but also ensures that even specialized applications can benefit from the deep, generalized understanding that pre-training provides.

Advantages of Pre-Trained Models

Pre-trained models significantly reduce the need for massive annotated datasets and extensive training time, as they come with a wealth of linguistic knowledge acquired from large-scale data. Their ability to generalize across diverse tasks leads to improved accuracy and efficiency, making them invaluable for rapid prototyping and scalable NLP solutions.

- **Resource Efficiency and Accelerated Training:** One of the most immediate advantages of using pre-trained models is their unparalleled efficiency. Traditional model training from scratch demands enormous amounts of annotated data and extensive computational power. In contrast, pre-trained models have already performed the heavy lifting during the pre-training phase. Fine-tuning these models for specific tasks requires far fewer resources and less time, making them an ideal choice for organizations with limited infrastructure. This efficiency translates directly into reduced operational costs and faster development cycles, enabling rapid prototyping and deployment of NLP solutions.
- **Enhanced Accuracy and Robust Performance:** Pre-trained models excel in delivering high accuracy across various NLP tasks. Their exposure to large and diverse datasets during pre-training allows them to learn complex language features that would be difficult to capture in task-specific training alone. As a result, when these models are fine-tuned, they tend to generalize better and achieve superior performance–even when the available labeled data is sparse. The robustness of these models is evident in their ability to handle the intricacies of human language, such as idiomatic expressions, polysemy, and contextual shifts, which are often stumbling blocks for models trained from scratch.

- **Versatility Across Multiple Domains:** A key strength of pre-trained models lies in their versatility. Once a model has mastered general language understanding, it can be fine-tuned for a multitude of applications without starting the learning process anew. This adaptability allows the same model architecture to be applied to a range of tasks, from text summarization and machine translation to more nuanced applications such as sentiment analysis and domain-specific content processing. For instance, while a model might initially be trained on a broad corpus covering general language, subsequent fine-tuning on legal or medical texts enables it to learn the specialized vocabulary and stylistic conventions of those fields. This cross-domain flexibility streamlines the development process and fosters innovation by reducing the need for multiple specialized models.
- **Rapid Prototyping and Iterative Innovation:** Pre-trained models also empower rapid prototyping, a crucial factor in today's fast-paced technological environment. The availability of models that already possess a deep understanding of language allows researchers and developers to experiment with new ideas quickly. Fine-tuning these models for emerging tasks or innovative applications can be accomplished in a fraction of the time required to build a model from scratch. This agility not only accelerates research and development cycles but also encourages iterative refinement. As new data becomes available, models can be updated and fine-tuned continuously, ensuring they remain state-of-the-art and responsive to evolving needs.

Llama Models: A Detailed Examination

Llama models exemplify the cutting edge of NLP, utilizing transformer architectures to capture intricate linguistic patterns and context dependencies. Their scalable design and efficient fine-tuning process allow them to adapt seamlessly across various domains, setting a new benchmark for robust language understanding and application.

Architectural Excellence of Llama Models

The Llama series stands at the forefront of modern NLP, exemplifying the advances in pre-training and transfer learning. Built upon transformer architectures, Llama models leverage self-attention mechanisms to effectively capture long-range dependencies within text. This architectural choice is central to their ability to understand context and maintain coherence across extended sequences of language—a critical requirement for tasks such as text generation and comprehension.

Llama models are meticulously pre-trained on diverse datasets that span multiple domains and languages. This extensive training ensures that they not only understand general language structures but also possess the flexibility to adapt to a variety of specialized applications. Their design inherently supports scalability, enabling the models to grow in complexity and capacity as additional computational resources become available.

Specific Advantages of the Llama Series

The advantages offered by Llama models are manifold:

- **Robust Language Representations:** Llama models are trained on massive, diverse datasets that allow them to develop a deep understanding of language nuances. This robust representation is critical when fine-tuning for tasks that require sensitivity to context and subtle linguistic cues.
- **Scalability and Adaptability:** The architecture of Llama models is designed to scale, meaning they can be adapted to both large-scale applications and niche, domain-specific tasks. Their ability to handle varying sizes of data and adapt to different contexts makes them particularly valuable in dynamic environments.
- **Efficient Fine-Tuning:** Thanks to the rich knowledge embedded during the pre-training phase, Llama models require fewer training iterations during fine-tuning. This efficiency enables faster deployment of models into production environments and supports rapid experimentation with new tasks.
- **Cross-Domain Flexibility:** The extensive pre-training regimen allows Llama models to be fine-tuned for a broad spectrum of applications without compromising on performance. Whether adapting to a new language, tackling domain-specific jargon, or addressing unique problem settings, these models maintain a high level of versatility.

Technical Innovations in Llama Models

The success of Llama models is also a testament to several technical innovations in the field of pre-trained models. Techniques such as dynamic masking, layer-wise adaptive learning rates, and sophisticated regularization methods ensure that these models maintain a balance between general language understanding and task-specific adaptation. By continuously refining these techniques, researchers are able to push the boundaries of what pre-trained models can achieve, ensuring that Llama models remain competitive in an ever-evolving landscape of NLP research.

Overcoming Challenges and Enhancing Capabilities

Overcoming challenges in transfer learning involves strategies such as domain-adaptive pre-training, robust regularization techniques, and computational optimizations to tackle issues such as domain mismatch and overfitting. These approaches enhance model performance and broaden the applicability of pre-trained models across diverse NLP tasks.

- **Addressing Domain Mismatch:** One challenge inherent in transfer learning is the potential for domain mismatch—where the distribution of data used during pre-training differs significantly from that encountered during fine-tuning. This can lead to performance degradation when the model is applied to highly specialized tasks. To mitigate this issue, strategies such as domain-adaptive pre-training are employed. This involves additional rounds of training on data that more closely mirrors the target domain, effectively bridging the gap between general language models and specialized applications.
- **Preventing Overfitting and Maintaining Generalizability:** While pre-trained models provide a strong foundation, fine-tuning on very limited datasets can still lead to overfitting. To address this, techniques such as dropout, weight decay, and data augmentation are routinely applied during the fine-tuning phase. These regularization strategies help maintain a balance between leveraging the vast pre-trained knowledge and adapting to the specificities of new tasks, ensuring that the model remains both accurate and generalizable.
- **Optimizing Computational Efficiency:** Despite the efficiencies gained through pre-training, the fine-tuning process—especially for large models such as Llama—can still be computationally demanding. Researchers and practitioners continue to explore methods to optimize resource usage. Techniques such as model pruning, quantization, and knowledge distillation are being actively developed to reduce model size and inference time without significant losses in performance. These innovations are critical for deploying state-of-the-art models in environments with limited hardware capabilities or strict energy consumption constraints.

The Broader Impact on the NLP Landscape

Pre-trained models have revolutionized the NLP landscape by democratizing advanced language technologies and enabling organizations of all sizes to leverage state-of-the-art tools. Their efficient learning and adaptability have accelerated both research breakthroughs and practical applications, transforming how industries extract insights from text data.

- **Democratizing Access to Advanced NLP:** The advent of pre-trained models has democratized access to sophisticated NLP capabilities. By significantly lowering the barriers to entry—both in terms of data requirements and computational costs—pre-trained models empower a wider range of organizations to leverage advanced language processing tools. This democratization is particularly important for smaller companies and academic institutions that may not have the resources to train models from scratch. The widespread availability of models such as those in the Llama series fosters a more inclusive innovation ecosystem, driving research and application across diverse sectors.

- **Accelerating Research and Technological Advancements:** Pre-trained models have also served as a catalyst for rapid advancements in NLP research. With the heavy lifting of learning general language representations already accomplished, researchers can focus on fine-tuning and experimenting with new architectures, training paradigms, and applications. This has led to a surge in innovative approaches to language understanding, generation, and analysis. The iterative feedback loop between research and practical application ensures that improvements in model performance are quickly translated into real-world benefits, propelling the field forward at an unprecedented pace.
- **Transforming Industry Practices:** In industry, the impact of pre-trained models is evident in the widespread adoption of NLP solutions across sectors such as healthcare, finance, legal services, and customer service. By enabling rapid development and deployment, these models help businesses automate processes, extract valuable insights from text data, and improve decision-making processes. The efficiency gains and performance improvements offered by pre-trained models are not just theoretical—they translate into tangible business value, driving competitive advantage and operational excellence.

Fine-Tuning Llama Models for Custom Tasks

Fine-tuning Llama models for custom tasks stands at the forefront of modern Natural Language Processing (NLP) innovations. By adapting powerful, pre-trained models to specialized applications, researchers and practitioners can unlock significant performance gains with reduced data and computational requirements. This guide delves deeply into the fine-tuning process—from dataset preparation and hyperparameter optimization to addressing domain-specific challenges and future directions—providing detailed insights and actionable strategies for tailoring Llama, Llama2, and Llama3 models to meet your unique needs.

Transfer learning has revolutionized NLP by decoupling the heavy, resource-intensive pre-training phase from the task-specific fine-tuning stage. With Llama models serving as an exemplary base, fine-tuning allows you to adapt these models—originally trained on broad, diverse datasets—to perform custom tasks with high accuracy and efficiency.

Motivation Behind Fine-Tuning

Fine-tuning enables us to adapt a robust, pre-trained model to a specific task, leveraging its general language understanding while optimizing performance with limited task-specific data. This process minimizes computational costs and accelerates deployment, making specialized NLP solutions more accessible.

- **Resource Optimization:** Pre-trained models absorb general linguistic knowledge during extensive training. Fine-tuning leverages this "*head start,*" reducing the need for massive labeled datasets and high computational overhead.
- **Superior Performance with Limited Data:** When task-specific data is scarce, fine-tuning can yield impressive performance improvements because the model already possesses deep language understanding.
- **Flexibility Across Domains:** Whether you are developing sentiment analysis tools, customer service chatbots, or domain-specific classifiers (for example, legal or medical text), fine-tuning allows you to customize the model to the nuances of your target application.

Real-World Impact: Fine-tuned models are already powering applications across industries–from automating customer feedback analysis to improving the accuracy of language translation systems. The rapid prototyping enabled by fine-tuning translates directly into accelerated innovation cycles and improved business outcomes.

The Fine-Tuning Process

Fine-tuning Llama models involves adapting the pre-trained architecture to a specific task. This process can be broken down into several key stages:

1. **Data Collection and Preparation:** Data collection and preparation lay the foundation for fine-tuning Llama models by ensuring that only high-quality, domain-relevant data is used. This stage involves meticulous curation, cleaning, and tokenization to create a balanced dataset that accurately represents the target task.
    - **Domain Relevance:** Select or curate datasets that are highly representative of the target task. For instance, if you are fine-tuning a model for sentiment analysis in the finance sector, ensure your dataset contains financial news, reports, or customer reviews related to financial products.
    - **Annotation Quality:** Accurate labels are crucial. Collaborate with domain experts when possible, and consider multiple rounds of quality control to verify annotation consistency.

2. **Data Preprocessing and Tokenization:** It transforms raw text into a clean, structured format, converting it into tokens that align with the model's vocabulary. This process is crucial for ensuring the Llama model efficiently processes and understands the input data.
    - **Cleaning and Normalization:** Remove noise such as HTML tags, special characters, or extraneous whitespace. Normalize text by converting to lower case, handling contractions, and correcting common misspellings.
    - **Tokenization Strategies:** Use tokenizers that align with the Llama models' pre-training–typically subword tokenization such as Byte-Pair Encoding (BPE) or SentencePiece. Custom tokenizers may be developed for highly specialized vocabularies in niche domains.
    - **Data Augmentation:** For domains with limited data, apply augmentation techniques such as synonym replacement, back-translation, or paraphrasing to create additional training samples without compromising semantic integrity.
3. **Dataset Splitting and Balancing**
    - **Training, Validation, and Test Splits:** Split the dataset into distinct sets to ensure robust model evaluation. A common practice is an 80/10/10 split, but the proportions may vary based on dataset size and task complexity.
    - **Addressing Imbalance:** Use techniques such as oversampling, undersampling, or synthetic data generation to balance classes, especially in classification tasks where certain classes may be underrepresented.

Model Initialization and Architecture Adaptation

Model initialization involves loading a pre-trained Llama model checkpoint, which serves as the foundation for subsequent fine-tuning. Architecture adaptation then tailors this base model to the specific needs of the target task–often by modifying or replacing output layers and integrating task-specific components. This combination ensures that the powerful, pre-learned language representations are preserved while enabling precise customization for specialized applications.

1. **Loading the Pre-Trained Llama Model**
    - **Model Checkpoints:** Begin by loading a pre-trained Llama model checkpoint. These checkpoints encapsulate the model's learned language representations and are available through repositories such as Hugging Face's model hub.
    - **Compatibility Considerations:** Ensure that the tokenizer and model architecture align. Mismatches between tokenizers and model expectations can lead to suboptimal performance or runtime errors.

2. **Modifying the Architecture for Custom Tasks**

   - **Output Layer Adaptation:** For classification tasks, replace the default output layer with a task-specific layer (for example, a SoftMax layer corresponding to the number of classes). For regression tasks, a linear layer may suffice.
   - **Intermediate Layers:** In some cases, inserting additional intermediate layers (for example, fully connected layers) between the pre-trained representations and the output layer can help capture complex task-specific patterns.
   - **Multi-Task Learning:** Consider architectures that support multiple tasks simultaneously, enabling shared representations across related tasks. This is particularly useful when dealing with closely related applications.

Hyperparameter Optimization

Hyperparameter optimization is crucial in fine-tuning Llama models, as it systematically adjusts key parameters such as learning rate, batch size, and training epochs. Techniques such as grid search, random search, and Bayesian optimization are employed to explore the parameter space effectively. This careful tuning helps ensure faster convergence, better generalization, and enhanced stability, ultimately boosting model performance on custom tasks.

1. **Critical Hyperparameters**

   - **Learning Rate:** A smaller learning rate (for example, 1e-5 to 5e-5) is typically used for fine-tuning to avoid disrupting the valuable pre-trained weights. Learning rate schedules, such as warm-up phases followed by gradual decay, can be beneficial.
   - **Batch Size and Epochs:** Choose a batch size that maximizes GPU utilization while fitting into memory constraints. Monitor the number of epochs closely; early stopping based on validation loss can prevent overfitting.

2. **Automated Tuning Techniques**

   - **Grid Search and Random Search:** These methods systematically explore the hyperparameter space to identify optimal configurations.
   - **Bayesian Optimization:** More advanced techniques, such as Bayesian optimization, can provide efficient and effective hyperparameter tuning, especially in complex search spaces.

Training Strategies: Layer Freezing and Gradual Unfreezing

Layer freezing involves keeping the initial layers of a pre-trained model static to preserve their robust, general language features while fine-tuning the later layers for task-specific adaptation. Gradual unfreezing then progressively releases these frozen layers, allowing them to adapt slowly to the new data without losing foundational knowledge. This strategy helps maintain model stability, prevents catastrophic forgetting, and optimizes training efficiency.

1. **Freezing Early Layers**
   - **Core Preservation, Stability, Efficiency:** The early layers of Llama models capture foundational linguistic features. Freezing these layers preserves the general knowledge while focusing the training on task-specific adjustments in later layers.
   - **Implementation:** Initially, freeze all but the final few layers. Gradually unfreeze earlier layers as training stabilizes to allow more nuanced adaptation.
2. **Gradual Unfreezing Techniques**
   - **Progressive Unfreezing:** Start by fine-tuning only the output layer and then progressively unfreeze additional layers. This strategy helps mitigate the risk of catastrophic forgetting and allows for a smoother adaptation process.
   - **Layer-Specific Learning Rates:** Applying different learning rates to different layers can balance stability and adaptability. For example, lower learning rates for frozen layers that are unfreezed later and higher rates for newly added task-specific layers.

Regularization and Optimization Techniques

Regularization techniques such as dropout, weight decay, and data augmentation help prevent overfitting by ensuring that the model learns robust features without relying too heavily on any single neuron or pattern. Optimization methods, including adaptive learning rate algorithms such as AdamW and dynamic schedulers, facilitate efficient and stable convergence during fine-tuning. Together, these strategies maintain a balance between retaining valuable pre-trained knowledge and adapting effectively to task-specific nuances, ultimately leading to more reliable and generalizable model performance.

1. **Preventing Overfitting**
   - **Dropout:** Implement dropout in the fully connected layers to reduce overfitting by randomly deactivating neurons during training.

- **Weight Decay:** Incorporate weight decay to penalize large weights, encouraging simpler models that generalize better.
- **Data Augmentation Revisited:** Augment the training data on-the-fly during fine-tuning to expose the model to a broader variety of examples.

2. **Optimization Algorithms**
   - **Adam and Its Variants:** Optimizers such as Adam or AdamW are frequently used for fine-tuning due to their adaptive learning rate properties and effectiveness in handling sparse gradients.
   - **Learning Rate Schedulers:** Utilize schedulers (for example, cosine annealing or step decay) to dynamically adjust the learning rate during training, helping the model converge more smoothly.

Addressing Common Challenges in Fine-Tuning Llama Models

Addressing common challenges in fine-tuning Llama models involves mitigating domain mismatch and overfitting by employing strategies such as domain-adaptive pre-training, robust regularization, and gradual layer unfreezing. These techniques help preserve foundational language understanding while enabling effective adaptation to task-specific nuances.

Managing Domain Mismatch

Managing domain mismatch involves bridging the gap between the broad, general data used during pre-training and the specialized data of the target domain. This is typically achieved through domain-adaptive pre-training and tailored data curation to ensure the model captures domain-specific nuances effectively.

- **Domain-Adaptive Pre-Training:** Domain-adaptive pre-training involves further training a pre-trained model on domain-specific data to capture unique vocabulary and contextual nuances.
  - **Additional Pre-Training:** Before fine-tuning, consider an intermediate step of domain-adaptive pre-training on a corpus that is representative of the target domain. This step helps bridge the gap between the general pre-trained model and the specific domain requirements.
    - **Example:** For a legal document classifier, perform additional pre-training on a large corpus of legal texts to help the model grasp specialized terminology and stylistic nuances.
- **Data Curation and Augmentation:** Data curation involves the meticulous selection, cleaning, and organization of high-quality datasets to ensure they accurately represent the target domain.

- **Curating Representative Samples:** Ensure that the fine-tuning dataset covers the breadth of the domain. Including edge cases and rare examples helps improve the model's robustness.
- **Augmentation Strategies:** Employ domain-specific data augmentation to enrich the dataset. Techniques such as domain translation (for example, legal jargon paraphrasing) can enhance the model's understanding.

Tackling Overfitting

Tackling overfitting involves implementing strategies such as dropout, weight decay, and early stopping to ensure the model learns robust features instead of memorizing training data. These techniques help maintain generalizability and enhance performance on unseen data.

- **Cross-Validation Techniques:** Cross-validation techniques partition the dataset into multiple folds, allowing the model to be trained and evaluated on different subsets.
  - **K-Fold Cross-Validation:** Use cross-validation to evaluate the model on different subsets of the data. This approach helps in ensuring that the model's performance is robust and not just tailored to a particular split.
  - **Regular Monitoring:** Continuously track performance metrics on a validation set to detect early signs of overfitting.
- **Ensemble Methods:** Ensemble methods combine the predictions of multiple models to enhance overall performance and reduce individual model biases.
  - **Model Averaging:** Consider training multiple fine-tuned models and averaging their predictions. Ensembles can reduce variance and provide more stable performance.
  - **Stacking:** Combine the outputs of different models through a meta-learner to further improve prediction accuracy.

Optimizing Computational Resources

Optimizing computational resources involves techniques such as model pruning, quantization, and using cloud-based GPU acceleration to reduce training time and inference costs while maintaining high model performance.

- **Leveraging Cloud-Based Infrastructures:** Leveraging cloud-based infrastructures enables scalable access to powerful GPU/TPU resources, dramatically reducing hardware constraints and accelerating the fine-tuning process.
  - **Scalability:** Utilize cloud platforms equipped with GPUs or TPUs to handle intensive fine-tuning tasks without the need for on-premise hardware investments.

  - **Cost Efficiency:** Take advantage of spot instances or managed services to reduce the overall cost of training.

- **Model Compression and Distillation:** Model compression and distillation reduce the size of large models while preserving performance, enabling faster inference and lower computational resource usage.
  - **Pruning and Quantization:** After fine-tuning, consider compressing the model using pruning techniques or quantization to reduce inference time and energy consumption while maintaining performance.
  - **Knowledge Distillation:** Transfer the knowledge from a large fine-tuned Llama model to a smaller, more efficient model, enabling deployment in resource-constrained environments.

Best Practices and Strategies for Successful Fine-Tuning

Best practices include iterative experimentation with rigorous hyperparameter tuning, gradual unfreezing of layers, and robust regularization (for example, dropout, weight decay) to preserve pre-trained knowledge while adapting to specific tasks. Detailed documentation and continuous evaluation are essential for achieving optimal fine-tuning results.

- **Iterative Experimentation and Continuous Refinement:** It involves repeatedly testing, adjusting, and optimizing model parameters and architectures to achieve peak performance.
  - **Metric Monitoring:** Maintain dashboards that track key performance metrics–accuracy, precision, recall, F1 score, and loss–across training epochs. Use these insights to iterate on hyperparameter settings and architectural modifications.
  - **Feedback Loops:** Integrate domain expert feedback into the training loop. Regularly review misclassifications and error cases to refine data preprocessing and model parameters.
- **Documentation and Reproducibility:** Comprehensive documentation of experiments–including hyperparameters, dataset versions, and training configurations–is essential for ensuring reproducibility.
  - **Version Control:** Document every experiment with detailed records of hyperparameters, dataset versions, training configurations, and model checkpoints. This practice ensures reproducibility and facilitates troubleshooting.

    - **Experiment Tracking Tools:** Utilize tools such as MLflow, Weights & Biases, or Tensor Board to log experiments, visualize training progress, and compare different runs systematically.

- **Collaborative Development:** Collaborative development leverages shared expertise and open-source resources to accelerate innovation, enabling teams to iterate rapidly and refine transfer learning techniques with Llama models.
    - **Open-Source Libraries:** Leverage community-maintained libraries and repositories. Open-source projects offer a wealth of resources, scripts, and pre-configured models that can jumpstart your fine-tuning efforts.
    - **Community Engagement:** Actively participate in forums, research communities, and conferences. Sharing your findings and learning from others accelerates innovation and helps refine best practices.

Case Studies: Adapting Llama for Text Classification and Sentiment Analysis

Transfer learning has fundamentally altered the way we develop NLP solutions. By leveraging pre-trained models that have already internalized a vast amount of linguistic information, we can focus our efforts on fine-tuning these models for specific tasks. This approach is not only cost-effective but also significantly reduces the time and computational resources required for building specialized systems.

In these case studies, our objective is twofold:

- **Text Classification:** Categorizing texts such as news articles into predetermined topics (for example, politics, technology, sports, health) by understanding contextual and semantic cues.
- **Sentiment Analysis:** Assessing the emotional tone of textual inputs (for instance, determining whether product reviews are positive, negative, or neutral) to extract valuable insights about public opinion.

These tasks, though related, present unique challenges that require custom adaptations in the fine-tuning process. The following sections provide a detailed roadmap of our journey from data curation through to deployment and performance evaluation.

Case Study 1: Fine-Tuning Llama for Text Classification

Text classification is a pivotal task in NLP, aiming to assign predefined categories to textual documents. In our case study, we focus on categorizing news articles into topics such as politics, technology, sports, and health. This section outlines every stage of the process–from dataset curation to model evaluation–with meticulous attention to detail.

Dataset Preparation

Dataset preparation involves curating high-quality, representative data and rigorously cleaning, normalizing, and tokenizing the text to ensure optimal model performance. This foundational step is crucial for effectively training and fine-tuning models for specific NLP tasks.

1. **Data Collection and Curation**
    - **Source Diversity:** We sourced articles from multiple reputable news outlets to ensure a balanced representation of topics. Cross-referencing was employed to mitigate bias and ensure diverse writing styles.
    - **Annotation Quality:** Each article was labelled by domain experts. In ambiguous cases, multiple annotators were consulted to ensure consensus, leading to high-quality ground truth data.
2. **Data Cleaning and Preprocessing**
    - **Text Normalization:** The raw text underwent rigorous cleaning: removing HTML tags, special characters, and correcting typographical errors. The normalization process also involved converting text to lowercase and standardizing punctuation.
    - **Tokenization Strategy:** We used sub word tokenization (for example, Byte-Pair Encoding) in alignment with the Llama model's vocabulary. This approach allowed for efficient handling of rare words and out-of-vocabulary terms, particularly useful in domain-specific texts.
    - **Handling Imbalances:** Techniques such as oversampling minority classes and data augmentation (for example, paraphrasing, synonym replacement) were employed to address class imbalances and ensure robust training.
3. **Dataset Splitting**
    - **Training/Validation/Test:** The dataset was divided into training (70–80%), validation (10–15%), and test sets (10–15%). The splits were carefully stratified to preserve the class distribution across all subsets.

Model Adaptation and Architectural Modifications

Model adaptation and architectural modifications involve tailoring pre-trained models by adjusting their structure–such as replacing output layers or inserting intermediate layers–to better align with the specific requirements of a custom task. This targeted approach ensures that the model not only retains its robust pre-trained knowledge but also effectively learns task-specific patterns for enhanced performance.

- **Output Layer Customization:** Output layer customization involves tailoring the final layers of a pre-trained model to align with specific task requirements, such as adjusting for the number of classes in a classification task.
  - **Softmax Layer Replacement:** The original Llama model's output layer was replaced with a softmax classifier tailored to our four categories. This modification ensures that the final predictions directly correspond to the target classes.
  - **Additional Dense Layers:** To enhance the mapping between the pre-trained representations and our classification task, we introduced intermediate fully connected layers with activation functions such as ReLU, which helped in learning non-linear decision boundaries.
- **Incorporating Attention Mechanisms:** Incorporating attention mechanisms enhances the model's ability to focus on critical parts of the input, capturing nuanced relationships and contextual cues that are vital for accurate predictions.
  - **Enhanced Context Capture:** Although Llama already uses self-attention, we experimented with additional attention layers in the final few blocks to focus on keywords and phrases that are highly indicative of specific news topics.

Hyperparameter Tuning and Training Strategies

Hyperparameter tuning and training strategies are essential for refining model performance by balancing learning rates, batch sizes, and epochs to suit specific tasks. Techniques such as layer freezing and gradual unfreezing further ensure that Llama models adapt efficiently to new challenges without losing their pre-trained strengths.

Hyperparameter Selection

- **Learning Rate and Batch Size**: A conservative learning rate (for example, 2e-5 to 3e-5) was chosen to preserve the pre-trained knowledge. The batch size was optimized based on available GPU memory, balancing training speed with model convergence.
- **Epochs and Early Stopping**: The model was trained over multiple epochs with early stopping criteria based on validation loss. Cross-validation further refined these settings, ensuring robust performance.

Layer Freezing and Gradual Unfreezing

- **Initial Freezing**: The lower layers of the Llama model were frozen during the early phases of training to maintain the integrity of the general language representations.

- **Gradual Unfreezing:** In later stages, layers were progressively unfrozen to allow fine-tuning on more complex, task-specific patterns without destabilizing the model.

Evaluation and Performance Metrics

Evaluation and performance metrics, such as accuracy, precision, recall, and F1 scores, provide critical insights into model effectiveness and guide iterative refinements. These metrics ensure that fine-tuned models meet the desired standards for reliability and real-world application.

Quantitative Metrics

- **Accuracy and F1 Score:** The model was evaluated using overall accuracy, along with precision, recall, and F1 scores for each class. Confusion matrices were generated to analyze misclassification trends.
- **Error Analysis:** Detailed error analysis highlighted challenges, such as overlapping content between categories (for example, technology and health in articles discussing medical technology).

Qualitative Insights

- **Case-by-Case Analysis:** In-depth review of misclassified articles provided insights into subtle contextual nuances that were difficult for the model to capture. This feedback informed further data preprocessing and model adjustments.

Results and Observations

- **High Accuracy:** The fine-tuned Llama model achieved an overall accuracy exceeding 90%, with particularly strong performance in distinct categories such as technology and sports.
- **Incremental Improvements:** Iterative hyperparameter adjustments and enhanced attention mechanisms led to measurable performance gains over successive training cycles.

Case Study 2: Fine-Tuning Llama for Sentiment Analysis

Sentiment analysis involves the classification of text based on the emotional tone expressed within it. This case study focuses on analyzing product reviews to determine whether the sentiments expressed are positive, negative, or neutral.

Dataset Preparation

Dataset preparation is a crucial phase that involves curating, cleaning, and preprocessing raw text data to ensure it is balanced, representative, and optimized for fine-tuning Llama models on custom tasks. This step lays the foundation for robust model performance by ensuring that the data accurately reflects the nuances and complexities of the target domain.

Data Collection and Annotation

- **Diverse Reviews:** We collected product reviews from a leading e-commerce platform, ensuring a wide spectrum of sentiment expressions across various product categories.
- **Annotation Process:** Reviews were annotated manually with sentiment labels. Special attention was given to ambiguous reviews, with multiple annotations used to ensure reliability.

Preprocessing for Informal Language

- **Handling Slang and Emoticons:** The informal nature of reviews required additional preprocessing steps, including normalization of slang, expansion of contractions, and conversion of emoticons into textual sentiment cues.
- **Tokenization Considerations:** Given the informal style, tokenization was adjusted to better handle non-standard language, ensuring that the model could effectively learn from colloquial expressions.

Model Adaptation and Architectural Enhancements

Model adaptation involves modifying the pre-trained Llama architecture–such as replacing the output layer and adding intermediate dense layers–to tailor the model to specific tasks. Architectural enhancements, including additional attention mechanisms and custom activation functions, further refine its ability to capture task-specific nuances and improve overall performance.

Output Layer for Sentiment Classification

- **Custom Sentiment Classifier:** The Llama model's output layer was replaced with a classifier designed for three classes–positive, negative, and neutral. The classifier was optimized using cross-entropy loss, tailored for categorical outputs.

Enhanced Attention for Sentiment Detection

- **Focusing on Sentiment-Bearing Words:** Additional attention layers were implemented to prioritize key sentiment-laden words and phrases. This helped in capturing the intensity and polarity of emotions expressed in the reviews.

- **Intermediate Representation Layers:** To bridge the gap between generic language understanding and nuanced sentiment detection, we introduced intermediate layers that distilled sentiment-specific features.

Training and Hyperparameter Optimization

Effective training and meticulous hyperparameter optimization–tuning parameters such as learning rate, batch size, and employing techniques such as early stopping–are critical for achieving robust convergence and preventing overfitting during model fine-tuning.

Training Dynamics

- **Adaptive Learning Rates:** A very low learning rate was critical to fine-tuning on noisy, informal text data. Schedulers such as cosine annealing were employed to adjust the learning rate dynamically.
- **Regularization Techniques:** Dropout and weight decay were extensively used to mitigate overfitting, which is a common challenge when working with highly variable consumer-generated content.

Handling Ambiguity and Mixed Sentiments

- **Progressive Unfreezing:** Similar to text classification, a gradual unfreezing strategy was employed. This allowed the model to slowly adapt to the complex patterns in sentiment without losing the foundational linguistic representations.
- **Fine-Tuning on Ambiguous Data:** Special subsets of data featuring mixed or ambiguous sentiments were used during training to enhance the model's robustness in real-world scenarios.

Evaluation, Results, and Insights

Evaluation of the fine-tuned models demonstrated high accuracy and robustness, with detailed error analysis revealing critical insights that guided further optimization.

Quantitative Evaluation

- **Sentiment Metrics:** Evaluation was based on overall accuracy as well as precision, recall, and F1 scores for each sentiment category. Particular emphasis was placed on the neutral class, which often presents the greatest challenge.
- **Confusion Matrix Analysis:** Misclassifications were analyzed through confusion matrices to identify common errors, such as misinterpreting sarcasm or nuanced expressions of dissatisfaction.

Qualitative Evaluation

- **Review-Level Analysis:** Detailed qualitative analysis of misclassified reviews provided insights into specific linguistic cues that were misinterpreted. For example, reviews with mixed sentiments were scrutinized to understand how overlapping sentiment cues could be better differentiated.
- **Iterative Model Refinement:** Feedback from these analyses led to further refinements in preprocessing such as enhanced handling of exclamations and intensifiers, which improved the overall sentiment detection performance.

Results and Impact

- **Strong Performance:** The sentiment analysis model achieved an overall accuracy of approximately 88%, with particularly high performance in clearly positive and negative reviews.
- **Enhanced Sensitivity:** The incorporation of extra attention layers and additional intermediate layers significantly improved the model's sensitivity to subtle sentiment cues, reducing misclassifications in borderline cases.
- **Real-World Applicability:** The refined model proved effective in processing real-world product reviews, providing actionable insights for marketing strategies and customer service improvements.

Comparative Analysis and Lessons Learned

Comparative analysis shows that while both tasks benefit from fine-tuning Llama models, text classification requires careful handling of overlapping topics, whereas sentiment analysis demands nuanced processing of informal and ambiguous language. These insights emphasize the value of iterative refinement and domain-specific adaptations in achieving optimal performance.

Common Strategies across Tasks

Both text classification and sentiment analysis benefited from:

- **Leveraging Pre-Trained Knowledge:** The robust language representations in Llama models were pivotal in reducing the dependency on large task-specific datasets.
- **Iterative Experimentation:** Continual refinement of hyperparameters and model architecture through iterative experimentation was crucial to achieving optimal performance.
- **Customized Output Layers:** Tailoring the final layers to match the specific output requirements of each task significantly improved accuracy and overall model effectiveness.

Unique Challenges and Adaptations

- **Text Classification:** The main challenge was managing overlapping content between similar topics, necessitating more refined attention mechanisms and robust feature extraction layers.
- **Sentiment Analysis:** The informal, nuanced nature of consumer reviews required additional preprocessing and enhanced attention to capture sentiment nuances effectively. Handling ambiguous and mixed sentiment expressions was particularly challenging, prompting the use of advanced regularization and dynamic learning rate strategies.

Key Lessons for Future Applications

- **Importance of Domain-Specific Pre-Training:** In cases where the domain differs significantly from general text corpora, an intermediate phase of domain-adaptive pre-training can bridge the gap.
- **Dynamic Adaptation Techniques:** Gradual unfreezing and layer-specific learning rates provide a balanced approach that preserves pre-trained knowledge while allowing necessary adaptation.
- **Robust Evaluation:** Combining quantitative metrics with qualitative analysis is essential for understanding model behavior and guiding further refinements

Conclusion

In conclusion, leveraging transfer learning with Llama models has proven to be a transformative strategy in NLP, enabling the efficient and effective adaptation of robust pre-trained architectures to specialized tasks such as text classification and sentiment analysis. By meticulously preparing high-quality datasets, implementing targeted model adaptations and architectural modifications, and employing advanced strategies such as gradual layer unfreezing and dynamic hyperparameter tuning, practitioners can overcome domain-specific challenges and achieve high performance even with limited data. This collaborative, iterative approach not only underscores the versatility and strength of transfer learning techniques but also paves the way for continual advancements and innovation in the field of language processing.

In the next chapter, we will delve into the ethical challenges surrounding NLP and AI, examining how bias in language models can be addressed and mitigated, and exploring strategies to enhance privacy and data security in NLP applications. We will also discuss the critical aspects of transparency, fairness, and responsible AI deployment, supported by real-world case studies that highlight ethical dilemmas in practical settings. This exploration will equip you with the knowledge and frameworks needed to navigate and resolve the moral complexities inherent in the rapidly evolving landscape of artificial intelligence.

Multiple Choice Questions

1. What is the primary advantage of using pre-trained models such as Llama for fine-tuning in NLP tasks?
   a. They require no additional data.
   b. They reduce the need for extensive training data and computational resources.
   c. They eliminate the need for any further model modifications.
   d. They work only for sentiment analysis.
2. Which of the following best describes the process of fine-tuning a pre-trained model?
   a. Training a model from scratch on a small dataset
   b. Freezing all layers and not updating the model
   c. Adapting a pre-trained model with additional task-specific training
   d. Replacing the entire architecture of the model
3. In the context of Llama models, what is the role of layer freezing during fine-tuning?
   a. It accelerates training by updating all the layers simultaneously.
   b. It helps preserve the foundational language knowledge while allowing task-specific layers to adapt.
   c. It completely prevents any changes in the model during fine-tuning.
   d. It only applies to the output layer.
4. Which technique is commonly used to prevent overfitting during the fine-tuning process?
   a. Increasing the learning rate
   b. Removing the dropout layers
   c. Using regularization methods such as dropout and weight decay
   d. Avoiding data augmentation

5. What is the purpose of modifying the output layer when adapting Llama models for text classification?
    a. To speed up the pre-training process
    b. To match the number of output classes specific to the classification task
    c. To reduce the model size
    d. To disable the self-attention mechanism
6. In sentiment analysis, why might additional attention layers be incorporated into a fine-tuned Llama model?
    a. To ignore sentiment-bearing words
    b. To capture subtle emotional cues and focus on key sentiment-laden phrases
    c. To eliminate the need for tokenization
    d. To increase the number of output classes
7. Which of the following is an advantage of using collaborative development in fine-tuning Llama models?
    a. It limits the exchange of ideas among developers.
    b. It accelerates innovation by leveraging community expertise and shared resources.
    c. It makes the process of fine-tuning completely manual.
    d. It restricts the use of open-source libraries.
8. What does 'gradual unfreezing' refer to in the context of model adaptation?
    a. Immediately updating all layers during fine-tuning
    b. Slowly unfreezing layers so that the model can adapt progressively while retaining pre-trained knowledge
    c. Keeping all layers frozen throughout training
    d. Unfreezing only the output layer
9. How does domain-adaptive pre-training benefit the fine-tuning process?
    a. It reduces the need for any task-specific adjustments.
    b. It further aligns the model with domain-specific vocabulary and context, bridging the gap between general and specialized tasks.

   c. It eliminates the need for a validation set.

   d. It only improves performance on sentiment analysis.

10. Which hyperparameter is particularly critical to adjust when fine-tuning pre-trained models to avoid catastrophic forgetting?

    a. The number of layers in the model.

    b. The learning rate, often set to a lower value.

    c. The size of the input vocabulary.

    d. The dropout rate alone.

Answers

1. b
2. c
3. b
4. c
5. b
6. b
7. b
8. b
9. b
10. b

CHAPTER 11
Ethical Considerations in NLP with Llama

Introduction

In this chapter, we delve into the ethical considerations inherent in developing advanced NLP systems using models such as Llama 4. As technology continues to push the boundaries of natural language processing, it becomes increasingly important to understand the ethical responsibilities tied to its development. Readers will gain insights into how ethical practices not only enhance the reliability of these systems but also ensure that they serve a broader societal good.

Throughout the chapter, we will explore a range of critical topics—from mitigating bias in language models to addressing privacy concerns and ensuring transparency. By examining real-world examples and best practices, you will learn how to identify potential pitfalls and implement robust strategies for responsible AI usage. This exploration emphasizes the dual role of innovation and accountability in technology development.

Beyond theoretical discussions, the chapter is designed to be a practical guide. You will discover actionable approaches to building equitable and inclusive NLP models. Each section is tailored to help you not only grasp the ethical dimensions but also apply this knowledge in your projects—ensuring that your work aligns with ethical principles from inception to deployment.

Ultimately, the aim is to empower you as a developer to recognize the broader impacts of AI-driven NLP systems. By aligning technological advancements with ethical imperatives, you will be better equipped to create systems that not only excel in performance but also contribute positively to society as a whole.

Structure

In this chapter, we will cover the following topics:

- Overview
- Ethical Challenges in NLP and AI
- Addressing Bias in Language Models
- Privacy and Data Security in NLP Applications
- Transparency, Fairness, and Responsible AI Deployment
- Case Studies: Ethical Dilemmas in Real-World NLP Applications

Overview

In the realm of natural language processing and AI, ethical challenges are becoming increasingly prominent as these technologies evolve. Developers face significant hurdles, including addressing bias inherent in language models and ensuring that the data used does not inadvertently perpetuate inequalities. At the same time, privacy and data security remain critical, as the vast amounts of sensitive information processed by NLP systems demand robust safeguards. This overview sets the stage by examining how these challenges intersect, highlighting the need for careful scrutiny and proactive measures to protect user information while mitigating systemic biases.

Equally important is the commitment to transparency, fairness, and responsible AI deployment. As organizations strive to harness the power of advanced NLP tools, there is a growing emphasis on openly communicating model capabilities and limitations, ensuring that decision-making processes are both ethical and accountable. By integrating comprehensive guidelines and best practices, developers can build AI systems that not only perform effectively but also uphold the values of inclusivity and social responsibility. This approach ultimately contributes to a more balanced and ethical technology landscape, where innovation aligns with the broader interests of society.

Ethical Challenges in NLP and AI

The rapid evolution of natural language processing (NLP) and artificial intelligence (AI) has brought about revolutionary changes in industries ranging from healthcare and finance to entertainment and customer service. These technologies have enabled machines to interpret, generate, and interact with human language in ways that were once considered science fiction. However, as we integrate these advanced systems deeper into our societal fabric, a host of ethical challenges emerge. In this extended discussion, we explore these challenges in detail–delving into bias in language models, the intricacies of privacy and data security, the imperative for transparency and accountability, and the broader societal and regulatory implications. Through detailed analysis and real-world examples, this discussion offers insights into the ethical landscape of AI development and practical strategies for responsible innovation.

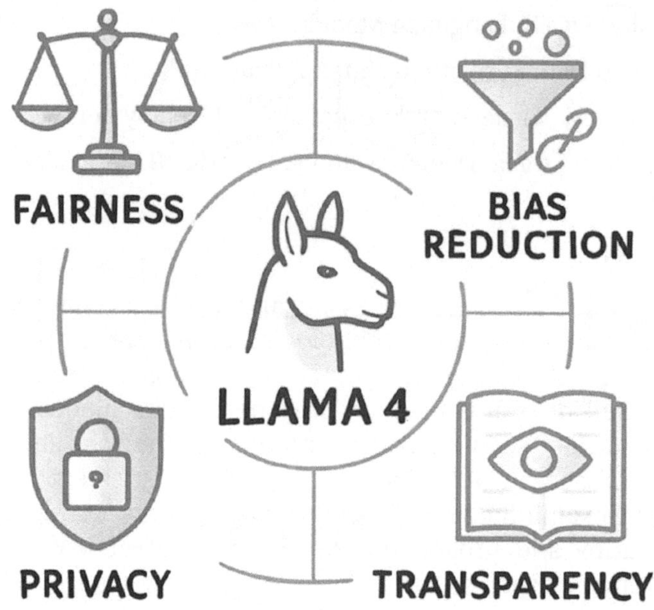

Figure 11.1: *Key Ethical Challenges in the Age of Advanced AI*

- **Fairness and Bias Reduction**: Models can absorb and amplify societal biases from their training data, leading to stereotypical or unfair outcomes.
- **Privacy**: There is a risk that models might inadvertently reveal sensitive personal information learned from their training data.
- **Transparency**: The complex, "black box" nature of these models makes it difficult to understand their decision-making process and assign responsibility when errors or harm occur.

Bias in Language Models: Origins, Manifestations, and Remedies

Bias in AI is not merely a technical flaw but a reflection of longstanding societal prejudices embedded in our data sources. NLP models, which rely on vast datasets scraped from the internet, inherently absorb both the positive and negative aspects of human discourse. For example, early research into word embeddings revealed that these models often associated certain professions or attributes with specific genders. When an algorithm that screens resumes learns from such biased data, it might disproportionately favor male candidates for technical roles or overlook equally qualified female candidates. Such biases can have profound consequences, especially in sectors such as recruitment, lending, or law enforcement, where decisions made by AI can perpetuate inequality.

Beyond gender bias, models have also demonstrated racial and cultural biases. A notable case involved a language model generating outputs that reinforced harmful stereotypes about certain ethnic groups. These outcomes highlight the need for rigorous oversight during both the data collection and model training phases. Developers are increasingly employing techniques such as data augmentation, bias detection algorithms, and fairness constraints during model training. For instance, debiasing techniques in word embeddings adjust the representation of words to minimize harmful associations, while adversarial training methods challenge models to produce more balanced outputs. Regular audits and continuous monitoring after deployment are equally critical, and hence, such measures ensure that any emergent biases are promptly identified and addressed.

Moreover, the challenge of bias extends into more subtle areas–such as sentiment analysis tools used in customer feedback systems. If a model interprets certain dialects or colloquialisms as negative due to biased training data, it can skew the understanding of customer satisfaction and lead to misinformed business decisions. Addressing bias, therefore, is not a one-time fix but an ongoing process that requires multidisciplinary collaboration among data scientists, ethicists, and domain experts. This collaboration is vital to develop standards that ensure AI systems not only perform effectively but also operate in a manner that promotes fairness and inclusivity.

Privacy and Data Security: Safeguarding Sensitive Information

Privacy and data security are at the heart of ethical challenges in NLP and AI. As these technologies advance, they increasingly rely on the collection, storage, and analysis of vast amounts of data, much of which is deeply personal or sensitive. Voice assistants, for example, continuously capture audio data to improve user experience. While these systems can offer remarkable convenience, they also raise significant privacy concerns. Without robust safeguards, there is a risk that personal conversations could be intercepted or misused by unauthorized parties.

A prominent example is the use of NLP in healthcare. Systems designed to analyze patient records and provide diagnostic support must handle sensitive medical information. The potential for data breaches in such contexts is alarming–not only can these breaches compromise patient privacy, but they can also have severe legal and ethical repercussions. To mitigate these risks, developers and organizations must adopt stringent data protection measures. This includes robust encryption protocols, comprehensive anonymization techniques, and adherence to international privacy regulations such as the General Data Protection Regulation (GDPR) in Europe and the California Consumer Privacy Act (CCPA) in the United States.

Data anonymization, in particular, is a critical component of safeguarding privacy. Techniques such as differential privacy allow AI models to learn from data without exposing identifiable information. However, achieving the right balance between data utility and privacy protection is a complex challenge that requires ongoing research and development. For instance, overly aggressive anonymization might strip data of its contextual richness, thereby reducing the effectiveness of the NLP system. Conversely, insufficient anonymization can lead to potential re-identification risks. This balance is particularly important when sensitive demographic or behavioral data is involved, necessitating transparent data governance policies that clearly articulate how data is collected, processed, and ultimately secured.

Furthermore, the rise of cloud-based AI services adds another layer of complexity to privacy and data security. When data is stored and processed on third-party servers, questions of jurisdiction, data ownership, and consent become even more pressing. Organizations must ensure that their partners adhere to the same high standards of data protection, implementing comprehensive audits and compliance checks. In an era where data is both a valuable asset and a potential liability, building trust through transparent and secure data practices is indispensable.

Transparency and Accountability: Demystifying the AI Black Box

One of the most significant ethical challenges in modern AI is the opacity of complex models. Many state-of-the-art NLP systems operate as "*black boxes*," making it difficult to understand how they arrive at specific decisions or outputs. This lack of transparency can have serious implications, especially when AI decisions affect areas such as criminal justice, hiring, or financial services. For instance, if a judicial system uses an AI tool to recommend sentencing, the inability to fully explain the model's reasoning could undermine public trust and lead to calls for accountability.

Explainable AI (XAI) has emerged as a promising solution to this problem. Techniques such as Local Interpretable Model-Agnostic Explanations (LIME) and SHapley Additive exPlanations (SHAP) provide insights into the decision-making processes of complex models. These methods work by highlighting the features and data points that most significantly influenced a particular decision, thereby offering a window into the model's "*thought process*." In practice, consider a scenario where an AI system flags potentially fraudulent transactions. An explainability tool might reveal that the model focused on unusual transaction amounts and deviations from typical spending patterns, thereby enabling human auditors to verify the decision-making process.

Beyond technical tools, transparency also encompasses clear communication and documentation of AI system design and training processes. Comprehensive documentation helps stakeholders–from developers and regulators to end-users–understand the underlying assumptions and limitations of a model. This documentation should include detailed records of the data sources, preprocessing steps, and training methodologies used, as well as the inherent limitations of the model. For example, a financial institution using AI for credit scoring must provide transparent explanations about how various factors–such as income levels, credit history, and demographic data–are weighted in the decision-making process.

Accountability is another essential aspect of ethical AI development. When AI systems cause harm or produce unintended consequences, it is vital to have clear mechanisms for assigning responsibility. This might involve establishing independent oversight committees or implementing audit trails that track every decision made by the system. By maintaining detailed logs and fostering a culture of responsibility, organizations can ensure that any issues are swiftly identified and rectified. In turn, these practices not only mitigate the risk of harm but also build public confidence in AI technologies.

Regulatory and Societal Implications: Aligning Innovation with Ethical Standards

The ethical challenges posed by NLP and AI extend far beyond the technical realm; they have profound implications for society and governance. As these technologies influence various aspects of public life, from media consumption to law enforcement, there is a growing need for regulatory frameworks that safeguard human rights and promote ethical practices. Regulatory bodies around the world are increasingly scrutinizing AI applications to ensure that they are deployed responsibly and with due consideration for their societal impact.

The European Union's guidelines for trustworthy AI serve as a leading example, emphasizing principles such as human oversight, accountability, and the protection of fundamental rights. These guidelines call for AI systems to be designed in a way that is not only technically robust but also ethically aligned with societal values. In the United States, ongoing legislative efforts are similarly aimed at creating standards for AI transparency, fairness, and accountability. Such frameworks encourage organizations to implement risk assessment procedures and establish clear lines of responsibility for AI-related decisions.

Societal implications of unethical AI practices are not theoretical. They have tangible consequences that can exacerbate social inequalities and undermine democratic processes. For example, the deployment of biased language models in social media platforms can influence public opinion by promoting certain narratives over others. This, in turn, can shape electoral outcomes or perpetuate misinformation. Similarly, AI systems used in predictive policing have come under fire for disproportionately targeting minority communities, highlighting how algorithmic bias can reinforce systemic injustices.

To address these challenges, policymakers, industry leaders, and civil society must work collaboratively. One promising approach is participatory design, where diverse stakeholders–including representatives from marginalized communities–are involved in the development and evaluation of AI systems. This inclusive approach ensures that the technology is shaped by a broad spectrum of perspectives and is responsive to the needs of all users. Additionally, public awareness campaigns and educational initiatives can help demystify AI for the general public, empowering citizens to engage in informed debates about its role in society.

Furthermore, international collaboration is essential to develop harmonized regulatory standards that transcend national borders. As AI technologies are inherently global, inconsistencies in regulation can create loopholes that undermine efforts to protect privacy, promote fairness, and ensure accountability. Cross-border initiatives and cooperative regulatory frameworks can help create a unified approach to the ethical deployment of AI, ensuring that technological innovation does not come at the expense of human rights.

Future Challenges and Opportunities in Ethical AI Development

As AI continues to evolve, the ethical challenges surrounding NLP and AI are poised to become even more complex. Emerging technologies–such as conversational AI that can mimic human empathy or autonomous systems that operate with minimal human intervention–raise new ethical questions which extend beyond traditional concerns. For instance, as AI systems begin to assume roles traditionally held by human experts, questions about the delegation of decision-making authority and the erosion of human agency come to the forefront.

Consider the case of AI-powered mental health applications. These systems are designed to offer immediate, accessible support to individuals in distress. However, relying solely on algorithms for mental health interventions raises significant ethical concerns. What happens when an AI misinterprets a user's emotional state, or when the nuances of human emotion are lost in translation? In such cases, the stakes are incredibly high–misguided advice or inappropriate interventions could have serious consequences for an individual's well-being. Addressing these challenges will require not only technical innovation but also the establishment of clear ethical guidelines and regulatory oversight, ensuring that AI-driven support systems are both effective and safe.

Future AI systems are also likely to blur the boundaries between human and machine interactions. As models become more sophisticated, the distinction between human-generated and machine-generated content may become less clear. This raises important questions about intellectual property, authenticity, and even what it means to be human. For example, if a conversational AI is capable of producing creative writing that rivals that of human authors, how should credit and responsibility be assigned? These are not merely technical issues but philosophical dilemmas that challenge our understanding of creativity and agency.

Moreover, the development of AI technologies will necessitate continuous investment in interdisciplinary research. By integrating insights from computer science, ethics, law, sociology, and psychology, we can develop comprehensive frameworks that address both the technical and ethical dimensions of AI. Educational initiatives will be crucial in this regard; universities and training programs must incorporate ethics into their curricula to prepare the next generation of AI practitioners for the complex moral landscape they will navigate. Workshops, seminars, and cross-disciplinary collaborations can help foster a culture where ethical considerations are as integral to innovation as technical prowess.

Looking ahead, opportunities for ethical AI development abound. Participatory design processes, where end-users and affected communities actively contribute to shaping technology, represent a promising avenue for ensuring that AI systems reflect diverse perspectives. Initiatives such as open-source AI projects and collaborative research networks can accelerate the development of ethical best practices. Ultimately, the future of ethical AI will depend on our collective ability to balance the transformative potential of these technologies with a steadfast commitment to fairness, accountability, and human dignity.

Addressing Bias in Language Models

The exponential growth of natural language processing has enabled groundbreaking advances in how machines understand and generate human language. However, alongside these technical innovations, the challenge of bias in language models has emerged as a critical concern. Bias in these systems can lead to unfair outcomes, perpetuate harmful stereotypes, and negatively impact various sectors–from recruitment and customer service to content moderation and beyond. This comprehensive exploration delves into the origins of bias in language models, examines its real-world consequences, and outlines practical strategies for detection, mitigation, and continuous improvement.

Understanding Bias in Language Models

Bias in language models arises from the very data and algorithms that power them. Since these models are trained on vast datasets collected from the internet and other sources, they inevitably absorb the biases present in those sources. These biases manifest in multiple ways:

- **Historical and Societal Prejudices:** Data scraped from the web reflects the existing societal prejudices. For example, if certain professions or roles are predominantly described using stereotypical language, the model may replicate and reinforce these associations.
- **Representation Bias:** Language models might underrepresent minority voices or overrepresent dominant narratives, leading to skewed perceptions in generated outputs.
- **Algorithmic Amplification:** Even subtle biases in training data can be amplified by complex algorithms, resulting in disproportionate impacts that extend well beyond the original data source.

Thus, by understanding these facets, developers can begin to trace the origins of bias and appreciate its far-reaching implications.

The Real-World Impact of Bias

The practical consequences of bias in language models are both diverse and profound. Consider the following examples:

- **Recruitment and Hiring:** An AI-driven resume screening tool might inadvertently favor candidates from certain demographics if historical data reflects imbalances in hiring practices. Such bias can lead to the perpetuation of inequality and limit opportunities for underrepresented groups.
- **Machine Translation and Localization:** Translation systems can embed gender biases when converting sentences between languages. For instance, a gender-neutral sentence in one language might be translated into a gendered form in another, reinforcing stereotypical roles–such as associating doctors with men and nurses with women.
- **Content Moderation:** Automated moderation tools may disproportionately flag or remove content written in dialects or non-standard language forms, mistaking cultural nuances for policy violations.
- **Customer Service and Chatbots:** Language models integrated into customer service can misinterpret user queries or generate biased responses, potentially alienating certain users and harming brand reputation.

These examples highlight how bias is not an abstract concept but a tangible issue that can have a wide-ranging impact on both individuals and society.

Methodologies for Identifying Bias

Addressing bias begins with its identification. Several methodologies and metrics have been developed to evaluate the extent and nature of bias in language models:

- **Quantitative Metrics:** Statistical measures such as disparity ratios, fairness scores, and word association tests can help quantify bias. For instance, researchers might evaluate how often certain adjectives are paired with male versus female names in model outputs.
- **Qualitative Auditing:** Beyond numbers, manual reviews and audits by human experts can uncover subtle biases that automated tests might miss. This might involve focus groups or expert panels examining the outputs of language models for content that reinforces stereotypes.
- **Benchmarking:** Standardized datasets and benchmarks (for example, the Winograd Schema Challenge) offer a way to systematically evaluate model performance on tasks designed to expose bias.
- **Crowdsourced Feedback:** Leveraging the insights of diverse user groups can provide real-world evidence of bias that technical evaluations might not fully capture.

Through these methodologies, developers gain a clearer understanding of where biases lie and how they might be mitigated.

Strategies for Mitigating Bias

Once identified, a range of strategies can be employed to mitigate bias in language models. These strategies often span multiple stages of the model development lifecycle.

Data Curation and Augmentation: Data curation involves the careful selection, organization, and management of data to ensure its quality and relevance for specific purposes, while data augmentation refers to techniques used to enhance existing datasets by generating additional samples through methods such as synthesis or transformation, thereby improving model performance and generalization.

- **Careful Data Selection:** Choosing diverse and representative datasets is paramount. Curators must critically assess data sources to ensure they do not unduly favor particular perspectives.
- **Data Augmentation:** Supplementing datasets with underrepresented voices or balanced representations can help counteract existing biases. For example, incorporating literature, news, and social media content from diverse cultural backgrounds can provide a more balanced training ground.

Algorithmic Debiasing: Algorithmic debiasing refers to techniques and processes used to mitigate biases present in machine learning models and algorithms.

- **Pre-Processing Techniques:** Before training, data can be transformed to minimize bias. Techniques such as re-weighting, re-sampling, or even removing overtly biased terms can be effective.
- **In-Processing Methods:** Modifying the training algorithms themselves to penalize biased outputs is another promising approach. For instance, fairness constraints can be added to loss functions so that the model is explicitly optimized for equitable performance.
- **Post-Processing Adjustments:** Even after a model is trained, its outputs can be adjusted or filtered. Techniques such as calibration or output re-ranking can reduce the propagation of biased responses.

Explainability and Transparency: Explainability and transparency in AI refer to the ability of algorithms to provide understandable and clear explanations for their decisions and actions, fostering trust and accountability in their deployment across various applications.

- **Explainable AI (XAI) Techniques:** By integrating methods such as Local Interpretable Model-Agnostic Explanations (LIME) or SHapley Additive exPlanations (SHAP), developers can better understand and interpret how a model makes decisions. This transparency aids in pinpointing bias.
- **Comprehensive Documentation:** Maintaining detailed records of data sources, preprocessing steps, model architectures, and training procedures ensures that every stage of development is open to scrutiny and continuous improvement.

Continuous Monitoring and Feedback Loops: Continuous monitoring and feedback loops are essential practices in AI and NLP development, ensuring ongoing evaluation and adjustment of models to maintain accuracy, fairness, and ethical integrity in real-world applications.

- **Regular Auditing:** Bias is dynamic, and what may not be evident at one point could emerge later. Ongoing monitoring and periodic audits are essential to catch and correct new biases as they arise.
- **User Feedback Integration:** Establishing channels for user feedback can provide valuable insights into biased behavior in real-world applications. This feedback can then be incorporated into iterative model updates.

By combining these strategies, developers can create a robust framework that not only minimizes bias during initial development but also adapts to evolving societal norms and ethical standards.

Case Studies and Real-World Examples

The following case studies and real-world examples provide concrete illustrations of theoretical concepts in action, offering valuable insights into how ethical principles are applied or challenged in practical scenarios involving NLP and AI technologies.

Recruitment Platforms: One notable case involves a recruitment platform that initially deployed an NLP-based resume screening tool. Early iterations of the model displayed a bias against female candidates, largely because the training data reflected historical hiring patterns in male-dominated industries. After identifying the issue through bias auditing and user feedback, the company implemented several corrective measures:

- They diversified the training data by incorporating resumes from industries with a higher representation of women.
- They introduced algorithmic constraints that penalized gender-biased associations during training.
- Continuous monitoring and periodic audits ensured that the bias was significantly reduced over subsequent iterations.

Machine Translation Systems: Another example is the evolution of machine translation systems. Early systems sometimes generated translations that inadvertently enforced gender stereotypes. For example, translating gender-neutral terms from languages such as Turkish or Finnish into English often resulted in gendered pronouns that aligned with societal stereotypes. In response, major tech companies refined their translation models by:

- Training on multilingual datasets that provided balanced gender representations.
- Incorporating context-aware algorithms that could better determine the intended gender-neutral usage.
- Engaging with linguistic experts to adjust and validate model outputs.

These real-world examples underscore the importance of proactive bias detection and intervention, demonstrating that with targeted strategies, it is possible to make significant improvements in fairness and accuracy.

Challenges and Limitations in Bias Mitigation

While many promising strategies exist, addressing bias in language models is not without its challenges:

- **Trade-offs Between Fairness and Accuracy:** In some cases, efforts to mitigate bias can inadvertently reduce a model's overall performance. Balancing fairness with accuracy is a delicate task that often requires iterative tuning and testing.

- **Complexity of Multidimensional Bias:** Bias is not monolithic. It can vary along dimensions of gender, race, culture, and more. Mitigation strategies must therefore be multifaceted, addressing each dimension without compromising others.
- **Evolving Societal Norms:** What is considered biased today may change as societal values evolve. Models must be designed with flexibility in mind, enabling them to adapt to new standards and expectations.
- **Resource and Expertise Constraints:** Developing and implementing sophisticated bias mitigation techniques requires significant computational resources and interdisciplinary expertise, which may not be readily available to all organizations.

Despite these challenges, continuous research and development, coupled with transparent practices, can drive steady progress toward more equitable language models.

Future Directions and Best Practices

Looking ahead, several emerging trends and best practices promise to further improve our ability to address bias in language models:

- **Interdisciplinary Collaboration:** The complexity of bias in language models necessitates collaboration across disciplines. By bringing together experts in computer science, sociology, psychology, law, and ethics, organizations can develop more holistic approaches to bias mitigation that are both technically sound and socially responsible.
- **Regulatory Frameworks and Ethical Guidelines:** Governments and regulatory bodies around the world are beginning to establish guidelines and frameworks that mandate fairness, transparency, and accountability in AI systems. Adhering to these frameworks not only helps mitigate bias but also builds public trust. Standards such as those proposed by the European Union's guidelines for trustworthy AI are setting important benchmarks for ethical AI development.
- **Enhanced User Engagement:** Incorporating feedback from a broad range of users is critical for identifying and addressing biases that might not be apparent in controlled testing environments. Crowdsourced evaluations and participatory design practices can ensure that the technology reflects the diversity of its user base.
- **Continuous Learning and Adaptation:** Bias is not a static challenge–it evolves over time as societal values shift and new data becomes available. Future models

will benefit from continuous learning systems that can adapt and recalibrate in real-time, using feedback loops to maintain fairness and accuracy.

- **Open Research and Collaboration:** Finally, fostering an open research culture where insights, datasets, and mitigation techniques are shared can accelerate progress. Open-source initiatives and collaborative platforms enable developers across organizations and geographies to contribute collectively toward addressing bias in language models.

Privacy and Data Security in NLP Applications

The proliferation of natural language processing (NLP) has transformed the way organizations and individuals interact with digital systems. From intelligent chatbots and virtual assistants to sophisticated sentiment analysis and machine translation systems, NLP applications rely on vast amounts of textual data to function effectively. However, this reliance on data brings with it a host of privacy and data security concerns. As NLP technologies continue to advance and permeate every sector of society, ensuring robust privacy measures and data security protocols is not just a technical challenge–it is an ethical imperative.

The Data-Driven Nature of NLP Applications

At the heart of every NLP application lies the need for large-scale data collection and processing. Whether it is social media posts, customer reviews, voice recordings, or confidential emails, these systems are built on extensive datasets that often contain sensitive personal information. The value of this data is undeniable–it fuels the machine learning algorithms that enable NLP systems to understand, interpret, and generate human language. However, the very characteristics that make this data useful also render it vulnerable to misuse.

For instance, consider a customer service chatbot that learns from historical conversation logs. These logs may contain personal identifiers, transaction details, and even sensitive financial information. Similarly, voice-activated assistants, which have become ubiquitous in homes and offices, continuously capture and process audio data to improve their performance. Without proper safeguards, this data can become a goldmine for cybercriminals and a potential source of privacy breaches.

Privacy Challenges: Consent, Anonymization, and Re-Identification

Privacy challenges in AI and NLP involve navigating issues such as obtaining informed consent, ensuring effective anonymization of data to prevent re-identification, and managing the delicate balance between data utility and individual privacy rights.

- **User Consent and Data Collection:** One of the foremost challenges in NLP data management is obtaining informed consent from users. Often, data is collected passively or through terms of service that users rarely read in detail. This practice raises significant ethical questions regarding the transparency of data collection processes. Users must be made aware of what data is being collected, how it will be used, and who will have access to it. Inadequate consent mechanisms can lead to legal ramifications under regulations such as the General Data Protection Regulation (GDPR) in Europe and the California Consumer Privacy Act (CCPA) in the United States.
- **Data Anonymization Techniques:** Once data is collected, protecting user identity becomes a top priority. Anonymization is the process of stripping personally identifiable information (PII) from datasets to safeguard user privacy. Techniques such as data masking, pseudonymization, and tokenization are employed to achieve this. However, anonymization is not foolproof. Sophisticated attackers may employ de-anonymization techniques by cross-referencing anonymized data with other datasets, thereby re-identifying individuals. For example, even when names, addresses, and social security numbers are removed from a dataset, patterns in user behavior, location data, or writing styles can sometimes reveal the identity of the original source.
- **Differential Privacy and Advanced Safeguards:** To combat the risks of re-identification, advanced techniques such as differential privacy are gaining traction. Differential privacy adds statistical noise to data, ensuring that individual data points cannot be reverse-engineered while still allowing for aggregate analysis. This method has been applied in various high-stakes scenarios, such as in healthcare analytics and public sector research, where the balance between data utility and privacy is crucial. By integrating differential privacy into NLP applications, organizations can significantly reduce the risk of privacy breaches while maintaining the value of the data for training and analysis.

Data Security: Protection Mechanisms and Technical Solutions

Data Security: Protection Mechanisms and Technical Solutions involve implementing robust encryption, secure data storage practices, access controls, and monitoring to safeguard sensitive information from unauthorized access or breaches.

- **Encryption and Secure Data Storage:** Encryption is one of the cornerstones of data security. When applied correctly, encryption converts data into a format that is unreadable without the appropriate decryption key. For NLP applications, encryption should be implemented at multiple levels–from data at rest on servers to data in transit between devices and cloud services. Modern encryption standards, such as AES-256, offer robust security against unauthorized access, ensuring that sensitive information remains protected even if a breach occurs.

Secure data storage practices extend beyond encryption. Organizations must also adopt stringent access controls and monitoring systems to prevent unauthorized access. Multi-factor Authentication (MFA) and Role-based Access Control (RBAC) are essential strategies that ensure only authorized personnel can access sensitive datasets. These measures are particularly important in environments where NLP applications handle sensitive customer data, such as financial services or healthcare.

- **Secure Data Transmission Protocols:** Data security is not only about how data is stored but also about how it is transmitted. Secure protocols such as HTTPS, TLS, and VPNs ensure that data moving between endpoints is encrypted and protected from interception. In the context of NLP applications that rely on cloud-based services, secure transmission protocols are critical for maintaining data integrity and confidentiality. For example, a language translation service that processes user queries must ensure that both the request and the response are transmitted securely to prevent eavesdropping or data tampering.
- **The Role of Auditing and Compliance:** Regular security audits and compliance checks are vital for maintaining data security in NLP applications. Audits help identify vulnerabilities and ensure that all security measures are up-to-date and effective against emerging threats. Compliance with international standards and regulations, such as ISO 27001 for information security management, is also crucial. These standards provide a framework for continuous improvement and help organizations align their data security practices with global best practices.
- **Regulatory Landscape: Navigating Legal and Ethical Standards:** The evolving regulatory landscape has a significant impact on how organizations manage privacy and data security in NLP applications. With the introduction of GDPR, CCPA, and other data protection laws, organizations are held to higher standards of accountability. These regulations mandate transparency in data collection, strict consent protocols, and robust security measures. Failure to comply can result in hefty fines and long-lasting reputational damage.
- **Case Study: GDPR Compliance in Healthcare NLP:** In healthcare, NLP applications are used to analyze patient records, support diagnostic decisions, and even facilitate personalized treatment plans. Given the sensitivity of medical data, GDPR compliance is paramount. A hospital deploying an

NLP-based diagnostic tool must ensure that all patient data is anonymized, encrypted, and stored securely. Moreover, patients must be informed about how their data will be used and must provide explicit consent for its use in training AI models. Regular audits and transparent reporting are necessary to maintain compliance and build trust with patients.

- **Global Harmonization of Data Security Standards:** Beyond national regulations, there is an increasing push toward global harmonization of data security standards. International bodies such as the International Organization for Standardization (ISO) and the National Institute of Standards and Technology (NIST) provide guidelines that help organizations navigate the complex global landscape. Adopting these standards can simplify compliance, reduce legal risks, and enhance the overall security posture of NLP applications. As data flows across borders, harmonized standards ensure that privacy and security measures remain consistent, regardless of geographic location.

Emerging Challenges and Future Directions

Emerging challenges in the field of NLP and AI include tackling deep-rooted biases in increasingly complex language models, navigating ethical dilemmas posed by rapid technological advancements, and ensuring robust frameworks for transparent and responsible AI deployment.

- **The Growing Threat of Cyberattacks:** As NLP applications become more integral to everyday operations, they also become more attractive targets for cyberattacks. Cybercriminals are constantly evolving their tactics, and NLP systems are no exception. Attacks such as data breaches, ransomware, and sophisticated phishing schemes can compromise sensitive data and disrupt services. Proactive measures, including continuous threat monitoring, incident response planning, and employee training, are essential to counter these risks. Organizations must invest in advanced cybersecurity technologies and foster a culture of security awareness to stay ahead of potential threats.
- **Balancing Innovation with Privacy:** The rapid pace of innovation in NLP and AI often places pressure on organizations to deploy new applications quickly. However, this speed must be balanced with a rigorous approach to privacy and data security. There is a constant tension between leveraging large-scale data for improved AI performance and ensuring that individual privacy is not compromised. Future developments in privacy-preserving technologies, such as federated learning and secure multi-party computation, offer promising solutions. These methods allow models to be trained on decentralized data sources without transferring sensitive information to a central server, thereby reducing the risk of data breaches.

- **User-Centric Data Security:** A key direction for future research and development is enhancing user control over personal data. Empowering users to manage their data, understand how it is used, and revoke consent when desired can transform the relationship between individuals and NLP applications. Techniques such as blockchain for data provenance and secure data sharing protocols can enhance transparency and trust. By placing users at the center of data security efforts, organizations can foster a more ethical and sustainable approach to NLP development.

Transparency, Fairness, and Responsible AI Deployment

The integration of artificial intelligence into nearly every facet of modern life–from healthcare and finance to education and public safety–has accelerated innovation while also raising profound ethical and societal questions. Central to these debates are three interconnected pillars: Transparency, fairness, and responsible AI deployment. Together, they form the ethical backbone of AI systems that not only deliver robust performance but also maintain public trust and safeguard individual rights. In this detailed exploration, we examine the importance of these principles, the challenges they present, and practical strategies for ensuring that AI technologies serve society equitably and transparently.

The Imperative of Transparency in AI

The imperative of transparency in AI underscores the critical need for clear and understandable processes and outcomes in artificial intelligence systems. It ensures accountability, fosters trust among users and stakeholders, and enables informed decision-making in the deployment and use of AI technologies.

Defining Transparency in AI: Transparency in AI is about more than simply sharing information–it is an ongoing commitment to clarity in every phase of the AI lifecycle. This encompasses everything from the raw data used to train models to the algorithms and parameters that drive decision-making, and even to the potential limitations and risks associated with an AI system. For instance, when a financial institution deploys an AI-based credit-scoring system, stakeholders should have access to clear explanations regarding how creditworthiness is assessed. This level of openness demystifies the "*black box*" nature of complex algorithms and builds a foundation of trust.

Explainability and Interpretability Techniques: Explainability is a practical subset of transparency. It involves using methods and tools that help both technical and non-technical stakeholders understand why an AI model reached a particular decision. Some commonly used techniques include:

- **Local Interpretable Model-Agnostic Explanations (LIME):** LIME approximates the model locally to explain individual predictions, such as why a loan application was approved or denied.
- **SHapley Additive exPlanations (SHAP):** SHAP values quantify the contribution of each feature in a model's prediction, making it easier to identify which factors–such as income level or credit history–are most influential.
- **Counterfactual Explanations:** These offer insights into what changes in input data would lead to different outcomes, helping users understand decision boundaries.

For example, consider an AI system used in healthcare diagnostics. If an algorithm suggests a particular treatment, explainability techniques can reveal which patient metrics (for example, blood pressure, test results) were most influential. This not only supports clinical decision-making but also provides a safeguard against erroneous or biased recommendations.

Comprehensive Documentation and Open Communication: True transparency goes beyond explainability. It involves comprehensive documentation throughout the AI development process. This documentation should include:

- **Data Provenance:** Detailed records of the data sources, collection methods, and any preprocessing steps taken.
- **Model Architecture:** Information about the algorithms used, model parameters, and training protocols.
- **Limitations and Risks:** A clear discussion of potential pitfalls, biases, and performance limitations.

Organizations that commit to open communication–by publishing white papers, technical reports, or even open-sourcing parts of their code–invite independent audits and peer reviews. In regulated industries such as finance and healthcare, such openness can be critical to meeting legal standards and ensuring that AI systems are both reliable and ethically sound.

Ensuring Fairness in AI Systems

Ensuring fairness in AI systems involves mitigating biases in data and algorithms to ensure equitable outcomes for all individuals, regardless of demographic or background factors.

Understanding Fairness in the Context of AI: Fairness in AI involves the commitment to equitable treatment across diverse populations. It demands that AI systems do not reinforce existing social biases or create new forms of discrimination. Fairness can be conceptualized in various ways:

- **Individual Fairness:** Ensuring that similar individuals receive similar outcomes.
- **Group Fairness:** Guaranteeing that different demographic groups (for example, by race, gender, age) experience comparable outcomes.
- **Procedural Fairness:** Focusing on the fairness of the processes that lead to decisions, not just the outcomes themselves.

Sources and Consequences of Bias: Bias in AI is often a reflection of historical and systemic issues embedded within the training data. For example, if a recruitment algorithm is trained on historical hiring data from an industry with gender imbalances, the algorithm may inadvertently favor male candidates. Similarly, an AI tool used in law enforcement may target specific communities if it relies on skewed crime statistics. Such biases have real-world consequences, including perpetuating economic disparities and eroding public trust.

Real-World Examples:

- **Recruitment Algorithms:** Companies have faced criticism when their AI-driven resume screening tools favored candidates from traditionally dominant demographics. In response, several organizations have revamped their data sources and implemented fairness constraints.
- **Predictive Policing:** Early implementations of predictive policing algorithms have been shown to disproportionately target minority neighborhoods, sparking debates about accountability and the ethical use of AI in public safety.

Strategies for Mitigating Bias

Mitigating bias requires a multi-pronged approach:

- **Data Curation and Augmentation:**
    - **Diverse Data Collection:** Ensure that training datasets are diverse and representative of the populations the AI system will serve.
    - **Data Augmentation:** Actively seek out and include underrepresented voices or demographic groups to balance skewed data.
- **Algorithmic Adjustments:**
    - **Fairness Constraints:** Incorporate constraints into the model training process that penalize unfair outcomes.
    - **Re-Weighting:** Adjust the importance of certain data points during training to counteract historical biases.

- **Regular Audits and Feedback:**
    - **Quantitative Metrics:** Use fairness scores, disparate impact ratios, and other metrics to measure bias.
    - **Qualitative Reviews:** Engage domain experts and community representatives to identify subtle biases that quantitative methods might miss.

Institutionalizing Fairness

Establishing fairness is not a one-time project–it requires continuous effort. Organizations can institutionalize fairness by:

- **Setting up Ethics Committees:** Dedicated bodies that oversee AI projects and ensure that fairness is considered at every stage.
- **Stakeholder Engagement:** Involve a broad range of stakeholders, including end users and affected communities, to provide ongoing feedback.
- **Transparent Reporting:** Regularly publish fairness audits and update stakeholders on the progress of bias mitigation efforts.

Responsible AI Deployment: Governance, Oversight, and Ethical Considerations

It involves establishing clear policies, regulatory frameworks, and ethical guidelines to ensure AI systems operate transparently, fairly, and accountably. It includes continuous monitoring, bias mitigation, and aligning AI practices with societal values to prevent harm and promote trust.

Defining Responsible AI Deployment: Responsible AI deployment is about ensuring that AI systems are designed, developed, and deployed with a holistic view of their societal impact. It requires balancing innovation with ethical considerations and regulatory compliance. Responsible deployment addresses not only technical performance but also the broader implications for human rights, safety, and social justice.

Governance Structures and Accountability: Effective governance is the backbone of responsible AI. It involves:

- **Clear Accountability:**
    - **Ethics Officers and Oversight Committees:** Designate individuals or groups responsible for overseeing AI initiatives and ensuring ethical compliance.

    - **Audit Trails:** Maintain detailed logs that document every stage of development, deployment, and decision-making. This transparency supports accountability when issues arise.

- **Policy and Regulation:**
    - **Compliance with Laws:** Adhere to data protection regulations (such as GDPR and CCPA) and emerging AI-specific guidelines.
    - **Industry Standards:** Align with international standards (such as ISO or NIST frameworks) to ensure consistency and robustness.

Human Oversight and Continuous Monitoring: While AI can automate decision-making, human oversight remains critical. Responsible AI deployment integrates human-in-the-loop systems that allow for:

- **Regular Performance Reviews:** Experts should periodically review AI outputs to detect anomalies or biased outcomes.
- **Real-Time Monitoring:** Continuous monitoring systems can alert developers to unexpected behavior, enabling timely interventions.
- **Feedback Mechanisms:** Channels for end users to report issues, ask questions, or provide suggestions help refine and improve the AI system over time.

Ethical and Societal Considerations: Responsible AI is inherently linked to broader ethical considerations. Some key aspects include:

- **Non-Maleficence:** The principle of "*do no harm*" should guide all AI deployments, ensuring that systems do not cause unintended negative consequences.
- **Beneficence:** AI should be designed to benefit society, promoting positive outcomes such as increased efficiency, improved healthcare, and enhanced public services.
- **Justice and Inclusivity:** AI systems must be developed with a focus on fairness and inclusion, ensuring that all societal groups benefit equitably from technological advances.

Overcoming Challenges and Implementing Best Practices

Overcoming challenges in NLP and AI requires a proactive approach that includes bias mitigation strategies, robust privacy safeguards, and transparent, fair, and accountable deployment practices.

Balancing Transparency with Proprietary Interests: One of the significant challenges in promoting transparency is reconciling it with the need to protect proprietary information. Organizations may be reluctant to share details about their algorithms for competitive reasons. However, several strategies can help strike this balance:

- **Third-Party Audits:** Independent audits can verify claims without requiring full public disclosure.
- **High-Level Summaries:** Providing detailed overviews of methods and results without exposing trade secrets can build trust while maintaining competitive advantage.
- **Controlled Access:** Establish secure environments where selected stakeholders can review detailed documentation under non-disclosure agreements.

Harmonizing Fairness with Performance: Efforts to improve fairness sometimes come with trade-offs in model accuracy or performance. To manage these trade-offs:

- **Iterative Testing:** Conduct extensive testing to understand the impact of fairness interventions on overall performance.
- **Adaptive Models:** Develop models that can recalibrate themselves based on new data and evolving fairness standards.
- **Collaborative Research:** Engage with academic and industry partners to share insights and develop methods that optimize both fairness and performance.

Strategies for Sustainable and Ethical AI Deployment: For AI systems to remain ethically sound over time, organizations must adopt a proactive and sustainable approach:

- **Interdisciplinary Collaboration:** Bringing together computer scientists, ethicists, legal experts, and social scientists ensures that multiple perspectives inform AI development.
- **Stakeholder Engagement:** Involve communities, industry groups, and regulatory bodies early in the design process to create systems that meet diverse needs.
- **Iterative Improvement:** Establish robust feedback loops that allow for continuous learning and improvement of AI systems.
- **Transparency Portals:** Create public dashboards or portals that provide ongoing updates about AI performance, fairness metrics, and audit results, thereby fostering ongoing dialogue with the public.

International Collaboration and Harmonized Standards: AI technologies often operate across borders, making it essential to harmonize ethical standards internationally:

- **Global Regulatory Frameworks:** Encourage international cooperation to create frameworks that ensure responsible AI practices across different jurisdictions.

- **Cross-Border Initiatives:** Participate in global forums and consortia dedicated to AI ethics, such as the Partnership on AI, to share best practices and drive collective progress.
- **Cultural Sensitivity:** Recognize and incorporate regional differences in ethical standards and cultural norms, ensuring that AI systems are adaptable and sensitive to local contexts.

Case Studies: Ethical Dilemmas in Real-World NLP Applications

The transformative power of Natural Language Processing (NLP) has spurred remarkable innovations across industries–from automated customer service and recruitment to healthcare diagnostics and content moderation. Yet, as these technologies become integral to daily operations and decision-making, they also expose organizations to a host of ethical dilemmas. These challenges, ranging from unintended biases and privacy breaches to misinformation and misinterpretation of context, underscore the need for a rigorous ethical framework in NLP development and deployment. In this exploration, we delve into several case studies that illustrate the multifaceted ethical dilemmas encountered in real-world NLP applications, examining both the challenges and the lessons learned.

Introduction: Navigating the Ethical Landscape of NLP

At its core, NLP involves teaching machines to understand, interpret, and generate human language. This capability has revolutionized industries by enabling applications that can analyze massive volumes of text, provide automated insights, and even mimic human conversation. However, the same technologies that unlock unprecedented opportunities also harbor ethical pitfalls. Consider the potential harm of an algorithm that inadvertently reinforces gender or racial stereotypes, or a chatbot that, without proper context, offers harmful advice to a vulnerable user. These scenarios are not merely hypothetical; they represent real challenges faced by organizations striving to balance innovation with responsibility.

Ethical dilemmas in NLP typically stem from two principal sources. First, the data used to train these models often reflect historical prejudices and imbalances, leading to biased outcomes that can perpetuate inequality. Second, the inherent complexity and opacity of many NLP models can obscure decision-making processes, complicating efforts to audit or challenge problematic outcomes. The following case studies provide detailed insights into these issues, highlighting both the technical and human dimensions of ethical challenges in NLP applications.

Case Study 1: Bias in Recruitment and Hiring Tools

An AI-driven recruitment tool trained on historical hiring data exhibited bias by favoring certain demographic groups over others, reflecting past prejudices in hiring practices. This case highlights the ethical challenges of biased training data and the need for fairness and transparency in AI-driven decision-making.

The Scenario

Imagine a multinational corporation that deploys an NLP-based recruitment tool designed to streamline the hiring process by scanning resumes and ranking candidates based on perceived suitability. The algorithm, trained on decades of historical hiring data, quickly becomes an indispensable part of the company's talent acquisition strategy. However, soon after implementation, human resource managers begin to notice a concerning trend: candidates from certain demographic groups are consistently ranked lower, even when their qualifications match the job requirements.

Uncovering the Ethical Dilemma

The root of the problem lies in the training data. Historical hiring records, reflecting past biases and discriminatory practices, had inadvertently taught the algorithm to favor candidates who fit a narrow profile. For example, the system might have learned to associate technical competence with male-oriented language or to prioritize candidates from elite educational institutions, inadvertently sidelining equally qualified individuals from diverse backgrounds.

The ethical dilemma here is multifaceted:

- **Fairness and Equity:** The tool, intended to eliminate human bias, ends up reinforcing historical inequities. This not only perpetuates discrimination but also denies talented individuals equal opportunities.
- **Transparency:** The decision-making process of the algorithm is opaque, making it difficult for candidates or HR managers to understand why certain resumes are ranked lower.
- **Accountability:** In cases of discriminatory outcomes, it becomes challenging to assign responsibility–should the fault lie with the data, the algorithm's design, or the lack of oversight?

Mitigation and Lessons Learned

In response to these issues, the company undertakes a thorough audit of its recruitment system. Steps taken include:

- **Data Rebalancing:** Curating a more diverse dataset that better reflects the current labor market and mitigates historical biases.
- **Algorithmic Adjustments:** Implementing fairness constraints during the model training process to penalize skewed associations.
- **Transparency Measures:** Publishing detailed documentation and explanation reports that outline how the algorithm works and the steps taken to mitigate bias.
- **Human Oversight:** Establishing a review committee that continuously monitors the tool's outputs and intervenes when anomalies are detected.

This case study underscores that while automation can enhance efficiency, it must be accompanied by robust ethical oversight to ensure fairness and accountability.

Case Study 2: Privacy and Misinformation in Mental Health Chatbots

Mental health chatbots, designed to provide support and guidance, pose significant ethical challenges related to user privacy and misinformation. In some cases, these AI-driven systems have mishandled sensitive user data or provided inaccurate medical advice, potentially leading to harmful consequences for vulnerable individuals.

The Scenario

A startup launches a mental health chatbot designed to provide immediate support and resources for individuals experiencing anxiety and depression. Powered by advanced NLP algorithms, the chatbot is available 24/7 and quickly gains popularity due to its accessibility and non-judgmental tone. However, as usage increases, concerns emerge about the chatbot's handling of sensitive user data and the accuracy of its responses.

Uncovering the Ethical Dilemma

Two critical ethical challenges come to the forefront:

- **Privacy and Data Security:** The chatbot collects extensive personal data, including users' emotional states, personal experiences, and in some cases, identifiers that could link to their identity. Although data anonymization techniques are applied, there remains a risk of re-identification through sophisticated cross-referencing with other datasets. Users are often unaware of the depth of data collection and the potential vulnerabilities inherent in such systems.

- **Misinformation and Misinterpretation:** Given the high stakes of mental health support, even a slight misinterpretation of a user's input can lead to inappropriate or even harmful advice. For instance, a user in crisis might receive a generic response that fails to address the urgency of their situation. The chatbot's inability to understand the nuance and context of human emotions raises ethical questions about its deployment in sensitive domains.

Mitigation and Lessons Learned

To address these dilemmas, the startup implements several strategies:

- **Enhanced Data Protection:**
    - Adopting stronger encryption methods for data storage and transmission.
    - Implementing differential privacy techniques to ensure that individual data points remain obscured.
    - Revising the consent process to clearly communicate what data is collected and how it will be used.
- **Improved Response Mechanisms:**
    - Incorporating human oversight into the chatbot's operations, where critical responses are reviewed by qualified mental health professionals.
    - Integrating context-aware algorithms that can better discern the severity of a user's input.
    - Establishing a robust escalation protocol, wherein the chatbot directs users to live support if certain high-risk phrases or sentiments are detected.

This case study highlights the delicate balance required when deploying AI in areas that touch on human well-being. The integration of ethical safeguards is not just a technical necessity but a moral imperative, especially when dealing with vulnerable populations.

Case Study 3: Misinformation and Content Moderation in Social Media

The rise of NLP-driven content moderation on social media platforms has led to challenges in distinguishing harmful misinformation from legitimate discourse. Bias in training data and algorithmic decision-making can result in the over-removal of certain viewpoints while failing to curb the spread of misleading or harmful content, raising ethical concerns about free speech, fairness, and accountability.

The Scenario

A global social media platform leverages NLP algorithms to automate the moderation of user-generated content. The goal is to swiftly identify and remove hate speech, misinformation, and harmful content. Initially, the system appears successful, significantly reducing the volume of objectionable posts. However, over time, users and advocacy groups begin to report instances where the moderation tool disproportionately flags content from certain cultural or political groups, while other harmful content goes undetected.

Uncovering the Ethical Dilemma

This scenario presents several intertwined ethical challenges:

- **Bias and Discrimination:** The algorithm's training data, drawn from a wide range of online interactions, includes inherent biases that may lead to over-policing of certain communities. For example, the nuances of dialects or cultural expressions may be misinterpreted as hate speech.
- **Freedom of Expression versus Harm Reduction:** The moderation system must balance the need to curb harmful content with the imperative to protect free speech. Overzealous filtering can silence legitimate voices, stifling public discourse and disproportionately affecting minority groups.
- **Transparency and Accountability:** Users often have little insight into why their content was flagged, creating a sense of arbitrariness and eroding trust in the platform. This lack of transparency makes it difficult to contest decisions or suggest improvements.

Mitigation and Lessons Learned

In response, the platform undertakes several corrective measures:

- **Algorithmic Refinement:**
  - Conducting regular audits to identify and correct biased behavior.
  - Incorporating community feedback into the moderation process to better understand cultural contexts.
  - Training the model on a more diverse dataset that reflects a broader spectrum of expressions and dialects.
- **Human-in-the-Loop Systems:**
  - Combining automated moderation with human review for borderline cases.
  - Establishing an appeals process where users can contest decisions, ensuring accountability and continuous improvement.

- **Enhanced Transparency:**
  - Publishing detailed reports on moderation policies, methodologies, and performance metrics.
  - Creating educational resources to help users understand the complexities and limitations of automated content moderation.

This case study emphasizes that while automation can significantly enhance efficiency, it must be carefully managed to avoid infringing on individual rights and to maintain the delicate balance between safety and freedom.

Case Study 4: Ethical Challenges in Healthcare NLP Applications

The use of NLP in healthcare, such as automated diagnostics and clinical decision support, raises ethical concerns related to patient privacy, data security, and potential biases in medical recommendations. Ensuring fairness, accuracy, and transparency in these AI-driven systems is critical to maintaining trust and preventing harmful outcomes.

The Scenario

Hospitals and healthcare providers are increasingly turning to NLP to analyze patient records, extract valuable clinical insights, and support diagnostic decision-making. An advanced NLP system is deployed to sift through electronic health records (EHRs), identify patterns in patient data, and flag potential medical issues. While the technology promises improved diagnostic accuracy and patient outcomes, several ethical dilemmas soon arise.

Uncovering the Ethical Dilemma

Key ethical concerns in this scenario include:

- **Patient Privacy and Data Security:** EHRs contain highly sensitive personal and medical information. The risk of data breaches, unauthorized access, and inadvertent exposure of patient details poses significant ethical and legal challenges. Even when data is anonymized, the possibility of re-identification through cross-referencing with other datasets remains a concern.
- **Bias in Medical Decision-Making:** If the training data for the NLP system includes biased or incomplete information, the system may produce skewed results. For instance, underrepresentation of certain demographic groups in clinical studies can lead to diagnostic models that are less effective for those populations, potentially exacerbating health disparities.

- **Transparency and Trust:** Healthcare providers and patients alike need to understand how the NLP system reaches its conclusions. Without clear explanations, clinicians may be hesitant to rely on its recommendations, and patients may question the integrity of their diagnoses.

Mitigation and Lessons Learned

To address these challenges, healthcare institutions implement a multi-layered approach:

- **Robust Data Protection Protocols:**
  - Utilizing state-of-the-art encryption, secure data storage, and strict access controls to safeguard patient records.
  - Implementing differential privacy techniques and continuous monitoring to mitigate risks of re-identification.
- **Bias Auditing and Inclusive Data Collection:**
  - Regularly auditing the system for biases and updating the training datasets to include diverse patient populations.
  - Collaborating with clinical experts to validate the system's recommendations and adjust for any disparities.
- **Enhanced Transparency and Clinician Collaboration:**
  - Providing detailed documentation and real-time explanations for diagnostic outputs.
  - Integrating clinician feedback into iterative system improvements, ensuring that the AI supports rather than supplants medical expertise.

This case study illustrates that while NLP can revolutionize healthcare, its deployment must be accompanied by rigorous safeguards to protect patient privacy and ensure equitable care.

Lessons Learned and Best Practices

The case studies presented reveal common themes and challenges:

- **Data Integrity is Paramount:** The quality, diversity, and representativeness of training data are crucial to preventing biases. Continuous data curation and augmentation are essential to adapting models to changing societal contexts.
- **Human Oversight is Critical:** Whether in recruitment, mental health support, content moderation, or healthcare, incorporating human judgment into the loop provides a necessary counterbalance to automated decision-making.

- **Transparency Builds Trust:** Open communication, comprehensive documentation, and user feedback mechanisms are key to ensuring that stakeholders understand and trust AI systems.
- **Ethical Frameworks Must Evolve:** As NLP technologies continue to advance, ethical guidelines and regulatory frameworks must be flexible enough to accommodate new challenges while safeguarding individual rights.

Conclusion

As NLP and AI continue to redefine the landscape of technology, addressing their inherent ethical challenges requires a multifaceted strategy that meticulously tackles bias in language models, reinforces robust privacy and data security measures, and upholds transparency, fairness, and responsible deployment practices. Balancing innovation with ethical considerations means actively mitigating historical prejudices embedded in training data, ensuring that sensitive user information is rigorously protected, and fostering an environment where AI systems operate with clear accountability and equitable outcomes. This comprehensive approach not only enhances trust among users and stakeholders but also lays the groundwork for sustainable, socially responsible technological advancements that honor the principles of justice and human dignity.

The next chapter will delve into practical methodologies and real-world case studies that illustrate how these principles are implemented in practice. We will explore innovative strategies for bias mitigation, advanced privacy-preserving techniques, and robust frameworks for ensuring accountability in AI systems, providing you with actionable insights and tools to build technology that not only performs effectively but also upholds the highest ethical standards.

Multiple Choice Questions

1. Which of the following is NOT one of the ethical challenges highlighted in our discussion on NLP and AI?

    a. Bias in language models

    b. Privacy and data security issues

    c. High computational cost

    d. Transparency, fairness, and responsible deployment practices

2. Mitigating bias in language models typically involves which of the following approaches?
   a. Removing all training data
   b. Data rebalancing and algorithmic debiasing
   c. Increasing model complexity without addressing data issues
   d. Discarding human oversight
3. Which technique adds statistical noise to data in order to protect individual privacy without significantly compromising overall utility?
   a. Data masking
   b. Differential privacy
   c. Data augmentation
   d. Role-based access control
4. What is an example of an explainability technique used to enhance transparency in AI systems?
   a. Federated learning
   b. LIME (Local Interpretable Model-Agnostic Explanations)
   c. Multi-factor authentication
   d. Data encryption
5. Responsible AI deployment emphasizes which of the following principles?
   a. Focusing solely on technical performance
   b. Transparency, fairness, and accountability
   c. Increasing data collection without regard for ethics
   d. Reducing human oversight in decision-making
6. In the case study on recruitment tools, what was the primary ethical dilemma encountered?
   a. The tool processed too many resumes
   b. Historical hiring data led the tool to favor certain demographics
   c. The tool had low technical performance
   d. There was an issue with data storage

7. What ethical challenge is illustrated by biased content moderation on social media platforms?

    a. Insufficient internet connectivity

    b. Over-filtering content from certain communities due to biased training data

    c. Excessively fast content delivery

    d. Inability to process a high volume of posts

8. Which of the following best describes a key aspect of transparency in AI systems?

    a. Keeping model architectures secret to protect intellectual property

    b. Providing detailed documentation and clear explanations of decision-making processes

    c. Relying solely on automated outputs without human intervention

    d. Avoiding external audits to maintain competitive advantage

9. In healthcare NLP applications, what is a major ethical concern that must be addressed?

    a. The speed of diagnostic processing

    b. Patient privacy and potential data breaches

    c. The visual design of the user interface

    d. High operational costs

10. To balance fairness with performance in AI systems, organizations should implement which of the following practices?

    a. Eliminate audits to maintain maximum performance

    b. Incorporate human oversight and iterative feedback loops

    c. Reduce training data diversity

    d. Ignore ethical considerations in favor of speed

Answers

1. c
2. b
3. b
4. b
5. b
6. b
7. d
8. b
9. b
10. b

CHAPTER 12
Practical Applications of Llama4

Introduction

In this chapter, we delve into the practical applications of Llama 4, a state-of-the-art language model that is revolutionizing natural language processing. Readers will embark on a journey to understand how Llama 4 builds upon the successes of its predecessors, offering improved performance and versatility in a range of NLP tasks. From text generation to sophisticated dialogue systems, the chapter is designed to provide both theoretical insights and actionable steps that empower you to leverage this model in your projects.

We explore how Llama 4 is tailored for real-world use cases across various industries such as healthcare, finance, and customer support. By examining hands-on examples and detailed case studies, you will gain a clear understanding of how to implement Llama 4 to solve complex challenges. The content emphasizes its efficacy in text summarization, language understanding, question answering, and more, illustrating how these capabilities can translate into tangible improvements in accuracy and efficiency.

Furthermore, this chapter is structured to equip you with practical skills that you can immediately apply. Whether you are developing a new customer support chatbot or refining your text analysis workflows, the lessons here provide a step-by-step guide to integrating Llama 4 into your solutions. Through real-world scenarios and detailed walkthroughs, you will discover best practices for maximizing the potential of this cutting-edge model.

Structure

In this chapter, we will cover the following topics:

- Overview
- Text Generation

- Text Summarization
- Language Understanding for Complex NLP Tasks
- Implementing Llama 4 for Question Answering Systems
- Conversational AI Applications

Overview

Llama 4 stands at the forefront of modern natural language processing, redefining how machines understand and generate human language. Its prowess in text generation allows for the creation of engaging, coherent, and contextually accurate content, making it a valuable tool for automated content creation and creative applications alike. Moreover, the model's advanced capabilities in text summarization enable it to distill complex information into concise, readable summaries, streamlining data interpretation and decision-making processes. These features are complemented by its strong foundation in language understanding, which equips Llama 4 to handle even the most complex NLP tasks with precision.

Beyond these core functionalities, Llama 4 is instrumental in the development of sophisticated question answering systems and conversational AI applications. By implementing Llama 4, developers can build interactive platforms that not only provide accurate responses to user queries but also engage in natural, dynamic conversations. This integration paves the way for innovative solutions in customer support, digital assistants, and beyond, ensuring that user interactions are both efficient and intuitively responsive. Together, these capabilities make Llama 4 a versatile and transformative tool in the evolving landscape of AI-driven language technology.

Text Generation

Below is a detailed example that demonstrates how to use **meta-llama/Llama-4-Maverick-17B-128E** for text generation in Python. In this practical application, we leverage the Hugging Face Transformers library to load the pre-trained Llama 4.3 model, tokenize a given prompt, and generate coherent text. You can customize various generation parameters–such as maximum length, temperature, and top-p sampling–to fine-tune the creativity and control of the output. This setup is ideal for applications such as creative writing, automated content generation, or as a component in conversational AI systems.

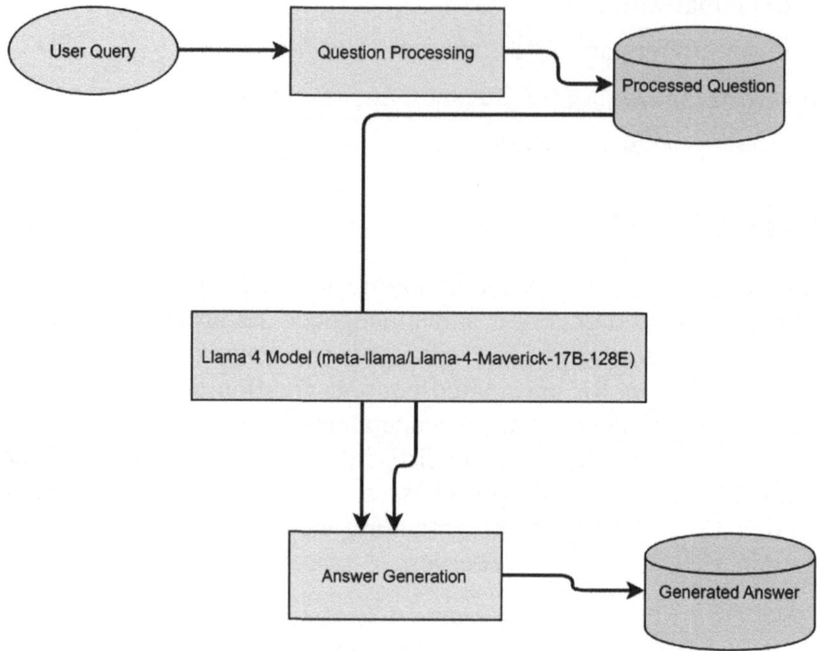

Figure 12.1: *Text Generation Architecture using Llama 4*

The data flow steps for text-generation are as follows:

1. Input Prompt → Tokenization
2. Tokenization → Tokenized Input
3. Tokenized Input → Text Generation
4. Llama 4 Model → Text Generation
5. Text Generation → Generated Text
6. Generated Text → Decoding

The code provided not only shows how to implement text generation but also includes a helper function that encapsulates the generation process. By running the code, you will see how to input a prompt, process it through the model, and then output the generated text. This example is designed to be a strong starting point for integrating **meta-llama/Llama-4-Maverick-17B-128E** into your projects, especially when you are working on chatbots, narrative generators, or any system that benefits from dynamic text creation.

Source Code: Please refer to this GitHub link for the source code for text generation:

https://github.com/OrangeAVA/Ultimate-Llama-for-NLP/blob/main/text_generation.py

Execution Steps(Windows)

1. **Create a Virtual Environment (Optional):**

   ```
   python -m venv venv
   venv\Scripts\activate
   ```

2. **Install Dependencies:** Create a requirements.txt file with the content provided below and install:

   ```
   transformers>=4.0.0
   torch>=1.7.0
   pip install -r requirements.txt
   ```

3. **Authenticate with Hugging Face:** Either replace "**`your_token_here`**" in the script with your Hugging Face token,

   Or log in via the CLI using: **`huggingface-cli login`**

   Then set **`auth_token=True`** in the script.

4. **Run the Script:**

   ```
   python text_generation.py
   ```

Execution Steps(Mac OS)

1. **Install Python (if not already installed):** macOS usually comes with Python 2.x, so it is recommended to install Python 3 using:

   Homebrew.

   Open Terminal and run: brew install python

   Confirm the installation with: python3 -version

2. **Create and Activate a Virtual Environment:**

   a. Open Terminal and navigate to your project directory.

   b. Create a virtual environment using Python 3:

      ```
      python3 -m venv venv
      ```

      Activate the virtual environment: **`source venv/bin/activate`**

3. **Prepare the requirements.txt File:** Create a file named requirements.txt with the following content:

   ```
   transformers>=4.0.0
   torch>=1.7.0
   ```

4. **Install Dependencies:** With your virtual environment activated, run:

   ```
   pip install -r requirements.txt
   ```

5. **Authenticate with Hugging Face:**

   a. Either update the script to replace "**your_token_here**" with your actual Hugging Face access token,

   b. **OR** log in via the Hugging Face CLI by installing it (if you haven't already) and then logging in:

   ```
   pip install huggingface_hub
   huggingface-cli login
   ```

   Follow the prompts; then, in the script, you can set **auth_token=True**

6. **Run the Script:** Ensure you are in the project directory with your virtual environment activated, then run:

   python3 text_generation.py

Sample Terminal Output

The following is an example of what you might see on your console/terminal:

Input Prompt:

In a futuristic metropolis where neon lights blend with the echoes of forgotten legends, a solitary inventor unveils a machine that can capture dreams and transform them into reality.

Generating text...

Generated Text:

In a futuristic metropolis where neon lights blend with the echoes of forgotten legends, a solitary inventor unveils a machine that can capture dreams and transform them into reality. As the machine whirred to life, beams of light danced across the dark skyline, revealing visions of a past long buried and a future yet to be written. The inventor, with eyes full of wonder, realized that every dream held the power to reshape destiny.

Text Summarization

Below is a detailed use case that demonstrates how to use **meta-llama/Llama-4-Maverick-17B-128E** for a **text summarization** use case in Python. In this practical application, we leverage the Hugging Face Transformers library to load the pre-trained Llama 4.3 model, construct a prompt that instructs the model to summarize a long text, and generate a concise summary. You can customize generation parameters–such as maximum new tokens, temperature, and top-p sampling–to fine-tune the summary's length and creativity. This setup is ideal for applications such as summarizing lengthy articles, reports, or any extensive text into a clear and concise summary. The code not only shows how to implement the summarization but also includes a helper function that encapsulates the process, making it easy to integrate into larger projects such as chatbots or automated reporting systems.

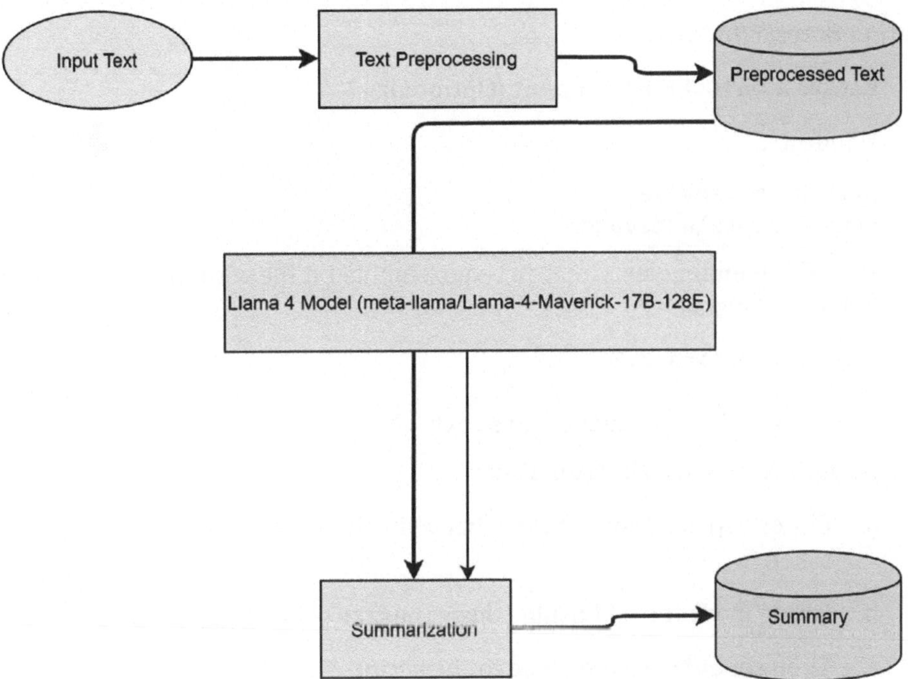

Figure 12.2: *Text Summarization Architecture using Llama 4*

The data flow steps for text-summarization are as follows:

1. Input Text → Text Preprocessing
2. Text Preprocessing → Preprocessed Text
3. Preprocessed Text → Summarization
4. Llama 4 Model → Summarization
5. Summarization → Summary

In this use case, we harness the power of **`meta-llama/Llama-4-Maverick-17B-128E`**—a model fine-tuned for instruction-following tasks—to summarize long texts effectively. By integrating with the Hugging Face Transformers library, we load a pre-trained model, construct a tailored prompt, and generate a concise summary. This process is ideal for summarizing detailed articles, technical reports, or any extensive text.

Source Code: Please refer to this GitHub link for the source code for text summarization:

https://github.com/OrangeAVA/Ultimate-Llama-for- NLP/blob/main/text_summarization.py

Execution Steps(Windows)

1. **Create a Virtual Environment (Optional):**

   Windows:

   ```
   python -m venv venv
   venv\Scripts\activate
   ```

2. **Install Dependencies:** Create a requirements.txt file with the content provided below and install:

   ```
   transformers>=4.0.0
   torch>=1.7.0
    pip install -r requirements.txt
   ```

3. **Authenticate with Hugging Face:**

   a. Either replace "**`your_token_here`**" in the script with your Hugging Face token,

   b. Or log in via the CLI using: **`huggingface-cli login`**

   c. Then set **`auth_token=True`** in the script.

4. **Run the Script:**

   ```
   python text_summarization.py
   ```

Execution Steps(Mac OS)

1. **Install Python (if not already installed):** macOS usually comes with Python 2.x, so it is recommended to install Python 3 using:

   Homebrew.

   a. Open Terminal and run: **`brew install python`**

   b. Confirm the installation with: **`python3 -version`**

2. Create and Activate a Virtual Environment:

   a. Open Terminal and navigate to your project directory.

   b. Create a virtual environment using Python 3:

      ```
      python3 -m venv venv
      ```

   Activate the virtual environment: **`source venv/bin/activate`**

3. **Prepare the `requirements.txt` File:** Create a file named requirements.txt with the following content:

   ```
   transformers>=4.0.0

   torch>=1.7.0
   ```

4. **Install Dependencies:** With your virtual environment activated, run:

   ```
   pip install -r requirements.txt
   ```

5. **Authenticate with Hugging Face:**

   a. Either update the script to replace "**`your_token_here`**" with your actual Hugging Face access token,

   b. **OR** log in via the Hugging Face CLI by installing it (if you haven't already) and then logging in:

      ```
      pip install huggingface_hub
      huggingface-cli login
      ```

   Follow the prompts; then, in the script, you can set **`auth_token=True`**

6. **Run the Script:** Ensure you are in the project directory with your virtual environment activated, then run:

   ```
   python3 text_summarization.py
   ```

Sample Terminal Output

The following is an example of what you might see on your console/terminal:

Input Text to Summarize:
As technology continues to transform every facet of modern society, the need for robust cybersecurity has never been greater. Companies around the globe are investing heavily in advanced defense mechanisms to protect their digital assets from evolving cyber threats. This digital arms race has spurred innovation in encryption techniques, network monitoring, and real-time threat intelligence. With hackers employing more sophisticated methods every day, maintaining a secure digital environment demands continuous improvement and vigilance. The stakes are high, as breaches not only compromise sensitive data but also erode public trust and damage reputations.
Generated Summary:
Robust cybersecurity is critical in today's tech-driven world as companies invest in advanced defense measures and innovative encryption and monitoring techniques to safeguard against ever-evolving cyber threats.

Language Understanding for Complex NLP Tasks

Language understanding for complex NLP tasks has become a cornerstone in developing intelligent systems that can interpret and process human language with remarkable nuance and accuracy. By leveraging models such as meta-llama/Llama-4-Maverick-17B-128E, practitioners can address challenges such as semantic disambiguation, context preservation, and intricate syntactic parsing. This model's robust architecture allows it to capture subtle language nuances, making it highly effective for applications that require deep understanding–ranging from advanced question answering and sentiment analysis to nuanced dialogue systems and contextual reasoning in multi-turn conversations.

Integrating meta-llama/Llama-4-Maverick-17B-128E into complex NLP workflows not only enhances language comprehension but also facilitates more interactive and responsive applications. Its instruction-tuned capabilities enable developers to craft tailored prompts that guide the model towards precise interpretations, ensuring that the output is both relevant and insightful. As a result, organizations can build systems that not only process vast amounts of textual data efficiently but also understand the underlying intent, paving the way for more intuitive human-computer interactions in domains such as customer service, automated content analysis, and beyond.

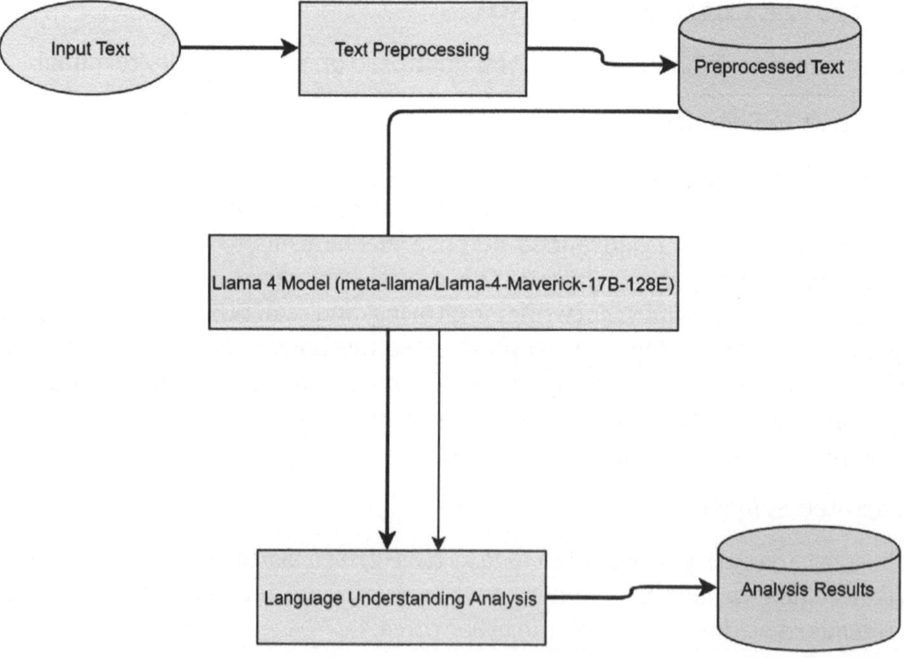

Figure 12.3: *Language Understanding Architecture using Llama 4*

The data flow steps for language understanding are as follows:

1. Input Text → Text Preprocessing
2. Text Preprocessing → Preprocessed Text
3. Preprocessed Text → Language Understanding Analysis
4. Llama 4 Model → Language Understanding Analysis
5. Language Understanding Analysis → Analysis Results

Below is a comprehensive example that demonstrates how to use **`meta-llama/Llama-4-Maverick-17B-128E`** for advanced language understanding–tailored for complex NLP tasks. This example shows how to analyze a piece of text to extract its underlying meaning, tone, sentiment, and key topics, all in a cohesive narrative form.

Source Code: Please refer to this GitHub link for the source code for the language understanding related usecase:

https://github.com/OrangeAVA/Ultimate-Llama-for-NLP/blob/main/language_understanding..py

Execution Steps(Windows)

1. **Create a Virtual Environment (Optional):**

   ```
   python -m venv venv
   venv\Scripts\activate
   ```

2. **Install Dependencies:** Create a **`requirements.txt`** file with the content provided below and install:

   ```
   transformers>=4.0.0
   torch>=1.7.0
   pip install -r requirements.txt
   ```

3. **Authenticate with Hugging Face:**

   a. Either replace "**`your_token_here`**" in the script with your Hugging Face token,

   b. Or log in via the CLI using: **`huggingface-cli login`**

   c. Then set **`auth_token=True`** in the script.

4. **Run the Script:**

   ```
   python language_understanding..py
   ```

Execution Steps(Mac OS)

1. **Install Python (if not already installed):** macOS usually comes with Python 2.x, so it is recommended to install Python 3 using:

   Homebrew.

   a. Open Terminal and run: **`brew install python`**

   b. Confirm the installation with: **`python3 -version`**

2. Create and Activate a Virtual Environment:

   a. Open Terminal and navigate to your project directory.

   b. Create a virtual environment using Python 3:

      ```
      python3 -m venv venv
      ```

   Activate the virtual environment: `source venv/bin/activate`

3. **Prepare the requirements.txt File:** Create a file named **`requirements.txt`** with the following content:

   ```
   transformers>=4.0.0

   torch>=1.7.0
   ```

4. **Install Dependencies:** With your virtual environment activated, run:

   ```
   pip install -r requirements.txt
   ```

5. **Authenticate with Hugging Face:**

   a. Either update the script to replace "**`your_token_here`**" with your actual Hugging Face access token,

   b. **OR** log in via the Hugging Face CLI by installing it (if you have not already) and then logging in:

      ```
      pip install huggingface_hub
      huggingface-cli login
      ```

   Follow the prompts; then, in the script, you can set **`auth_token=True`**

6. **Run the Script:** Ensure you are in the project directory with your virtual environment activated, then run:

   ```
   python3 language_understanding..py
   ```

Sample Input/Output Screen

The following is an example of what you might see on your console/terminal:

```
Input Text for Analysis:

In an era marked by rapid technological evolution, the fusion of human creativity with digital innovation has transformed the way we perceive art and communication. Modern digital platforms empower individuals to share their visions, resulting in a cultural shift that values both originality and collaborative expression. This transformative landscape is characterized by dynamic exchanges of ideas, where traditional boundaries are blurred and new forms of artistic dialogue emerge.

Performing language understanding analysis...

Generated Analysis:

The text explores the profound impact of technology on human creativity, emphasizing how digital innovation has redefined traditional art forms and communication methods. It highlights a cultural shift where individual expression is amplified through collaborative digital platforms, creating a dynamic environment that transcends conventional boundaries. The narrative reflects an optimistic tone, celebrating the emergence of new artistic dialogues and the transformative power of technology in shaping modern culture.
```

Implementing Llama 4 for Question Answering Systems

Implementing Llama 4 for question answering systems opens up a powerful avenue for creating interactive applications that deliver precise and context-aware responses. By utilizing the **`meta-llama/Llama-4-Maverick-17B-128E`** model, developers can tap into a state-of-the-art language processing tool specifically fine-tuned for instruction following. This model excels at understanding and generating detailed answers from complex queries, making it an ideal choice for systems ranging from chatbots to enterprise-level support platforms. Leveraging the Hugging Face Transformers library, one can seamlessly integrate the model into a QA pipeline where user questions are transformed into structured prompts, enabling the model to produce succinct and accurate responses.

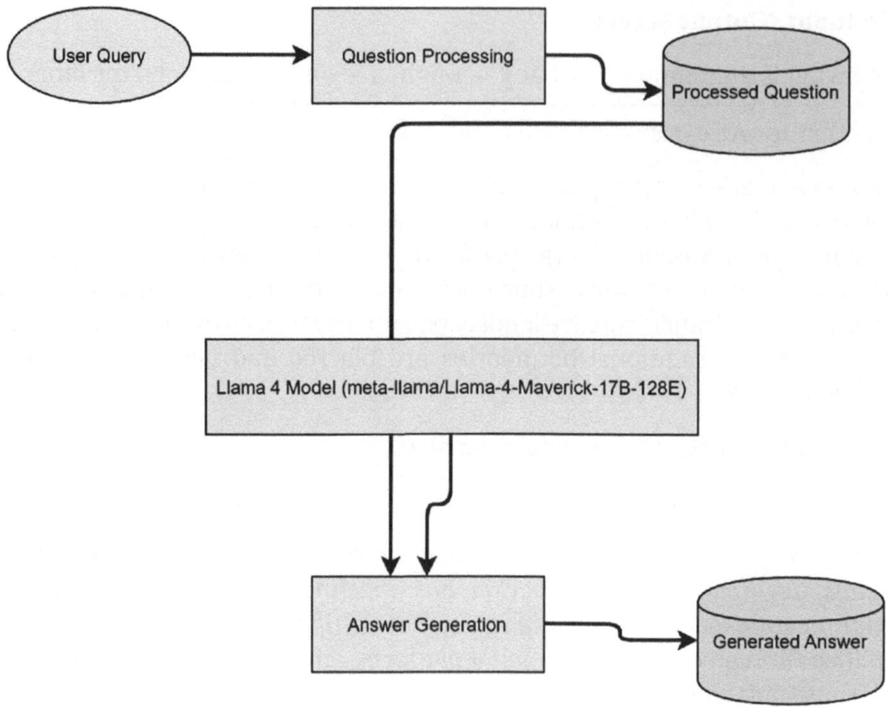

Figure 12.4: *Question Answering System Architecture using Llama 4*

The data flow steps for the question-answering system are as follows:

1. User Query → Question Processing
2. Question Processing → Processed Question
3. Processed Question → Answer Generation
4. Llama 4 Model → Answer Generation
5. Answer Generation → Generated Answer

In practical applications, the flexibility of Llama 4 becomes a key asset, as it allows fine-tuning of generation parameters such as maximum tokens, temperature, and top-p sampling to suit different domains and response styles. This level of control not only enhances the precision of the answers but also tailors the output to align with the desired conversational tone and specificity. Additionally, integrating Llama 4 into existing systems can streamline the handling of diverse and dynamic queries, ensuring that end users receive reliable, real-time information. Overall, the meta-llama/Llama-4-Maverick-17B-128E model is a cornerstone for modern QA systems, merging advanced natural language understanding with customizable response generation.

Source Code: CDE's. Please refer to this GitHub link for the source code for the question and answering system:

https://github.com/OrangeAVA/Ultimate-Llama-for-NLP/blob/main/question_answer_system.py

Execution Steps(Windows)

1. **Create a Virtual Environment (Optional):**

   Windows:

   ```
   python -m venv venv
   venv\Scripts\activate
   ```

2. **Install Dependencies:** Create a requirements.txt file with the content provided below and install:

   ```
   transformers>=4.0.0
   torch>=1.7.0
   pip install -r requirements.txt
   ```

3. **Authenticate with Hugging Face:**

   a. Either replace "**`your_token_here`**" in the script with your Hugging Face token,

   b. Or log in via the CLI using: **`huggingface-cli login`**

   c. Then set **`auth_token=True`** in the script.

4. **Run the Script:**

   ```
   python question_answer_system..py
   ```

Execution Steps(Mac OS)

1. **Install Python (if not already installed):** macOS usually comes with Python 2.x, so it is recommended to install Python 3 using:

   Homebrew.

   a. Open Terminal and run: brew install python

   b. Confirm the installation with: python3 –version

2. Create and Activate a Virtual Environment:

   a. Open Terminal and navigate to your project directory.

   b. Create a virtual environment using Python 3:
   ```
   python3 -m venv venv
   ```

   Activate the virtual environment: **`source venv/bin/activate`**

3. **Prepare the requirements.txt File:** Create a file named requirements.txt with the following content:

```
transformers>=4.0.0
torch>=1.7.0
```

4. **Install Dependencies:** With your virtual environment activated, run:

```
pip install -r requirements.txt
```

5. **Authenticate with Hugging Face:**

    a. Either update the script to replace "**your_token_here**" with your actual Hugging Face access token,

    b. **OR** log in via the Hugging Face CLI by installing it (if you haven't already) and then logging in:

    ```
    pip install huggingface_hub
    huggingface-cli login
    ```

    Follow the prompts; then, in the script, you can set **auth_token=True**

6. **Run the Script:** Ensure you are in the project directory with your virtual environment activated, then run:

```
python3 question_answer_system..py
```

Sample Input/Output Screen

The following is an example of what you might see on your console/terminal:

Question: What are the main challenges in implementing robust cybersecurity measures in modern organizations? Generating answer... Generated Answer: *Implementing robust cybersecurity measures involves tackling challenges such as evolving threat landscapes, budget constraints, employee training, and ensuring real-time monitoring and rapid incident response to mitigate risks effectively.*

Conversational AI Applications

Conversational AI applications have emerged as a pivotal use case for meta-llama/Llama-4-Maverick-17B-128E, enabling developers to build highly interactive and context-aware systems. By leveraging the advanced capabilities of this model, designers can create chatbots and virtual assistants that not only understand user queries but also maintain nuanced multi-turn conversations. Integrating this model with frameworks such as Hugging Face Transformers allows for seamless deployment and scalability, making it easier to customize the dialogue flow, adjust generation parameters, and fine-tune responses to reflect specific conversational styles. This approach ensures that interactions are both natural and informative, enhancing user engagement across various platforms.

Furthermore, the inherent flexibility of Llama 4.3-70B-Instruct in handling diverse linguistic contexts makes it a formidable tool for crafting personalized conversational experiences. Whether deployed in customer support, personal assistants, or educational tools, the model adapts to dynamic scenarios by leveraging contextual cues and maintaining coherent dialogue threads. Fine-tuning parameters such as temperature and top-p sampling empowers developers to strike the right balance between creativity and factual accuracy, ensuring that responses are not only relevant but also engaging. As conversational AI continues to evolve, the application of meta-llama/Llama-4-Maverick-17B-128E represents a significant leap towards more intuitive and human-like digital interactions.

Source Code: Please refer to this GitHub link for the source code for the conversational ai related usecase:

https://github.com/OrangeAVA/Ultimate-Llama-for-NLP/blob/main/conversational_ai.py

Execution Steps(Windows)

1. **Create a Virtual Environment (Optional):**

   Windows:

   ```
   python -m venv venv
   venv\Scripts\activate
   ```

2. **Install Dependencies:** Create a requirements.txt file with the content provided below and install:

   ```
     transformers>=4.0.0
   torch>=1.7.0
   pip install -r requirements.txt
   ```

3. **Authenticate with Hugging Face:**

   a. Either replace "**`your_token_here`**" in the script with your Hugging Face token,

   b. Or log in via the CLI using: **`huggingface-cli login`**

   c. Then set **`auth_token=True`** in the script.

4. **Run the Script:**

   ```
   python conversational_ai..py
   ```

Execution Steps(Mac OS)

1. **Install Python (if not already installed):** macOS usually comes with Python 2.x, so it is recommended to install Python 3 using:

   Homebrew.

   a. Open Terminal and run: **`brew install python`**

   b. Confirm the installation with: **`python3 -version`**

2. Create and Activate a Virtual Environment:

   a. Open Terminal and navigate to your project directory.

   b. Create a virtual environment using Python 3:

   ```
   python3 -m venv venv
   ```

   Activate the virtual environment: **`source venv/bin/activate`**

3. **Prepare the requirements.txt File:** Create a file named requirements.txt with the following content:

   ```
   transformers>=4.0.0
   torch>=1.7.0
   ```

4. **Install Dependencies:** With your virtual environment activated, run:

   ```
   pip install -r requirements.txt
   ```

5. **Authenticate with Hugging Face:**

   a. Either update the script to replace "**`your_token_here`**" with your actual Hugging Face access token,

   b. **OR** log in via the Hugging Face CLI by installing it (if you haven't already) and then logging in:

   ```
   pip install huggingface_hub
   huggingface-cli login
   ```

   Follow the prompts; then, in the script, you can set auth_token=True

6. **Run the Script:** Ensure you are in the project directory with your virtual environment activated, then run:

   ```
   python3 conversational_ai..py
   ```

Sample Input/Output Screen

Below is an example of what you might see on your console/terminal:

Welcome to the Conversational AI. Type '*exit*' to quit. User: Hi there, how are you today? AI: I'm doing well, thank you! How can I help you today? User: Can you tell me what the weather is like in New York? AI: I'm not able to fetch live weather updates, but New York is usually vibrant and dynamic during this time of year. Is there anything else you'd like to know? User: exit

Conclusion

In conclusion, this chapter has demonstrated the transformative potential of Llama 4 across a spectrum of NLP tasks, from text generation and summarization to sophisticated language understanding, question answering, and conversational AI applications. By examining hands-on examples and real-world case studies, we have highlighted how Llama 4's advanced capabilities not only elevate the performance of NLP solutions but also drive significant improvements in industries such as healthcare, finance, and customer support. Equipped with this knowledge, you are now better prepared to harness the power of Llama 4 to tackle complex business challenges and deliver more accurate, efficient, and engaging language-driven experiences.

The next chapter highlights how emerging trends, groundbreaking research, and a rigorous focus on ethical governance are converging to establish best practices that ensure both innovation and responsibility. These advancements promise not only to expand the capabilities of Llama models but also to foster transformative breakthroughs across diverse applications, paving the way for a new era of safe, efficient, and equitable AI solutions.

Multiple Choice Questions

1. Which industries are highlighted as ideal candidates for deploying Llama 4 applications?

    a. Retail, Manufacturing, Agriculture

    b. Healthcare, Finance, Customer Support

    c. Entertainment, Sports, Tourism

    d. Education, Logistics, Real Estate

2. What is the primary function of Llama 4 in text generation tasks?
    a. To translate text between different languages
    b. To generate coherent and creative text based on given prompts
    c. To extract keywords from a text
    d. To identify sentiment in text
3. In the context of text summarization with Llama 4, what is the main benefit of using this model?
    a. It only increases the length of the text
    b. It extracts irrelevant details
    c. It generates concise summaries from lengthy content
    d. It replaces the original text entirely
4. How does Llama 4 enhance language understanding for complex NLP tasks?
    a. By relying solely on static rule-based methods
    b. By leveraging deep learning techniques to capture context and semantics
    c. By using pre-defined templates without modification
    d. By ignoring contextual nuances in the text
5. Which practical application of Llama 4 is best exemplified by its use in question answering systems?
    a. Converting audio files into text
    b. Building chatbots that provide precise, context-aware answers to user queries
    c. Generating random facts
    d. Translating texts between languages
6. What role does Llama 4 play in Conversational AI applications?
    a. It only performs sentiment analysis
    b. It supports dialogue systems by generating human-like, interactive responses
    c. It solely focuses on text classification
    d. It encrypts user data during conversations

7. When fine-tuning Llama 4 for various NLP tasks, which of the following generation parameters can be adjusted?
    a. Maximum tokens
    b. Temperature
    c. Top-p sampling
    d. All of the above
8. How can real-world case studies of Llama 4 applications benefit businesses?
    a. They offer theoretical models with no practical insights
    b. They demonstrate how Llama 4 can automate and enhance tasks like report generation, customer support, and content summarization
    c. They only focus on improving hardware performance
    d. They replace human decision-making entirely without oversight
9. What factor is primarily responsible for Llama 4's improved performance compared to its predecessors?
    a. A reduction in model parameters
    b. Enhanced fine-tuning capabilities and architectural optimizations
    c. Simplified language processing techniques
    d. Exclusive reliance on rule-based algorithms

Answers

1. b
2. b
3. c
4. b
5. b
6. b
7. d
8. b
9. b

Chapter 13
Future Directions and Advancements in Llama

Introduction

In this chapter, we embark on an exploration of future directions and advancements in Llama models, setting the stage for a deep dive into the evolving landscape of natural language processing and artificial intelligence. Readers will gain insights into emerging trends that are reshaping the AI frontier and learn about groundbreaking research advancements in Llama models. The discussion will address not only the technical innovations but also the ethical implications and challenges of AI governance, offering a balanced view of the potential breakthroughs and considerations that accompany this rapidly advancing field.

Furthermore, this chapter is designed to equip you with practical strategies for implementing cutting-edge developments in your own work. As you navigate through topics such as best practices in using Llama models and future prospects for these technologies, you will discover how to integrate theoretical knowledge with real-world applications. By highlighting key areas such as emerging trends in NLP and AI, research advancements, ethical considerations, and best practices, the content provides a comprehensive roadmap to help you drive innovation and make informed decisions in both academic and professional settings.

Structure

In this chapter, we will cover the following topics:

- Overview
- Emerging Trends in NLP and AI
- Research Advancements in Llama Models

- Ethical Implications and AI Governance
- Best Practices Using Llama Models
- Future Prospects for Llama Models

Overview

Emerging trends in NLP and AI are rapidly reshaping the landscape of language processing, with Llama models standing at the forefront of these innovations. As research advancements push the boundaries of what is possible, these models are being fine-tuned to handle more complex linguistic tasks, from nuanced language generation to real-time conversational interfaces. The evolution of Llama models is not just about enhancing performance; it also involves a deep exploration of ethical implications and the development of robust AI governance frameworks. By addressing concerns such as algorithmic bias, transparency, and accountability, researchers and practitioners alike are setting the stage for responsible AI deployment that benefits society while mitigating risks.

At the same time, best practices for using Llama models are emerging as a crucial aspect of leveraging these advancements effectively. Practitioners will learn how to integrate state-of-the-art research into practical applications, ensuring that these models are used to their full potential while adhering to ethical standards. From optimizing model training techniques to implementing rigorous evaluation protocols, the future prospects for Llama models are promising. This chapter will guide readers through current research breakthroughs, offer insights into ethical considerations, and present actionable strategies for harnessing the power of Llama models in both academic and professional settings.

Emerging Trends in NLP And AI

The fields of Natural Language Processing (NLP) and Artificial Intelligence (AI) have witnessed transformative growth over the past decade. Innovations driven by deep learning and novel architectures have not only redefined how machines understand and generate human language but also enabled the creation of systems that can interact with humans in increasingly natural ways. This evolution is best exemplified by the advent of transformer-based models—architectures that have become the backbone of state-of-the-art systems such as GPT, BERT, and other large-scale language models. These developments have allowed computers to process complex language patterns, comprehend context, and even exhibit elements of creativity and reasoning. As organizations and researchers continue to push the boundaries of what AI can achieve, the emerging trends in NLP are paving the way for applications that are both more dynamic and responsive to real-world demands.

One of the key emerging trends in NLP is the integration of multi-modal capabilities, where language models are not only confined to text but can also process and generate insights from images, audio, and even video. This convergence of data types opens up possibilities for more holistic AI systems that mirror human sensory integration—improving everything from automated content moderation to interactive educational tools. For instance, virtual assistants powered by such models can now interpret user queries accompanied by images or voice commands, offering more comprehensive responses that better reflect the nuances of human communication.

Advances in Deep Learning and Transformer Architectures

Recent research advancements in transformer architectures have drastically improved the scalability and performance of NLP models. These models have enabled AI systems to handle longer contexts, manage subtleties in language, and even generate text that is contextually coherent over extended passages. One real-time scenario that highlights this progress is in customer support. Companies are deploying advanced chatbots that not only provide immediate responses to user queries but can also engage in meaningful follow-up questions, ensuring that complex customer issues are addressed without human intervention. This evolution is particularly significant for industries such as e-commerce and banking, where customer satisfaction and rapid response times are paramount.

Another remarkable application can be found in content creation and curation. News agencies and media outlets are increasingly leveraging NLP models to draft articles, generate summaries, and even suggest edits for clarity and engagement. These systems use real-time data feeds to ensure that the information is not only accurate but also aligned with current events, thereby enhancing the efficiency of journalistic workflows. Moreover, academic research has seen the integration of AI tools that assist in literature review by summarizing extensive texts and identifying emerging trends in specific domains—all powered by advancements in transformer models.

Real-Time Applications and Industry Impact

In today's fast-paced digital environment, real-time applications of NLP and AI are becoming indispensable. One striking example is in the healthcare industry, where NLP is used to analyze patient records, clinical notes, and even voice recordings to assist in diagnosis and treatment planning. By extracting key insights from unstructured data, healthcare professionals can identify trends and anomalies that might otherwise go unnoticed. For instance, a hospital may deploy an AI system that continuously monitors patient records to flag early signs of complications, ensuring timely intervention and improved patient outcomes.

Similarly, the finance sector benefits significantly from these emerging trends. Real-time sentiment analysis of financial news, social media chatter, and market reports can offer traders and analysts a competitive edge. AI-driven models can analyze vast amounts of textual data in milliseconds, providing actionable insights into market trends and investor sentiments. This allows for more informed decision-making and risk management strategies, particularly in volatile economic climates where every second counts.

Moreover, the rise of conversational AI in retail and customer service is transforming the way businesses interact with consumers. Virtual assistants and chatbots, equipped with the latest NLP advancements, can now handle a diverse range of tasks–from answering frequently asked questions to processing complex transactions. These systems learn and adapt from every interaction, continuously improving their responses and offering personalized customer experiences. For example, a retail chatbot might integrate with a company's inventory system to provide real-time product recommendations based on a customer's browsing history and current trends.

Ethical Implications and AI Governance

As the capabilities of NLP and AI continue to expand, so too do the ethical considerations and challenges surrounding their use. One of the most critical concerns is the potential for algorithmic bias. Large-scale models trained on vast amounts of internet data can inadvertently learn and propagate societal biases, which in turn can lead to unfair outcomes in applications ranging from hiring processes to law enforcement. Addressing these issues requires not only technical solutions–such as bias detection and mitigation algorithms–but also a robust framework for AI governance. Governments, industry bodies, and research institutions are actively collaborating to develop ethical guidelines and regulatory policies that ensure the responsible deployment of AI technologies.

Transparency and explainability in AI decision-making are also vital components of ethical AI governance. Users and stakeholders need to understand how and why AI systems make certain decisions, especially in high-stakes environments such as healthcare and finance. Efforts to create more interpretable models are underway, with researchers exploring methods to visualize the decision-making processes of complex NLP systems. In a real-time scenario, consider the use of AI in legal document analysis, where lawyers rely on NLP tools to sift through massive volumes of case law. Ensuring that these tools provide clear explanations for their recommendations not only builds trust among legal professionals but also supports fairer outcomes in judicial processes.

Furthermore, data privacy concerns are at the forefront of discussions on ethical AI. With the increasing integration of personal data into AI systems, it is crucial to implement measures that protect user privacy while still enabling the benefits of advanced analytics. Real-time systems that monitor social media trends or financial markets must strike a balance between effective data utilization and adherence to stringent privacy regulations. The development of federated learning and privacy-preserving algorithms is a direct response to these challenges, ensuring that while AI systems become more powerful, they do not compromise individual rights or security.

Future Directions and Prospects

Looking ahead, the future of NLP and AI is filled with exciting possibilities and challenges. Researchers are now focusing on building more robust models that can not only process multiple data types but also understand context at a deeper, more human-like level. The integration of multi-modal data–where text, audio, images, and even video are analyzed in unison–represents a significant leap forward in creating AI systems that can operate with a comprehensive understanding of the world around them.

One promising area of development is edge computing, which involves processing data locally on devices rather than relying solely on centralized cloud systems. This trend is particularly relevant for applications requiring real-time analysis and response, such as autonomous vehicles, smart home devices, and wearable health monitors. By reducing latency and improving data security, edge computing enables NLP and AI systems to deliver faster, more personalized experiences to users. Imagine a smart wearable that not only tracks your health metrics but also uses NLP to provide personalized health advice based on your daily routines and real-time data analysis.

In addition, the convergence of NLP with augmented reality (AR) and virtual reality (VR) is set to redefine interactive experiences. In educational settings, for instance, AI-driven virtual tutors can provide immersive learning experiences that combine real-time language processing with interactive visual aids. These systems can adapt to a learner's pace and style, offering tailored content that makes complex subjects more accessible. In the realm of entertainment, conversational AI integrated with VR platforms is opening up new possibilities for interactive storytelling and gaming, where narratives evolve based on the user's interactions and real-time decisions.

The journey toward fully autonomous and context-aware AI systems also brings challenges that will require ongoing research and collaboration across disciplines. Issues such as energy efficiency, scalability, and the ethical deployment of AI technologies remain at the forefront of the discussion. Future research will likely focus on creating models that are not only more powerful but also more sustainable and ethically sound. As we continue to explore these frontiers, the importance of cross-disciplinary collaboration–spanning computer science, linguistics, ethics, and beyond–will be key to unlocking the full potential of emerging trends in NLP and AI.

Research Advancements in Llama Models

The realm of artificial intelligence has witnessed remarkable progress over the last few years, with transformer-based architectures playing a pivotal role in advancing natural language processing. Among these, the Llama models have emerged as a notable breakthrough, balancing efficiency, scalability, and versatility. This article delves into the recent research advancements in Llama models, exploring the innovations that are driving their development, the novel training techniques being employed, and the extensive efforts to refine their performance across various tasks.

Innovations in Model Architecture and Scaling

One of the most significant areas of research advancement in Llama models is the continuous refinement of their underlying architecture. Researchers have focused on several key innovations:

- **Optimized Transformer Blocks:** Advancements in transformer block design have allowed Llama models to better capture long-range dependencies and contextual nuances. By experimenting with variations in self-attention mechanisms and feed-forward networks, researchers have succeeded in reducing model redundancy while increasing expressive power. This has resulted in models that are not only more efficient but also more robust when applied to diverse NLP tasks.
- **Parameter Efficiency and Scaling Laws:** The principle of parameter efficiency has been central to Llama's design philosophy. Through rigorous experimentation, scientists have uncovered new scaling laws that explain how performance improvements correlate with increases in data and model size. This has guided the creation of Llama variants optimized for specific tasks, striking an ideal balance between computational demands and performance outcomes. Researchers have demonstrated that by leveraging techniques such as weight sharing and sparsity-inducing regularization, models can be scaled up without a proportional increase in computational cost. These insights have important implications for deploying language models in resource-constrained environments.
- **Distributed and Parallel Training Techniques:** Training large-scale models is a computationally intensive endeavor. Recent research has focused on developing distributed training frameworks that allow Llama models to be trained efficiently across multiple GPUs and even across clusters of machines. Innovations in parallel processing, including pipeline parallelism and model parallelism, have been instrumental in reducing training times while maintaining model fidelity. These advancements not only accelerate the

research cycle but also enable the deployment of Llama models in real-time applications where rapid response times are critical.

- **Novel Training Strategies and Fine-Tuning Methods:** In addition to architectural improvements, considerable research attention has been dedicated to refining the training strategies and fine-tuning methods used with Llama models. These strategies are crucial for maximizing the potential of pre-trained models and adapting them to specific domains.
- **Self-Supervised and Unsupervised Learning:** A cornerstone of modern NLP research is self-supervised learning, where models learn useful representations from vast amounts of unlabeled data. Llama models have benefited from innovative pre-training strategies that exploit the inherent structure of language data. Researchers have experimented with novel masking techniques and dynamic context windows that enable models to better understand semantic relationships and syntactic structures. The outcome is a model that exhibits improved generalization across a variety of downstream tasks, from text classification to sentiment analysis.
- **Transfer Learning and Domain Adaptation:** One of the most promising directions in Llama research involves the application of transfer learning. Fine-tuning pre-trained models on domain-specific datasets has proven effective in tailoring the model's capabilities to niche applications such as legal document analysis, medical report summarization, and financial forecasting. Research in this area has led to the development of adaptive fine-tuning protocols that minimize the risk of overfitting while maximizing performance gains. For instance, in scenarios where data is scarce or highly specialized, techniques such as few-shot learning have allowed Llama models to adapt quickly and efficiently, offering impressive performance with minimal training data.
- **Reinforcement Learning and Human-in-the-Loop Approaches:** Beyond conventional supervised learning, reinforcement learning (RL) has emerged as a valuable tool in further refining Llama models. By incorporating feedback loops where models learn from human evaluators or simulated environments, researchers have created systems that can iteratively improve their outputs. This human-in-the-loop approach ensures that the models not only learn from static datasets but also adapt dynamically to real-world interactions. Applications in conversational AI and automated customer support have particularly benefited from these techniques, where models must continuously refine their responses based on user feedback.
- **Benchmarking and Performance Evaluation:** To ensure that advancements in Llama models translate into tangible benefits, rigorous benchmarking and performance evaluation have become integral components of the research

process. Researchers are continually developing new metrics and evaluation protocols to assess various dimensions of model performance.

- **Standardized Benchmarks:** Benchmarks such as GLUE, SuperGLUE, and other domain-specific evaluation sets are routinely used to measure the effectiveness of Llama models. These benchmarks assess a range of capabilities–from basic language understanding to complex reasoning tasks–and provide a standardized basis for comparison with other state-of-the-art models. Research papers detailing Llama's performance often include comprehensive evaluations across these benchmarks, highlighting areas where the model excels and where further improvements are needed.
- **Real-World Testing and Pilot Studies:** Beyond synthetic benchmarks, real-world testing plays a crucial role in validating the effectiveness of Llama models. Pilot studies in industrial settings, such as customer support centers, financial analytics platforms, and healthcare diagnostic tools, have provided valuable insights into how these models perform under practical constraints. For example, a recent pilot study in the retail sector demonstrated that a Llama-based chatbot was able to reduce response times and improve customer satisfaction by dynamically adjusting its responses based on ongoing conversations. Such real-world evaluations are essential for translating academic research into practical, scalable solutions.
- **Comparative Analyses:** Comparative studies have been conducted to assess the strengths and limitations of Llama models relative to other contemporary architectures. These analyses consider factors such as inference speed, memory consumption, and adaptability to new tasks. By systematically comparing performance metrics across different models, researchers are able to identify key areas for further optimization. This iterative process of evaluation and refinement has contributed significantly to the rapid evolution of Llama models, fostering a competitive environment where continuous improvement is the norm.
- **Multi-Modal Integration and Application Expansion:** The frontier of Llama research is increasingly shifting towards multi-modal integration, wherein models are designed to process not only text but also images, audio, and even video. This multi-modal approach is critical for developing AI systems that can interact with the world in a manner akin to human perception.
- **Bridging Text with Vision and Audio:** Recent studies have explored the extension of Llama architectures to handle multi-modal inputs, enabling the creation of systems that can interpret and generate content across different media types. For instance, integrating visual data with textual analysis has led to improved performance in applications such as image captioning, where the model not only describes the content of an image but also contextualizes it within a broader narrative. Similarly, combining audio inputs with text allows

for the development of more sophisticated virtual assistants that can better understand and respond to spoken commands. These innovations are paving the way for richer, more interactive user experiences across a variety of platforms.

- **Cross-Disciplinary Applications:** The versatility of Llama models is being harnessed in numerous cross-disciplinary applications. In the field of healthcare, for example, multi-modal models are used to analyze medical images alongside patient histories to provide more accurate diagnoses. In education, integrated systems are being developed that combine text-based tutoring with interactive visual aids, offering personalized learning experiences that adapt to the needs of individual students. These real-time applications underscore the potential of Llama models to transform industries by bridging the gap between diverse data modalities.
- **Collaborative Frameworks and Open Research:** The push towards multi-modal integration has also spurred the development of collaborative research frameworks, where academic institutions, industry leaders, and government bodies work together to set standards and share best practices. Open-source initiatives have played a crucial role in this collaborative environment, allowing researchers worldwide to contribute to the continuous improvement of Llama models. These collective efforts not only accelerate the pace of innovation but also ensure that advancements are accessible to a broader community of practitioners.
- **Ethical Considerations and Responsible AI:** As research advancements in Llama models continue to evolve, so do the ethical considerations associated with their deployment. Ensuring that these powerful tools are used responsibly has become a critical area of focus within the AI research community.
- **Mitigating Algorithmic Bias:** One of the foremost challenges in deploying advanced language models is mitigating algorithmic bias. Since Llama models are often trained on vast datasets that may contain inherent biases, researchers have developed specialized techniques to detect and mitigate these issues. These include methods for de-biasing training data, incorporating fairness constraints during model optimization, and continuously monitoring model outputs for signs of unintended bias. Addressing these challenges is essential not only for improving the reliability of Llama models but also for ensuring that their applications do not inadvertently reinforce societal inequalities.
- **Transparency and Explainability:** Transparency in model decision-making is another crucial aspect of responsible AI. Efforts to make Llama models more interpretable involve developing visualization tools and explainability frameworks that allow users to understand the underlying reasoning behind the model's outputs. In high-stakes applications such as healthcare or finance, this transparency is vital for building trust and ensuring accountability.

Researchers are exploring techniques that enable end-users to trace how specific inputs lead to particular outputs, thereby demystifying the "*black box*" nature of deep learning models.

- **Governance and Regulatory Frameworks:** Beyond technical solutions, ethical research in Llama models also involves the development of governance frameworks and regulatory guidelines. Collaboration among policymakers, industry stakeholders, and academic researchers has led to the formulation of ethical guidelines aimed at balancing innovation with societal responsibility. These frameworks address issues such as data privacy, consent, and accountability, ensuring that as Llama models become more pervasive, they do so in a manner that respects individual rights and societal norms.
- **Future Directions and Ongoing Research:** The landscape of research in Llama models is dynamic, with new challenges and opportunities emerging as the technology evolves. Future research directions are likely to focus on several key areas:
- **Enhanced Adaptability and Personalization:** Researchers are actively exploring methods to make Llama models even more adaptable to user-specific contexts. This includes developing techniques for real-time fine-tuning based on user interactions, which could lead to highly personalized experiences in applications such as virtual assistants, customer service, and interactive learning platforms. By incorporating continuous feedback mechanisms, future iterations of Llama models may be capable of evolving their responses dynamically, tailoring their performance to meet individual user needs more effectively.
- **Integration with Edge Computing and Real-Time Processing:** As AI moves closer to deployment in real-time environments, the integration of Llama models with edge computing is a promising area of research. By enabling these models to operate on local devices rather than relying solely on centralized cloud infrastructure, latency can be reduced and data privacy can be enhanced. This is particularly relevant for applications in autonomous vehicles, smart home devices, and wearable health monitors, where real-time decision-making is critical. Research in this domain is expected to yield models that are not only more responsive but also more energy-efficient and secure.
- **Cross-Lingual and Cross-Domain Capabilities:** Expanding the reach of Llama models to support a diverse range of languages and dialects remains a top priority. Researchers are working on cross-lingual models that can transfer learning across languages, enabling the same underlying architecture to perform robustly in multiple linguistic contexts. Additionally, cross-domain research is underway to ensure that the models can adapt to various industry-specific requirements without extensive re-training. This universality will play a key role in democratizing access to advanced AI capabilities on a global scale.

- **Collaborative Research and Open-Source Initiatives:** The success of Llama models so far has been driven in large part by a collaborative research ecosystem. Moving forward, open-source projects and shared research initiatives are expected to continue fostering innovation, with researchers across the globe contributing to incremental improvements. These collaborative efforts will be critical in addressing challenges such as data scarcity, model interpretability, and ethical deployment, ensuring that the advancements in Llama models benefit a broad spectrum of society.

Ethical Implications and AI Governance

Let us get real about where Llama (Large Language Model Meta AI) is headed, especially when it comes to ethics and governance. As these models flex insane capabilities–chatting with us, drafting essays, even whipping up code–we have got to pause and ask: "*What are the vibes on responsibility*?" This is not just some boardroom buzzword; it is the foundation for making sure Llama and its AI cousins do not go off the rails. Over the next few pages, we will spill the tea on the ethical implications of deploying Llama at scale and unpack frameworks for keeping it all on the up-and-up. No cap, balancing innovation with accountability is super crucial if we want AI to serve everybody, not just a select crew.

Understanding Ethical Implications

First off, ethics in AI is not a one-and-done checklist–it is an ongoing convo about values, fairness, and respect. When Llama splits out text, it is remixing patterns learned from massive data feeds. That means biases lurking in that data can sneak into generated content, perpetuating stereotypes or misinformation. Plus, privacy concerns are real: if Llama's training data contains sensitive info, we risk unintended leaks. Real talk? It is not about blaming the model but recognizing that designers, data curators, and end-users all share the accountability. We have gotta keep checking for hidden biases, respect user privacy, and ensure outputs align with inclusive, human-centered values. This way, we can vibe with progress without ghosting ethical duties.

Deep Dive into Ethical Implications

No cap, when Llama flexes its generative power, it is remixing trillions of tokens. But with great token power comes major responsibility. Here is the lowdown:

- **Bias Amplification**
  - **What is Up:** If your training data over-represents one group or viewpoint, Llama's outputs can skew the narrative–such as always suggesting male names for STEM roles.

  - **IRL Example:** Back in 2018, Amazon's AI recruiting tool downgraded résumés with words such as "*women's*" because its data was male-heavy. They had to scrap it entirely once they caught the bias.

- **Misinformation and Hallucinations**
  - **What is Up:** Llama can confidently "*make up*" facts when it is unsure.
  - **IRL Example:** In early 2025, a healthcare chatbot built on a sibling of Llama suggested the wrong drug dosage for a fictional scenario—triggering an industry-wide recall of unverified AI prescriptions.

- **Privacy Leaks**
  - **What is Up:** If you train on scraped web data, sensitive nuggets can resurface.
  - **IRL Example:** A legal-advice bot accidentally regurgitated a snippet of a real client's contract details last summer, prompting a GDPR complaint.

Staying woke on these issues means auditing data pipelines, flagging weird outputs, and keeping humans in the loop.

Potential Risks and Challenges

Let us not sugar-coat it—here are the most significant (and concerning) risks:

- **Malicious Use Cases**: Crafting hyper-convincing phishing emails or deepfake scripts.
- **Environmental Footprint**: Training Llama-scale models can burn megawatts of power.
- **Accountability Black-Hole**: When something goes wrong, who is the "*bad actor*"? The developer? The deployer? The user?

IRL Case: In 2024, a gaming studio used an LLM for NPC dialogue. Fans noticed the AI dropped micro-aggressive slurs—turned out the moderation filters were not up to scratch. The backlash was real, and the studio paused the rollout.

Building Robust AI Governance Frameworks

Governance is not just red tape—it is your AI's seatbelt. Here is your improvement roadmap:

- **Policy Alignment and Regulatory Sandboxes**: Sync with the EU AI Act (effective 2025) and tap into "*regulatory sandbox*" programs in the UK and Singapore to test safely.
- **Transparency Playbook**: Publish **Model Cards** detailing training corpora, known blind spots, and performance metrics across demographics.

- **Stakeholder Co-Creation**: Circle in ethicists, minority-group reps, and domain experts from day one—no gate-keeping.
- **Continuous Audits & Red-Teaming**: Run simulated attacks and bias-hunting exercises quarterly.

IRL Example: A European fintech startup launched a Llama-based credit-scoring assistant in May 2025—but before going live, they invited an independent "*AI ethics coalition*" to probe for bias. The coalition spotted a skew against gig-economy workers, so the team retrained on a balanced income dataset.

Best Practices for Ethical Deployment

Ready to deploy? Here is your checklist for responsible deployment:

- **Bias Mitigation Pipelines**: Integrate tools such as IBM's AI Fairness 360 to pre- and post-process predictions.
- **Human-in-the-Loop (HITL)**: For any "*high-stakes*" domain (medicine, law, finance), require a human sign-off before the final answer drops.
- **Privacy-First Data Handling**: Use **differential privacy** or **federated learning** so raw data never leaves the user's device.
- **Explainability Dashboards**: Offer users an "*Explain My Answer*" button that visualizes which data points influenced the response.
- **Real-Time Monitoring & Alerting**: Hook into logging pipelines that flag unusual behavior—such as a sudden spike in toxic outputs.

IRL Example: Shutterstock's generative art tool now tags every AI-created image with a "*Generated by AI*" watermark, and they publicly share monthly "*Content Safety Reports*" showing how many flagged images were removed.

Looking Ahead: The Next-Gen of Governance

Llama vNext is going to be even more fire, so our governance game must level up too:

- **Adaptive Policy Engines**: Automated rule updates that merge global regulation changes (such as GDPR, CCPA, Brazil's LGPD) with internal guardrails.
- **Decentralized Governance Models**: DAO-style committees where token-weighted stakeholders vote on new ethical standards.
- **Community-Driven Audits**: Open-source bias bounties: crowdsource "*Find the Bias*" challenges and reward contributors.
- **Cross-Sector Ethical Councils**: Blend voices from environmental science, sociology, and indigenous communities to surface blind spots.

- **AI "Ethics AI"**: Meta-tools that use smaller LLMs to scan outputs from Llama and grade them on an "*Ethical Scorecard*."

Best Practices Using Llama Models

Llama models come in different sizes–7B, 13B, 30B, and 65B parameters–each with its own flex. Here is how to choose:

Picking the Perfect Llama

- **Use-Case and Resource Balance**
  - **Lightweight tasks** (for example, simple chatbots, quick prototyping): Go for **Llama-7B**. It is lean, fast, and runs on modest GPUs.
  - **General-purpose assistants** (for example, FAQ bots, coding helpers): **Llama-13B** hits that sweet spot between speed and quality.
  - **High-stakes or creative tasks** (for example, summarization of long docs, nuanced content generation): Consider **Llama-30B or 65B**–they pack more world knowledge and nuance.
- **Infrastructure and Budget**
  - Cheaper GPUs (such as A10) can handle 7B & 13B comfortably.
  - For 30B+, you need beefy hardware (A100s or H100s) or cloud instances–plan your cloud budget accordingly.
- **Latency vs. Quality Trade-offs**
  - If sub-second responses are critical (for example, live chat), stick with smaller models.
  - If you can tolerate a few seconds of latency for premium quality, bump up the parameter count.

Data Curation and Fine-Tuning Fundamentals

Fine-tuning is where the true value emerges – but poor-quality data undermines the results. Here are the key details:

Curate Clean, Task-Specific Data

- **Diversity and Representativeness**
  - Ensure your dataset covers the range of inputs your end-users will throw at the model.
  - **Example**: For a customer-support bot, include tickets from different regions, languages, and issue types.

- **Data Hygiene**
  - Remove duplicates, irrelevant noise, and personally identifiable info (PII).
  - Normalize formats (dates, currencies) so the model learns consistency.

Fine-Tuning Strategies

- **Full-Model vs. Parameter-Efficient Approaches**
  - **Full-Model Fine-Tuning (FT)**: All parameters update–best quality but heavy.
  - **Parameter-Efficient Fine-Tuning (PEFT)**: Techniques such as LoRA or adapters update a small subset–cheaper, faster, and often nearly as good.
- **Hyperparameter Tuning**
  - Start with learning rates around 1e-5 to 3e-5.
  - Use small batch sizes (4–16) if GPU memory is tight.
  - Monitor validation loss and implement early stopping to avoid overfitting.
- **Mixed-Precision Training**
  - Use FP16 or BF16 to speed up training and lower memory footprint–just watch for potential stability issues.

Prompt Engineering and Inference Best Practices

Even the most advanced model can fail with a weak prompt. Use the following strategies to improve your prompt design.

Prompt Design Patterns

- **Instruction Style**: "*You are an expert medical assistant. Summarize the following patient case notes in bullet points:*"
- **Chain-of-Thought (CoT)**: For reasoning tasks, ask the model to "*think step by step*" before giving the answer.
- **Few-Shot Examples**: Provide 2–3 input–output pairs to demonstrate the desired format.

Temperature and Decoding Controls

- **Temperature**
  - **0.0–0.3** for factual, deterministic outputs.
  - **0.7–1.0** for creative, diverse generations.
- **Top-k / Top-p (Nucleus Sampling)**: Use **top-p = 0.9** to let the model draw from the most plausible 90% probability mass–balances creativity and coherence.
- **Maximum Tokens**: Set a reasonable limit to avoid runaway responses.

Inference Optimization

- **Batching Requests**: Process multiple prompts in parallel to maximize GPU throughput.
- **Quantization**: Model size shrinks (for example, to 4-bit or 8-bit) with minimal quality loss–hugely boosts speed and reduces RAM usage.
- **Serving Frameworks**: Use Triton Inference Server, NVIDIA TensorRT, or Hugging Face's Accelerate to handle scaling, GPU allocation, and auto-batching.

Evaluation and Monitoring

Deploying a model is half the battle; keeping it healthy is the other half.

Pre-Deployment Evaluation

- **Automated Metrics**
  - *Perplexity* for general fluency.
  - *ROUGE / BLEU* for summarization or translation tasks.
- **Task-Specific Tests:** Build unit tests: for example, for a code-generation model, check that generated snippets compile.
- **Bias and Safety Checks:** Run your model through bias-detection suites (such as IBM AI Fairness 360) and toxicity filters (such as Detoxify).

Post-Deployment Monitoring

- **Logging and Analytics**: Capture input-prompt, output, and metadata (timestamp, user ID) for auditing and retraining.
- **Drift Detection:** Track shifts in input distributions or sudden spikes in error rates–trigger retraining when thresholds exceed.
- **Feedback Loops:** Let users flag problematic responses. Incorporate that data back into your fine-tuning pipeline.

Protip: Build dashboards (Grafana, Kibana) that visualize metrics such as average response time, error rates, and fairness scores in real time.

Security, Privacy, and Ethical Safeguards

Best practices are not just about performance–they are about trust and safety.

- **Access Controls:** Authenticate and authorize every request. Use API keys, OAuth, or JWT tokens.
- **Rate Limiting**: Throttle requests to prevent abuse or runaway costs.

- **Data Privacy**
  - For user-sensitive prompts, employ on-prem or VPC-isolated deployments.
  - Implement data retention policies: purge logs after a set period or anonymize them.
- **Adversarial Robustness:** Test with "*jailbreak*" prompts to ensure the model does not leak its system instructions or generate disallowed content.
- **Ethical Guardrails:** Integrate safety layers such as OpenAI's Moderation API or custom classifiers to block hate speech, violence, or PII disclosures.

Real-World Case Study: Llama in Customer Support

To bring this home, here is a quick IRL snippet of Llama flexing responsibly:

Context: A global e-commerce brand needed a 24/7 support assistant that could handle queries in English, Spanish, and French.

Approach:

1. **Model Choice:** Llama-13B, quantized to 8-bit for inference speed.
2. **Fine-Tuning:** 50K multilingual support transcripts, PEFT with LoRA, 3 epochs, early stopping.
3. **Prompting:** Few-shot examples for each language and "*assistant persona*" instructions.
4. **Monitoring:** Kibana dashboards tracking response accuracy and customer feedback ratings.

Outcome:

- 40% reduction in average handling time.
- Customer satisfaction score jumped from 72% to 88%.
- Zero major incidents of hallucinated info or biased replies, thanks to periodic bias scans and human-in-the-loop verifications.

Future Prospects of Llama Models

Prepare for the road ahead with Llama, as its potential is highly promising. As these models level up, they will reshape everything from on-device assistants to ultra-specialized industrial workflows—while still staying open and community-driven. Here is a sneak peek at what is coming next.

Next-Gen Architectures: Bigger, Better, Smarter

- **Massive Context Windows:** Llama's original context limit (~4K tokens) was adequate, but future variants will stretch that to 100K+ tokens. Imagine summarizing entire books, multi-day chat histories, or even real-time legal transcripts without losing the thread—no cap, that is next-level coherence.
- **Mixture-of-Experts and Sparse Models:** Instead of every neuron firing all the time, future Llamas will route queries through specialized "*expert*" subnetworks. This means you get top-tier performance on diverse tasks with a fraction of the compute—and a much lighter carbon footprint.
- **Multimodal Fusion:** Combine Llama's text-gen prowess with vision (think LLaVA), audio (such as Whisper), and maybe even sensory data from IoT devices. You could point your phone camera at a plant, and an assistant would both identify the species and draft a care guide—seamless image+text synergy.

Edge-Ready and On-Device Intelligence

- **Tiny Llama for Your Pocket:** Thanks to quantization, distillation, and parameter-efficient fine-tuning (LoRA, QLoRA), we will see 1–2 GB Llama variants running on smartphones, AR glasses, and embedded systems. Real-time language translation, personal mental-health check-ins, or even kids' homework help—offline, private, and super speedy.
- **Federated & Privacy-First Learning:** Your device becomes an active learner, updating its Llama-powered assistant without uploading raw data. That means better personalization (your email style, your slang), with privacy preserved via on-device differential privacy.

Hyper-Specialized Domain Models

- **Vertical-Tailored Llamas:** Beyond "*generalist*" Llama: think "*Llama-Health*," "*Llama-Law*," "*Llama-Fin*." With domain-adaptive pretraining on medical journals, legal filings, or financial reports, these variants will speak jargon fluently and flag hallucinations in high-stakes contexts.
- **Real-Time Knowledge Updates:** Integrating retrieval-augmented generation (RAG) pipelines so your domain Llama ingests the latest research papers or regulatory changes on the fly. A pharma R&D team could ask for the newest trial outcomes, and the model would source, synthesize, and cite them instantly.

Democratized Innovation and Community Power

- **Open Weights, Open Minds:** Meta's open-source ethos means anyone—from academic labs to solo devs—can spin up Llama experiments. Expect a surge of plugins, fine-tuned forks, and community-driven safety layers.

- **Ethics-as-a-Service:** Community-maintained "AI *trust marks*" will tag each Llama model with bias scores, energy-use metrics, and provenance info. Before deploying, you will pick a model that has been peer-audited for fairness, security, and environmental impact.

Integration with Agents and Autonomous Systems

- **Llama-Powered Agents:** Combine Llama with planning frameworks (AutoGPT, LangChain) to build agents that not only understand language but also execute multi-step tasks–booking flights, running code, or orchestrating IoT devices. Imagine a smart office where your Llama agent handles meeting invites, drafts agendas, and adjusts room lighting–all via natural conversation.
- **Robotics and AR/VR:** Give robots the gift of the gab: service robots in hotels could handle check-in, cleaning requests, and concierge services through Llama dialogue. In AR/VR spaces, avatars will speak, adapt, and learn from you naturally, making virtual worlds truly immersive.

Sustainable and Responsible AI

- **Green AI Initiatives:** With sparse training, mixed-precision, and recycled compute credits, future Llamas will lean into carbon-neutral certifications–letting organizations pick models that match their sustainability goals.
- **Continuous Governance:** Expect dynamic policy engines that auto-update compliance settings as data privacy laws evolve (GDPR, CCPA, LGPD). Your dev console will flag potential privacy leaks or bias drifts in real-time, so governance isn't a quarterly chore–it is embedded in every API call.

What This Means for You

- **For Developers:** Easier fine-tuning recipes, edge-deployment toolkits, and a plugin marketplace where you can sell or share Llama extensions.
- **For Enterprises:** More domain-specialized models that slice deployment costs and deliver razor-sharp accuracy in regulated industries.
- **For End-Users:** Smarter, more personalized assistants that respect your privacy, keep you in the loop with real citations, and run even when you're offline.

Conclusion

As you wrap up this chapter, you have journeyed through the most exciting frontiers of Llama–from spotting emerging trends in NLP and AI to diving into cutting-edge research advancements that push these models further, from unpacking the ethical implications and AI governance frameworks to mastering best practices for fine-tuning and deployment, and finally, envisioning the future prospects that will redefine what Llama can do. You now understand how context-window expansions, mixture-of-experts architectures, multimodal fusion, responsible data strategies, and robust governance models all weave together to create a powerful, trustworthy Llama ecosystem.

Armed with these insights, you are ready to implement what you have learned: you will experiment with domain-adaptive pretraining to tailor models to your own use cases, integrate human-in-the-loop checks for high-stakes applications, adopt dynamic policy engines for ongoing compliance, and prototype those edge-ready, privacy-first assistants you have been dreaming about. In short, this chapter does not just tell you what is on the horizon—it gives you the playbook to shape that future yourself.

Multiple-Choice Questions

1. Which technique refers to continuing Llama's pretraining on a large, unlabeled corpus specific to your domain?
   a. Task-Adaptive Fine-Tuning (TAFT)
   b. Retrieval-Augmented Generation (RAG)
   c. Domain-Adaptive Pretraining (DAPT)
   d. Parameter-Efficient Fine-Tuning (PEFT)
2. What is the main benefit of using Parameter-Efficient Fine-Tuning (PEFT) methods such as LoRA or adapters?
   a. They improve inference latency by 10×.
   b. They allow fine-tuning with far fewer trainable parameters.
   c. They increase a model's context window.
   d. They automatically detect bias in outputs.
3. In an AI governance framework, which document transparently describes a model's training data, capabilities, limitations, and intended use cases?
   a. Model Card
   b. Datasheet for Datasets
   c. API Reference Guide
   d. Prompt Template Library

4. Which decoding strategy balances creativity and coherence by sampling tokens until their cumulative probability reaches a threshold?
   a. Greedy Search
   b. Beam Search
   c. Top-k Sampling
   d. Top-p (Nucleus) Sampling
5. What is a key real-time monitoring practice for catching sudden shifts in model behavior or input characteristics post-deployment?
   a. Active Learning Loop
   b. Drift Detection
   c. Few-Shot Prompting
   d. Zero-Shot Evaluation
6. Which of the following is an example of multimodal fusion—an emerging trend for future Llama models?
   a. Combining RAG with vector databases
   b. Merging text generation with image understanding
   c. Using mixed-precision training (FP16/BF16)
   d. Applying PEFT on legal text
7. Which ethical risk arises when Llama replicates and even amplifies stereotypes hidden in its training data?
   a. Model Drift
   b. Bias Amplification
   c. Latency Degradation
   d. Context Window Overflow
8. In high-stakes applications (for example, medical advice), which best practice ensures a human reviews AI outputs before they reach the end user?
   a. Few-Shot Prompting
   b. Chain-of-Thought Generation
   c. Human-In-The-Loop (HITL)
   d. Mixed-Precision Inference

9. What future Llama advancement aims to route different types of queries through specialized parts of the network to save compute?
   a. Extended Context Windows
   b. Mixture-of-Experts (MoE)
   c. Quantized Distillation
   d. Adaptive Token Sampling
10. Which technique creates a smaller "student" model that learns to imitate a larger "*teacher*" Llama, reducing inference cost?
    a. Quantization
    b. Model Distillation
    c. Prefix Tuning
    d. Checkpoint Averaging

Answers

1. c
2. b
3. a
4. d
5. b
6. b
7. d
8. c
9. b
10. b

Index

A

AI, trends
  AI Governance 393
  Deep Learning/Transformer Architecture 392
  Future Directions/Prospects 394
  Industry Impact 392
Architectural Innovations 42
Architectural Innovations, components
  Adaptive Computation 42
  Mixed Precision Training 43
  Modular Design 43
  Sparse Attention 42

B

Batch Processing 207
Batch Processing, architecture 215
Batch Processing, benefits
  Overhead, reducing 215
  Resource Utilization, optimizing 216
  Throughput, enhancing 216
Batch Processing, challenges 217
Batch Processing, implementing 216
Batch Processing, insights
  E-commerce Recommendation Engine 220
  Fault Tolerance/Error Handling 221
  GPU/TPU Acceleration 219
  Performance Testing 222
  Real-Time Translation Application 220
  Software Tools 220
Batch Processing, parallelism
  I/O Overhead, reducing 208
  Requests Aggregation 207
  Vectorized Computations 207
Bias 343
Bias, challenges 347
Bias, consequences
  Content Moderation 344
  Customer Service 344
  Machine Translation/Localization 344
  Recruitment/Hiring 344
Bias, methodologies 345
Bias, practices 348
Bias, strategies 345
Bias, ways
  Algorithmic Amplification 344
  Historical/Societal Prejudices 344
  Representation 344

C

Chatbot Interaction 218
Chatbot Interaction, terms
  Data Transformation/Padding 219
  Efficient Data Preparation 218
Cloud Deployment 257
Cloud Deployment, approaches
  Edge 256
  Hybrid 257
  On-Premise 255
Cloud Deployment Architecture 260

Cloud Deployment Architecture, terms
Hybrid/Multi-Cloud 261
Monitoring/Logging 262
Multi-Tier 261
Security/Compliance 262
Cloud Deployment Landscape 258
Cloud Deployment Landscape, architecture 258
Cloud Deployment Landscape, purpose
Cost-Efficiency 258
Global Accessibility 258
Maintenance 258
Scalability 258
Cloud Deployment Landscape, terms
Containerization/ Orchestration 259
Managed AI Services 260
Serverless Architecture 259
Cloud Deployment, strategies
Cloud Deployment Architecture 260
Cloud Deployment Landscape 258
Cloud Deployment, terms
Compute Costs 254
GPU Instances 254
Horizontal Scaling 255
Inference Latency 254
Cloud Deployment, trends 263
Comparative Analysis 331
Comparative Analysis, adaptations
Sentiment Analysis 332
Text Classification 332
Comparative Analysis, applications 332
Comparative Analysis, strategies 331
Computational Layers 49
Computational Layers, types
Embedding Layer 49
Multi-Head Self-Attention Layer 50
Continuous Improvement 280, 294
Continuous Improvement, architecture 295
Continuous Improvement, flow 294
Continuous Improvement, impacts 297
Continuous Improvement, implementing 296, 297
Continuous Improvement, methodologies 296
Continuous Improvement, strategies
AI Ops, leveraging 281
Collaborative Problem Solving 281
Feedback Loops 281
Continuous Improvement, trends
Data-Driven Decision Making 295
Employee Empowerment 295
Iterative Processes 295
Conversational AI Applications 384
Conversational AI Applications, integrating 385, 386
Customer Service, characterictics
Education 172
Energy/Utilities 174
Government/Public Administration 173
Logistics/Supply Chain 172
Manufacturing 174
Media/Content Creation 173
Retail 173
Customer Services 183
Customer Services, case study
Advanced Sentiment Analysis 186
Global User Management 184
Intelligent Ticketing 185

D

Data Pipeline 208

Data Pipeline, strategies
Asynchronous Data Handling 208
Caching Mechanisms 208
Efficient Data Preprocessing 208
Data Preprocessing/Augmentation 147
Data Preprocessing/Augmentation, scenarios 147
Debugging Llama 282
Debugging Llama, challenges
Complex Model 282
Data Pipelines 282
Distributed/Heterogeneous 282
Resource Constraints 282
Debugging Llama, impact
Accelerated Development Cycle 287
Cost Efficiency 287
Performance, improving 287
Reliability, enhancing 287
User Experience 287
Debugging Llama, techniques
Automated Error/Anomaly Detection 285
Comprehensive Logging/Monitoring 283
Interactive Debugging 283
Profiling/Performance Analysis 284
Reproducibility/Environment Replication 286
Unit Testing 286
Decoder-Only Structure 34
Decoder-Only Structure, advantages
Efficiency 34
Specialization 34
Deployment Architecture 239
Deployment Architecture, components
CI/CD 246
Data/Model Pipelines 246
Infrasfructure as Code (IaC) 246
Model Versioning/Experimentation 246
Preprocessing Modules 246
Deployment Architecture, concepts
Data Ingestion/Preprocessing 240
Disaster Recovery/Compliance 243
Maintenance/Logging 242
Model Serving/Inference 240
Scalability/Load Balancing 241
Deployment Architecture, strategies
Cloud-Based Deployment 244
Hybrid Deployments 245
On-Premises Deployments 245
Deployment Architecture, tips
Performance/Resource Utilization 239
Reliability/Fault Tolerance 239
Scalability/Flexibility 239
Security/Compliance 239
Document Summarization Service 219
Domain Adaptation 144
Domain Adaptation, approaches
Data Preprocessing/Augmentation 147
Domain-Sensitive Loss Functions 147
Domain-Specific Datasets 146
External Knowledge Bases 148
Incremental/Continual Learning 149
Domain Adaptation, architecture 145
Domain Adaptation, strategies
Continual Learning 145
Data Processing/Augmentation 145
Domain-Sensitive Loss 145
Domain-Specific Datasets 144
External Knowledge Bases 145
Domain-Sensitive Loss Functions 147
Domain-Sensitive Loss Functions, scenarios 148
Domain-Specific Datasets 146

Domain-Specific Datasets, scenarios 146
Dynamic Batch Sizing 217

E

Education 192
Education, case study 192
Effective Monitoring 263
Effective Monitoring, architecture 264
Effective Monitoring, metrics 264, 265
Effective Monitoring, practices 268
Effective Monitoring, purpose
  Consistent Performance, ensuring 264
  Model Drift, detecting 264
  Operational/Infrastructure Health 264
Effective Monitoring, strategies 266, 267
Effective Monitoring, tools 265, 266
Embedding 35
Embedding Layer 49
Embedding, layers
  Positional 35
  Token 35
Energy/Utilities 194
Energy/Utilities, case study 194
Ethical Implications 400
Ethical Implications, architecture 400
Ethical Implications, level up 402
Ethical Implications, practices 402
Ethical Implications, terms
  AI Governance Frameworks 401
  Deep Dive 400
  Potential Risks 401
Evaluation/Benchmark 45
Evaluation/Benchmark, components
  Ablation Studies 46
  Benchmark Suites 45
  Comparative Analysis 46
  Generate Coherent 47
External Knowledge Bases 148
External Knowledge Bases, scenarios 149

F

Feed-Forward Neural Networks (FFN) 36
FFN, pattern
  Activation Functions 38
  Activation Functions/ Normalization 36
  Deep/Wide Layers 36
  Layer Normalization 37
  Optimization Techniques 40
  Parameter Efficiency 39
  Parameterization/Scaling 38
  Regularization 41
  Residual Connections 37
  Training Methodologies 39
  Training Objectives 40
Finance 179
Finance, cases study
  Automated Financial Reporting 180
  Personalized Client Engagement 182
  Proactive Risk Management 179
Fine-Tuning 134, 307
Fine-Tuning, case studies
  Education 159
  Financial Services 157
  Healthcare 155
  Legal Industry 156
  Retail/E-commerce 158
  Text Classification System 160
Fine-Tuning, domain
  Curated Domain-Specific 135
  Data Augmentation 135
  Domain-Sensitive Loss 135

Fine-tuning Llama Models 317
Fine-tuning Llama Models, approaches
  Optimization Algorithms 322
  Preventing Overfitting 321
Fine-tuning Llama Models, architecture 318
Fine-tuning Llama Models, case studies
  Sentiment Analysis 328
  Text Classification 325
Fine-tuning Llama Models, challenges
  Computational Resources 323
  Domain Mismatch, managing 322
  Tackling Overfitting 323
Fine-tuning Llama Models, practices 324, 325
Fine-tuning Llama Models, sources
  Hyperparameter Optimization 320
  Model Initialization/Architecture Adaptation 319
Fine-tuning Llama Models, stages
  Data Collection/Preparation 318
  Data Preprocessing/Tokenization 319
  Dataset Splitting/Balancing 319
Fine-tuning Llama Models, strategies
  Freezing Layers 321
  Gradual Unfreezing 321
Fine-Tuning, methods
  Continuous Evaluation 136
  Hyperparameter Optimization 136
  Regularization/Dropout 136
Fine-Tuning, strategies
  Layer-Wise 135
  Progressive Unfreezing 135
  Task-Specific Adaptation 135

G

Government/Public Administration 190
Government/Public Administration, case study 190

H

Hardware Optimizations 228
Hardware Optimizations, strategies
  Hardware Accelerators, utilizing 228
  Hardware-Specific Tuning 230
  Memory/Data Transfer Optimization 229
Hardware/Software Optimizations, approach
  Integrated Pipelines 233
  Synergistic Effects 232
Hardware/Software Optimizations, practices 233, 234
Healthcare 175
Healthcare, approach
  Automated Knowledge Extraction 176
  Patient Data Management 175
  Virtual Health Assistants 177
Hyperparameter Tuning 149, 150
Hyperparameter Tuning, advantages
  Efficient Resource 151
  Generalization 152
  Model Accuracy 151
  Stability 152
Hyperparameter Tuning, aspects 151
Hyperparameter Tuning, considerations 154
Hyperparameter Tuning, process 155
Hyperparameter Tuning, strategies
  Adaptive Learning Rates 154
  Bayesian Optimization 153
  Grid Search 152
  Manual Tuning 152
  Random Search 153

I

Incremental/Continual Learning 149

Incremental/Continual Learning, scenarios 149
Inference Speed 207
Inference Speed, strategies
  Batch Processing 207
  Data Pipeline 208

L

Language Understanding 378
Language Understanding, integrating 378-380
Large Language Model
  Meta AI (Llama) 2
Llama2 2
Llama2, highlights
  Advanced Training 10
  Architectural Improvements 10
  Cross-Domain Proficiency 10
  Ethical/Responsible AI 10
Llama2, terms
  Algorithms, enhancing 3
  Multilingual Proficiency 3
  Optimize Training 3
  Safety/Alignment 3
Llama3 3
Llama3, innovations
  Adaptive Learning 3
  Contextual Awareness 3
  Customization/Fine-Tuning 4
  Interdisciplinary Integration 3
  Robust Security Measures 4
Llama3, models
  Acadamic Research 4
  Business/Industry 4
  Creative Industries 4
  Healthcare/Eduction 4
Llama3, terms
  Advanced Training Paradigms 11
  Contextual/Semantic 11
  Ethical AI 12
  Innovative Model 11
  Robust Customization 11
Llama 4 78
Llama4 4
Llama 4, applications 79
Llama 4, features 78
Llama 4, highlights
  Contextual Awareness 80
  Energy Efficiency 81
  Multilingual Support 80
  Multi-Modal Capabilities 80
  NLP Task 80
  Real-Time NLP 80
Llama4, highlights 12, 13
Llama4, terms 4
Llama, achievements
  AI Ecosystem 73
  Ethical/Responsible Initiatives 72
  Multilingual Proficiency 71
  Parameter Milestones 70
  Training Efficiency 71
Llama, advancements
  Architectural Innovation 81
  Continuous Learning/ Adoptation 86
  Data Management/ Preprocessing 83
  Ethical/Responsible Enhancements 85
  Hardware/Infrastructure Innovation 85
  Multimodal Integration 84
  Optimization Algorithms 83
  Prospects 87
  Security/Privacy Enhancements 87
  Training Methodologies 82
Llama, architecture 2
Llama, aspects
  Advanced Reasoning 15
  Global/Inclusive AI 15
  Seamless Human-AI 15
  Social Intelligence 15
  Sustainable AI 15
Llama, capabilities 15, 17
Llama, categories
  Llama2 2
  Llama3 3
  Llama4 4
Llama, challenges 14
Llama, ensuring 5

Llama, evolution
 Benchmark Performance 14
 Community/Ecosystem 14
 Ethical AI 14
 Research Contributions 14
 Widespread Adoption/ Integration 13
Llama, features
 Open Accessibility 2
 Scalability 2
 Versatile Application 2
Llama, foundations
 AI Landscape 66
 Meta Vision 67
Llama, history 6
Llama, milestones
 Architecture Design/ Training 9
 Community Engagement 9
 Conceptualization/Objectives 9
Llama Model Dependency, challenges
 Debugging/ Troubleshooting 278
 Hardware/Resource Contraints 275
 Integration/Environment Issues 276
 Performance Bottlenecks 277
 Security/Compliance 280
Llama Model, industry
 Customer Service 171
 Finance 171
 Healthcare 170
Llama Models 32, 63
Llama Models, advantages 315
Llama Models, benefits
 Adaptability 66
 Resource Efficiency 65
 Scalability 65
 Versatility Across Tasks 65
Llama Models, challenges 316
Llama Models, components
 Decoder-Onlu Structure 34
 Self-Attention 34
 Transformer Architecture 32
Llama Model, sectors
 Customer Services 183
 Education 192
 Energy/Utilities 194
 Finance 179
 Government/Public Administration 190
 Healthcare 175
 Manufacturing 196
 Retail 188
Llama Models, ensuring 64
Llama Models, evolutions
 Begin Era 74
 Code Llama 75
 Llama 2 75
 Llama 3 76
 Llama 3.1 77
 Llama 3.2 77
 Llama 3.3 78
 Llama 4 78
Llama Models, foundations
 Multi-Head Attention 48
 Positional Encoding 49
 Self-Attention Mechanism 48
Llama Models, history 64, 65
Llama Models, parameters
 Data Curation 403
 Evaluation/Monitoring 405
 Perfect Llama 403
 Prompt Engineering 404
 Security/Privacy 405
Llama Models, points 57, 58
Llama Models, prospects
 Antonomous Systems 408
 Democratized Innovation 407
 Hyper-Specialized Domain 407
 Next-Gen Architectures 407
 On-Device Intelligence 407
Llama Models, scenarios
 Customer Service 168
 Finance 167
 Healthcare 167
 Horizon Expanding 168
 Versatility Demonstrating 169

Llama, phase
Conceptualization/Initial Development 67
Public Deployment/Iterative Improvement 69
Scaling/Optimization 68
Llama, scenearios
Cloud Infrastructure 8
Competitive Impact 7
Economic Impact 8
Market Landscape 6
Market Positioning 8
Llama, use cases
Education 92
Entertainment 93, 94
Finance 90
Healthcare 88, 89
LLM, challenges
Data Quality/Integration 198
Ethical/Bias Mitigation 200
Legacy System, integrating 201
Model Adaptation/Domain-Spccific Tuning 199
Scalability/Real-Time Processing 200

M

Manufacturing 196
Manufacturing, case study 196
Multi-Head Self-Attention Layer 50
Multi-Head Self-Attention Layer, parts
Feed-Forward Neural Network (FFN) 50
Layer Normalization 51
Multi-Head Attention 50
Residual Connections 51
Self-Attention 50

N

Named Entity Recognition (NER) 125
Natural Language Processing (NLP) 101, 337
NER, architecture 126
NER, components 127
NER, entities
Business Intelligence 128
Content Management 128
Healthcare 128
Socail Media Monitoring 128
NER, levels
Cross-Lingual 128
Explainability 129
Multimodal Data, integration 129
NER, metrics
F1-Score 128
Precision 127
Recall 128
NER, process
Entity Annotation 127
Relevant Data, curating 126
Tokenization/Text Cleaning 126
NLP, advancements 352
NLP, architecture 349
NLP, case study
Bias/Recruitment 360
Content Moderation 362
Ethical Challenges 364
Privacy/Misinformation 361
NLP, challenges
Data Anonymization 350
Differential Privacy 350
User Consent/Data Collection 350
NLP, mechanisms
Auditing/Compliance 351
GDPR Compliance 351
Global Harmonization 352
Regulatory Landscape 351
Secure Data Storage 350
Secure Data Transmission 351
NLP, prerequisites
Hardware Requirements 102

Software Requirements 102
NLP, roles
Advanced Test Generation/ Creative Assistance 18
Automated Financial 23
Cognitive Behavioral Therapy (CBT) 25
Cultural Heritage Preservation 26
Deep Sentiment/Emotion Analysis 19
Diverse Applications 26
Dynamic Machine Translation 19
Hyper-Personalized Recommendation 21
Information Retrieval/ Contextual Question 19
Innovative Creative Industries 24
Integrative Speech Recognition 21
Intellectual Property Analysis 25
Intelligent Code Generation 22
Intelligent Text Summarization 20
Intelligent Tutoring Systems 23
Legal/Regulatory Compliance 24
Named Entity Recognition (NER) 20
Personalized Patient Care 22
Proactive Content Moderation 22
Sophisticated Conversational Agents 18
Supply Chain, enhancing 25
NLP, setting up
Conda 103
Data Preparation 106
Dependencies, installing 103
Docker/Containerization 109
Evaluation 108
Fine-Tuned Service, deploying 108
Fine-Tuning 107
Large Model, handling 105
Llama Model, obtaining 104
Performance, optimizing 110
Proper Configuration 105
REST API 109
Virtualenv/Pip 103
NLP, strategies
Bias/Language Models 338, 339
Ethical Challenges 342
Privacy/Data Security 339
Regulatory/Societal Implications 341
Transparency/ Accountability 340

O

Optimization Techniques 53
Optimization Techniques, strategies
Optimizer 53
Regularization 55
Optimizer 53
Optimizer, terms
Adam 53
Gradient Clipping 54
Learning Rate Schedules 54
Mixed Precision Training 55
Weight Decay 53

P

Parallelization 44, 208
Parallelization, architecture 222
Parallelization, case studies
Customer Service 213
Finance 213
Healthcare 212
Horizons Expanding 214
Versatility/Effectiveness, demonstrating 214
Parallelization, integrating 226
Parallelization, practices 227
Parallelization, purpose
Hardware Acceleration 209
Monitoring/Continuous Improvement 211
Software-Level

Optimizations 210
Parallelization, strategies
Asynchronous Execution 209, 225
Data Parallelism 44, 223
Distributed Training Frameworks 45
Model Parallelism 44, 224
Multi-Threading/Multi-Processing 209
Pipeline Parallelism 224
Task-Based Parallelism 209, 225
Parallelization, terms
Edge Computing 212
High-Volume Content Moderation 211
Real-Time Chatbot Deployment 211
Parallelization, tips
Efficient Resource 222
Performance Boost 222
Scalability 222
Performance Monitoring 288
Performance Monitoring, applications
E-Commerce Platforms 293
Financial Institutions 293
Healthcare Systems 293
Streaming Services 293
Performance Monitoring, architecture 288
Performance Monitoring, benefits
Data-Driven Decision 288
Problem Detection 288
Resource Optimization 288
User Experience 288
Performance Monitoring, strategies
Caching Mechanisms 291
Continuous Optimization/ Feedback Loops 292
Database Optimization 292
Hardware/Infrastructure Scaling 291
Load Balancing/Traffic Management 292
Performance Monitoring, techniques
Centralized Logging Systems 289
Real-Time Metrics Collection 289
Pre-Trained Models 304
Pre-Trained Models, advantages
Rapid Prototyping 314
Resource Efficiency/ Accelerated Training 313
Robust Performance 313
Versatility Across 314
Pre-Trained Models, architecture 312
Pre-Trained Models, benefits
Efficiency 304
Performance, improving 305
Rapid Deployment 305
Versatility 305
Pre-Trained Models, insights 316
Pre-Trained Models, steps 305

Q

QAS, implementing 382-384
QAS, steps 382
Question Answering Systems (QAS) 381

R

Regularization 55
Regularization, techniques
Data Augmentation 56
Distributed Training 56
Dropout 55
Early Stopping 57
Weight Sharing 56
Research Advancements 395
Research Advancements, innovations 395-399
Responsible AI Deployments 353
Responsible AI Deployments, configuring 356, 357

Responsible AI Deployments, implementing 357
Responsible AI Deployments, principles
  Establishing Fairness 356
  Fairness AI System, ensuring 354
  Imperative Transparency 353, 354
  Mitigating Bias 355
Retail 188
Retail, case study 188

S

Scalability Considerations 247
Scalability Considerations, architecture 247
Scalability Considerations, challenges 252, 253
Scalability Considerations, resources
  Computational Complexity 250
  Data Heterogeneity/Bias 251
  Distributed Systems 251
  Energy Consumption 251
  Reliability/Reproducibility 251
Scalability Considerations, terms
  Data Management/Quality 248
  Distributed Systems 249
  Parameter Growth 248
  Real-Time Applications 250
Self-Attention 34
Self-Attention, features
  Multi-Head 34
  Relative Positional 35
  Scaled Dot-Product 34
Sentiment Analysis 119, 328
Sentiment Analysis, advantages
  Adaptability/Fine-Tuning 120
  Contextual Nuance 119
  Scalability/Efficiency 120
Sentiment Analysis, applications
  Customer Feedback Analysis 122
  Financial Market Insights 123
  Product/Market Research 123
  Social Media Monitoring 123
Sentiment Analysis, architecture 119
Sentiment Analysis, datasets
  Data Collection 120
  Data Processing 120
  Labeling Sentiment 120
Sentiment Analysis, importance 119
Sentiment Analysis, phase
  Architecture Adaptation 120
  Fine-Tuning 121
  Function/Regularization 121
  Hyperparameter Optimization 121
Sentiment Analysis, techniques
  Explainability/Interpretability 122
  Multimodal 122
  Robustness 122
  Transfer Learning/Domain Adaptation 122
Sentiment Analysis, terms
  Dataset Preparation 329
  High Accuracy/Robustness 330
  Hyperparameter Optimization 330
  Model Adaptation 329
Software Optimizations 230
Software Optimizations, strategies
  Code-Level 231
  Framework/Library, enhancing 230
  Model-Level 231

T

Text Classification 111, 325
Text Classification, advantages
  Adaptability 112
  Contextual relationships 112
  Scalability 112
Text Classification, applications
  Fraud Detection 117
  Healthcare/Medical Text 116
  Legal Document Analysis 116
  New/Media Categorization 116

Sentiment Analysis 115
Spam/Toxic Content Detection 115
Text Classification, foundation
Data Preparation 112
Fine-Tuning 113
Model, evaluating 113
Model Preparation 112
Text Classification, implementing 118
Text Classification Input, types
Data Sources 114
Llama 3.3 114
Preprocess Stages 114
Text Classification, process
Dataset Preparation 326
Hyperparameter Tuning 327
Model Adaptation 326
Performance Metrics 328
Text Classification, role
Intent Recognition 111
Sentiment Analysis 111
Spam Detection 111
Topic Categorization 111
Text Generation 51, 371
Text Generation, capabilities
Context Awareness 52
Decoding 52
Text Generation, implementing 372, 373
Text Generation, steps 372
Text Summarization 374
Text Summarization, demonstrating 375-377
Text Summarization, steps 375
Transfer Learning 134, 303
Transfer Learning, architecture 137, 303
Transfer Learning, benefits 308
Transfer Learning, case studies
Domain-Specific Application 308
Sentiment Analysis 308
Text Classification 307
Transfer Learning, challenges
Computational Demands 309
Domain Mismatch 309
Interpretability 309
Risk Overfitting 309
Transfer Learning, evaluating 310
Transfer Learning, evolutions 306
Transfer Learning Integration, techniques 309
Transfer Learning, opportunities 311, 312
Transfer Learning, phases
Fine-Tuning 304
Pe-Training 304
Transfer Learning, preventing 141, 142
Transfer Learning, scenarios
Financial Services 141
Legal Document Analysis 140
Social Media Sentiment 141
Transfer Learning, strategies
Community/Collaboration 309
Iterative Refinement 309
Rigorous Evaluation 309
Transfer Learning, techniques
Continual Learning 139
Domain Adaptation 139
Few-Shot/Zero-Shot 139
Layer-Wise Adaptation 138
Progressive Unfreezing 138
Task-Specific Optimization 138
Transfer Learning, term
Custom NLP Applications 139
Data Augmentation, implementing 140
Domain-Specific Datasets 139
Hyperparameter Tuning 140
Transformer Architecture 32
Transformer Architecture, dependecies 32, 33